From Paris
To Sèvres

From Paris To Sèvres

The Partition of the Ottoman Empire at the Peace Conference of 1919-1920

Paul C. Helmreich

Ohio State University Press
Columbus

Library of Congress Cataloging in Publication Data

1. Paris. Peace Conference, 1919. Turkey.
2. European War, 1914-1918—Territorial questions—Turkey. I. Title.
D651.T9H44   949.6   73-12812
ISBN 0-8142-0170-9

TO MY PARENTS ❀ ERNST CHRISTIAN
AND LOUISE ROBERTS HELMREICH

Table of Contents

PREFACE

DURING 1919 AND the first
months of 1920, statesmen representing the victorious powers in
World War I gathered in Paris, London, and San Remo to draft
peace terms that were to be imposed upon their defeated enemies.
Of the five pacts that were negotiated, the one that took the longest
by far was the treaty with the Ottoman Empire. It involved not only
the drafting of peace terms for Turkey but also the division of vast
territorial spoils among the powers themselves. The negotiation of
this Near East peace settlement, incorporated in the document known
as the Treaty of Sèvres, is the topic of this study.

The Treaty of Sèvres constituted Europe's solution to a nineteenth-century problem in international relations, the Eastern Question. This book is essentially a history of the negotiations between
the European powers (and, for a time, the United States). It has
been constructed as a study of World War I peace-conference diplomacy, and is not intended to be an examination of Near Eastern
history as such. In general, external forces and events in the Near
East have been considered only with a view to determining the extent
of their influence on the course of the negotiations and the reasons
for it. All too often what emerges is a picture of an internal *realpolitik*
around the negotiating table that was sadly out of touch with the
realities of external events. Traditional imperial ambitions and national rivalries, supplemented by personal conflicts and prejudices
on the part of the negotiators, dominated the negotiations between

the leaders of various Western powers as they proceeded, both glee-
fully and acrimoniously, to partition the Ottoman Empire along
nineteenth-century imperialistic lines.

This study had its origins in a doctoral dissertation that was presented at Harvard University in 1964. Since then the account has
been thoroughly revised in the light of material gained from extensive
additional archival research. Of particular import has been the wealth
of new material made available by the opening of the British archives
for the interwar period. Without these Foreign Office and Cabinet
Papers, completion of this study would have been impossible.

I have been fortunate in receiving financial aid from a number
of sources. A Summer Stipend Fellowship from the National Endowment for the Humanities enabled me to spend the summer of 1967
in London. Smaller grants, financed by the Danforth and Ford
Foundations and awarded by Wheaton College, allayed research
expenses during other summer periods. Funds provided to Wheaton
College by the Ford Foundation also allowed me to take a leave
of absence from teaching in the fall of 1971. In addition, I have
received extensive aid from Wheaton College in the form of typing
and duplicating services, a sabbatical leave in the spring of 1968,
and financial assistance from the College's Faculty Research Fund.

It is impossible for me to acknowledge everyone to whom I am
in debt for help during the course of my work. I would, however,
like to thank the staffs of several institutions for their assistance
and cooperation. In London, I am indebted to the British Museum,
the Public Record Office, the India Office Library, and the Beaverbrook Library. In the United States, I have an equally great obligation
to the National Archives, the Library of Congress, the Columbia
University Library, the Yale University Library, and, in particular,
the Harvard University Library. I am especially indebted to Miss
Hilda Harris and the staff of the Wheaton College Library.

Four persons have been kind enough to read all of the manuscript
at various stages in its development, and I have benefited greatly
from their comments and criticisms. Only in the most inadequate
way can I express my thanks to my parents, Professor Ernst C.
Helmreich of Bowdoin College and Dr. Louise Roberts Helmreich,
to Professor Ernest R. May of Harvard University, and to Professor

Ernest J. Knapton of Wheaton College. To all of them I am also heavily indebted for help and encouragement in matters that extend far beyond anything having to do with this particular work.

My greatest obligation, however, is to my wife, Dorothy, whose editorial criticisms, patience, and understanding have been a constant source of help and support. I must also express my thanks to my colleague Professor Vaino Kola, who prepared the maps, and to Mr. Vincent Cuccaro, who assisted me in examining the Sonnino papers. I am in debt as well to Mrs. Helen Durant, Mrs. Barbara Wilson, and Mrs. Nancy Shepardson for their typing services, and to Mrs. Sarah T. Millett of the Ohio State University Press for her editorial assistance.

Portions of this study relating to oil rights have appeared as an article in *Middle East Forum*. They have been substantially revised for inclusion in the present text. Reference has been made to a standard gazetteer, *The Columbia Lippincott Gazetteer of the World* (New York, 1952). In cases where more than one spelling was declared acceptable, the one most closely approaching that used at the time of the negotiations has been chosen.

Unfortunately, a word of warning to those who would use the microfilmed reels of the Sonnino Papers must be included. As originally distributed by University Microfilms in 1969, the numbered listing of the reels in the Sonnino Papers catalog did not always match the actual numbering on the reels. This was rectified in the summer of 1971, when the reel numbers were changed so as to correspond with those listed in the catalog. All references in this book are based upon this revision, and all reels sold by University Microfilms since that time may be used directly if further consultation on matters referred to in this work is desired. However, to my knowledge the company has made no effort to change reel numberings on those sets that were sold prior to August 1971. Therefore, before, using any of the reels one should ascertain when they were purchased and, if necessary, make the appropriate corrections through reference to the catalog.

Paul C. Helmreich

Norton, Massachusetts

From Paris
To Sèvres

I ❊ THE AIMS AND ATTITUDES
OF THE GREAT POWERS

WHEN the Paris Peace Conference convened on January 12, 1919, there was little real agreement among the Allied and Associated Powers on the specific demands that would be made on the defeated nations. In fact, even within the national delegations little concord existed as to policy or plans. On no question was this vagueness of policy more complete than that of the disposition of the Ottoman Empire.

The Armistice of Mudros

The armistice that had been signed with Turkey on October 30, 1918, served only to complicate matters.[1] Throughout the fall of 1918, the British and French had been engaged in a bitter quarrel over the command of the Allied fleet in the Aegean. Therefore, when the Turks sent General Townshend, commander of the forces captured at Kutal Imara in 1916, to Mudros with a message requesting that negotiations be opened, the British commander in the Aegean, Admiral Calthorpe, was instructed to exclude his French counterpart, Admiral Amet, from any part in the discussions and to proceed alone with the negotiation and signing of an armistice. This action by the British government was taken despite the fact that the Allies had already received peace feelers from the Ottoman government through Spanish and American sources. It was clearly an effort to assert British primacy in Near Eastern affairs.[2]

The negotiation of the armistice was thus a purely Anglo-Turkish affair. Although the majority of the terms negotiated by Calthorpe had been approved previously by an inter-Allied conference on October 7, two significant differences appeared in the final document. The original draft had called for the immediate evacuation of Cilicia by Turkish troops; the armistice terms gave Turkey the right to maintain any forces in the area that were necessary for the preservation of law and order. Since Cilicia was part of the area that the French regarded as their sphere of influence, this exclusion appeared to constitute a deliberate attack on French interests in the Near East. In addition, the original proposal had simply asserted the right of Allied troops to occupy important strategic points; the armistice added, "in the event of any situation arising which threatens the security of the Allies," a distinctly qualifying condition in terms of Turkish internal affairs, but one that opened the possibility of action taken to meet external threats, particularly the spread of Bolshevism south from Russia.[3]

Since the armistice laid down no conditions for the negotiation of the peace treaty, the Turkish surrender was in this respect unconditional. Moreover (and this undoubtedly reflected Great Britain's special interest in naval affairs), though eight of the clauses dealt with naval matters, the armistice failed to deal precisely with such important issues as disarmament and the disbanding of troops, nor did it impose any penalties against, or call for the removal of, the leaders of the Young Turk party known as the Committee of Union and Progress.[4] Failure to undertake immediately these steps added to the difficulties the Allies subsequently had to face in their efforts to enforce the final peace settlement.

Arno Mayer, in his excellent study of external and domestic influences working on the peacemakers of World War I, has asserted that the Turkish armistice clauses were formulated primarily "with the strategic access to Russia rather than with internal order" in mind, the aim being to prevent the penetration of Bolshevism into the defeated areas.[5] Although it is true that Allied control of the Straits did provide direct access to anti-Bolshevik forces fighting in the Ukraine and Caucasus, it is clear that at least the British regarded control of Constantinople and all ports, railroads, and wireless systems, along with naval domination of the entire Anatolian coastline, as more than enough to ensure the imposing of their will upon a totally crushed enemy. Certainly at the time there was little concern over the lack of the specific clauses mentioned above. As British Foreign Secretary Arthur Balfour commented to the Italian ambassador to London: "Having opened the Straits, and communication with the Black Sea, having occupied Constantinople, and having reduced Turkey to absolute military impotence, the conditions left out of the armistice could be imposed by any of the Allies at the peace negotiations." [6]

Wartime Agreements and Commitments

The circumstances surrounding the signing of the armistice intensified France's distrust of British intentions in the Near East, yet the terms themselves failed to provide any guidelines for an ultimate solution. This is not to say that such guidelines did not exist. Their very profusion and seeming contradictions served more to complicate and confuse the issue than to cast any light upon it. The fate of the outwardly "sick" Ottoman Empire had been the source of European diplomatic negotiation and intrigue for much of the nineteenth century. It was hardly surprising that settlement of the "Eastern Question" had been the topic of many statements and agreements, both public and secret, by the Allied powers during the course of the war. These may be summarized briefly.

Constantinople Agreement, March–April, 1915

In a series of diplomatic exchanges, the British and French governments recognized Russia's right to annex Constantinople, European Turkey to the Enos-Midia line, the Ismid peninsula, and the islands of the Sea of Marmara. These claims were recognized with the provisos that the war should first be successfully concluded and that British and French "desiderata in the Ottoman Empire and elsewhere" should be attained. [7]

Treaty of London, April 26, 1915

This agreement, concluded between Italy and the Entente powers, served to bring Italy into the war on the Allied side. In clauses pertaining to the Eastern settlement, Italy was accorded sovereignty over the Dodecanese Islands. More important:

In the event of the total or partial partition of Turkey in Asia, she [Italy] ought to obtain a just share of the Mediterranean region adjacent to the province of Adalia, . . . If France, Great Britain and Russia occupy any territories in Turkey in Asia during the course of the war, the Mediterranean region bordering on the Province of Adalia within the limits indicated above shall be reserved to Italy, who shall be entitled to occupy it.[8]

Hussein-McMahon Correspondence, July, 1915–March, 1916

In a series of communications[9] over a protracted period of time, Sir Henry McMahon, British high commissioner in Egypt, successfully negotiated an Arab uprising against the Turks, equipped and supported by the British. The Arabs demanded recognition and support of Arab independence in an area stretching from Persia to the Mediterranean, and from the Indian Ocean to the thirty-seventh parallel. To this McMahon agreed, with three equally significant and ambiguous "modifications."

The two districts of Mersina and Alexandretta and portions of Syria lying to the west of the districts of Damascus, Homs, Hama and Aleppo cannot be said to be purely Arab, and should be excluded from the limits demanded . . . .
Great Britain will guarantee the Holy Places against all external aggression and will recognize their inviolability . . . .
As for those regions lying within those frontiers wherein Great Britain is free to act without detriment to the interests of her ally, France, . . . subject to the above modifications, Great Britain is prepared to recognize and support the independence of the Arabs in all the regions within the limits demanded by the Sherif of Mecca, Hussein.[10]

Sykes-Picot Agreement, May 9–16, 1916

This agreement, ratified by an exchange of notes between Paul Cambon, French ambassador in London, and British Foreign Secretary Sir Edward Grey, constituted the division of spoils that had been envisaged in the Constantinople Agreement of 1915. Subsequently ratified by Russia, the agreement called for the establishment of an international regime in Palestine, French annexation of coastal Syria with an extended zone of influence in the interior, and British annexation of lower Mesopotamia with a similar zone of influence that would border on that allotted to France. Within the zones of influence, both states were prepared to "recognize and uphold an independent Arab State or a Confederation of Arab States." However, each nation reserved the right to be the sole provider of any foreign advisers requested for the area within its own zone of influence.[11]

Saint Jean de Maurienne Agreement, August 18, 1917

This agreement[12] gave to Italy a designated area for eventual annexation in Asia Minor as well as a much more extensive zone of influence. It served to bring Italy within the scope of the earlier Sykes-Picot Agreement. The failure of Russia to assent to this agreement, due to the events of the revolution, eventually led to a severe dispute between Italy and the other powers as to its legal validity.

Balfour Declaration, November 2, 1917

A declaration on the part of the British government to the leaders of the World Zionist Organization stated that:

His Majesty's Government view with favour the establishment in Palestine of a national home for the Jewish people, and will use their best endeavors to facilitate the achievement of this object, it being clearly understood that nothing shall be done which may prejudice the civil and religious rights of existing non-Jewish communities in Palestine, or the rights and political status enjoyed by Jews in any other country.[13]

Hogarth Message, January, 1918

The release of the terms of the Constantinople and Sykes-Picot agreements by the new Bolshevik government in Russia prompted the British government, in an effort to reassure the Arabs of its good intentions, to state that the Entente powers were fully committed to the concept of Arab independence. It stressed that the Balfour Declaration did not conflict with previous promises and would be implemented only inasmuch as it was "compatible with the freedom of the existing population both economic and political . . . . " [14]

Fourteen Points, January 8, 1918

In President Wilson's fundamental statement of American peace aims, Article 12 dealt with the Ottoman Empire.

The Turkish portions of the present Ottoman Empire should be assured a secure sovereignty, but the other nationalities which are now under Turkish rule should be assured an undoubted security of life and an absolutely unmolested opportunity to autonomous development, and the Dardanelles should be permanently opened as a passage to the ships and commerce of all nations under international guarantees. [15]

Four Principles, February 11, 1918

These principles constituted a reiteration and further definition by Wilson of the right of self-determination of nations. Statements such as the following left little doubt as to Wilson's fundamental position: "Peoples and provinces are not to be bartered about . . . ."; "Every territorial settlement involved in this war must be made in the interests and for the benefit of the populations concerned. . . . "; "All well-defined national aspirations shall be accorded the utmost satisfaction possible . . . without introducing new or perpetuating old elements of discord and antagonism. . . ." [16]

Declaration to the Seven, June, 1918

This was a statement by the British government to seven Arab leaders that Britain recognized the "complete and sovereign independence of the Arabs" who inhabited territories that had been independent before the war or that had been liberated from Turkish control by Arab forces during the course of the war. Territories occupied by the Allies or remaining under Turkish control would be handled in conformity with the "principle of the consent of the governed." [17]

Four Ends, July 4, 1918

Here again, President Wilson stressed that the peace settlement must be based upon "the settlement of every question . . . upon the basis of the free acceptance of that settlement by the people immediately concerned." [18]

Five Particulars, September 27, 1918

This was the last of the great pronouncements of President Wilson, in which he stated, among other things, that the peace must be based on "impartial justice . . . between those to whom we wish to be just and those to whom we do not wish to be just. It must be a justice that plays no favorites and knows no standard but the equal rights of the several peoples concerned." [19]

Anglo-French Declaration, November 7, 1918

This policy statement reiterated in the most definite terms the determination of the two powers to do everything possible in the Near East to aid the establishment of governments "deriving their authority from the initiative and free choice of the indigenous populations." The two governments specifically disclaimed any desire "to impose on the populations of these regions any particular institutions." [20]

Taken together, all these agreements and policy statements did not provide any clear outline for a Near East settlement. The spirit, if not the letter, of the Sykes-Picot Agreement was clearly in conflict with the British promises to the Arabs. The withdrawal of Russia

from the war removed the cornerstone on which much of the subsequent network of agreements had been built. The Balfour Declaration promised the formation of a homeland for Jews in a territory
with only a ten percent Jewish population. President Wilson's promise of equal justice for victor and vanquished was nowhere to be
found in the secret treaties that partitioned both Turkish and non-
Turkish areas into spheres of influence for European states. Finally,
the Wilsonian concept of the self-determination of nations, explicitly
agreed to by the British and French in their joint declaration of
November 7, 1918, would, if ultimately followed, ensure the over-
throw of many of the provisions that had been agreed to secretly
by the statesmen of France, Great Britain, and Italy.

Aims of the Great Powers

Before beginning discussion of the work of the Peace Conference
itself, it is necessary to examine briefly the political situation within
the major countries and the attitudes of the various delegations
toward the Ottoman Empire at the time the Peace Conference
opened.

Great Britain

The British delegation, headed by Prime Minister David Lloyd
George, arrived in Paris buoyed by an overwhelming victory at the
polls for Lloyd George's coalition government in November, 1918.
Although this election, the first in eight years and including eight
million newly enfranchised voters, three-fourths of them women,
gave Lloyd George a clear vote of public confidence, it also placed
him in a difficult political position. For not only did this election
signal the Labour party's withdrawal from the wartime coalition,
it also resulted in a complete split within Liberal party ranks between
those supporting former Prime Minister Herbert Asquith and those
willing to follow Lloyd George in a coalition government. Although
Asquith's group suffered a thoroughgoing defeat, to achieve it Lloyd
George had to throw in his lot with the Conservatives; in fact, the

famous "coupon" letter certifying candidates supported by the government was issued to 364 Conservatives as opposed to only 159 Liberals. The result was that within the victorious coalition Conservatives outnumbered Liberals by two and one-half to one. The Conservatives generally tended to take a more vindictive attitude than did the Liberals toward the enemy and the peace settlements to be imposed, an attitude that reflected with reasonable accuracy the feeling of the electorate. Lloyd George may well have been aware of this popular attitude when he decided to run on a coalition rather than a party ticket.

During the election campaign, Lloyd George had personally tended to take a relatively calm and moderate view of the coming peace negotiations, though he made little effort to control his more vindictive supporters or disavow their belligerent statements. Yet the results of the election created a situation in which he, though a Liberal, had to depend on support from a predominantly Conservative, and what has been described as "jingo," House of Commons.[21] In other words, Lloyd George found himself in the strange and rather uneasy position of heading a coalition government at a time when party politics had returned with a vengeance, a coalition in which, because his own party was a minority, he found himself as much prisoner as leader. It is therefore understandable that he felt at his back the considerable pressure of what both the press and government understood to be right-wing popular and parliamentary demand for a harsh peace. Naturally, most of this vindictiveness was directed at Germany and to a lesser extent Austria rather than at belligerents such as Bulgaria and the Ottoman Empire. In fact, Near East questions, on which Lloyd George himself tended to take a rather forceful anti-Turk position, played no real role in the election campaign and were of comparatively little concern to the general public and the press.[22]

Despite this fact there is no question but that the Conservative-dominated government which emerged from the election saw Britain's future in the greatness of its empire. During the last years of the war, the Lloyd George War Cabinet had been dominated by men such as Milner and Curzon who regarded a consolidated and powerful empire as the sine qua non of British participation in the war. The election only strengthened the imperialists' position. Thus while public pressure for a peace that would force the defeated continental powers to pay the costs of the war and reconstruction was great, the chief aims of the government, both before and after the election, were the destruction of Germany's navy and the relinquishment of all colonies held by the defeated nations. In this pro-imperial policy Britain was strongly supported by its overseas dominions.[23]

To say that complete agreement existed on Near East questions within the British peace delegation would be a gross oversimplification. Yet there were certain fundamental and incontestable principles to which all the delegates unquestionably subscribed. Chief among these was the conviction that the crown jewel of the British Empire, India, must be protected at all costs, and that it was therefore necessary to obtain in one way or another British control of the various land and sea routes to India. On the protection of the empire there could be no compromise. Thus the core of British policy was founded in cold reality on an imperial concept of the power struggle.

This attitude was hardly new; it had been the basis for Britain's nineteenth-century policy of supporting the territorial integrity of the Ottoman Empire, while making sure that British influence remained supreme at the Sublime Porte. Now, however, the events of the war had made impossible a continuation of that policy. Therefore, new measures to ensure continued British control of the "lifeline" of the empire were in order.[24]

Yet, while new ways of implementing an old policy might be called for, the opponent remained the same: France. For centuries France and Britain had been commercial and imperial rivals in the Near East. Now, with the threat of German imperialism gone and the war in Europe at an end, Britain was in no way ready to sacrifice its imperial supremacy in the Near East because of wartime commitments to France. In fact, the likelihood of a shift in the balance of continental power toward French supremacy was all the more reason for building up the British Empire at the expense of French power elsewhere.[25]

The demands and claims of the British delegation to the Peace Conference centered on three basic concepts. The first was the necessity of establishing as great a degree of British supremacy as possible in the Near East. Second, there was the equal necessity of reducing the competitive position of France to the lowest possible level. Finally, there was the belief that the traditional policy of supporting the government at Constantinople would no longer suffice to satisfy these ends.

It was the first two of these aims that had led Britain during the war to insist upon the naval command of the Aegean fleet as well as command of a planned expedition against Constantinople. These were not unreasonable demands, since Britain and its dominions were furnishing most of the ships and troops. It was to further these same aims that Britain froze France out of the armistice negotiations and proceeded to send British troops to Constantinople immediately following the signing of the armistice. These measures were all designed to ensure that during the time when the final disposition of the Ottoman Empire was being made at Paris, the old tradition of British political domination in the Near East would be preserved.[26]

However, it was the addition of the third concept to the first two that guided the British delegation in deciding to support the Arab cause at the Peace Conference. A government decision in December, 1918, that British, rather than international or American control of Palestine, should be sought can be at least partly ascribed to the same reasoning.[27] Similarly, the formation of an independent Armenian state would remove control of the northern gateway to India from Turkey and provide a buffer against Russian expansion, and thus Britain enthusiastically supported this aim.

Although the British wanted no part of an Armenian mandate, they were not happy over the prospect of French domination in the area. They also recognized that France would never consent to British supervision of the Straits. However, these areas, originally promised to Russia, obviously were not to be turned over to a Bolshevik regime whose ideology preached uncompromising hostility to Western political systems. Even if the Bolsheviks were ultimately defeated, Russia had forfeited any claim to these territories by failing to remain in the war until its conclusion. Thus, in January, 1919, it became one of the basic aims of British policy to place these areas under the authority of the United States.[28]

It was not generosity or some sort of overwhelming feeling of friendship for America that prompted this attitude. Lloyd George's comment at the December meeting in which he and Curzon reversed their position supporting an American mandate in Palestine is indicative of his view of the United States when its presence might threaten British interests. "As regards Palestine, he had been in favour of entrusting that to the United States originally, but had changed his mind. It would involve placing an absolutely new and crude Power in the middle of our complicated interests in Egypt, Arabia, and Mesopotamia. Everyone with a complaint to make against the British administration would rush off to the United States, who would not be able to resist the temptation to meddle." [29]

However, the British recognized that by appealing to the Wilsonian brand of idealism, they might obtain acceptable solutions to issues that otherwise might be resolved in ways distinctly distasteful to them. The United States would help Britain avoid fulfilling its wartime commitments and perhaps even aid in fighting British battles at the negotiating table. The British also saw no long-range threat to their own imperial interests in the United States's acceptance of a role in affairs concerning Armenia and the Straits, for they were convinced that America would never assume the competitive position of a rival such as France.[30]

In short, the sources of British policy lay neither in humanitarian concern for rising nations and nationalities nor in international cooperation and lofty self-sacrifice. That these motives were present and in tune with certain aspects of public opinion (particularly in the case of Armenia) cannot be denied.[31] But it is questionable whether general humanitarian concepts or specific concern for national or ethnic groups would have meant much to those in control had these concerns not coincided with the new tactical position taken by the British government in January, 1919.

On one issue, however, there was no agreement at all. This was the ultimate political fate of Constantinople and the Straits. The War Office and the Government of India bitterly opposed forcing the Turks out of Constantinople. The War Office believed that such a step would create serious opposition among the Turks and make any subsequent peace treaty nearly unenforceable. The India Government was opposed because of the opposition such a move would arouse within the large Moslem population of India. In January, 1918, Lloyd George had indicated his support for this position. Now, however, backed by the Foreign Office, he adamantly insisted that the Turk must be totally expelled from Europe, that the "bag and baggage" policy of Gladstone, so recently reiterated by Lord Curzon, should be fulfilled.[32] In this he was in accord with popular opinion, which was deeply influenced by a well-organized flow of anti-Moslem propaganda of a religious nature that poured from the pulpits and the press.

Any British hopes that the United States might agree to accept a Straits mandate were greatly diminished upon President Wilson's arrival in Europe. When Lloyd George broached the question, Wilson immediately refused, stating that he did not wish the United States to become involved in territorial questions and that besides "it would be difficult to persuade them [the American people] that such a mandate was not a profit, but really a burden." [33] Ultimately, in a meeting of department representatives on January 30, the War Office reluctantly agreed to the expulsion of Turkey from Europe in return for a Foreign Office commitment that control of the area should be vested in an international commission rather than a single power. Given President Wilson's blunt refusal of a Straits mandate, this indeed seemed a logical compromise. Nonetheless, both Lloyd George and Balfour remained firm in their belief that an American mandate was the best possible solution, and they continued to advocate this both within the British delegation and at the peace Conference.[34]

France

French interest in the Near East was based as much on historical and emotional grounds as it was on practical issues. Traditionally, Frenchmen saw their nation as "the great Christian power of the Orient; it is France that amidst the misery and ruins of Turkish barbarism remained the hope of the oppressed and who saved their future for them." [35] The aura of history and of long-standing French moral, political, educational, and economic influence formed the foundation for French interests in the Near East. Practically speaking, France had invested sums totaling approximately three and a quarter billion francs in the Ottoman Empire.[36] It is easy to understand French Foreign Minister Stéphen Pichon's statement to the Chamber of Deputies that France had "incontestable rights to safeguard in the Ottoman Empire." [37] While agreeable to the expulsion of Turkey from Constantinople, France was no more willing to concede British control of the Straits area than the British were to admit France to a similar position.[38]

Territorially, the French claimed Syria, Cilicia, Lebanon, and Palestine. They based these claims not only on historical rights but more concretely on Allied wartime commitments. Like the British, they professed a willingness to revise these agreements. Unlike the British, they had no real interest in actually doing so. Since the only revision that could benefit France would be an extension of French authority eastward from Syria, and since in any revision the British would be likely to give them less rather than more, the French held meticulously to the 1916 Sykes-Picot Agreement, arguing that it must remain in force in all aspects until a new arrangement was reached. This had been the stated French policy for some time, and it would not vary appreciably during the early weeks of the Peace Conference.[39]

However, there were complicating factors. The issue of preeminent import for France was the European settlement, so much so that all other concerns played a secondary role. Although France did not hold parliamentary elections in the fall of 1918, the political atmosphere in the French assembly indicated clearly a move to the right, which paralleled the results of the British and American elections.[40] While this in one sense strengthened those favoring French imperial aims, it provided even greater support for those whose primary concern was the settlement in Europe.

Public and parliamentary demand for terms that would permanently disable Germany and assure French military and economic supremacy on the continent was tremendous. The war in the west had been fought primarily on French soil, resulting in incredible destruction of property and loss of life. Added to this was the desire for *revanche* against Germany that had dominated French politics since the Franco-Prussian war of 1870. Small wonder that in 1919 France was obsessed with the need for the emasculation of Germany and the creation of future security for itself.

As a result, Near Eastern problems necessarily occupied less time, energy, and concentration at the Quai d'Orsay than at the British Foreign Office. Paul Cambon, French ambassador in London, believed that Clemenceau was simply not interested in the Near East, quoting the premier as stating that it was good only "for storybooks." [41] Although this judgment seems overly harsh, there is much to indicate that Clemenceau was willing, if necessary, to sacrifice French interests elsewhere in order to obtain a more favorable European settlement.[42]

Evidence to substantiate this can be found in Lloyd George's account of Clemenceau's visit to London in December, 1918.

When Clemenceau came to London after the War I drove with him to the French Embassy through cheering crowds who acclaimed him with enthusiasm. After we reached the Embassy, he asked me what it was I specially wanted from the French. I instantly replied that I wanted Mosul attached to Irak, and Palestine from Dan to Beersheba under British control. Without any hesitation he agreed.[43]

Since this agreement was never recorded on paper, the question of whether reciprocal British concessions of some sort were part of the agreement was to be an issue of great debate in subsequent months. In June, 1920, Victor Berard defended Clemenceau in the French Senate by asserting that the concessions had been made partly to ensure British cooperation in regard to French demands for "Metz and Strasbourg without a plebiscite, the Saar basin, Rhine occupation, complete security, and coal without a money advance." [44] The truth of this allegation is hard to ascertain; certainly Clemenceau later maintained that the cession of Mosul had been made only in return for promises guaranteeing the fulfillment of French interests in the Near East. Nonetheless, Berard's statement in general reflected a position that the vast majority of Frenchmen would have supported, at least in the early stages of the peace negotiations. Clemenceau was determined that the wartime entente should be preserved at all costs, and undoubtedly realized that if he wished to obtain the Saar Basin and some form of control in the Rhineland, a moderate, soft-line approach to British demands elsewhere would necessarily be in order.[45]

Italy

Basing their claims on the promises made in the Treaty of London and the Saint Jean de Maurienne Agreement, the Italians sought, above all else, the preservation of a "Mediterranean equilibrium" following the projected breakup of the Ottoman Empire. Aside from Libya, which had for all intents and purposes been a closed Italian preserve since the Italian-Turkish War of 1911–12, this meant that Italy was less concerned with obtaining specific rights and privileges than with the maintenance and even extension of its position as a Mediterranean and colonial power. Thus any extension of territorial influence on the part of any other power in the Near East must of necessity bring a concomitant extension of Italian control or spheres of influence. As Tommaso Tittoni put it in a speech to his colleagues in the Italian Senate: "If the others have nothing, we will demand nothing. This is not an imperialist criterion, it is only the criterion of distributive justice." [46]

But it was clear that "the others" were going to obtain a good deal, and as the Peace Conference approached, the Italians became increasingly alarmed over the weakness of their Near East position. In particular they recognized that the territory they had staked out for themselves in Anatolia could in no way be justified in terms of any of the Wilsonian principles. The British and French claims were in non-Turkish Arab territories that would in any case be separated from Turkey. This was not true for Anatolia. Moreover, the British and French had troops in occupation of many of the territories they claimed; in fact the French had even occupied some of the territory claimed by the Italians. Yet when Italy proposed to send troops to the Adana and Adalia regions, the British and French strongly protested that there was no legitimate reason to do so under the armistice terms because nothing that was happening there in any way threatened the security of the Allies. Thus the Italians found themselves shut out from the areas they regarded as their legitimate share in the spoils of the Ottoman Empire, nor did it seem likely that any scheme of mandates or other form of supervision would subsequently justify their claims.[47]

Not only did the Italians see their rewards jeopardized by the actions of the great powers, they also regarded fearfully the aspirations of the Greek government. For the Greeks could claim in Anatolia what the Italians could not, a sizable national population native to the area, at least in the cities along the seacoast. Thus, from the Wilsonian point of view, the Greek claim was stronger, and the Italians recognized it. Moreover, nothing would endanger Italy's position in the eastern Mediterranean as much as the extension of Greek control to the Mediterranean littoral of Asia Minor.[48]

Thus by the time the conference opened the Italians were both bitter and suspicious of what they regarded as the moralizing interference of the United States and the power politics of France and Britain. The tone of Italian dispatches indicates a belief that the other powers were not taking Italy and Italian claims as seriously as they should.[49] More likely than not these suspicions were correct. Italy's entrance into the war had come late, and in a sense had been bought in hard bargaining sessions by the British and French. Moreover, the course of the war had placed Italy in a secondary military role, one in which it could hardly claim to have acquitted itself brilliantly. If the British saw their future security in the strength of their empire, and the French saw it in the disablement of Germany and the preservation of their alliance with Britain, certainly neither saw Italy as very important in their future plans. While recognizing that certain promises made in return for services would have to be kept, the other victorious powers seemed to evidence no real concern for the preservation and retention of Italy as a strong ally. Although one can more easily sense than prove that this attitude existed in January, 1919, the events of the following months and the subsequent growth of open hostility toward Italy on the part of the other major powers serves to strengthen rather than weaken the case.

The domestic political situation in Italy also helped intensify Italian territorial demands at the Peace Conference. Although Prime Minister Orlando was considered somewhat of a political moderate, in Italy as elsewhere, victory brought with it an upsurge of nationalism and chauvinism, which was reflected in a political swing to the conservative right. By the time the Peace Conference opened, these forces, led by Italian Foreign Minister Baron Sidney Sonnino, were firmly in control of parliament and the cabinet. They regarded the territorial concessions promised to Italy in the wartime agreements as minimal rather than maximal, ones that should be expanded now that Russia had been removed from the diplomatic equation. Moreover, opposition to extensive imperial claims centered in the socialist and liberal parties, who also sought domestic reforms that were bitterly opposed by the conservatives. The fact that these opposition groups regarded Wilson as their champion only intensified Sonnino's determination to gain Italy's imperial aims at the conference, for both he and Orlando recognized that failure to do so would create a severe political crisis at home.[50]

United States

Unlike the major Allied powers, the United States had never declared war on Turkey. Although there had been a certain amount of public and congressional agitation for such action, both Wilson and the State Department vigorously opposed these proposals. The reasons were several. At no time had the Ottoman government taken any provocative action similar to the submarine sinkings that had brought the United States into the war with Germany. American diplomatic experts were convinced that Turkey was little more than a tool in German hands, and a declaration of war would only serve to increase Germany's control over the Ottoman government. Moreover, the United States at no time contemplated any action in the war that would have involved it in the Near East front. A declaration of war would have led to the closing of several American educational institutions in Turkey and the confiscation of their considerable property. American aid to Syrians and Armenians, which amounted to close to a million dollars a month, would have been cut off since it was channeled through missionary sources in Turkey. Finally, aside from religious, educational, and humanitarian concerns, America was thought to have no real interest in Near Eastern affairs.[51]

Nonetheless, in the fall of 1917, as part of a general study of problems relating to the forthcoming peace settlements, a committee of American experts examined the problem of a peace treaty with Turkey. The recommendations of this "Inquiry," dated December 22, 1917, provided President Wilson with information that he used as a guide in framing point twelve of the Fourteen Points. In January, 1919, these recommendations still remained the basis of American policy in the Near East.[52]

> It is necessary to free the subject races of the Turkish Empire from oppression and misrule. This implies at the very least autonomy for Armenia and the protection of Palestine, Syria, Mesopotamia and Arabia by the civilized nations. It is necessary also to establish free intercourse through and across the straits. Turkey proper must be justly treated and freed from economic and political bondage.[53]

A definite program was worked out in Paris by the American delegation during January, 1919. The cardinal point was the contention that all agreements or treaties that conflicted with the armistice terms had been abrogated because all the Allies had agreed that the peace treaties should be based on the Fourteen Points.[54] Throughout the peace negotiations the United States would hold to this position in regard to the secret treaties. This attitude was certainly justified when it concerned Germany, which had surrendered on the basis of an agreement that the final peace settlement would be based upon the Fourteen Points. But the extension of this interpretation to include a nation with which the United States was not at war and whose armistice terms, unilaterally negotiated by the British, had been those of unconditional surrender with no mention of the famed Wilsonian principles, appears questionable.[55] In reality, the only possible case that could be made for including Turkey within the confines of the Wilsonian declarations lay in the fact that the powers were bound, not by any commitment to the Turkish government, but on the one hand by the Anglo-French Declaration of November, 1918, and on the other by a purely inter-Allied moral obligation to fulfill points five and twelve of the Fourteen Points.

These called for adjustment of colonial claims giving "equal weight" to the wishes of the imperial governments and the native populations, and the freeing of minorities from Turkish control.[56]

Popular attitude in America toward Turkey in the winter of 1918–19 was one of intense hostility, based chiefly on religious and humanitarian grounds. This vindictive attitude was reflected by the members of the American peace delegation, and was most aptly summarized by the former United States minister to Turkey, Henry Morgenthau: "So long as the Koran makes murder a part of the Mohammedan religion, the Moslem must not be permitted to rule over Christians or Jews." [57]

On January 21, 1919, the American intelligence section of the Peace Conference submitted a series of recommendations concerning Turkey that reflected this anti-Turk position.[58] The report urged the creation of an international state at the Straits under the supervision of the League of Nations. It would include the "entire littoral of the Straits, and of the Sea of Marmora" [59] and in Asia would incorporate Panderma and Brusa. The latter was to be included in order to keep a city so near the Straits from becoming the new Turkish capital and a center of intrigue. Large enough to have its own truck garden and water supply facilities, the international state would remain small enough to be easily administered. The actual form this administration would take was not discussed, and for good reason. It appears that there was a difference of opinion between Wilson and the rest of the delegation on this issue. Wilson favored control by a small power or a group of small powers, while the American Near East experts, Clive Day, Charles Seymour, and Albert Lybyer, inclined toward a great power, preferably Britain or the United States. They were in agreement with Wilson, however, that it was highly improbable that the United States could undertake such an obligation, for public opinion in America was not ready for such a step.[60] The report also approved the formation of new Arab states and the creation of an Armenian state, on condition that they be put under a League of Nations mandatory system. Great Britain was specifically named as the most suitable power to administer a mandate in Palestine.

One final point is of extreme import in considering the position of the American delegation to the peace conference. The congressional elections in November, 1918, had produced a Republican majority in both houses of Congress. This had been achieved in the face of strong pleas by Wilson for a Democratic victory as a vote of confidence in his leadership and peace program. The Republicans had openly taken a hard-line position in the electoral campaign, favoring total military victory and stringent peace terms. Moreover, the Republican victory elevated to the position of Senate majority leader and chairman of the Foreign Relations Committee Henry Cabot Lodge of Massachusetts, a man whose personal and political antipathy towards Wilson was long standing and of such intensity that he could write to Theodore Roosevelt in 1915, "I never expected to hate anyone in politics with the hatred I feel towards Wilson." [61] So vehement had the Republican leadership been in refusing to support Wilson's peace program that he in turn refused to include any prominent Republican from either the House or Senate as a member of the peace delegation, a diplomatic faux pas of the first order. Although Wilson apparently remained convinced that in the long run popular and congressional opinion in the United States would support any settlement based upon his peace principles, many within his own delegation and the governments of the Allied powers were not so sanguine. Thus, while the Italian and French delegations were in tune with the domestic swing to the right at home and Lloyd George had made his accomodation with a similar development in Britain, for Wilson, though he may not have fully realized it, the domestic political battlelines had been drawn and the obvious struggle at hand bode ill for the successful completion of his peace program. [62]

An overview of the general attitude of each of the great powers at the beginning of the Paris Peace Conference indicates that there was a fair amount of agreement on basic issues. All appeared ready to exclude the Turk from Europe and to establish some form of international control over Constantinople and the Straits, preferably (for all but Wilson) that of a great power. All agreed that the Arab portions of the Ottoman Empire should be liberated and that some sort of national recognition should be granted to the newly freed nationalities, albeit under the watchful care of the great powers. All four of the great powers had accepted the Balfour Declaration.

All were in accord with the creation of an Armenian state, and all recognized that this state would need a great deal of outside aid and advice of an economic, military, and political nature. Thus it would seem that the outline of a peace settlement had been formed and that only details were left.

But what details! If the Straits and Constantinople were to be internationalized, how would this affect Constantinople's religious role as the seat of the caliphate? If non-Turkish elements were to be freed, how was this freedom to be achieved; what sort of states created; what degree of independence or foreign control allowed; and under the protective wing of which European nation would each area be placed? What was meant by a "national home for the Jews"? How were Wilson's various declarations of purpose to be reconciled with the secret agreements of the war years? How could one determine the wishes of the peoples of the Near East, and, if they could be determined at all, were their aims economically and politically feasible? In regard to Armenian and Zionist aspirations, was the doctrine of majority rule and self-determination even just? How could the sizeable capital investment of European nations in the Ottoman Empire be safeguarded, and what provision would be made in regard to the enormous Ottoman debt? These were only a few of the more easily discernible problems that remained to be settled. Thus, when the various questions came before the Peace Conference a host of differences suddenly appeared concerning the practical implementation of accepted generalities.

New Friction in Paris

In Paris, friction between the powers quickly developed, chiefly over such problems as the German Treaty and the League of Nations (toward which all of the powers except the United States took a rather cool view). Even seemingly minor irritants, such as French indignation at the acceptance of English as one of the diplomatic languages of the conference, played a surprisingly important role in the development of antagonistic attitudes.[63]

Discord over Near Eastern affairs quickly appeared as well. The British and the Italians were annoyed by the blatantly pro-French stand of the Allied commander in chief in European Turkey, General Franchet d'Esperey.[64] The Italians, vexed by the French occupation of Mersina and Adana in Cilicia and furious at British unwillingness to allow similar Italian action in the area promised them in Adalia, began laying plans for unilateral action in the near future.[65] A decision to take over control of Turkish coastal trade produced a minor quarrel between France and Italy over supervision of the port of Smyrna, with the Italians at least temporarily winning the upper hand.[66] The British agreed to Greek requests for aid in repatriating their nationals to Asia Minor and asked France and Italy to join in sending a commission to investigate the situation. This they did with the greatest reluctance; the Italians in particular were opposed, since any Greek repatriation to Asia Minor could only strengthen Greek claims to that area.[67]

Both France and Italy were anxious to enter into secret negotiations with Britain on Near Eastern affairs. The overtures were bluntly refused. The British stated that they were in complete accord with President Wilson's spirit of open diplomacy, that with the Peace Conference at hand the time was hardly propitious for secret talks, and that the United States must be present at any further discussions on these matters.[68] This high-minded spirit was probably dictated by the consideration that separate discussions with either the French or Italians would of necessity have as a basis the wartime agreements, and the British, now in nearly total military control of the Near East, were far less enthusiastic about fulfilling these commitments than were the French or the Italians.[69]

Personal animosities also made their appearance in Paris. Clemenceau quickly came to the conclusion that Wilson was "too soft". Wilson, in turn, evidenced an almost instantaneous dislike of Orlando and Sonnino at the time of their first meeting in December, 1918, a feeling that Sonnino clearly reciprocated. Only Lloyd George seemed able to remain relatively clear of this clash of personalities.[70]

The League and the Mandate System

Despite all the tensions, large and small, it did appear as if the basic lines of a Near East settlement were fairly well established, and therefore the powers at first approached the problem with relative unconcern. The question of what areas should be taken from Turkey and what form of government they should have dominated the first few meetings of the Council of Ten.[71] For some time it had generally been accepted that a form of mandate rather than actual annexation of these territories by European states would be used. Wilson had been determined that the mandates should be placed under the authority of the League of Nations.[72] But the first concrete plan came from another source. On December 16, 1918, Jan Smuts, delegate from South Africa, asked that the League of Nations be given the right to dispose of the territories of the defunct empires of Austria-Hungary, Russia, and Turkey. He recommended that they be placed under the mandatory control of a single power that would be responsible to the League of Nations for its actions. Annexation would be forbidden, and the mandatory power would be required to follow an open-door policy in terms of economic development and trade. Eventually the mandated areas would become independent.[73] This suggestion proved acceptable to President Wilson.

No attempt will be made here to record the long and sometimes acrimonious discussions concerning the organization of the mandates and the areas to be included. Ultimately, the plan for mandating the territories of the Austro-Hungarian and Russian Empires was dropped in favor of recognizing the governments of the various independent states that had already been formed in these areas. Though the principle was accepted in regard to the Ottoman Empire and the German African colonies, neither the number and size of these mandates nor the powers to whom they would go were designated.[74]

No disagreement arose over the areas that should be completely severed from the Ottoman Empire; a British request that Kurdistan be added to the draft resolution that named Armenia, Syria, Mesopotamia, Palestine, and Arabia was readily accepted.[75] The naming of these areas was done "without prejudice to the settlement of other parts of the Turkish Empire." [76] Mandates were to be divided into three types, A, B, and C, based upon the extent of their economic and political development. Those formed from territory formerly belonging to the Ottoman Empire were to be placed in the A group, since they had "reached a stage of development where their existence as independent nations can be provisionally recognized subject to the rendering of administrative advice and assistance by a mandatory power until such time as they are able to stand alone. The wishes of these communities must be a principal consideration in the selection of a mandatory power." [77]

The addition of Kurdistan to the list of territories to be taken from Turkey was indicative of a recent British policy decision. Ever since the previous summer the idea of an independent Kurdish state under British supervision had been under consideration. This would prevent Turkey from retaining control of the territorial gap between Armenia and Mesopotamia. Moreover, it would give the British a firmer hold on the Mosul vilayet, which was ethnically half Kurd, as well as provide a buffer zone for that oil-rich province. Arnold Wilson, acting civil commissioner for Mesopotamia, recounts in his memoirs that by January of 1919, local government through tribal chieftains had been initiated under British guidance. "We were charged with the foundation of an independent Southern Kurdish state under British auspices." [78] However, Wilson believed that the only solution lay in Kurdistan's incorporation into Mesopotamia as an autonomous province.

The decision to install League of Nations mandates in the Near East was one that can be attributed chiefly to President Wilson and the American delegation, and it was an achievement of great magnitude. It constituted an enormous step forward, not so much because the territories that were to be separated from the Ottoman Empire were named, for this had never been a great source of discussion or conflict, but rather because by accepting the mandatory principle and by placing the mandates under the authority and supervision of the League of Nations, some of the provisions of the wartime agreements, particularly the Sykes-Picot Agreement, were automatically superseded. These agreements had called for open annexation of certain areas by France and Britain. Under a mandate system this could not occur.

It is easy to see why this shift was welcomed by the British, for they saw in it a means of gaining unfettered jurisdiction over Palestine as well as a possible way out of the moral dilemma that they faced due to conflicting French and Arab claims. Moreover, it did much to bolster the British claims in subsequent talks that none of the Sykes-Picot terms were valid any longer. Harder to understand is the fact that Clemenceau did not raise his voice in at least nominal protest against a scheme that deprived France of its annexationist ambitions in Syria, especially when he had to face the opposition of the French colonial office, which favored a policy of direct annexation.[79] Yet even here an explanation can be found.

Under the terms of the Sykes-Picot Agreement, the four interior cities of Damascus, Homs, Hama, and Aleppo and all of eastern Syria were to be under Arab control and subject only to a vaguely defined French sphere of influence. Now, under the mandate system, the French could contend that Syria should be treated as a whole and France should have the League mandate and the right of occupation for it. In other words, in return for giving up a provision that allowed the annexation of a limited area, the French could now insist on a single mandate over a much larger territory.[80]

Having settled the general principles on which the future formation of mandates would be based, the Council of Ten turned to the temporary occupation and administration of the Ottoman Empire until such time as the final treaty terms were worked out. The question was raised by Orlando, who was anxious that Italy should occupy some territory. Three possible alternatives were proposed by Lloyd George:

> They could leave things as they were—leave the mandatories to be settled by the League of Nations and the occupation to go on exactly as at the present moment—or they could have a provisional mandate, leaving the definite final thing to be settled by the League of Nations; or they could now say they were the League of Nations and settle the business finally.[81]

Lloyd George advocated deciding once and for all, as a settlement at any time would be made by the same powers and perhaps even by the same people. Moreover, he stated that it was impossible for the British to support indefinitely the 1,084,000 British and imperial troops then in the Turkish Empire while waiting for a settlement that seemed very far away. Britain must have relief, and a permanent designation of mandates seemed the best and quickest way to achieve this.

Such a solution raised immediate problems for Wilson, for the creation of the mandates system greatly complicated America's position vis à vis the Near East settlement. Despite the well-founded reservations regarding American participation in the mandatory system that he had expressed to Lloyd George in December, Wilson recognized that it was next to impossible for him to be the chief instigator and supporter of the scheme and at the same time refuse to participate in it.[82] Moreover, he regarded the successful implementation of the mandate system as necessary in order to provide the League of Nations with an important, concrete task from the moment of its inception. Yet, there was no way that he could guarantee that America would accept a mandate, for such a decision rested exclusively with the Senate, which was dominated by a hostile Republican party led by his arch-foe, Henry Cabot Lodge.

Therefore Wilson vehemently opposed Lloyd George's proposal for an immediate assignment of mandates. Determined to avoid any undermining of the functions of the League, he had from the beginning of the discussion accepted the whole mandates plan "subject to re-consideration when the full scheme of the League of Nations was drawn up." [83] This policy was particularly necessary if the United States was to take a mandate in the Near East. America had never declared war on the Ottoman Empire and therefore could assume a role in Near Eastern affairs only on the basis of League of Nations membership. Therefore, he made it clear that if an immediate decision were to be made, political and legal reasons would make it impossible for him to accept any mandate for the United States. He therefore suggested redividing the territory between the great powers in order to obtain a temporary but more equitable division of occupation responsibilities. Final decisions relating to permanent mandates would be taken at a later date. This recommendation was accepted and the question was referred to the military representatives of the Allied and Associated Powers to determine the best method of deciding the equitable distribution of occupying forces.[84]

The report of the military representatives was submitted to the Council of Ten on February 5. It was discussed briefly on February

10 and placed on the agenda for the following day. The report recommended that British troops occupy Palestine and Mesopotamia and that the Italians be allowed to occupy the Caucasus region and the area around Konia. Syria (with the exception of Cilicia and Palestine), including the Adana, Aleppo, Homs, Damascus railroad, should be occupied by French troops. If subsequently it were found that an occupation of Armenia and Kurdistan was needed and the United States was willing, American troops might be despatched to these areas.[85]

However, the discussion scheduled for February 11 never took place, nor was any decision as to a redistribution of territories reached until the fall of 1919. Interestingly, the reasons for this delay rested partly in the acceptance of the mandates scheme itself. The larger Syria now eyed by France as a future mandate included territories that Britain had promised the Arabs. Recognizing the importance of de facto control, the British particularly feared French military occupation of the area, however temporary it might be in theory, before an agreement acceptable to the Arabs and safeguarding their own interests was reached. Therefore, on the morning of February 11, Lord Milner met with Clemenceau and laid the matter on the line.

[He] made it clear that we did not want Syria, and that we had not the slightest objection to France being there, but that we were anxious about the peace if the French rushed to occupy it at once. What we wanted . . . was an arrangement which both the French and the Arabs could accept, and it was impossible for us to move our troops until that had been arranged. . . . Meanwhile, the question is to be taken off the Agenda today.[86]

Two days later Philip Kerr informed Lloyd George that "the question of altering the military occupation is blocked. Milner has made that clear to Clemenceau and the U.S.A. are determined to support us on this." [87] Kerr noted that this meant that the Syrian question would therefore be postponed unless Milner could arrange an agreement between Feisal and Clemenceau. This would probably be possible only if the French would be content with Lebanon, which was unlikely. Nonetheless Kerr felt that "the French realize that we are not trying to get them out of Syria, and that the Arab difficulty is a genuine one not fomented by us." [88] Thus the British, who had originally asked for relief from the burdens of military occupation, had taken the initiative in suspending the negotiations aimed at providing exactly that relief.

Nonetheless, despite Anglo-French differences over Syria, in January of 1919 the Eastern Question, so long a source of strife among the European powers, appeared on the verge of a quick and easy solution. Moreover, the mandates plan offered a formula that would still allow the European states, which had eyed the riches of the Ottoman Empire for over a century, to gratify their desires. That there were problems remaining to be solved was apparent to all, but none of them seemed of great magnitude or capable of providing any lasting controversy or discord.

Turkey's provinces were gone; her allies were crushed; and, except for her champions among the Indian Muslims, she was friendless even in the camp of Islam. Constantinople was held by the victors, Turkey was encircled by enemies. Like wolves about the camp fire the Powers were prowling at the threshold with hungry eyes, for Turkey by nature is rich, and imperialism is greedy.[89]

1. For the text of the Armistice of Mudros, see Appendix A.

2. Britain's unilateral action was undoubtedly influenced by the fact that France had only recently acted similarly in regard to an armistice with Bulgaria. Great Britain, Cabinet Papers, Cab. 23/14, W.C. 489A, 10/21/18; W.C. 491A, 10/25/18; Sidney Sonnino, Papers relating to World War I in the Archive of Baron Sidney Sonnino (hereafter cited as Sonnino Papers) (Ann Arbor, Mich.: University Microfilms), Reel 20, no. 2046, Cellere to Rome, 10/16/18; no. 2162, Bonin Longare to Rome, 10/24/18; no. 2225, Cellere to Rome, 10/30/18; Reel 49, Rodd to Sonnino, 10/22/18; F. B. Maurice, The Armistices of 1918, pp. 17-26; D. Lloyd George, War Memoirs, 6:275-79; S. Leslie, Mark Sykes, His Life and Letters, p. 291; L. M. Adkisson, Great Britain and the Kemalist Movement for Turkish Independence, 1919-1923, pp. 71-75. For an extremely pro-French account, see M. Milleff, La Bulgarie et les Detroits, p. 144. The Turkish role in the negotiations is best recounted in Lord Kinross, 'Ataturk, A Biography of Mustafa Kemal, Father of Modern Turkey, pp. 146-51. Permission to reprint from the Sonnino Papers granted by Baron Lodovico de Renzis Sonnino and Professor Benjamin F. Brown.

3. Cabinet Papers, Cab. 23/14, W.C. 482A, 10/3/18; Cab. 28/5, I.C. 77, 10/7/18; Cab. 23/8, W.C. 484, Annex I, 10/11/18; A. J. Balfour Papers, British Museum, MSS 49744, Derby to Balfour, 10/23/18; MSS 49745, Cambon to Balfour, 10/27/18. Permission to reprint all quotations from the Balfour Papers granted by the Trustees of the British Museum.

4. See C. Sforza, Diplomatic Europe Since the Treaty of Versailles, p. 51.

5. A. J. Mayer, *Politics and Diplomacy of Peacemaking: Containment and Counterrevolution at Versailles, 1918–1919*, pp. 95–96.

6. Sonnino Papers, Reel 20, no. 2145, Imperiali to Rome, 10/24/18.

7. J. C. Hurewitz, *Diplomacy in the Near and Middle East, A Documentary Record, 1535–1956*, 2:7–11.

8. Ibid., pp. 11–12; Great Britain, *Parliamentary Papers, 1920*, Cmd. 671, "Agreement between France, Russia, Great Britain and Italy, Signed at London, April 26, 1915."

9. Great Britain, *Parliamentary Papers, 1939*, Cmd. 5957, "Correspondence between Sir Henry McMahon, His Majesty's High Commissioner at Cairo and the Sherif Hussein of Mecca, July 1915–March 1916"; Cmd. 5974, "Report of the Committee set up to consider certain correspondence which took place in the years 1915 and 1916 between Sir Henry McMahon, . . . and the Sherif of Mecca." See also Cabinet Papers, Cab. 24/68, G.T. 6185, "Memorandum on British Commitments to King Hussein," November, 1918. For a discussion based on an examination of Arab sources, see Z. N. Zeine, *The Struggle for Arab Independence*, chap. 1.

10. Hurewitz, *Diplomacy*, 2:15.

11. See Appendix B. The failure to include Italy in these negotiations, given the provisions of the Treaty of London and the fact that Italy had been at war with Turkey since June, 1915, has always seemed strange. According to Sir Eric Drummond, Grey was often urged to include the Italians, but he steadfastly refused because Italy had not declared war on Germany, "and he therefore would not regard them as a full Ally." (Italy did not declare war on Germany until August, 1916.) Drummond stated that he thought the Italian ambassador in London was told this later, privately and unofficially. Balfour Papers, MSS 49751, Drummond to Balfour, 5/6/19.

12. Cabinet Papers, Cab. 24/16, Memorandum by Lord Cecil for Italian ambassador, 6/7/17; E. L. Woodward and R. Butler, eds., *Documents on British Foreign Policy, 1919–1939*, Series 1 (hereafter cited as *Br. Doc.*), 4:638–41; A. Giannini, *I Documenti per la Storia della Pace Orientale, 1915–1932*, pp. 12–13.

13. Hurewitz, *Diplomacy*, 2:26.

14. Ibid., p. 29; See also, Great Britain, *Parliamentary Papers, 1939*, Cmd. 5964, "Statements Made on behalf of His Majesty's Government During the Year 1918 in regard to the Future Status of certain parts of the Ottoman Empire."

15. United States, *Congressional Record*, 65th Cong., 2d sess., 1/8/18, 56:680-81.

16. Ibid., 2/11/18, p. 1937.

17. Hurewitz, *Diplomacy*, 2:29–30; Great Britain, *Parliamentary Papers, 1939*, Cmd. 5964, "Statements during 1918."

18. *Congressional Record*, 65th Cong. 2d sess., 7/5/18, 56:8671.

19. Ibid., 9/28/18, p. 10887.

20. Hurewitz, *Diplomacy*, 2:30.

21. S. P. Tillman, *Anglo-American Relations at the Paris Peace Conference of 1919*, p. 64.

22. R. B. McCallum, *Public Opinion and the Last Peace*, pp. 27–60; C. L. Mowat, *Britain Between the Wars, 1918–1940*, pp. 2–13; Tillman, *Anglo-American Relations*, pp. 62–65; T. Jones, *Lloyd George*, pp. 158–64; Mayer, *Politics of Peacemaking*, chap. 5; H. Nicolson, *Peacemaking* (Boston, 1933), pp. 18–24; A. Marwick, *The Deluge: British Society and the First World War*, pp. 257–66; T. Wilson, "The Coupon and the British General Election of 1918," pp. 28–42, and *The Downfall of the Liberal Party, 1914–1935*, pp. 135–83. Permission to reprint from Harold Nicolson, *Peacemaking*, granted by Harcourt Brace Jovanovich, Inc., New York, and Nigel Nicolson, executor of the estate of Harold Nicolson, Kent, England.

23. M. Beloff, *Imperial Sunset: Britain's Liberal Empire, 1897–1921*, pp. 275–80; P. Guinn, *British Strategy and Politics, 1914–1918*, pp. 192–93; Italy, Ministero degli Affari Esteri, *I*

documenti diplomatici italiani, Sesta serie (hereafter cited as *Ital. Doc.*), 1:76, Avezzana to Sonnino, 11/14/18.

24. Cabinet Papers, Cab. 24/72, G.T. 6506, "The Settlement of Turkey and the Arabian Peninsula," Memorandum by Political Intelligence Department, 11/21/18; Great Britain, Foreign Office, Historical Section, *Handbooks prepared under the direction of the Historical Section of the Foreign Office*, no. 76, "Persian Gulf," p. 76.

25. At a cabinet meeting on October 3, 1918, Lloyd George commented that "he had been refreshing his memory about the Sykes-Picot Agreement, and had come to the conclusion that it was quite impracticable to present circumstances, and was altogether a most undesirable agreement from the British point of view." Cabinet Papers, Cab. 23/14, W.C. 482A, 10/3/18. See also Cab. 29/2, P. 83, Foreign Office Minute, 12/19/18; P. 97, Eastern Committee Resolutions Regarding the Disposal of Middle East Territories, 1/16/19. A Political Intelligence Department memorandum stated bluntly: "British desiderata in the Arab countries may be summed up as a British Monroe Doctrine, but with certain qualifications." Cab. 24/72, G.T. 6506, 11/21/18. See also Beloff, *Sunset*, pp. 183-85; E. Kedourie, *England and the Middle East: the Destruction of the Ottoman Empire 1914-1921*, pp. 136-37; J. Nevakivi, *Britain, France and the Arab Middle East, 1914-1920*, pp. 98-101.

26. Cabinet Papers, Cab. 23/14, W.C. 500A, 11/10/18, App. 3, Calthorpe to Admiralty, 11/10/18; Maurice, *Armistices*, pp. 16-17; P. Azan, *Franchet d'Esperey*, p. 217; H. Cumming, *Franco-British Rivalry in the Post War Near East*, pp. 51-52; H. Howard, *The Partition of Turkey, 1913-1923*, pp. 208-10.

27. Cabinet Papers, Cab. 27/24, Eastern Committee minutes, no. 42, 12/9/18; no. 43, 12/16/18; Cab. 24/72, Political Intelligence Department memorandum, G.T. 6506, 11/21/18; Cab. 23/42, I.W.C. 44, 12/20/18; D. Lloyd George, *The Truth About the Peace Treaties*, pp. 1146-47. During 1917 and the first part of 1918, opinion in Britain was quite strong in favor of an American mandate in Palestine. See L. Stein, *The Balfour Declaration*, pp. 606-11; Cabinet Papers, Cab. 23/42, I.W.C. 44, 12/20/18.

28. D. H. Miller, *My Diary at the Conference of Paris, with Documents*, 1:74, 1/11/19. Miller states that some members of the British delegation even wanted American control over Syria. See also Lloyd George, *Truth*, pp. 189-90; Cabinet Papers, Cab. 29/2, P. 97. Eastern Committee Resolutions, 1/16/19; Cab. 29/2, P. 84, Memorandum on Armenia and Transcaucasia, 1/1/19; David Lloyd George Papers, Beaverbrook Library, London, England, F89/2/3, Kerr to Lloyd George, n.d. [1918]; F6/6/5, Cecil to Lloyd George, 2/4/19; G. L. Beer, Diary at the Paris Peace Conference, December, 1918-August, 1919, 1/15/19; W. L. Westermann Papers, Personal Diary at the Peace Conference in Paris, December, 1918-July, 1919, Meeting with Vansittart, Mallett, and Toynbee, 1/15/19; *Ital. Doc.*, 1:342, Imperiali to Sonnino, 12/23/18; Nevakivi, *Arab Middle East*, p. 101. Permission to reprint material from the David Lloyd George Papers has been granted by the First Beaverbrook Foundation.

29. Cabinet Papers, Cab. 23/42, I.W.C. 44, 12/20/18.

30. Churchill alone was opposed to any American involvement in Near East territorial affairs, for he was afraid that the United States would then seek to become a Mediterranean naval power. W. R. Louis, "Great Britain and the African Peace Settlement," p. 879.

31. Popular opinion was generally anti-Turk, and seemed to center on three basic objectives: an independent Armenian state; the expulsion of the Turks from Europe; the "return" of the Mosque of Santa Sophia to its original Christian builders. See discussion of these issues in subsequent chapters.

32. Cabinet Papers, Cab. 27/24, Eastern Committee minutes, no. 46, 12/23/18; Cab. 28/5, I.C. 101, Allied Conference, 12/3/18; Cab. 29/2, P. 85, Curzon memorandum, 1/2/18 [*sic*] circulated January, 1919; Cab. 29/2, P. 91, Montagu memorandum, 1/8/19; Great Britain, Foreign Office, Class 608, "Peace Conference of 1919-1920: British Delegation Correspondence," F.O. 608/109/685-1-6/1500, Montagu memorandum, 2/5/19. See also Lloyd George, *Truth*, pp. 1014-15; H. Temperley, *A History of the Peace Conference*, 1:190; D. Lloyd George, *British War Aims; statement by the Rt. Hon. David Lloyd George, January*

5, *1918*, p. 11; G. L. Dickenson, *Documents Relating to Peace Proposals and War Aims, December, 1916-November, 1918*, p. 118; *Times* (London), 1/8/19, 1/20/19.

33. Lloyd George, *Truth*, pp. 189–90.

34. Foreign Office, F.O., 608/109/385-1-6/1096, Meeting of representatives of departmental missions of the British delegation, 1/30/19; F.O., 608/83/342-8-4/7442, "Statement of British Policy in the Middle East for Submission to the Peace Conference (if required)," 2/18/19; Nicolson, *Peacemaking*, pp. 252–53, 1/30/19. If, as it appears, the India Office delegate, Sir Arthur Hirtzel, did not oppose the decision on January 30, the India Office made up for it subsequently by consistently leading the fight for the retention of Constantinople by the Turks. A published summary of the British policy statement of February 18 may be found in H. N. Howard, *The King-Crane Commission*, pp. 12–20.

35. E. Driault, "Before Constantinople," p. 9. For similar emotional statements relating to a French "mission" in the Near East, see H. Richard, *La Syrie et la guerre*, passim; "La question de Syrie et la paix," pp. 119-31; Saint René Taillandier, "La France et la Syrie, notre ouvre dans le Levant et son avenir," pp. 771–804; G. Samné "French Interests in Syria," pp. 608–13.

36. J. B. Gidney, *A Mandate for Armenia*, pp. 98–99, n. 5.

37. S. Pichon before Chamber of Deputies, 12/29/18, as quoted in J. Pichon, *Le Partage du Proche Orient*, p. 164: See also *Le Temps* as quoted by the *Times* (London), 11/2/18; L. Evans, *United States Policy and the Partition of Turkey, 1914-1924*, p. 115. See also Premier Clemenceau's statement in *Le Matin*, as quoted by the *Times* (London), 12/11/18.

38. Cabinet Papers, Cab. 28/5 I.C. 101, Allied Conference, 12/3/18; Balfour Papers, MSS 49744, Derby to Balfour, 12/14/18; *Le Temps*, 1/22/19.

39. Cabinet Papers, Cab. 29/2, P. series, Foreign Office memorandum regarding French and Arab claims, 12/19/18; Sonnino Papers, Reel 24, no. 389, Soragna to Rome, 1/25/19; *Echo de Paris*, as quoted by the *Times* (London), 12/13/18; Howard, *King-Crane Commission*, pp. 9 10, Evans, *U.S. and Partition*, p. 115.

40. Mayer, *Politics of Peacemaking*, p. 186.

41. P. Cambon, *Correspondence, 1870-1924*, 3:275, 10/9/18.

42. See P. Miguel, "Le Journal des Débats et la paix de Versailles," p. 382. Clemenceau, who was known as an antiimperialist, has been bitterly criticized for the lack of French policy in this period. Gontaut-Biron has charged that instead of insisting on the immediate fulfillment of the provisions of the Sykes-Picot Agreement, France was content to rely on "the good will of friends whom we knew had interests different from ours." The English could not be blamed for pushing for what they wanted. "The English proposals to the Peace Conference scarcely favored us; they reflected the view of the English in contrast to which we proposed nothing." Instead, according to Frangulis, the biggest characteristic of French Near Eastern policy was Clemenceau's complete docility when he was faced with the claims of Lloyd George and Venizelos. Clemenceau was so concerned with the Rhine that he knew or cared little about anything else. R. de Gontaut-Biron, *Comment la France s'est installée en Syrie (1918-1919)*, p. 63; A. Frangulis, *La Grèce et la Crise Mondiale*, 2:133-34. See also Evans, *U.S. and Partition*, pp. 114–15; G. Suarez, *Briand*, 4:382–85, 382 n.1.

43. Lloyd George, *Truth*, p. 1038.

44. V. Berard to French Senate, 7/28/20, as quoted by Howard, *Partition*, p. 212.

45. Mayer, *Politics of Peacemaking*, pp. 184–85; Zeine, *Arab Independence*, pp. 57–59. A year later Clemenceau categorically denied that he had ever made such a one-sided unilateral concession. Yet there is much to indicate that at least an oral commitment was given. Great Britain, Foreign Office, Class 406, "Confidential Prints: Eastern Affairs," F.O. 406/41/169, Clemenceau to Lloyd George, 11/9/19; Class 371, "General Correspondence, 1920," F.O. 371/5109/E6304-56-44, Derby to Curzon, 6/10/20. For further discussion of this question, see below, Chapter 9.

46. Tittoni to Italian Senate, 12/14/18, as quoted by Pichon, *Partage*, p. 166. See also Sonnino Papers, Reel 42, no. 56, Sonnino to London and Paris, 1/8/18; no. 293, Sonnino to London

and Paris, 2/18/18; no. 1073, Sonnino to Supreme Command, 7/24/18; no. 1600, Sonnino to Naval Ministry, 10/30/18; Reel 20, no. 2456, Bonin Longare to Rome, 11/30/18; no. 2498, Sforza to Rome, 12/11/18; Reel 50, Promemoria, Asiatic Turkey, 1/30/19; Reel 49, Memorandum of Italian peace conference delegation, 2/1/19; Reel 53, Map, Desireable Boundary of Italian Asia Minor; *Ital. Doc.*, 1:335, Sonnino to Imperiali, 12/21/18; p. 398, Sonnino to Paris, London and Constantinople, 1/2/19; Foreign Office, F.O. 608/93/362-1-1/414, Rodd to Balfour, 12/10/18; Balfour to Rodd, 12/27/18; F.O. 406/41/15, Martino to Hardinge, 2/6/19; Hardinge to Martino, 2/11/19; United States, Department of State, "Papers of the American Commission to Negotiate Peace" (hereafter cited as A.C.N.P.) 185.513/20, Report of the Committee on Italian Colonial and Oriental Interests, 3/21/18. For a general discussion of Italian claims, see R. Albrecht-Carrié, *Italy at the Paris Peace Conference*, pp. 205-7.

47. Sonnino Papers, Reel 20, no. 2161, Bonin to Rome, 10/24/18; Reel 52, Imperiali to Sonnino, 10/28/18; Reel 49, Rodd to Sonnino, 12/15/18; Reel 44, Sonnino to Imperiali and Bonin Longare, 1/9/19; *Ital. Doc.*, 1:343, Sonnino to Imperiali, 12/28/18; p. 347, 12/24/18; p. 371, Imperiali to Sonnino, 12/28/18; p. 415, Sonnino to Imperiali and Bonin Longare, 1/5/19.

48. Sonnino Papers, Reel 17, no. 2036, Bosdari to Rome, 7/23/17; Reel 42, no. 114, Sonnino to Paris, 1/16/18; no. 1423, Sonnino to Paris and London, 10/1/18; no. 4481, Sonnino to Paris and London, 10/11/18. For a detailed examination of the Greek claims, see below, Chapter 2.

49. Sonnino Papers, Reel 18, no. 2966, Imperiali to Rome, 11/4/17; Reel 42, no. 970, Sonnino to Paris and London, 6/29/18; Reel 20, no. 1441, Imperiali to Rome, 7/16/18; no. 2341, Cellere to Rome, 11/4/18; Reel 42, no. 1611, Sonnino to London, 11/6/18; Reel 43, no. 1668, Sonnino to London, 12/16/18; *Ital. Doc.* 1:97, Imperiali to Orlando, 11/16/18; p. 267, Sonnino to Imperiali, 12/7/18; p. 287, Imperiali to Sonnino, 12/11/18; p. 447, Elia to Sonnino, 1/10/19.

50. For a discussion of Italian domestic politics in late 1918 and early 1919, see Mayer, *Politics of Peacemaking,* chap. 3; also C. Seton-Watson, *Italy from Liberalism to Fascism, 1870-1925,* pp. 505-27.

51. Evans, *U.S. and Partition,* pp. 32-42; H. M. Sachar, *The Emergence of the Middle East, 1914-1924,* pp. 340-47.

52. For a critical study of the work of the Inquiry, see L. Gelfand, *The Inquiry: American Preparations for Peace, 1917-1919,* pp. 239-58. See also H. M. Sachar, "The United States and Turkey, 1914-1927—The Origins of Near Eastern Policy," pp. 82-94; Evans, *U.S. and Partition,* pp. 71-85.

53. United States, *Papers Relating to the Foreign Relations of the United States, The Paris Peace Conference, 1919* (hereafter cited as *U.S. Doc., P.P.C.*), 1:52, "The Inquiry," memorandum dated 12/22/17.

54. Miller, *Diary,* 3:237, Miller to House, 1/11/19.

55. Miller recognized this problem in a memorandum dated 11/29/18. Ibid., 2:133.

56. For the best discussion of this problem see Temperley, *Peace Conference,* 4:120-29.

57. *Times* (London), 1/17/19. For a summary of American press attitudes, see R. Robinson, *The First Turkish Republic,* pp. 35-36; Westermann Papers, Diary, 12/14/18.

58. Miller, *Diary,* 4:254-67, 1/21/19. See also Hurewitz, *Diplomacy,* 2:40-45; Howard, *King-Crane Commission,* pp. 10-12.

59. Miller, *Diary,* 4:255, 1/21/19.

60. Charles Seymour Papers, "George Washington" file, Conference with Woodrow Wilson, 12/10/18; Beer, Diary, 12/11/18; Nicolson, *Peacemaking,* pp. 226-29, 1/7/19-1/9/19; Lloyd George, *Truth,* pp. 189-90; *Ital. Doc.,* 1:275, Imperiali to Sonnino, 12/9/18.

61. J. A. Garrety, *Henry Cabot Lodge: A Biography,* p. 312. For a study of the Lodge-Wilson conflict, see chaps. 17-21.

62. For an excellent discussion of the November, 1918, congressional elections, see Mayer, *Politics of Peacemaking,* pp. 55-60, 119-32. See also, Great Britain, General Staff of the British

War Office, *Daily Review of the Foreign Press: Allied Press Supplement* (hereafter cited as *D.R.F.P.: Allied Press Supplement*) 5:1/1/19, 1/8/19.

63. Nicolson, *Peacemaking*, p. 240, 1/17/19; D. Garnett, *The Letters of T. E. Lawrence*, p. 273.

64. *Ital. Doc.*, 1:366-67, Diaz to Sonnino, 12/28/18; p. 398, Sonnino to Paris, London and Constantinople, 1/2/19; pp. 413-14, Diaz to Sonnino, 1/5/19; p. 470, Biancheri to Diaz, 1/16/19; p. 472, Sforza, 1/17/19; Balfour Papers, MSS 49749, Hohler to Balfour, 2/6/19. For a long series of dispatches beginning in February 1919, dealing with the so-called Franchet d'Esperey affair, see Foreign Office, F.O. 608/108/385-1-1; Cabinet Papers, Cab. 24/66, G.T. 5972, Minutes, Supreme War Council.

65. *Ital. Doc.*, 1:343, Sonnino to Imperiali, 12/23/18; p. 344, Imperiali to Sonnino, 12/23/18; p. 351-52, Bonin Longare to Sonnino, 12/25/18; p. 371-72, Imperiali to Sonnio, 12/28/18; p. 385, 12/30/18; pp. 415-16, Sonnino to Paris and London, 1/5/19; pp. 441-42, 1/9/19; p. 447, Italian commander at Rhodes to Sonnino, 1/10/19; Sonnino Papers, Reel 20, no. 2257, Imperiali to Rome, 11/6/18; no. 2577, 12/31/18; *U.S. Doc.*, *P.P.C.*, 2:277-78, British Foreign Office to British ambassador at Rome, 12/13/18; Lloyd George Papers, F56/2/18, Rodd to Balfour, 12/29/18; F56/2/20; Cecil to Rodd, 1/3/19; F56/2/22, Rodd to Balfour, 1/5/19.

66. *Ital. Doc.*, 1:452, Sforza to Sonnino, 1/11/19.

67. Ibid., p. 404, 1/3/19; p. 425, Sonnino to Sforza, 1/6/19.

68. *Ital. Doc.*, 1:373, Imperiali to Sonnino, 12/28/18; p. 427, 1/6/19; Lord Robert Cecil of Chelwood Papers, MSS 51094, Draft memorandum by Cecil, 10/8/18; Lloyd George Papers, F3/3/45, Balfour to Lloyd George, 11/29/18; Foreign Office, F.O. 608/93/362-1-1/1512, Martino to Hardinge, 2/6/19; Hardinge to Martino, 2/11/19; Cabinet Papers, Cab. 24/3, G. 110, Milner note, 1/16/17.

69. Lloyd George, *Truth*, p. 1232.

70. Balfour papers, MSS 49744, Derby Diary, 1/27/19. In December, 1918, Derby commented that Wilson was "very anti Italian. . . . He said he was sick to death of Orlando and Sonnino and all their ways and he particularly did not want to have any conversation with them." Sonnino, when asked about Wilson after their December meeting, commented, "Specie di clergyman." Ibid., MSS 49744, Derby to Balfour, 12/22/18; MSS 49745, Rodd to Balfour, 12/28/18. See also V. Orlando, *Memorie, 1915-1919,* pp. 353-54; Mayer, *Politics of Peacemaking*, p. 212.

71. This council, composed of the two chief delegates from Great Britain, France, Italy, Japan, and the United States, was the center of work during the first two months of the Peace Conference.

72. For a thorough documentary and narrative coverage of the drafting of the League Covenant, see D. H. Miller, *The Drafting of the Covenant.*

73. Ibid., 2:24-37; doc. no. 5; G. Curry, "Woodrow Wilson, Jan Smuts and the Versailles Settlement," pp. 968-86. Gelfand has established that a year prior to Smut's presentation, George L. Beer had formulated a more general scheme along quite similar lines. Gelfand, *Inquiry*, pp. 231-39.

74. Miller, *Drafting the Covenant,* 1:101ff. See also C. T. Thompson, *The Peace Conference Day by Day*, pp. 73ff.

75. *U.S. Doc., P.P.C.,* 3:805, C. of Ten, 1/30/19; Miller, *Diary,* 4:103; Miller, *Drafting the Covenant,* 2:220, doc. no. 18.

76. *U.S. Doc., P.P.C.,* 3:795, C. of Ten, 1/30/19, Appendix.

77. Ibid., p. 796; Miller, *Drafting the Covenant,* 1:109-10.

78. A. T. Wilson, *Loyalties, Mesopotamia,* 2:133; also p. 126ff; Howard, *Partition*, pp. 220-21.

79. *U.S. Doc., P.P.C.,* 3:758-71, C. of Ten, 1/28/19.

80. Foreign Office, F.O. 608/107/384-1-6/1562, French draft of a proposed new Anglo-French agreement on Syria, with comments by the F.O. section at the Peace Conference, 2/5/19; Cabinet Papers, Cab. 29/7, W.C.P. 67, 2/5/19; *Le Temps*, editorial, 1/14/19. In

addition, given British and American opposition to territorial annexations, Clemenceau undoubtedly saw little sense in alienating Wilson by pursuing this issue in view of France's paramount interest in the European settlement still to be negotiated.

81. *U.S. Doc., P.P.C.*, 3:806, C. of Ten, 1/30/19.

82. For a fuller discussion of the shift in Wilson's attitude regarding American acceptance of a Near East mandate, see below, Chapter 2.

83. *U.S. Doc., P.P.C.*, 3:791, C. of Ten, 1/30/19; Miller, *Drafting the Covenant*, 2:199.

84. *U.S. Doc., P.P.C.*, 3:805–8, C. of Ten, 1/30/19. In this discussion Wilson was not clear as to the role the United States could or would play in such a military occupation. The following day the American Commissioners Plenipotentiary discussed the question and decided that the decision should be left to General Bliss, one of the commissioners, but that any judgment he reached should be prefaced, "if it is considered advisable, and the consent of the Turkish Government is given thereto, the number of American troops etc., etc." This proviso, it was thought, would give the United States many avenues of retreat should this be deemed necessary. Ibid., 11:1, Commissioners Plenipotentiary, 1/31/19; Tasker Bliss Papers, Library of Congress, Washington, D.C., Box 65, Diary, 1/31/19. Permission to reprint granted by the heirs of Tasker Bliss. Woodrow Wilson Papers, Series V-A, Peace Conference, 1919, Box 12, Wilson to Sec. War. 2/8/19.

85. Cabinet Papers, Cab. 29/7, W.C.P. 63, Report on the military occupation of the Turkish territories and Transcaucasia, 2/5/19; Cab. 21/129, Minutes of meeting of military representatives, 2/5/19, also Annex A; Bliss Papers, Box 65, Diary, 2/4/19; *U.S. Doc., P.P.C.*, 3:837–83, C. of Ten, 2/1/19; pp. 955–56, 2/10/19; 5:4, C of Four, 3/20/19; Sonnino Papers, Reel 46, no. 107, Sonnino to ambassadors in London, Paris, and Constantinople, 2/11/19.

86. Lloyd George Papers, F89/2/7, Kerr to Lloyd George, 2/11/19. Also F89/2/9, Kerr to Lloyd George, 2/12/19; *U.S. Doc., P.P.C.*, 5:4–5, C. of Four 3/20/19; Cabinet Papers, Cab. 29/28, Minutes, British Empire delegation meeting, 2/7/19.

87. Lloyd George Papers, F/89/2/11, Kerr to Davies (for Lloyd George), 2/13/19.

88. Ibid.

89. A. Toynbee and K. Kirkwood, *Turkey*, pp. 67–68.

II ❀ THE CLAIMS OF THE NEAR EASTERN DELEGATIONS

IN JANUARY of 1919, Paris was swarming with delegations from all over the world, each pleading its special cause. The members of these delegations flooded the Entente representatives with literature and statistics backing their claims, and pressed their views on anyone who would listen. Isaiah Bowman brilliantly described these lobbying techniques:

> Each of the national delegations . . . had its own bagful of statistical and cartographical tricks. When statistics failed, use was made of maps in color. It would take a huge monograph to contain an analysis of all the types of map forgeries that the war and the peace conference called forth. A new instrument was discovered . . . the map language. A map was as good as a brilliant poster, and just being a map made it respectable, authentic. A perverted map was a life-line to many a foundering argument.[1]

The Near East provided its share of these lobbying groups. Greek, Armenian, Syrian, and Zionist delegations were active in Paris. It was in response to the claims submitted by these delegates during the first two months of the Peace Conference that increasing signs of real discord appeared among the great powers over a Near East settlement.

Greek Claims

The most formidable of the petitioning groups at the Peace Conference was the Greek delegation, headed by Prime Minister Eleutherios Venizelos. Greece had remained neutral throughout the early stages of the war, entering only in June, 1917, as a result of an antiroyalist rebellion. This successful attack on the monarchy had been led by Venizelos and supported, both diplomatically and militarily, by France and Britain.[2] The overwhelmingly favorable impression created by Venizelos at the Paris Conference cannot be overemphasized. Even those delegates who bitterly opposed his claims professed great personal admiration and liking for the man. Without question, the Allied leaders at Paris felt a heavy debt of personal gratitude to Venizelos for his efforts in behalf of the Allied cause during the war—much more obligation, certainly, than they felt to Greece. Perhaps Harold Nicolson best expressed the almost bewildered adulation that seemed to grip the Peace Conference when he wrote to his father, "I cannot tell you the position that Venizelos has here! He and Lenin are the only two really great men in Europe." [3]

Large-scale pretensions as to Greece's future role in the Near East had been evidenced by Venizelos long before the end of the war, and he reiterated them prior to the convening of the Peace Conference and in personal appearances before the Council of Ten.[4] These may be summarized as follows.

1. Northern Epirus was claimed on the grounds that it had a population of 120,000 Greeks and 80,000 Albanians. "Greece maintains that this mixed population ought necessarily to be allotted to her, for it would be contrary to all equity that a majority with a higher civilization should have to submit to a minority with an inferior civilization." [5] Venizelos maintained that even though the Greeks in the area spoke Albanian, their loyalty was to Greece, as exemplified by the thousands who had joined Greek military forces during the war.

2. Venizelos also asserted Greece's right to Thrace, which, with Constantinople, had a Greek population of 730,822, the majority concentrated in eastern Thrace. Venizelos admitted that the Turkish population of western Thrace far surpassed that of Greeks and Bulgarians combined, but he maintained that the Turks would prefer Greek to Bulgarian rule if it were impossible for Turkey to govern the territory. Pointing out that Bulgaria had fought on the side of

the Central Powers, he claimed that it sought "to play the part in the Balkan peninsula that Prussia played on the vast European stage." [6] He added that the only reason he had been willing to give Thrace to Bulgaria after the first Balkan war was that he had envisioned the creation of a Balkan confederation of Christian states, and had wanted Bulgarian cooperation in this scheme. Even this had not satisfied Bulgaria. Now he no longer had such hopeful illusions concerning this treacherous state. Nevertheless, he was willing to grant Bulgaria special rights in an international commercial outlet either at Kavalla or Salonika, although in reality Bulgaria was a continental country with no need for any outlet other than those it already had on the Black Sea. [7]

3. In Western Asia Minor, Venizelos asked for the islands off the coast, part of the vilayet of Brusa, and all of the vilayet of Aidin with the exception of the sanjak of Denizli. The center of this area was the allegedly all-Greek city of Smyrna. He claimed that these territories had a population of 1,188,359 Greeks and 1,042,050 Mohammedans, and he advanced statistics and data to prove that the area was not only ethnically but also climatically and geographically related to an Aegean, and hence Greek, culture and civilization, rather than to the Asiatic hinterland.

4. Venizelos also maintained Greece's right to the island of Cyprus. The British had offered the island to King Constantine in 1915 as an inducement to enter the war; and Venizelos evidently assumed that despite Greece's failure to join in the hostilities at that time, he would have little difficulty in obtaining this territory from Great Britain.

In the case of Constantinople and the isolated Greek towns of Trebizond and Adana, Venizelos, though maintaining Greece's right to these areas, advanced no claim to them. He asked only that the Turks be deprived of control of all three, expressing his support for international administration of Constantinople and the Straits, while suggesting that the other two towns be included in the new Armenian state. This apparent magnanimity probably was carefully calculated to arouse the sympathies and gain the support of the leaders of the big powers. No one would have been willing to grant Greece sole control of the Straits in any case, and all were committed to the formation of a separate Armenia. Thus, Venizelos was in reality conceding nothing, and he could point out that relinquishing these claims should serve to strengthen Greek pretensions to all of Thrace.

The Greek claims presented obvious difficulties. Clearly they were in direct conflict with the Treaty of London, which had given Italy the right to annex Rhodes and the Dodecanese. They were also at cross purposes with the Saint Jean de Maurienne Agreement, which had given territory in Anatolia, including Smyrna, to Italy as its share in the partitioning of Turkey. The acquisition of all the territory sought by Greece would automatically make it the dominant power in the Aegean and eastern Mediterranean. It is hardly surprising that the initial reaction of the great powers to these demands was either noncommital or distinctly hostile.

The French government was most careful to take a neutral position regarding the Greek claims. At no point did Greek ambitions conflict directly with French aims. Moreover, there was little love lost between France and Italy, which was also claiming the Smyrna area, and the French probably welcomed a counterbalancing claim. Totally preoccupied with the attempt to achieve its claims against Germany, France undoubtedly saw no point in committing itself on a matter in which it had no direct interest, especially as by doing so it might unwittingly antagonize either Britain or the United States, upon whose support France depended for fulfillment of its continental ambitions.

As for the United States delegation, Nicolson gained the impression from his discussions with Day, Seymour, and Lybyer that it was unalterably opposed to giving western Thrace to Greece, vague as to the fate of eastern Thrace, but favorable to a Greek zone at Smyrna.[8] So far as Thrace was concerned, this impression was basically true. The report of the intelligence section of the American delegation said:

No change is recommended in the northern frontier of Greece. The claims of the Greeks to the territory along the whole northern coast of the Aegean is [sic] inadmissable because they would block Bulgaria from direct access to the Aegean for the sake of a shallow fringe of Greeks along the shore.[9]

Instead, the report recommended that the boundaries of 1913 should

be retained with a possible extension in favor of Bulgaria to the
Enos-Midia line.

A difference of opinion, however, existed within the American
delegation over Greece's Asia Minor claims. While asking that Italy
turn over Rhodes and the Dodecanese to Greece, the intelligence
section opposed the recognition of Greek claims in Asia Minor.

> The possession of the Dodecanese puts Greek people, Greek ships and
> Greek merchants at the very doors of the new state. To give her a foothold
> upon the mainland would be to invite immediate trouble. Greece would
> press her claims for more territory; Turkey would feel that her new bounda-
> ries were run so as to give her a great handicap at the very start.[10]

Moreover, Smyrna was the chief commercial outlet for all the Ana-
tolian uplands, and therefore a necessary part of Anatolia as a whole.
This position was in direct conflict with the view that Seymour,
Lybyer, and Day had expressed to Nicolson.

The Italians understandably were disturbed by the Greek proposals, especially since Italy had been promised the same territory as
Asia Minor by the Allies. Both the Greeks and the Italians recognized
that something would have to give way, and it was with this in mind
that Venizelos met with Sonnino in Rome in December, 1918, and
proposed the negotiation of a provisional agreement regarding the
Dodecanese and northern Epirus. Sonnino, however, refused, prefer-
ring to keep his hands free for the bargaining he was certain would
take place at the Peace Conference. However, as the Greeks mounted
an ever intensifying campaign for fulfillment of their claims, the
Italian attitude changed. Taking the initiative, the Italian ambassador
in Paris, Count Lelio Bonin Longare, discussed the matter on January
5 with the Greek minister in Paris, Athos Romanos, and with Venizelos on January 6. It appeared, Bonin Longare reported to Rome,
that the Greeks were willing to recognize Italian claims of any type
in Asia Minor so long as Smyrna was left to them. Venizelos had
said to him that Greece did not wish to press its legitimate claims
from Adalia to the Black Sea, for this would mean becoming an
instrument of French and British policy. An Italian-Greek accord
would do much to bring about Greece's ultimate aim, which was
to be independent of everyone. Also, Venizelos had assured him

that Greece had no desire to be a great Mediterranean power. On the basis of these interviews, Bonin Longare was convinced that Italian concession of the Dodecanese and Smyrna to Greece would bring about the desired agreement. He suggested that such an agreement would prevent the Greeks from forming a united front with the Yugoslavs regarding claims in the Adriatic.[11]

Not everyone was as optimistic as Bonin Longare. Romano Anezzana, Italian ambassador to Greece, took a rather negative view of such a settlement. Although he admitted that the city of Smyrna was Greek, he pointed out that the vilayet of Aidin was not and that it was next to impossible to separate the two. Should the Greek claim to Smyrna be recognized by the Peace Conference, it would inevitably lead to conflict over the surrounding areas. It was therefore imperative that Italy immediately stake out a claim in fact, as well as in theory, in Asia Minor. An agreement with Greece, Anezzana stated, would serve no useful purpose.[12]

Nevertheless, negotiations continued. On January 19, Sonnino called upon Venizelos and suggested that Italy might accede to limited Greek claims in the Dodecanese and Smyrna in return for the cession of most of northern Epirus to Albania. Despite Italian desires for strictest secrecy, Venizelos quickly communicated this proposal to the British. Nicolson, one of several who were told, believed that Greece would be able to get both areas at the Peace Conference without giving up anything. He therefore advised a friend of Venizelos, Gerald Talbot, to tell Venizelos not to make any agreement, but rather to take "grateful note" of Sonnino's concession and promise to submit the Albanian question to the Council of Ten.[13]

Subsequently, Venizelos discovered that the Italians were willing to discuss in detail only the territory Italy would receive in Epirus. Unable to accept an agreement that would provide detailed terms on one side but only general promises of support on the other, Venizelos broke off the conversations. Despite continued Italian protestations of good intentions, the talks were not resumed. Venizelos, undoubtedly recognizing the developing hostility to Italy at Paris over Italian claims to Fiume, decided that more could be gained at the Peace Conference than from treating directly with Italy.[14]

Thus the attempt to reach an Italian-Greek understanding came

to naught. The Italians, unaware of Britain's knowledge of the negotiations, immediately reverted to demands based upon the secret
treaties, a policy they would continue to follow from then on as
far as Asia Minor was concerned. Coupled with this was a total
opposition to Greek claims for anything, anywhere.

British reaction to the Greek demands was surprisingly hostile.
Both the Foreign Office and the War Office General Staff had
considerable reservations and submitted critical reports on this subject. Although both departments supported the creation of an international zone at Constantinople and the Straits, as well as the cession
of eastern Thrace to Greece, they took sharp exception to Greek
claims to western Thrace. The Foreign Office report stated:

> . . . The claim to Western Thrace should be resisted strongly, since there
> are few Greeks in Western Thrace, . . . while the assignment of the corri-
> dor [to Eastern Thrace] would cut off Bulgaria territorially from the Ae-
> gean.[15]

What was in effect being suggested was that eastern Thrace should
become a Greek "island," to be reached only by sea.

Moreover, both reports were agreed that the recognition of this
limited claim should be conditional upon Greece's renunciation of
its Anatolian claims, claims that the War Office report termed "eth-
nologically indefensible."[16] At the same time the General Staff
pointed out that Italian claims to the area were even less defensible
and that in a struggle between the Greeks and the Italians in Asia
Minor, the Greeks "could count on British, French and Russian
sympathy."[17] In any case, the Turks had shown themselves unfit
to govern or develop the area. Therefore, the General Staff suggested
"some kind of autonomy under international guarantee, and that
the civil rights of Greek minorities in Turkish districts shall be
protected."[18] Stressing the strategic importance of Cyprus, the report
stated that although Greek control was acceptable, once Britain gave
it up there would always be the danger that it might fall under
the control of a stronger power. Presumably, this was a not-so-veiled
reference to Italian ambitions in the Mediterranean.

Despite these adverse reports, at the end of January the British
peace delegation decided to support the Greek claims in Asia Minor.

Nicolson, a third secretary of the Foreign Office and a member of the British delegation, had been assigned to study and report on Venizelos's claims. On January 27, he noted in his diary: "I take the line that North Epirus justified, except for Karitza. Thrace, both East and West justified. Asia Minor justified, but not with the whole of the Aidin vilayet and the Meander [Menderes] valley." [19] This was a stand quite different from that taken in the Foreign Office and War Office reports.

On January 31, the day after the British delegation had agreed to support the expulsion of Turkey from Constantinople, the delegation decided, upon the recommendation of Sir Eyre Crowe, assistant under-secretary of state for foreign affairs, to accept Nicolson's recommendation relative to a Greek zone in Asia Minor. This was done in the face of vehement opposition from the military and also from Lord Hardinge, permanent under-secretary for foreign affairs and Crowe's superior, who wished the area to be left in Turkish hands.[20] Although Nicolson attributes the ultimate decision to Crowe, one somehow senses a stronger hand behind the scenes, perhaps that of Lloyd George. Seeing that Crowe's own superior opposed giving Smyrna to the Greeks, certainly some very high support was needed to bring the delegation to such a swift and radical change in policy, especially in the face of the recommendations of both the War Office and Foreign Office reports. Lloyd George, an open and avowed Grecophile, explicitly indicates in his memoirs his strong, personal support of Greek claims from the very beginning.[21] In any case, from this time on, despite considerable dissension within its own ranks, the British delegation was to be the chief supporter of Venizelos's claims at the Peace Conference.[22]

Perhaps partly responsible for this change in British attitude was the fact that the Greek delegation made it very clear that the future of Venizelos's government at home depended on his success in obtaining the areas that he had promised to the Greek people. Since Venizelos had long been recognized as a friend of the Allies, and particularly of Great Britain, his fall from power would in no way help British interests or influence in the area.[23]

More important, however, was the fact that support of Greek claims made good sense in terms of the underlying principles of traditional British Near Eastern policy. The chief object of this policy had always been twofold: to prevent the predominance of any other great power in the Near East; and to secure the ascendance of Great Britain in that area, preferably through indirect rather than direct control. Throughout most of the nineteenth century, by supporting the integrity of the Ottoman Empire, Britain had successfully carried out this policy. Now, with the Ottoman Empire at an end and what was left of the Turkish state seemingly weak and impotent, it made good sense to cultivate the friendship and support the growth of a state that could serve both as a commercial counterpart to French commerce in the Levant and as a naval and territorial counterweight to Italian ambitions in the Mediterranean. The dominance of Britain in the Near East would be secured even more thoroughly than in the days of the Turkish Empire, but it would be done through the new techniques of friendship with Greece and guidance of the Arab states.

On February 4, immediately following Venizelos's appearance before the Council of Ten, Lloyd George proposed the creation of a committee of experts to examine and recommend on the Greek claims.[24] Realizing that both Italy and the United States were opposed to many of the demands, Lloyd George may well have believed that his plan would be more likely to succeed if it could be thoroughly presented and discussed in a lower echelon rather than put directly to the Council of Ten. The proposal met with a favorable reception, and all discussion of the Greek claims was postponed until the report of the committee was received.

Armenian Claims

Nowhere had the great powers made firmer commitments and nowhere were they less eager to become involved directly than in Armenia. Prior to the Peace Conference, all had stated publicly their support for the creation of an autonomous Armenian state, and the British and Americans had even drafted specific territorial proposals.[25] However, the problem was complicated by the fact that in no area did the Armenians constitute a distinct majority of the population, and their total in any sizeable state would run as low as 30–35 percent. Hatred between Turk and Armenian ran deep, and any suggestion that Turkish territory should be taken to form a separate Armenia brought sharp opposition from all non-Armenian elements.

Thus, when French detachments consisting mainly of Armenian troops were landed at Mersina following the armistice, Turkish reaction was swift. On January 4, a *Times* Constantinople dispatch stated that "individual Turks have openly acknowledged that their intention is to deal a final blow at the Armenians and to consummate the Turkish policy of exterminating that unfortunate race." [26] Throughout January, dispatch after dispatch chronicled an increasingly defiant attitude in the interior of Anatolia. United States Commissioner at Constantinople Lewis Heck reported that some officials guilty of the worst atrocities had not been removed from their posts. The "Moslem population is as arrogant as ever, not realizing defeat, because of lack of show of force by Allies." [27] Turkish officers were reported engaged in black-market profiteering. Armenians returning to their former homes met with Turkish opposition, both military and local. Their rights to the lands they had formerly owned were denied. Having nowhere to go, they concentrated in the cities, totally dependent on the aid that the Americans were providing. [28]

In the area, Turkish military forces refused to evacuate the territory and disband. By promising land to both Armenians and Georgians, they provoked fights between these two elements. Only the dispatch of British troops brought an end to Turkish occupation and established an uneasy peace. [29]

So great was the disorder and so lacking was Allied authority and control in the interior, that Heck felt constrained as early as January 4 to send a warning note to Paris.

If an independent Armenia is to be established, official announcement should be kept in abeyance until either firm Allied Military Control is established in Asia Minor, or until a large number of persons guilty of previous massacres have been placed under arrest in order to show to the Turkish population the danger of indulgence in further massacres. [30]

Initially, two Armenian delegations appeared at the Peace Conference. The one officially recognized by the Allies was the Armenian National delegation, headed by Boghos Nubar Pasha, representing the Turkish Armenians and the Armenian colonies in the various nations of the world. The other delegation, with Avetis Aharonian at its head, represented the Republic of Armenia, which had been proclaimed in May, 1918, as a result of the collapse of the Russian Empire. The two leaders could not tolerate one another, and it was only after the head of the Armenian Church intervened and ordered them to cooperate that the two delegations joined and formed a single, if rather disunified, group.[31]

In addition to these two main delegations, there were some forty independent Armenian delegations from various nations at the Peace Conference. The result was that the lobbying was intense.

> They held conferences and meetings at which hundreds of journalists, writers, singers, professors, senators, and ex-ministers, made long speeches in support of the Armenian cause. The Armenian delegates followed Wilson, Lloyd George, and Clemenceau, reminding them every minute of the debt they owed Armenia. Their importunity annoyed everyone, and they began to lose friends. . . . Loris-Melikov. . . writes that when the conference opened Armenia had the wholehearted sympathy of everybody at Paris [but] . . . the excessive demands and the tone in which they were made finally drove most people to dislike them. . . . [They] were bound to antagonize those whom it was their purpose to win over.[32]

These demands, as presented to the Council of Ten, were for an immense Armenian state that would touch upon the Mediterranean, Black, and Caspian Seas. It would include the Republic of Armenia and the seven Turkish vilayets of Van, Bitlis, Diarbekr, Kharput, Sivas, Erzerum, and Trebizond except for those areas south of the Tigris and west of the Ordu-Sivas line. All of Cilicia, including Alexandretta, was also demanded.[33]

Although admitting that Armenians did not constitute a popular majority in the area claimed, the delegation laid the blame directly on Turkish atrocities before and during the war. Armenia had "proportionately paid in this war a heavier tribute to death than any other belligerent nation," with losses estimated as exceeding 1,000,000 out of a worldwide "nation" of 4,500,000 persons.[34] Besides, once the state was established, all Armenians then in Russia and America would return, and within a few years the Armenians would have a popular majority.

Statistics also were presented to show the industriousness and economic worth of the Armenians. It was claimed that before the war Armenians, though only 10 percent of the population, had controlled more than 35 percent of the total commerce of the Ottoman Empire. But that was not all; of the 2,000,000 Armenians resident within the empire in 1914, 85 percent had been farmers and small craftsmen.[35] It would seem, according to the delegation, that not only had the Armenians been all things to all men but had been so at all times.

The claim to Cilicia was based on the geographical argument that it was part of the Armenian plateau. Moreover, since the Armenians maintained that they were religiously and culturally Westerners it followed naturally that they should have an outlet on the Mediterranean. Assuming that the territory would be taken from Turkey, the delegation clinched its argument by pointing out that only 300 to 400 Syrians had fought for the Allies, while about 5,000 Armenians had fought with the Allied forces in Palestine.[36]

The powers showed a great reluctance to make any specific commitment on the Armenian question. Although pledged to the general concept of an Armenian state, neither Britain, France, or Italy had any desire to become too directly involved in the actual creation and support of this state. It was obvious that an Armenian state, whatever its territorial boundaries, would require a great deal of political supervision and military and economic aid. To support it too openly would undoubtedly alienate not only the Turks but the whole Moslem population of the Near East. Thus, the Armenian mandate promised to be a very expensive headache with little or no material or strategic benefits to recompense the mandatory power. Moreover, acceptance of the Armenian mandate by Britain, France, or Italy would upset the agreed-upon partition of the Ottoman Empire.[37]

The easiest solution, therefore, seemed to be for America to take on those areas originally promised to Russia, and the Allies eagerly sought an American commitment to undertake the Armenian mandate. Nor was this any longer the faint hope it had seemed the previous December when Wilson had rejected Lloyd George's suggestion that the United States take a mandate for Constantinople.

With the acceptance of the plan for a mandate system under the supervision of the League of Nations, Wilson had warmed perceptively to the idea of American participation. On January 30, he commented in a meeting of the Council of Ten that though the American public would be "most disinclined" to accept a mandate, "he himself had succeeded in getting the people of America to do many things, and he might succeed in getting them to accept this burden also." [38] Later that same day he returned to the subject again, this time stating that although it would take a good deal of time and persuasion on his part to convince the American people to assume a mandate, he was "disinclined to see her [the United States] shirk any burden or duty." [39]

Certainly many members of the American delegation openly confirmed American willingness to undertake mandates and in particular an Armenian one. American missionary and humanitarian concern for the Armenians was of a recognized and long-standing nature, and it seemed logical that if any mandate were to receive popular support at home it would be one supporting the creation of an eventually independent Armenian state. The assumption among almost all Americans connected with the Peace Conference was that, like it or not, America would have to participate in making the mandatory system work. [40]

Thus, when Colonel Edward M. House, President Wilson's most trusted advisor and the man who replaced Wilson as chief American delegate when Wilson returned to the United States for the adjournment of Congress, was questioned privately on March 7 by Lloyd George and Clemenceau about America's acceptance of Armenian and Constantinople mandates, he had no compunctions about replying in the affirmative. "I thought the United States would be willing when the proposal was bought before them," he cabled to Wilson in his account of the meeting. [41]

Although a statement of this nature could hardly be regarded as binding, Wilson did nothing subsequently to disavow House's statement concerning Armenia. That this assurance was welcomed by the British and French is unquestionable. Both saw it as a golden opportunity to fulfill pledges and at the same time pass the responsibility on to someone else. That they regarded the question of the

Armenian mandate as settled from that time forward is evidenced by the fact that serious consideration of a possible alternative only commenced close to a year later, when it became apparent beyond all doubt that the United States would refuse to undertake the mandate.

Arab Claims: Syria

The Arab territories were of great concern to France and Great Britain, but not to the other powers. The United States's interest was limited to a vague desire to ensure a degree of political self-determination for the native population, while Franco-British claims were used by Italy as a guide to the extent and type of demands it could make in Anatolia and Albania.

France and Britain differed sharply concerning the disposition of the Arab lands. As a result of the Sykes-Picot Agreement, the French regarded Syria, including Damascus, Homs, Hama, and Aleppo, as rightfully theirs to control, either directly through annexation or indirectly as part of a political and economic sphere of influence in the guise of a League mandate.[42] To the British, however, this agreement no longer seemed desirable. In 1916, at a time when a traditional imperial partition of the Ottoman Empire between Russia, France, and Britain had been accepted British policy, the agreement had seemed both logical and necessary. In 1919, the collapse of Russia, plus the complete British military domination of wartime campaigns and postwar occupation in the Near East, put the situation in a new light. The British, now anxious to consolidate their preeminent position through friendship with the Arabs, were reluctant to evacuate Syria until they were sure that their claims to Palestine and those of the Arabs to control Damascus, Homs, Hama, and Aleppo would be recognized. So opposed were the British to any real French control in the Near East that some of the members of the British peace delegation openly advocated United States administration of the coastal areas of Syria.[43] The Sykes-Picot Agreement, originally formulated to prevent postwar Franco-British rivalry in the Near East, now seemed more likely to create than to dispel friction between the two powers.

Pursuing this policy of Arab friendship, Lloyd George proposed to the Council of Ten the recognition of the Hedjaz delegation and obtained, over French objections, two seats at the Peace Conference for the kingdom of the Hedjaz instead of one. The British openly supported the pretensions of the Arab leader Emir Feisal, brought him and his delegation to France on an English battleship, and paid all expenses incurred by the Hedjaz delegation while in Paris.[44]

There is much to indicate that Feisal's reception in Paris was not as warm as he had hoped it would be. The French made little effort to conceal their hostility.[45] Much more upsetting to Feisal was the rather constrained and noncommital attitude taken by President Wilson when they met privately prior to Feisal's appearance before the Council of Ten.[46] Considering Wilson's oft-expressed disapproval of the existing Allied secret commitments concerning the Near East, and his equally publicized dislike for authoritarian, hereditary rulers, this attitude was hardly surprising. Although Wilson supported the concept of self-determination, it is unlikely that he regarded Feisal as the representative of popular will. In fact, the general American policy position regarding the claims of the Husseini family was anything but enthusiastic. Without referring to Feisal, the United States intelligence report clearly stated that the Husseini family should be allowed to rule only those who wished to be under its control. The report advocated a separate Syria and Mesopotamia, both under mandates, and an independent Arabia.[47]

It was in this semihostile, questioning atmosphere that Feisal presented his claims. The handsome Arab in his distinctive dress created a favorable impression in Paris, although he never commanded the sympathy that was felt for Venizelos. Representing himself as the spokesman for Arab unification, he demanded independence for all territories south of the Alexandretta line. He justified his claim on the basis of natural frontiers that formed a unit "socially and economically." [48] Moreover, all its inhabitants spoke the same language, were of the same religion, and over 99 percent were of Semitic stock. The Arabs had fought valiantly in the Allied cause, losing some 20,000 men. "At the end of the war the Allies promised them independence. The Allies had now won the war, and the Arabic-speaking peoples thought themselves entitled to independence and worthy of it." [49]

While emphasizing his own personal desire for Arab unity under a single mandate, Feisal admitted that this was impossible at that time because of temporary social and economic differences. He recognized the desire of some people in Lebanon for French protection, and was willing to see Lebanon independent, asking only that it not be bound so closely to a foreign nation that future admittance into an Arab confederation would be impossible. He conceded that the Syrians did not favor membership in an Arab confederation but rather sought independent status, free of any foreign control. They were willing to pay for the outside technical aid they admittedly would need, and they should be free to choose the country from which it came. He suggested that an international board of inquiry should be sent to Syria to determine the exact wishes of the population. A separate state under some form of political guidance would be best for Mesopotamia, whereas the Hedjaz should be an independent state organized along tribal lines. As for Palestine, the worldwide tensions and interests involved there were unique, and he was willing to accept the trusteeship of a European power in that area.[50]

In sum, Feisal indicated Arab willingness to accept economic ties with the West, but not exploitation or political subservience. Yet the final goal of Arab unity remained.

> In our opinion, if our independence be conceded and our local competence established, the natural influence of race, language and interest will soon draw us together into one people; but for this the Great Powers will have to insure us open internal frontiers, common railroads and telegraphs and uniform systems of education. To achieve this they must lay aside the thought of individual profits, and of their old jealousies. In a word, we ask you not to force your whole civilization upon us, but to help us pick out what serves us from your experience. In return we can offer you little but gratitude.[51]

During the course of Feisal's appearance before the Council of Ten, French Foreign Minister Pichon went to great lengths to point out that a small French artillery group had fought with the Arab forces. Although Pichon was understandably anxious to stress any French military action in the Near East, in doing so he hurt his own cause, for he also succeeded in calling attention to how small that token contribution had been in comparison to British and Arab efforts.[52]

The Hedjaz delegation was not the only one in Paris concerned with Syrian affairs. On February 13, the Council heard Dr. Howard Bliss, president of the Syrian Protestant College in Beirut. He supported Feisal's plea that a commission of inquiry be sent to Syria, for he maintained that censorship there was preventing freedom of expression. This allegation irritated the British, who were in control in Syria, and terms such as "national honor" were used somewhat heatedly by Lloyd George and Lord Milner. On further questioning, it turned out that the actual censorship was being carried out by French military authorities who were under the direct authority of General Allenby, and therefore, Dr. Bliss assumed, were acting with Allenby's approval. This little discussion left neither the British nor the French very happy and provided an opening for an argument over British censorship in Syria, an issue that ultimately would be the chief obstacle to sending the commission that Dr. Bliss so eagerly advocated.[53]

Following Dr. Bliss, a statement in direct opposition to Feisal's was presented by the chairman of the Central Syrian Committee, Chekri Ganem.[54] This committee was composed of men who purported to represent each of the main religious groups in Syria—Moslem, Greek Orthodox, Hebrew, Greek Melchite, and Maronite—and also claimed to represent more than a million Syrians around the globe. Maintaining that despite similarities in language and religion the Syrian was really not an Arab, and that Arab conquerors had long since been absorbed into a superior Syrian civilization, Mr. Ganem argued that any Syrian state must of necessity be completely separate from the other Arabic-speaking countries. Unlike the Arabs, the Syrians were politically mature enough to recognize that they were not ready to govern themselves completely and that foreign help and supervision, both political and economic, would be needed to combat the poverty and ignorance of the masses. In determining which country should supply this aid, it would be dangerous to consult the people because of the religious, emotional, and political chaos resulting from the war. Rather, the choice should fall on that country which before the war would have been their unanimous, or nearly unanimous, selection. That country was France.

Citing the age-old traditions tying Syria and France together, Mr. Ganem emphasized the geographical closeness and the affinities of temperament and culture between the two peoples; as an example, French was the Syrian's "second mother tongue." The educational system in Syria was entirely French, except for the American University at Beirut. France could conciliate Christian and Moslem elements because it had twenty to twenty-five million Moslem subjects and traditionally had been the protector of Christianity in the Near East. Finally, Ganem stated that France lacked any imperialist faction, and therefore its role in Syria would be purely that of a "guide or arbitrator." In conclusion, he noted that his committee had made this statement because it believed that the French would be too bashful to come into Syria unless they were urged.

This report merits close attention, for Mr. Ganem, who had apparently been away from Syria for thirty-five years and was now reportedly a French citizen, had offered the official French view in its entirety, and his statement constitutes the best single summary of French attitudes and claims to Syria.[55] Moreover, by having this come from a Syrian, the French had laid the groundwork for a claim, which they subsequently advanced, that Syrian pro-British manifestations occurred only because the British were the military force in occupation. This French position regarding British military occupation and censorship in Syria would reach its climax with the refusal of France to participate in a commission of investigation.

Ganem, however, had failed to mention one of the chief elements motivating France's drive for territory in the Near East. This was the ephemeral image of French overseas imperial power that had been a part of France's historical tradition for centuries. In the sixteenth century France had been the first Western nation to establish commercial relations with the Ottoman Empire, and its commercial interests had grown steadily throughout the empire over the centuries. By the outbreak of World War I France's influence not only predominated both politically and culturally in the Syrian area, but its economic investments throughout the Ottoman Empire exceeded those of any other power. Even the majority of the bonds of the renowned Ottoman Debt were in French hands. Having lost one empire to the British in the eighteenth century, the French government was not anxious to lose control of the African and Near Eastern territories that had come under its direct or indirect influence during the wave of imperialism in the last years of the nineteenth century. Though the European settlement and continental security remained the government's primary concern in 1919, it should not be thought that the traditional concept of a Mediterranean and African empire had lost its political or popular appeal.[56]

To round out the claims from this area, the Council of Ten heard the statement of Daoud Bey Mammon, president of the Great Administrative Council of Mount Lebanon. He asked for an independent state of Lebanon under French guidance, but was willing to consider a loose type of federal union with Syria, if Syria were also under French supervision. His request was seconded by a Druse and a Moslem delegate.[57]

The conflicting claims of the various delegations seemed to warrant an investigation, and on February 18, United States Secretary of State Robert Lansing formally proposed the sending of an inter-Allied commission of inquiry to Syria. The Council of Ten, however, postponed the question without any discussion.[58] Although the reasons are not definitely known, a good idea may be obtained from a discussion eight days later between the American Commissioners Plenipotentiary and Dr. Bliss. At that time Lansing assured Bliss that if Britain would support it he would try again to have a commission sent, even though it had been "refused by Pichon under orders from Clemenceau." However he warned that "no decision was imminent." [59]

Thus, by the end of February signs of imminent friction were plainly visible. However, a month would pass before it broke out into the open.

Zionist Claims: Palestine

The problem of Palestine was great in itself. The British view was that Palestine, separated from Syria, should be a British mandate, should not be under international administration, and above all, for strategic reasons should not fall into the hands of France or Italy.[60] This, of course, was not at all in accordance with the Sykes-Picot Agreement. In fact, Palestine was one of the chief reasons for British anxiety to get clear of the secret commitments. The British government was therefore quite pleased when the American intelligence report specifically recommended a British mandate in Palestine.[61]

France, despite Clemenceau's December promises to Lloyd George, still offically maintained its claim for the inclusion of Palestine in a greater Syria or the creation of an international administration for the area.[62]

The Zionist leaders at the Peace Conference were intent on cashing in the pledges regarding a Jewish national home that the major powers had made when they subscribed to the Balfour Declaration. Recognizing France as their greatest potential foe, the Zionist leaders attempted to isolate the French before the Peace Conference began by reaching agreements with both Italy and the Arabs. In return for Italian support of Jewish and British claims in Palestine, the Zionists offered their support for an Italian mandate in Armenia and assured the Italians that the British would internationalize the Holy Places and include French and Italians in the administration.[63] The Italian reaction was completely noncommittal. Actually, Italy had been offered little. Zionist support would be of little meaning in deciding Anatolian issues, whereas French acquiescence would be of great value. Moreover, Italy's chief territorial ambitions lay in central and southern Anatolia rather than in Armenia.

Much more important and much more successful were the Arab-Zionist negotiations, which early in January resulted in a written agreement between Feisal and Dr. Chaim Weizmann, leader of the Zionist movement.[64] Feisal recognized both the separation of Palestine from Syria and the Zionist program for immigration. In return, Weizmann guaranteed the political, civil, and religious rights and freedom of the Moslem population of Palestine and promised help in the planning and development of economic resources in the whole Near East area, Jewish or Arab. Any and all matters of dispute were to be referred to the British government for arbitration.[65]

This agreement constituted a master stroke of diplomacy for both sides. The agreement did much to relieve British and American fears regarding the compatibility of the two groups, fears that had been the greatest obstacle to the furtherance of the Zionist cause. By negotiating with Feisal, Weizmann had granted him recognition as the leader of the Arab world and as the responsible Arab negotiator in Syrian affairs. Certainly this could only strengthen Feisal's position in his conflict with France.[66] In addition, Feisal's acceptance of a separate Palestinian state removed the last source of friction between him and the British. However, Feisal stipulated that he would not be bound by the terms of the agreement unless all his other claims in the Near East were fully achieved at the Peace Conference. Although this condition should have raised doubts as to the long-range worth of the agreement, the document nevertheless served to enhance the reputation of both negotiators as responsible statesmen. At the same time, by so openly supporting British wishes in the matter, both Feisal and Weizmann had placed Great Britain under even more of an obligation to them and their causes.

Thus, by the time Weizmann appeared before the Council of Ten to present formally the Zionist claims, the attitudes of the great powers and the lines of conflict were already clearly drawn. In presenting his claims. Weizmann sought to justify the Zionist demand for a Jewish national home in Palestine by the following arguments.

1. Palestine was the historic home of the Jewish people, Their culture had originated there, and they had been driven from Palestine by force.

2. Palestine would provide a needed outlet for surplus Jewish population, especially from eastern Europe.

3. Palestine would be the base of another diverse civilization and would serve as a focal point and source of inspiration to Jews all over the world.

4. The land in Palestine needed redemption, The Jews had already invested huge sums there and possessed the people, energy, and money to complete the project.

5. Great Britain, France, Italy, the United States, Japan, Greece, Serbia, China, and Siam had recognized these historic rights by virtue of their approval of the Balfour Declaration. Therefore, Weizmann asked that Great Britain be given a separate mandate for Palestine under the auspices of the League of Nations.[67]

In the questioning that followed, Lansing asked Weizmann if the term Jewish national home meant "an autonomous Jewish Government." Weizmann firmly replied in the negative:

The Zionist organization did not want an autonomous Jewish Government, but merely to establish in Palestine, under a mandatory Power, an administration, not necessarily Jewish, which would render it possible to send into Palestine 70 to 80,000 Jews annually. The Association would require to have permission at the same time to build Jewish schools, where Hebrew would be taught, and in that way to build up gradually a nationality which would be as Jewish as the French nation was French and the British nation British. Later on, when the Jews formed the large majority, they would be ripe to establish such Government as would answer to the state of the development of the country and to their ideals.[68]

It would seem that Weizmann's ultimate aim was unquestionably the creation of just the autonomous Jewish state that he was so thoroughly disclaiming.

With the appearance of the Zionist delegation before the Council of Ten, the presentation of formal claims by delegations concerned with Near Eastern affairs came to a close. Some of the major stumbling blocks to a Near Eastern settlement were involved in the claims set forth by these delegations. Greek, Armenian, and Syrian claims would be among the basic issues to which the negotiators would return again and again in subsequent months. It was clear that though the Council of Ten had thought it necessary to hear these petitions, little action was contemplated for the immediate future except possibly on Greek claims. The complexity of the problems and the interconnection of claims and aspirations, both on the part of the lobbying delegations and the great powers themselves, made it impossible to settle one issue conclusively before agreement was reached on the others. Negotiation and compromise on a quid pro quo basis would be necessary in order to reach a final settlement.

1. E. M. House and C. Seymour, eds., *What Really Happened at Paris: the Story of the Peace Conference, 1918–1919* p. 142.

2. For a general discussion of Greek politics during the war, see Sachar, *Emergence,* pp. 279–306.

3. Nicolson, *Peacemaking,* p. 271, 2/25/19. See also R. Lansing, *The Big Four and others at the Peace Conference,* pp. 142–60; Sachar, "U.S. and Turkey," pp. 104–5.

4. E. Venizelos, *Greece before the Peace Congress of 1919.* For Venizelos's appearance before the Council of Ten, see *U.S. Doc., P.P.C.,* 3:859–75, C. of Ten, 2/3/19, 2/4/19. See also Cabinet Papers, Cab. 27/7, W.C.P. 33, Venizelos memorandum 12/30/18; W.C.P. 58, Memorandum presented to Peace Conference by M. Venizelos, 1/28/19; Westermann, Diary, 12/19/18. For a sampling of the many pro-Greek pamphlets circulating in Paris, see A. Andreades, "La Grèce devant le Congrès de la Paix"; *The Liberation of the Greek People in Turkey;* A. Lugan, *Les Problèmes Internationaux et le Congrès de le Paix;* Anatole France, "Greece and the Peace"; *Hellas and Unredeemed Hellenism;* Z. D. Ferriman, *Greece and Tomorrow.*

5. Venizelos, *Greece*, p. 2.

6. Ibid., p. 17.

7. For Bulgarian counterclaims, see Bulgaria, Delegation to the Peace Conference, (1) *Western Thrace*, (2) *Eastern Thrace*.

8. Nicolson, *Peacemaking*, pp. 226, 229, 1/7/19, 1/9/19. See also Clive Day Papers, Letters to Mrs. Day, 1/8/19, 1/9/19.

9. Miller, *Diary*, 4:249, 1/21/19,

10. Ibid., p. 258. See also Hurewitz, *Diplomacy*, 2:40–45. On February 2, General Bliss commented to the Greek ambassador to Rome that Venizelos would have a hard time convincing the powers to give Greece as much of the Smyrna hinterland as he wanted. Whether this implied an acceptance by Bliss that Smyrna itself should be Greek is hard to say. Bliss Papers, box 65, Diary, 2/2/19. See also State Department, A.C.N.P., 185.513/26, Memorandum by Morgenthau, Westermann and Buckler, (n.d.); 185/5/2, Recommendation in Regard to Settlements in the Ottoman Empire, (n.d.).

11. Foreign Office, F.O. 608/37/92-1-3/1411, Talbot to Naval Intelligence (Paris), 2/3/19; *Ital. Doc.*, 1:417, Bonin Longare to Sonnino, 1/5/19; pp. 423–24, 1/6/19. See also France, Ministères de la Guerre et des Affaires Étrangeres, *Bulletin périodique de la presse italienne*, no. 103, no. 104.

12. *Ital. Doc.*, 1:450, Anezzana to Sonnino, 1/11/19.

13. Sonnino Papers, Reel 53, "Conversations with Venizelos at the Hotel Edward VII," 1/10/19, 1/19/19; Foreign Office, F.O. 608/37/92-1-3/1411, Talbot to Naval Intelligence (Paris), 2/3/19; F.O. 608/37/92-1-1/883, Hardinge to Balfour, 1/21/19; Nicolson, *Peacemaking*, p. 246, 1/22/19.

14. Sonnino Papers, Reel 53, "Conversations with Venizelos at the Hotel Edward VII," 1/24/19; Memorandum 1/27/19; Reel 26, Bonin Longare to Rome, 2/7/19; Foreign Office, F.O. 608/37/92-1-3/1411, Talbot to Naval Intelligence (Paris), 2/3/19; F.O. 608/37/92-1-3/2295, Granville (Athens) to Curzon, 2/5/19; Nicolson, *Peacemaking*, p. 246, 1/24/19. For a somewhat different account of these discussions see Orlando, *Memorie*, pp. 386–87.

15. Lloyd George, *Truth*, p. 1234, report of the Near East experts, 1/2/19.

16. Ibid., p. 1237, War Office memorandum, 1/16/19.

17. Ibid., p. 1236.

18. Ibid., p. 1237. See also Foreign Office, F.O. 608/82/342-6-1/777, Ramsay to Mallet, and minutes, 1/20/19.

19. Nicolson, *Peacemaking*, p. 250, 1/27/19. For the report, see Foreign Office, F.O. 608/37/92-1-1/775, 1/26/19. It should be noted that Nicolson made no attempt to conceal his admiration for Venizelos, whom he had met several times and with whom he had discussed the Greeks claims at length. F.O. 608/37/92-1-1/161, Nicolson, memorandum *in re* conversation with Venizelos, 1/16/19. Nicolson also was incensed at Crowe's refusal to give Cyprus to the Greeks, and this may somewhat account for his pro-Greek attitude on other matters.

20. Cabinet Papers, 29/8, W.C.P. 118, Conference of representatives of departmental missions, 1/31/19; also in F.O. 608/37/92-1-3/1411; Nicolson, *Peacemaking*, p. 253, 1/31/19. See also. F.O. 608/82/342-6-1/777, Ramsay to Mallet, Hardinge minute, 1/20/19. The disagreement was only over the question of Turkish versus foreign administration. All were agreed that Greek rather than Italian control was preferable.

21. For a private memorandum dated November 2, 1918, from Venizelos to Lloyd George, see Lloyd George Papers, F55/1/11; also Lloyd George, *Truth*, pp. 1228–31. See also A. Toynbee, *The Western Question in Greece and Turkey*, pp. 73–74, 87.

22. The War Office and the General Staff continued to oppose the decisions regarding Asia Minor. Foreign Office, F.O. 608/37/92-1-1/1242, War Office memorandum regarding Greek claims, 2/1/19; F.O. 608/37/92-1-1/1575, General Staff memorandum regarding Greek claims, 2/7/19.

23. Venizelos said this directly in a lengthy meeting with Lloyd George on February 5. Cabinet Papers, Cab. 21/153. Nicolson also recognized this in his own favorable report on Greek claims. "It is a direct British interest that M. Venizelos' personal influence in Greece should be maintained and strengthened." F.O. 608/37/92-1-1/775, Nicolson memorandum, 1/26/19. See also S. Bonsal, *Suitors and Suppliants, the Little Nations at Versailles,* p. 179, 1/22/19; A. Pallis, *Greece's Anatolian Venture and After,* p. 63.

24. *U.S. Doc., P.P.C.,* 3:875, C. of Ten, 2/4/19. The technique used by Clemenceau in running the Council of Ten meetings (and the plenary sessions as well) is well shown in the adoption of this proposal as described by Nicolson. "I stay behind for a few minutes while they discuss whether they shall appoint a Committee of Experts to examine the Greek claims. Lloyd George proposes it, President Wilson seconds it. Clemenceau concludes abruptly—'Objections? . . . Adopte.' The Italians gasp, as they do not want a Committee of Experts in the least." Nicolson had little liking for Clemenceau, describing him "as usual wearing the half-smile of an irritated, skeptical and neurasthenic gorilla." Nicolson, *Peacemaking,* pp. 256–57, 2/4/19.

25. For a concise summation of Allied plans and promises regarding Armenia, see R. Hovannisian, "The Allies and Armenia, 1915–1918," pp. 145–68; idem., *Armenia on the Road to Independence,* pp. 247–54; Gidney, *Mandate,* chaps. 3,4.

26. *Times* (London), 1/4/19.

27. Miller, *Diary,* 4:180, Heck to Paris delegation, 1/19/19.

28. Ibid., 4:259–60, 1/21/19; 17:366–68, American delegation to the Peace Conference, 4/1/19; 18:7–9, Venizelos to Peace Conference, 4/12/19; Foreign Office, F.O. 608/83/342-8-4/7442, "Statement of British Policy in the Middle East. . . . ", 2/18/19; State Department, A.C.N.P., 185.5/58, Report of commission on boundaries of future Armenian State, 2/24/20; R. de Gontaut-Biron, *Comment la France s'est installée en Syrie (1918-1919),* pp. 53–57; *U.S. Doc., P.P.C.,* 2:282, Heck to Sharp, 1/14/19; *Times* (London), 1/4/19, 1/16/19, 1/22/19, 1/23/19, 1/24/19; Frangulis, *Crise Mondiale,* 2:59; E. Pech, *Les Alliés et la Turquie,* p. 51, 4/27/19; A. Williams, "Armenia, British Pledges and the Near East," p. 421. For accounts of American relief work among the Armenians see *U.S. Doc., P.P.C.,* 10:14,32,94,169,171,227,429,457,500,501, Supreme Economic Council; Sachar, "U.S. and Turkey," pp. 125–46; H. Hoover, *Memoirs,* 3:389.

29. *Times* (London), 1/10/19, 1/24/19. See also F. Kazemzadeh, *The Struggle for Transcaucasia, 1917-1921,* pp. 163–73, 176–77, 180–82.

30. *U.S. Doc., P.P.C.,* 2:282, Heck to Sharp, 1/4/19.

31. Kazemzadeh, *Transcaucasia,* pp. 253–54; S. Atamian, *The Armenian Community,* pp. 204–34; A. Aharonian, "Republic of Armenia; Memorandum of Avetis Aharonian," pp. 526–27; Gidney, *Mandate,* p. 85. Boghos Nubar Pasha, it later developed, had never been to Armenia. Ibid., p. 171.

32. Kazemzadeh, *Transcaucasia,* p. 257. See also Atamian, *Armenian Community,* p. 212.

33. For the minutes of the Council of Ten meeting with the Armenian delegates, see *U.S. Doc., P.P.C.,* 4:147–57, C. of Ten, 2/26/19. For Aharonian's account, see A. Aharonian, "From Sardarapat to Sèvres and Lausanne; a political diary," p. 7, 2/26/19.

34. *The Armenian Question before the Peace Conference, a memorandum presented officially by the representatives of Armenia to the Peace Conference at Versailles on February 26, 1919,* p. 4. It is interesting to note that in his oral statement to the Council of Ten, Boghos Nubar Pasha maintained that an Armenian majority did exist. He based this on the supposed fact that the Armenians had been in a majority prior to World War I and that Turkish and Armenian casualties had been approximately the same in the area involved. This is the only instance on record in which such a claim of an existing majority was attempted by the Armenians. All other information clearly indicates that this was not the case. Ibid., p. 10.

35. Ibid., p. 27.

36. In the memorandum presented by the delegation to the Council of Ten, a reference

was made to a 1916 agreement between France and Armenia in which some form of guarantee regarding Cilicia was alleged to have been given (presumably favorable to Armenia). The veracity of this statement may well be doubted, for no other record of such an agreement can be found. See ibid., p. 10.

37. Evidence of Britain's reluctance to commit itself to any definite action can be seen in Foreign Secretary Balfour's statement in the House of Commons on November 6, 1918. Despite considerable pressure Balfour refused to say that Britain would "insist on" the removal of Turkish sovereignty over Armenian provinces. Instead he stated that "it will perhaps suffice to say that we have always regarded the freeing of the Armenian from Turkish misrule as an important part of our Middle East policy, and that we confidently look forward to its accomplishment." Great Britain, *Parliamentary Debates* (Commons), 5th ser., 110:2087-88, 11/6/18. See also Gidney, *Mandate*, pp. 77-79; *Le Temps*, 2/28/19.

38. *U.S. Doc., P.P.C.*, 3:788, C. of Ten, 1/30/19.

39. Ibid., p. 807. Moreover, when Wilson returned to the United States in February he met with a group of congressmen and, according to press reports, told them that he favored an American mandate over Armenia. *D.R.F.P.: Allied Press Supplement*, 5:3/26/19.

40. Thompson, *Peace Conference Day by Day*, p.73; Nicolson, *Peacemaking*, p. 226, 1/7/19; p. 229, 1/9/19; Sachar, *Emergence*, pp. 346-52; Gidney, *Mandate*, pp. 41-45, 79-80; *New York Times*, 2/16/19; Howard, *Partition*, p. 232.

41. C. Seymour, *The Intimate Papers of Colonel House*, 4:358-59, 3/7/19. See also Lloyd George, *Truth*, p. 288; Woodrow Wilson Papers, V-A, Box 15, House to Wilson, 3/8/19; Lloyd George Papers, F89/2/33, Kerr to Lloyd George, 2/26/19; F23/4/28, Hankey to Lloyd George, 3/1/19; House and Seymour, *What Really Happened*, p. 187.

42. Foreign Office, F.O. 608/107/384-1-3/2983, Curzon to Balfour, 2/21/19; also found in F.O. 406/41/17; Cambon, *Correspondance*, 3:309, 2/10/19; *Times* (London), 2/7/19; *Le Temps*, 2/1/19; William Yale Papers, Sterling Memorial Library, Yale University, New Haven, Connecticut, II-24, Feisal-Westermann conversation, 1/20/19. Permission to reprint from the William Yale Papers granted by Yale University Library.

43. Miller, *Diary*, 1:74, 1/11/19. The men were Lawrence, Curtis, and Westongard. See also Westerman, Diary, 1/12/19.

44. *U.S. Doc., P.P.C.*, 3:487, C. of Ten, 1/12/19; pp. 599, 616, 1/17/19; Garnett, *Lawrence Letters*, p. 273; Kedourie, *England and the Middle East*, p. 138; House and Seymour, *What Really Happened*, p. 190.

45. Foreign Office, F.O. 406/41/14, Curzon to Derby, 2/12/19; F.O. 608/92/360-1-1/1694, Derby to Curzon, 2/7/19; *Le Temps*, 2/7/19, 2/11/19; *Ital. Doc.*, 1:244, Imperiali to Sonnino, 12/5/18; Zeine, *Arab Independence*, p. 53.

46. Bonsal, *Suitors and Suppliants*, p. 40, 2/6/19. For the negotiations leading to this meeting on February 6, see Evans, *U.S. and Partition*, p. 121.

47. Miller, *Diary*, 4:260-65, 1/21/19.

48. *U.S. Doc., P.P.C.*, 3:889, C. of Ten, 2/6/19.

49. Ibid.

50. Ibid., pp. 889-91, C. of Ten, 2/6/19. See also Miller, *Diary*, 4:297-99, 1/1/19; p. 300, 1/29/19; Bonsal, *Suitors and Suppliants*, pp. 39-40; F.O. 608/92/360-1-1/1551, Feisal memoranda, 1/1/19, 1/29/19.

51. Miller, *Diary*, 4:297-99, 1/1/19.

52. *U. S. Doc., P.P.C.*, 3:893, C. of Ten, 2/6/19.

53. Ibid., pp. 1016-21, C. of Ten, 2/13/19. Neither Feisal nor Dr. Bliss was responsible for initiating the idea of a commission of inquiry. It apparently had been broached some time earlier by King Hussein and had been taken up and recommended in the report of the United States intelligence section at the Peace Conference. Miller, *Diary*, 4:267, 1/21/19.

Dr. Bliss told General Bliss privately that the Arabs wanted an American mandate. Tasker Bliss Papers, Box 65, Diary, 1/23/19. See also Zeine, *Arab Independence*, p. 69 n.3.

54. *U.S. Doc., P.P.C.,* 3:1024-38, C. of Ten, 2/13/19.

55. Foreign Office, F.O. 608/106/384-1-2/822, Henderson memorandum; J. Shotwell, *At the Paris Peace Conference,* p. 178; House and Seymour, *What Really Happened,* p. 189; Pichon, *Partage,* pp. 180-81; S. Longrigg, *Syria and Lebanon under the French Mandate,* p. 88; Westermann, Diary, 2/14/19.

56. For a discussion of French interests in the Near East, see Cumming, *Franco-British Rivalry,* chap. 1; Sachar, *Emergence,* pp. 156, 259-60; Longrigg, *Syria and Lebanon,* pp. 41-45. See also *D.R.F.P.: Allied Press Supplement,* 5:1/22/19, 1/29/19, 2/19/19.

57. *U.S. Doc., P.P.C.,* 4:2-5, C. of Ten, 2/15/19; *Le Temps,* 2/1/19.

58. *U.S. Doc., P.P.C.,* 4:56, C. of Ten, 2/18/19.

59. Ibid., 11:76-77, Commissioners Plenipotentiary, 2/26/19. See also Howard, *King-Crane Commission,* p. 26. Bliss assured Lansing that Balfour was favorably inclined toward sending a commission.

60. Cabinet papers, Cab. 29/2, P. 97, "Eastern Committee Resolutions Regarding the Disposal of Middle East Territories," 1/16/19; Cab. 24/72 G.T. 6506, Political Intelligence Department memorandum, 11/21/18; Foreign Office, F.O. 608/83/342-8-4/7442, Statement of British Policy, 2/18/19; Lloyd George, *Truth,* pp. 1142-55.

61. Miller, *Diary,* 4:263, 1/21/19. Wilson also told Weizmann in a personal interview that he could count on United States support for British control in Palestine. Foreign Office, F.O. 608/98/375-2-1/157, "Memorandum on Dr. Weizmann's Account of his Interview with President Wilson, the 14th Jan. 1919." See also Stein, *Balfour Declaration,* p. 595; F. Manuel, *The Realities of American Palestine Relations,* p. 218.

62. Little love was lost between Clemenceau and Chaim Weizmann, the Zionist leader. Weizmann recounted that Clemenceau told him that Christians could not forgive the Jews for crucifying Christ, to which Weizmann retorted that Clemenceau's France would refuse Christ a visa because he was a "political agitator." R. Meinertzhagen, *Middle East Diary, 1917-1956,* p. 22, 6/14/19.

63. *Ital. Doc.,* 1:387-88, Imperiali to Sonnino, 12/31/18; p. 403, 1/3/19.

64. The negotiations had been going on in some form since the previous June. Evans, *U.S. and Partition,* pp. 119-21; *Times* (London), 10/29/18.

65. Foreign Office, F.O. 608/98/375-2-2/159, "Text of Feisal-Weizmann agreement, 1/3/19"; G. Antonius, *The Arab Awakening: The Story of the Arab National Movement,* pp. 437-39; Miller, *Diary,* 3:188-89; 1/3/19; C. Weizmann, *Trial and Error,* 1:247.

66. This same point is made by Stein, *Balfour Declaration,* pp. 639-40.

67. Miller, *Diary,* 5:15-19; 2/3/19; *U.S. Doc., P.P.C.,* 4:161-64, C. of Ten, 2/27/19.

68. *U.S. Doc., P.P.C.,* 4:169, C. of Ten, 2/27/19.

III ❀ THE DISPATCH OF A COMMISSION OF INQUIRY TO THE NEAR EAST

WHEN President Wilson returned to Paris on March 14, after a month's absence, Lloyd George proposed that the heads of state of the four major powers should meet together privately to discuss the German treaty.[1] From that time on the Council of Four supplanted the Council of Ten, which continued to meet irregularly, as the decision-making body of the Peace Conference. The meetings were conducted in the strictest secrecy, so much so that for many sessions no secretary was present, the only other person attending being an interpreter, Paul Mantoux. Thus the fundamental policies of the conference were worked out in an atmosphere of privacy as thorough and complete as could be achieved.

Decision to Send a Commission of Inquiry

Despite the primary concern with Germany, the first recorded session of the Council of Four was devoted almost entirely to Syrian affairs. During the month since the last of the Syrian delegations had been heard, Franco-British discord on this issue had increased considerably. France, though recognizing the rights of the Arabs to a limited degree of local autonomy, insisted that the entire territory allotted to French influence in the Sykes-Picot Agreement should become a single French mandate. Clemenceau steadfastly refused to meet with Feisal or to recognize him as having any legitimate concern in Syrian affairs.[2] Britain clearly indicated that it entertained no direct ambitions in Syria, but was equally firm in supporting the demands of the Arab delegation and the rights of the Arabs to a "free choice of the Power whose assistance they desire."[3] Although the British were willing to end their military occupation of Syria and turn it over to the French, they maintained that this would be impossible until some agreement was reached directly between Feisal and Clemenceau. Therefore, they exerted constant pressure upon Clemenceau to treat directly with the Arab prince.[4]

At a meeting with Lloyd George on March 10, Clemenceau insisted on French control of all Syria. Lloyd George countered with a plan that had been conceived by the British ambassador to France, Lord Milner. It called for a French administrative mandate over the coastal area, leaving a narrow corridor to the sea for an interior autonomous Arab state governed by Feisal in which France would have the role of economic advisor. The French refused even to consider such a proposal, for as Lord Milner observed, "What they have been looking for, despite their own Sykes-Picot Agreement, is the virtual ownership of Syria."[5] Two days later Lloyd George remarked that war was inevitable if the French demands for all of Syria continued.[6]

In this rather strained atmosphere the Council of Four began discussion of the problem on March 20. In a long introductory statement, French Foreign Minister Pichon declared that during the past month Britain had twice proposed plans whereby there would be "a great limitation of the territory to come under French influence."[7]

These plans would be absolutely indefensible in the Chamber. It was enough for the Chamber to know that the Government were in negotiation with Great Britain for the handing over of Mosul to create a movement that had resulted in a proposal in the Budget Committee for a diminution of credit in Syria. This . . . represented a real movement of public opinion. French opinion would not admit that France could be even partly excluded after the sacrifices she had made in the War, even if she had not been able to play a great part in the Syrian campaign.[8]

Pichon demanded that the whole of Syria should be treated as a unit, and that France should be put in charge of the League of Nations mandate for the area.

In reply, Lloyd George asserted that Britain had no interest in Syria; rather, "It was a question between France and an agreement which we had signed with King Hussein." [9] He did not intend to see the League of Nations used to get around that agreement. Britain had done the fighting in Syria and intended to see its commitments to the Arabs fulfilled. Pichon, obviously irritated, retorted that France had never had any agreement with the Arabs. Although he admitted that France and Britain had agreed to the formation of an Arab state or a confederation of states that would include the areas of Damascus, Homs, Hama, and Aleppo, he argued that at no time had France made any commitment to accept Hussein or his family as the rulers of the Arab state. What the French obviously envisaged was an interior province, possibly with a limited amount of local autonomy under French supervision but constituting a single political and economic unit with coastal Syria rather than with other Arab areas outside the French sphere of political and economic control.

At this point President Wilson intervened. Although "he was not indifferent to the understanding which had been reached between the British and French governments, and was interested to know about the undertakings of King Hussein, . . . the point of view of the United States of America was . . . indifferent to the claims of both Great Britain and France over peoples unless those peoples wanted them." [10] He had been informed that Arab public opinion was opposed to French occupation of Damascus and Aleppo. Therefore, he suggested the sending of an inter-Allied commission to Syria and perhaps beyond to "elucidate the state of opinion and the soil to be worked on by any mandatory." [11]

Neither Clemenceau, Lloyd George, or Orlando could refuse to accept a proposition put this way without openly rejecting the basic principles under which the Peace Conference purported to operate. They therefore agreed to the formation of the commission, and it was decided, at Clemenceau's suggestion, that the investigation should include Palestine, Mesopotamia, and Armenia as well. Wilson undertook to draft a set of instructions for the commission, which were subsequently approved by the Council of Four on March 25. [12]

American desire to send an investigating commission was undoubtedly enhanced by the fact that there was reason to believe the results would be such as to strengthen America's hand in negotiating a Near East settlement. During the latter part of January, Feisal, though remaining a thoroughgoing Anglophile, had adopted an equally enthusiastic attitude toward the United States, calling America "the most powerful protector of the freedom of man." [13] On February 13, he told William Yale, an American expert attached to the Division of Western Asia, that he favored a United States mandate in Syria, because America was the "most disinterested Power," but that "he did not dare to say so openly as he received no encouragement from America." [14] When news of the Council of Four's decision to send an investigatory commission reached him, Feisal was beside himself with delight and immediately wrote Wilson thanking him for giving the Arabs the chance to express "their own purposes and ideals for their national future." [15] Subsequently, Feisal bluntly asked House whether America would consider taking a mandate in Syria, to which House in effect replied, "No comment." [16] This reply was misleading, for there is no indication that America ever seriously considered assuming such a mandate. Wilson was highly averse to any American involvement in a mandate that might bring charges at home of national profiteering at the expense of others. A Straits mandate could conceivably be seen not only as legitimate punishment of the enemy but also as control over an international waterway analogous to that already exercised by the United States in Panama. An Armenian mandate could possibly be justified as a mission of mercy to the persecuted and downtrodden. But acceptance of a Syrian mandate could all too easily be construed as acceptance of a share in the victor's spoils. Nevertheless, it must have been apparent to all concerned that a vote in favor of an American mandate by the Syrian population (and this was considered a distinct possibility) would greatly increase America's influence in determining a final settlement as well as provide definite impetus for the promulgation of Wilsonian principles in the Near East. [17]

French and British Attempts to Reverse the Decision

It is evident that neither the British nor French statesmen, despite their initial support of Wilson's proposal, were in the least bit happy about it. They feared, with some reason, that the investigation might prove embarrassing. Clemenceau, in accepting, complained about the British occupation of Syria and Feisal's pro-British attitudes, which he indicated would make a fair investigation very difficult. He also commented rather sourly that "he had made every effort to bring himself to agree with the principles propounded by President Wilson, but something must be said for the historical claims and for the efforts that nations had made in different regions." [18] Balfour, in turn, objected that the investigation would delay a peace with Turkey. Moreover, Feisal's preference for an American mandate in Syria was well known, and the British obviously did not relish the thought that similar attitudes might well appear in areas such as Mesopotamia. Lloyd George even commented that "he supposed that if the evidence were so overwhelming that, for example, the British Empire was ruled out of Mesopotamia, they would be free to consider whether they could take a mandate elsewhere in Turkey." [19] The British also were acutely aware that in Palestine the "existing population" would oppose strongly any large-scale Jewish immigration. Balfour noted in a memorandum to the British delegation that the "task of countries which, like England and America, are anxious to promote Zionism will be greatly embarrassed." [20]

Thus, despite bitter attacks in the French press regarding Britain's support of Feisal [21] and Clemenceau's adamant insistence that there was only one possible Syrian solution, Lloyd George was willing to enter into private negotiations with the French in an effort to prevent the outside interference of an investigatory commission. On March 25, a group of British and French experts met informally to consider the Syrian question. "There was general recognition . . . that the effect of sending an international commission to Syria would be to unsettle the country, to make it appear that the Conference had been unable to reach any decision and to open the door to intrigues and manifestations of all kinds." [22] It was recognized that the whole affair had come about because of British and French inability to reach a settlement, particularly French failure to come to an agreement with Feisal. The experts, therefore, worked out a settlement to which they thought Feisal would agree, and the French experts promised to bring this to the attention of the French government. The plan called for the installation of Feisal as ruler of all Syria, the creation of a Syrian National Assembly, and French mandatory control of the same type that Britain exercised in Egypt or over the native states in India.[23]

The favorable results of this meeting were probably responsible for an attempt by Lloyd George, on March 27, to convince Wilson that the commission should not be sent. He maintained that it would only stir up trouble and that the Arabs would never confide in strangers. Wilson, however, was of the opinion that merely sending the commission would make a very favorable impression and that by specifically limiting the commission's duties it could accomplish its mission quickly and efficiently. Clemenceau, using a tactic of seeming to give something when he really was not, agreed with Wilson that the commission's work should be done speedily, thereby purposely giving Wilson the impression that the French supported sending it. Then in the same breath, making the best use of this rare moment of Franco-American cordiality, he queried, "Now, what about the left bank of the Rhine?" (a matter very dear to his heart).[24]

The British and French made their combined opposition to the commission clear to Wilson on April 11. In response to Wilson's inquiry concerning the delay in naming the French and British delegates to the commission, Lloyd George and Clemenceau responded that it was necessary first for them to reach a preliminary agreement on the territories to be mandated, in order to have propositions that the people might accept. This, of course, was not the purpose of the commission, as Wilson immediately pointed out; it was intended simply to sound out popular sentiment. Nevertheless, he reluctantly agreed to the Franco-British plea for further discussions. To emphasize Franco-British unity, Lloyd George declared "that he had no interest in this question [of a Syrian mandate] and that he desired to tell Feisal that he must not count on a disagreement between France and England." [25]

One week later the American delegation came into possession of a "secret" French document "accidentally" left by an official of the Quai d'Orsay at the headquarters of the American Near East experts. This memorandum indicated that the French were not going to participate in the commission under any circumstances and that

Britain would probably join them in their refusal if a Franco-British agreement on Syria could be reached. On April 18 the American Commissioners Plenipotentiary decided to give up the idea of the commission altogether.[26] Thus it appeared that the Franco-British policy was going to be successful.

Britain's determination to avoid a break with France over Syria became even more apparent on April 25. At that time Wilson bitterly complained that in discussing the Syrian mandate, Britain and France were settling League of Nations' business between them. This prompted Lloyd George to state: "For us, the friendship of France is worth ten Syrias." [27] Britain, he went on, would "absolutely not accept a mandate in Syria." [28] Wilson was left in a bad position, for he had to admit that the last outcome he wanted was an American mandate there. This seemed to leave only France. To escape such a conclusion, Wilson almost deliberately tried to provoke an argument by suggesting a single mandatory for all the Arab states, to which Lloyd George calmly remarked that they had never been united before, and then changed the subject.

Negotiations Between Feisal and Clemenceau

Meanwhile, efforts to bring Feisal and Clemenceau together for discussions based on the plan devised by the British and French experts on March 25 seemed to be meeting with exceptional success. Once Clemenceau was prevailed upon to meet with Feisal, negotiations proceeded quite rapidly. Although the details of the conversations are not available, it appears that an agreement was reached on April 13, for four days later Clemenceau sent Feisal a draft letter confirming their discussion. In it he stated that France

recognized the right of Syria to independence in the form of a federation of autonomous local communities corresponding to the traditions and wishes of their populations.

France is prepared to give material and moral assistance to this emancipation of Syria.

Your highness Feisal recognized that France is the Power qualified to give Syria the assistance of the various advisors.[29]

On April 22, at a meeting of the Council of Four, Clemenceau gave a copy of the letter to Lloyd George and said that Feisal had replied that "he was satisfied."[30]

An agreement thus had been reached on the basis of terms quite similar to those agreed on informally by the British and French on March 25—or had it? Copies of the correspondence between Feisal and Clemenceau were given to the British shortly thereafter. The letter from Feisal, written on April 20, proved to be a very noncommittal dispatch, proclaiming Syrian friendship for France and thanking Clemenceau for being the first to suggest the sending of an inter-Allied commission to Syria. (Feisal certainly knew better; he was either diplomatically telling a lie, or outwardly accepting one that had been told him.) The dispatch ended by stating that the conversations with Clemenceau "have convinced me of the need there is for us to come to a complete understanding on the points that interest us."[31] No reference was made to the specific proposals mentioned in Clemenceau's letter, nor was there any confirmation of Clemenceau's assurance to Lloyd George that Feisal "was satisfied." It was also learned that before sending the relatively mild letter described above, Fcisal had submitted an earlier one in which he stated what Syria wanted and what it was willing to concede to France. This letter had been rejected out of hand by the French.

Still further factors were involved. T. E. Lawrence, who was both confidant and adviser to Feisal and who had been present at the April 13 meeting with Clemenceau, stated explicitly on three separate occasions that no agreement had been concluded.[32] Thus, on May 8, when French Ambassador to London Paul Cambon commented to Curzon that the Feisal-Clemenceau conversations had been "thoroughly satisfactory" and that Feisal would welcome French troops, Curzon politely refused to believe him and suggested that Cambon examine the documents.[33] Cambon, who had never seen the correspondence, thereupon investigated, and on May 26 gave to Curzon what constituted the first official French recognition that indeed no such agreement had ever been reached.

It appeared that there had been a proposal to make an exchange of letters between M. Clemenceau and Feisal, but the former was only willing to write on the clear understanding that Feisal's reply to his letter would be of a satisfactory character. A draft letter from M. Clemenceau was communicated to Feisal on the 17th of April with a request to communicate the answer which it was proposed to return. When Feisal's draft reply was received its terms were not considered to be satisfactory, and therefore M. Clemenceau's letter was never sent to him.[34]

Thus it turned out that the letter that Clemenceau had given to Lloyd George in the Council of Four meeting of April 22, had been nothing more than a draft, to which a satisfactory reply had not been received.

It is clear that no formal agreement had been reached between Feisal and Clemenceau. Then on what basis had Clemenceau stated that an arrangement did exist? The answer lies in the fact that a verbal agreement had indeed been achieved. Feisal told General Gilbert Clayton on May 20, that "on the advice of Lawrence he had agreed verbally with Clemenceau to use his efforts with the people to secure a French mandate for Syria on the understanding that France recognized Syrian independence."[35] In telling the Council of Four that an agreement had been attained, Clemenceau was undoubtedly relying on these verbal assurances, but there was no justification for his statement that Feisal's reply to his letter indicated acquiescence to, or satisfaction with, any definite terms regarding Syria.

Why, then, had Clemenceau led the Council of Four to believe that Feisal had accepted the French terms? Though there is no clear answer, it seems likely that two factors were involved. Clemenceau probably assumed that Feisal had told the British of his oral commitments. Considering the closeness of Feisal's relations with Britain this assumption would be warranted. Undoubtedly, Clemenceau thought that Britain, knowing about the verbal promises and more anxious than France for an Arab-French agreement, would choose to overlook the vagueness of Feisal's written reply.[36] Moreover, Franco-British acceptance of Clemenceau's letter to Feisal as constituting an agreement might force Feisal to honor his oral commitments. If not, Clemenceau at any time could repudiate the letters as drafts that had never been formally exchanged, an action, due to subsequent Anglo-French discord, that he was quite willing to take by the end of May.

Anglo-French Differences over Syria

Clemenceau also probably hoped that news of an agreement with Feisal would convince the United States that a commission was no longer necessary. Immediately after announcing the agreement to the Council of Four on April 22, he inquired as to the fate of the commission. Positive that Britain would join him in opposing it, Clemenceau sustained a tremendous shock when Lloyd George, rather than Wilson, blandly stated that he thought the Commission of Inquiry should proceed at once.[37] The next day the *Times* made public the news that Britain had appointed Sir Henry McMahon and Commander David Hogarth as its official representatives on the commission. The Americans, who a few days before had been ready to give up the whole idea of a Syrian investigation, were delighted, and took up the cause with renewed vigor.[38]

This seemingly sudden British reluctance to give up the idea of a commission stemmed from the fact that British-French efforts to reach an agreement on the boundaries of the mandated territories were not meeting with success. In fact, as early as April 12, Lloyd George was indicating privately that negotiations between Pichon and himself had broken down completely and that he was determined that the commission should go, and soon.[39] The argument centered on the old question of the theoretically temporary zones of military occupation. Whereas the British were willing to agree provisionally to a French mandate over all of Syria,[40] they maintained that only the area that both nations accepted as part of a future French mandate should be turned over to French occupation troops. Recognizing the old saying about possession being nine-tenths of the law, Britain refused to relinquish a strip of land along the southern boundary of Syria over which it wished to build a railroad connecting Mosul and Mesopotamia with the Mediterranean. Although the French were willing to allow the British to build the railroad, they refused to modify the southern boundary of Syria so as to place this area within the British mandated territory and maintained instead that they should be allowed to occupy the territory originally assigned to them in the Sykes-Picot Agreement.

This dispute finally broke out into the open on May 21, when President Wilson, tired of waiting, announced that his commissioners would leave on May 26, and Lloyd George stated that the British commissioners would do the same. Clemenceau, however, maintained that he could not send his delegates because promises made to him to work out differences first had not been kept. He would allow French representatives to go only when French troops had replaced the British as the occupying force in all of Syria. In effect, Clemenceau refused to recognize that any sampling of public opinion made while British troops were in sole occupation of Syria could be accurate. His attitude generally implied that the British would not withdraw because they would lose their means of influencing the population through intimidation, and he angrily charged the British with failure to honor the territorial promises made in 1916.[41]

In return, Lloyd George vehemently asserted that the French seemed more than willing to invoke the original map of the Sykes-Picot Agreement when it was to their benefit to do so, but refused to accept the provisions of the same agreement that called for an independent Arab zone in the interior with French influence limited to that requested by the native government. As far as the southern boundary question was concerned, it was impossible that a rail line whose only purpose was to connect areas under British influence with the Mediterranean should be controlled by France. Either France could accept the British map or the status quo could be maintained until the report of the investigatory committee became available. Britain pledged itself to accept this report even if the Americans went alone, for Lloyd George could not send delegates if the French did not.[42]

It is clear that Lloyd George was not talking here about delineating temporary zones of military occupation but was instead insisting on French acceptance of new Syrian boundary lines as the price for Britain's withdrawal of troops from Syria, lines that would guarantee that the proposed railroad would fall under British control. This Clemenceau refused to do, and he indicated that since no agreement could be reached for the replacement of British troops by French, he would not allow his commissioners to proceed to the Near East. However, he indicated a willingness to accept under protest the occupation status quo for the time being. He promised to make no attempt to send French troops into Syria as that would produce too much friction. But he added bitterly, "I will say this to you frankly, that I will not continue to associate myself with you in this part of the world if mutual engagements are not held to." [43] How serious Clemenceau finally had become on this issue can be seen from his statement to Cambon a few days later that if he did not get the backing of the French Chambers on his demand that France occupy all Syria, he would resign from the government.[44] The American delegation, headed by Charles Crane and Henry King, proceeded to the Near East alone.[45]

An examination of the policies of the three powers most involved in the Arab question during the early months of the Peace Conference leads to the conclusion that all were reasonably consistent in their attitudes and policies. In the course of the negotiations, however, Great Britain, much more than the other two, emerged as master of the situation at all times. Certainly, Lloyd George was highly successful in putting the American proposal for a commission of inquiry to effective use for British ends.

American policy was outwardly consistent. Basing his stand on disinterest in any American gain plus refusal to recognize any of the secret treaties, Wilson insisted on the right of Arab self-determination and pressed for an international commission of inquiry. He no doubt felt that the price he had to pay for French and British participation in such a commission was to assent, however reluctantly, to Anglo-French attempts to reach a separate territorial agreement dividing up the area. Apparently he did not realize that such an agreement would render meaningless any information the commission might secure.

The position of the French was equally straightforward. They demanded a single mandate for all Syria, which they defined territorially in terms of the area allotted to French control or influence in the 1916 Sykes-Picot Agreement (less Mosul). They insisted that Britain remove its troops from this territory immediately and that France be allowed to occupy all of it, pending the final decision on mandates and boundaries. Until this was accomplished, they refused to have anything to do with the Commission of Inquiry.

French opposition to a commission was based on a number of factors. Foremost was the belief that their claims in Syria were solidly founded, both in terms of past influence and investment and in terms of Allied wartime agreements. Thus they argued that all information necessary for making a decision regarding mandates was available in Paris; there was no need for a commission to make an on-the-spot inquiry. Moreover, Clemenceau vehemently maintained that no fair investigation could be made as long as British troops remained in occupation of Syria. In this view he was somewhat justified, if the example of action by Sir Arnold Wilson in Mesopotamia is an accurate indicator. In January, 1919, Wilson ordered a poll of native opinion regarding future British rule, stipulating that it be done "when opinion is favourable" and that the "right" answers should be sure to be obtained![46] Yet there is little to indicate that French occupation would have created a situation any more favorable to a truly open and free expression of public opinion in Syria. Probably Clemenceau recognized that anti-French feeling in Syria was so great that only if the French were there to "control" the investigation would there be any chance that a return favorable to France might be achieved.[47] Finally, there is evidence that Clemenceau was under a good deal of pressure at home not to give in any further on Syria. The French Chamber had shown itself to be particularly sensitive on this matter. On April 25, Clemenceau told the Council of Four in an almost pleading fashion, "I would like it better if this commission didn't leave until the Germans get here. That would enable me to do it more easily." [48]

In an effort to obtain British support in opposing the commission, Clemenceau, much against his will, agreed to enter into negotiations with Feisal and succeeded in reaching a fairly definite oral agreement. Having taken Lloyd George at his word that Britain had no interest in Syria and that the only question remaining to be settled was between France and Feisal, Clemenceau was understandably perturbed when Lloyd George, who a week and a half earlier had tried to persuade Wilson not to send a commission, greeted the announcement of Clemenceau's agreement with Feisal by stating that the commission should proceed as planned.

This seeming shift in British policy was really no shift at all. The British used their willingness to oppose the Commission of Inquiry as a lure to achieve two concessions, rather than one, from the French. What Clemenceau failed to realize was that the British were concerned not only about a Franco-Arab agreement. They were equally anxious that a permanent delineation of spheres of influence (mandates) should be agreed on before Britain turned over any territory to French military occupation. Although technically the argument concerned temporary military occupation, the tone of the conversations indicated that both sides recognized that in reality the temporary lines of occupation were intended to become permanent. The British in particular took this view, and as long as it appeared that there was some chance for a Franco-British agreement on this issue, Lloyd George was willing to support France in opposing a commission. Thus he made common cause with Clemenceau in the Council of Four and delayed for nearly two weeks the public announcement of the British commissioners who had been selected. However, when the Anglo-French discussions bogged down, as they apparently had by the third week in April, the British tune changed. Britain was in no way ready to renounce the commission or evacuate Syria just because Clemenceau claimed that he had reached an agreement with Feisal. Nor would the British have been willing to do so had the agreement been written and formal rather than oral and suspect. Concern for Arab claims remained secondary to Britain's primary objectives, which was to secure its own imperial position and limit France's role in the Near East as much as possible.

The French were unwilling to join the Commission of Inquiry unless France had military control of the territory it claimed. Britain was unwilling to oppose sending the commission unless France recognized Britain's right to the territory it wanted. Since both claimed the same area along the Syrian-Palestinian border, no agreement could be reached, and the attempt to provide a concerted front opposing the commission fell through.[49]

There is no indication that Britain relished the thought of a commission of inquiry. The British would have been pleased to avoid it, for they recognized the possibility of results that would be unfavorable to Britain in both Mesopotamia and Palestine. At the same same time, the British realized that although the commission might find anti-British sentiment in almost any area, anti-French feeling in the same area would be a good deal greater. The British were convinced that, given a choice, any Arab population, outside of the

Lebanese, would prefer a British to a French mandate; though the people might well choose the United States over either, Wilson had firmly renounced any active American role in the Arab world. Therefore, although the results of the commission's investigation might be somewhat embarrassing to British sensibilities, in comparison to France, Britain had little to lose. The findings that the British expected from the commission could only serve in the long run to force France toward an agreement on British terms.

Lloyd George's decision not to send the British delegates unquestionably was meant as a conciliatory gesture to the French, one the British could well afford. The purposes for which Britain supported the commission could be achieved as well or even better by the American delegates alone, for reports that put France at the bottom of a popularity poll would look better if a British delegation had not been involved.

One minor point should be made in passing. Although Lloyd George was correct in accusing Clemenceau of citing the Sykes-Picot Agreement only when it suited him, he was equally guilty of using the same tactic. Lloyd George had no compunctions about demanding alterations concerning Palestine and Mosul, yet his sporadic insistence that France should have only advisory rights in the area of the four cities was a condition based solely upon the Sykes-Picot Agreement. It is correct to assume, however, that Lloyd George, unlike Clemenceau, would have been glad to be rid of the whole agreement.[50]

Italy played no real role in the complex negotiations surrounding the creation of the commission. From the beginning the Italians had not been happy with the whole idea, for they recognized, as Sonnino put it privately, that "no population of Turkey or Asia shows itself favorable to Italian assistance, nor seeks it."[51] Sonnino did advise the Italian high commissioner in Constantinople to see if Italian agents could round up petitions from important citizens in Anatolia asking for Italian assistance, a technique that he asserted would be followed in other areas by the British and French. Though Orlando originally had agreed to participate in the work of the commission, it was undoubtedly with some relief that he used the failure of the French and British to send commissioners as justification for a decision to follow suit.[52]

By the time Wilson left Paris in June, 1919, Anglo-French hostility over Syria was manifest. Yet, despite the apparent deadlock, the situation was not nearly as serious as it appeared to be. To all intents and purposes the British had abandoned their original support of a separate Arab state in the interior of Syria and had implicitly agreed to the concept of a single French mandate for all Syria. It is true they still hoped that this could be achieved through a voluntary agreement between Feisal and the French, for in this way, both the British commitment to the Arabs and the Sykes-Picot Agreement could be fulfilled. The French, however, recognized that Feisal hardly would be the tractable native ruler they desired for Syria.

Wilson had admitted that the United States could not take a mandate in Syria. No one, not even the Italians, ever thought of giving Syria to Italy or to a small, disinterested nation. Lloyd George repeatedly told the Council of Four that Britain would not take a Syrian mandate under any circumstances, and by the end of May he had instructed British officials in the Near East to convey the same information to Feisal.[53] Thus, the real decision as to French domination in Syria had been made. Although Lloyd George and Wilson had stated that they would abide by the decision of the Commission of Inquiry, the general allocation of mandates had actually been decided before the commission ever left Paris. Georges Picot told Feisal that the commission's findings "would carry no weight at all at the Conference."[54] Despite British and American protestations to the contrary, he was basically correct.

---

1. Tillman, *Anglo-American Relations*, p. 84.

2. On February 11, at the time the British refused to allow French troops to occupy all of Syria, Clemenceau had agreed to meet with Feisal as long as Milner was also present. However, the attempted assassination of Clemenceau on February 19 occurred before Milner could arrange a meeting, and as Anglo-French relations over Syria worsened during March, Clemenceau became increasingly intransigent. Cambon, for one, was furious, commenting that "whether he [Feisal] was in good faith or not, he deserved to be heard." Feisal and Lawrence did have two completely fruitless meetings on February 24 and 25 with Gout and Briand respectively. Cambon, *Correspondance*, 3:320, 4/10/19; Lloyd George Papers, F39/1/10, Milner to Lloyd George, 3/8/19; Foreign Office, F.O. 608/92/360-1-1/1694, Derby to Curzon, 2/7/19; F.O. 608/93/360-1-8/3322, Lawrence minutes, 2/24/19, 2/25/19; *Le Temps*, 2/7/19, 2/11/19.

3. Foreign Office, F.O. 608/107/384-1-6/1562, "French Draft of a Proposed New Anglo-French Agreement regarding Syria, and comments by the Foreign Office section at the Peace Conference," 2/5/19; also in Cabinet Papers, Cab. 29/7, W.C.P. 67.

4. Lloyd George, *Truth*, p. 288; 3/7/19; Cambon, *Correspondance*, 3:320, 4/10/19.

5. Lloyd George Papers, F39/1/10, Milner to Lloyd George, 3/8/19; Lloyd George, *Truth*, pp. 1046–50; Miller, *Diary*, 6:317, 3/10/19.

6. Seymour, *House Papers*, 4:361, 3/12/19. For further evidence of increasing Anglo-French tension over Syria, see Foreign Office, F.O. 608/107/384-1-3/1333, Pichon to Balfour, 1/31/19; 2983; Curzon to Balfour, 2/21/19; 3927, Pichon memorandum, 3/8/19; 4961, Curzon to Cambon, 3/19/19; F.O. 496/41/8, Derby to Curzon, 1/23/19; 14, Curzon to Derby, 2/12/19.

7. *U.S. Doc., P.P.C.*, 5:5, C. of Four, 3/20/19. The second of the two was the Milner proposal referred to above.

8. Ibid.

9. Ibid., p. 7.

10. Ibid., p. 9.

11. Ibid., p. 12.

12. Howard, *King-Crane Commission*, pp. 32–34; Sonnino Papers, Reel 46, no. 315, Sonnino to Paris and London, 3/23/19. For the text of the instructions, see Cabinet Papers, Cab. 29/10, W.C.P. 375, 3/25/19. For the tangled and confusing story of American plans for a Near East commission, February–April, 1919, see Gidney, *Mandate*, pp. 136–44.

13. *Times* (London), 1/20/19.

14. Yale Papers, V-3; also in Kedourie, *England and the Middle East*, p. 142.

15. Howard, *King-Crane Commission*, p. 35; Evans, *U.S. and Partition*, p. 141.

16. Edward M. House Papers, Sterling Memorial Library, Yale University, New Haven, Connecticut, Diary, 3/29/19; Garnett, *Lawrence Letters*, p. 275; Bonsal, *Suitors*, pp. 48–49, 3/29/19. Permission to reprint from the Edward M. House Papers granted by Yale University Library.

17. Wilson was also under pressure from Near East missionary groups to send a commission, for they saw it as a way to foil Zionist ambitions in Palestine. For the same reason the Zionists generally were opposed to the idea of the commission. Manuel, *American-Palestine Relations*, pp. 223, 244; Nevakivi, *Arab Middle East*, p. 137. Not all members of the American delegation were happy with the decision. Westermann called it "extremely foolish"; Beer regarded it as "futile." Westermann, Diary, 3/23/19; Beer, Diary, 3/27/19.

18. *U.S. Doc., P.P.C.*, 5:13, C. of Four, 3/20/19; *Le Temps*, 3/26/19, 4/7/19.

19. *U.S. Doc., P.P.C.*, 5:14, C. of Four, 3/20/19.

20. Balfour Papers, Mss 49751, Memorandum, 3/23/19. See also Howard, *King-Crane Commission*, p. 326; Evans, *U.S. and Partition*, p. 144.

21. Foreign Office, F.O. 608/113/385-1-20/4923, Derby to Curzon, 3/20/19; 5064, 3/21/19; 5127, 3/21/19; *Times* (London), 4/5/19. See also E. Brémond, *Le Hedjaz dans la Guerre Mondiale*, p. 323; D.R.F.P.: *Allied Press Supplement*, 5:4/2/19.

22. Miller, *Diary*, 7:169–70, 3/25/19.

23. Ibid., This meeting was arranged by H. Wickham Steed, Paris correspondent and editor of the *Times* (London). H. Wickham Steed, *Through Thirty Years, 1892–1922, A Personal Narrative*, 2:300. See also Yale Papers, II-2; Howard, *King-Crane Commission*, pp. 34–35; Evans, *U.S. and Partition*, pp. 142–43; E. Bourgoyne, ed., *Gertrude Bell, from her personal papers, 1914–1926*, p. 110.

24. P. Mantoux, *Les Délibérations du Conseil des Quartre, (24 mars–28 juin, 1919)*, 1:49, 3/27/19.

25. Ibid., p. 228, 4/11/19. Jean Gout of the French delegation told Lybyer on April 10 that Lloyd George opposed sending the commission and that it would be far better to settle the matter of mandates in Paris, after which the commission could consider the form of government to be set up by investigating on the spot. Howard, *King-Crane Commission*, pp.

43–44. Wilson had selected his commissioners, Charles Crane and Henry King, immediately following the decision to send the commission. This was done without prior consultation with the American Commissioners Plenipotentiary, who were rather nonplussed when they were informed of this decision by Henry White, who added that "the President felt these two men were particularly qualified to go to Syria because they knew nothing about it." *U.S. Doc., P.P.C.*, 11:133–34, American Commissioners Plenipotentiary, 3/27/19; p. 140, 3/31/19. See also, Howard, *King-Crane Commission*, pp. 36–41; Evans, *U.S. and Partition*, pp. 145–46.

26. Yale Papers, II-1; *U.S. Doc., P.P.C.*, 11:155, American Commissioners Plenipotentiary, 4/18/19; Howard, *King-Crane Commission*, pp. 48–50; Bliss Papers, Box 101, Diary, 4/18/19; Westermann, Diary, 4/12/19, 4/15/19.

27. Mantoux, *Conseil des Quatre*, 1:379, 4/25/19.

28. Ibid.

29. *U.S. Doc., P.P.C.*, 5:115, C. of Four, 4/22/19, App. 1.

30. Ibid., 5:112, C. of Four, 4/22/19. See also Zeine, *Arab Independence*, pp. 80-81; Evans, *U.S. and Partition*, pp. 148-49.

31. Foreign Office, F.O. 406/41/38, Balfour to Curzon, 4/30/19, enclosure, Feisal to Clemenceau 4/20/19; also in F.O. 608/93/360-1-8/8653; *Br. Doc.* 4:252–53, Balfour to Curzon, 4/30/19.

32. Foreign Office, F.O. 608/93/360-1-8/7735, Derby to Curzon, 4/18/19, Lawrence minute, 5/1/19; 8653, Kerr to Mallet, 4/28/19, Lawrence minute, 5/3/19; 8810, Balfour to Curzon, 5/5/19; Evans, *U.S. and Partition*, p. 148.

33. Foreign Office, F.O. 406/41/40, Curzon to Derby, 5/8/19.

34. *Br. Doc.* 4:253, Curzon to Balfour, 5/26/19. See also Cambon, *Correspondance*, 3:331, 5/9/19.

35. *Br. Doc.*, 4:265, Clayton to Curzon, 6/5/19, n.3, Clayton to Foreign Office, 5/21/19. Feisal admitted that for the moment relations between himself and the French were good since the French thought that the conversations with Clemenceau meant something. But actually they did not. "He had never had any intention of carrying out this arrangement. . . ." See also Foreign Office, F.O. 608/106/384-1-1/13927, Cornwallis to Clayton, 5/16/19; Gontaut-Biron, *Comment*, p. 231.

36. Lawrence, who had participated in the meeting of French and British experts on March 25, undoubtedly urged Feisal to make this verbal commitment on April 13 in hopes of preventing the Commission of Inquiry from going. However, when no formal written exchange of notes resulted, Lawrence quite correctly indicated that no agreement had been reached.

37. *U.S. Doc., P.P.C.*, 5:112, C. of Four, 4/22/19; p. 115, App. 1.

38. *Times* (London), 4/23/19; Howard, *King-Crane Commission*, p. 51. The British had selected their commissioners shortly after it was decided to send a commission, but had chosen not to make this decision public. The Italians were ready to appoint theirs, but did not do so when the French continued to delay in naming their delegation. Foreign Office, F.O. 608/86/349-1-3/5422, Balfour to Curzon, 4/11/19; 8628, Toynbee minute, 4/29/19; Howard, *King-Crane Commission*, p. 85; Woodrow Wilson Papers, V-A, Box 28, King to House, 5/6/19; Beer, Diary, 4/19/19.

39. Foreign Office, F.O., 608/86/349-1-3/7030, Mallet minute, 4/12/19. Lloyd George's attitude was undoubtedly strengthened by reports received from Allenby that public opinion in the Near East necessitated that the commission proceed as announced. Howard, *King-Crane Commission*, p. 51.

40. Miller, *Diary*, 7:169-70, 3/25/19; Mantoux, *Conseil des Quatre*, 1:379, 4/25/19; *U.S. Doc., P.P.C.*, 5:763, App. 3, C. of Four; Cambon, *Correspondance*, 3:304, 2/6/19; pp. 337-38, 6/2/19.

41. Mantoux, *Conseil des Quatre*, 2:133–43, 5/21/19; *U.S. Doc., P.P.C.*, 5:13, C. of Four, 3/20/19; pp. 756–66, 5/21/19; Foreign Office, F.O. 608/107/384-1-3/2983, Curzon to Derby, 2/21/19; House Papers, Diary, 5/20/19; Gontaut-Biron, *Comment*, p. 65.

42. For the text of the debate see Mantoux, *Conseil des Quatre*, 2:159–64, 5/22/19; and *U.S. Doc., P.P.C.*, 5:807–12, 5/22/19.

43. Mantoux, *Conseil des Quatre*, 2:163, 5/22/19.

44. Cambon, *Correspondance*, 3:333, 5/24/19.

45. See also *Br. Doc.*, 4:256, Allenby to Balfour, 5/30/19; p. 257, Clayton to Balfour, 5/30/19; pp. 257–58, C. of Four, 5/31/19; p. 259, Balfour to Allenby, 5/31/19 (2); *U.S. Doc., P.P.C.*, 6:131–33, 137, C. of Four, 5/31/19.

46. Sachar, *Emergence*, p. 368.

47. Sir Harold Temperley states that the French were "conscious that the result of such an inquiry would be against their Syrian claims." Certainly the pro-French testimony of Chekri Ganem before the Council of Ten on February 13 indicated a fear of an inquiry into popular opinion in Syria at that time. See above, Chapter 2; Temperley, *Peace Conference*, 6:148.

48. Mantoux, *Conseil des Quatre*, 1:379, 4/25/19. For a sampling of French press views on this issue, see *Le Temps*, 5/4/16; *Times* (London), 1/4/19, 5/5/19, 5/17/19; Foreign Office, F.O. 608/113/385-1-20/9146, Derby to Curzon, 5/4/19; F.O. 608/114/385-1-20/10208, Derby to Curzon, 5/16/19; 10448, 5/18/19; 10773, 5/22/19. See also Lugan, *Problèmes Internationaux*, pp. 54–57; Mayer, *Politics of Peacemaking*, pp. 179–81; see above, pp. 54–55.

49. An argument can be made that Clemenceau was not that much concerned about the Syrian-Palestinian border issue, that he used it as a good, handy excuse to refuse to send his commissioners. The proof of this would be the fact that the following September, when an agreement was finally worked out, Clemenceau agreed to British occupation of the territory. Actually, this argument does not seem valid. The pressures on Clemenceau at home in the spring of 1919 made it totally impossible for him to accept any further revision of the Sykes-Picot territorial arrangements. Commission or no commission, Clemenceau was in no position at that time to give in to any more British territorial ambitions.

50. See above, Chapter 1; also Kedourie, *England and the Middle East*, p. 140.

51. Sonnino Papers, Reel 46, no. 47, Sonnino to Constantinople, 1/26/19.

52. Ibid.; *U.S. Doc., P.P.C.*, 6:133, C. of Four, 5/31/19; Howard, *King-Crane Commission*, pp. 85–86.

53. Foreign Office, F.O. 608-86/349-1-3/11565, Clayton to War Office, 5/15/19; Balfour to Clayton, 5/29/19. See also *Br. Doc.*, 4:276, Allenby to Curzon, 6/12/19; p. 277, Clayton to Curzon, 6/15/19; pp. 298–99, Balfour to Allenby, 6/26/19; Mantoux, *Conseil des Quatre*, 2:518, 6/25/19.

54. This was on June 18, 1919. *Br. Doc.*, 4:278–80, Cornwallis memorandum (n.d.). For a discussion of the King-Crane Commission and its report, see below, Chapter 6.

IV ❀ THE COMMITTEE ON GREEK AFFAIRS AND THE OCCUPATION OF SMYRNA

O_N FEBRUARY 12, the Committee on Greek and Albanian Affairs (generally referred to as the Greek Committee), which had been established a week before by the Council of Ten, began consideration of Greek claims. The question was made extremely difficult by the fact that reliable population statistics did not exist. Turkish persecution of Greeks in the Ottoman Empire during the war had altered the balance of population in favor of the Turks in many former Greek areas. Acceptance of the changes would seem to condone the atrocities committed, yet failure to recognize them would make it difficult to achieve a realistic and workable solution applicable to the future. Also, in many areas economic and ethnic considerations were not in harmony.

Any settlement of Greek claims automatically posed the problem of the validity of the 1915 and 1917 agreements between France, Britain, and Italy. Italy, of course, maintained that both of these were binding and that therefore the committee had no real right to discuss the question of Asia Minor because it had already been settled. France and Britain flatly stated that Russia's failure to sign the Saint Jean de Maurienne Agreement of 1917, as had been stipulated, released them from any commitment to it. This was the document that had defined the boundaries of Italy's sphere of influence in Asia Minor. The 1915 Treaty of London, which Britain and France did recognize, provided only that Italy would receive "a just share of the Mediterranean region adjacent to the province of Adalia,"[1] as compensation for French and British gains in the Near East. The United States refused to recognize either agreement "unless, by chance, they happen to contain certain provisions which we consider to be just and proper, in accordance with our declared principles." [2]

The Report of the Greek Committee

The conflict over the secret treaties proved insoluble and the final report of the committee to the Council of Ten reflected the division among the powers.[3] Britain and France for the most part accepted the Greek position; the United States took a more reserved stand; Italy bitterly opposed the majority of the Greek claims.

Northern Epirus

Britain and France were prepared to recognize Greek demands in northern Epirus, not because of the legitimacy of Greek ethnological claims, but rather for strategic reasons relating to control of transportation routes.[4] The United States was willing to grant to Greece only those areas which were economically dependent on it. Italy argued that the whole area was predominantly Moslem and Albanian, that many of those who were Christians were Albanian in national sentiment, and that therefore no part of the country should go to Greece.

The underlying assumption in this dispute was the well-recognized fact that geographical factors would inevitably bring Albania within an Italian sphere of influence, whether it was officially designated as such or not. The result was, as Nicolson put it, that Albania had the "terribly bad luck . . . to get her frontiers cut down merely because none of us trust Italy in the Balkans." [5]

Aegean Islands

All four powers agreed that, with the exception of the Dodecanese, the Aegean islands should be returned to Greece. The United States also advocated Greek control of the Dodecanese, but the other three powers maintained that these islands had been in Italian hands before the outbreak of the war, had also been promised to Italy in the Treaty of London, and therefore should play no part in the peace settlement.

Thrace

The four nations agreed to accept in principle the cession of western Thrace to Greece; all but Italy were also agreed on the boundaries. Although the majority population in western Thrace was Turkish, it was apparent that Turks did not count, and the committee maintained that "the ethnic claims of Greece are . . . superior to those of Bulgaria." [6]

Noting with approval Greece's declared willingness to grant Bulgaria commercial access to the Aegean, the American, French, and British members of the committee also agreed in principle that eastern Thrace should go to Greece. The Italians differed sharply. They felt that a corridor to the Aegean together with the port of Dedeagatch should be left to Bulgaria and that eastern Thrace, which would then be separated from western Thrace, should become part of the Constantinople zone that was to be placed under an international administration. The Italians pointed out that Dedeagatch was a predominantly Bulgarian city and that the people of Adrianople had also expressed their opposition to Greek military occupation. However correct these observations may have been, the population of eastern Thrace was predominantly Greek. To put it in the international zone would only have compounded the ethnological error made in giving western Thrace, with its Turkish population, to Greece.

Asia Minor

Britain and France accepted the Greek claims in the north and east but opposed the demand for the Menderes River valley in the south. With this reservation, they were ready to allow Greece to annex "the ports of Smyrna and Aivali, with a certain dependent region." [7] This position was based on British and French belief that Turkey would be placed under a mandate, and therefore it could not be expected that "a compact and civilized community such as that of the Hellenic colonies on the western seaboard of Asia Minor . . . [should be placed] under such tutelage." [8]

The United States was completely opposed to detaching these districts from Turkey. The committee report gave the reasons:

The American Delegation cannot accept the figures presented by the Greek government as to the Turkish population. Their own information leads them to place the Turkish population at a figure which puts the Greeks in a decided minority in every sandjak of the area claimed by Greece except in the Sandjak of Smyrna itself. . . .

They are also of the opinion that from an economic point of view it will be inequitable to separate the coastal districts of western Asia Minor from the central Anatolian plateau, and so to sever what remains of the Turkish Empire from its most natural exits to the sea. [9]

The Italians submitted a separate statement concerning Greek claims in Asia Minor. They maintained that the committee had no business discussing these claims as they could not be separated from discussion of the general settlement in Anatolia. Moreover, since much of the territory claimed by the Greeks had been apportioned to Italy in the 1915 and 1917 agreements, "it would appear that a preliminary exchange of views between the Allies ought to take place before coming to a decision on the merits of the Greek claims." [10] As a result, the Italians failed to make any formal recommendations, either positive or negative, on the Greek claims in Asia Minor.

Rejection of the Report

The Greek Committee's report came before the full Central Territorial Committee almost immediately. Whereas the British and French advocated acceptance of the report, the American delegate, Dr. Sidney Mezes, joined the Italian delegate in arguing that until the Supreme Council made a definite decision regarding the future of the Turkish state, no decision on Greek claims could be made.[11] Since at that time the possibility of an American mandate for the Constantinople zone, and even perhaps for all of Turkey,[12] was under consideration, it is understandable that Mezes was reluctant to agree to concessions in Thrace and Asia Minor that might hamper the administration of these mandates. Certainly this did not indicate that American and Italian views on Asia Minor were identical. Although their stands in the report of the Greek Committee were similar, American opposition stemmed basically from a reluctance to see the territory in Greek hands and was in no way coupled with any support for Italian ambitions.

The report was neither accepted nor rejected; instead action was deferred in the hope that coordination of the differing viewpoints could be obtained. Nicolson records that the Council of Ten was insistent that the Greek Committee should reach an agreement.[13] Moreover, shortly before the committee had submitted its report, the Council of Ten had instructed all committees to draw up draft articles implementing their recommendations and to submit them with their reports. This order had come too late to be complied with in the initial report; now the Greek Committee was faced with this task.[14]

United States Capitulation on Greek Claims

Since it was obvious that Italy would not alter its position, the solution of the problem of Greek claims became a question of achieving some sort of rapprochement between the British and French on the one hand and the Americans on the other. This accomplished, a united and forceful front could be presented to the Italians. On March 15, Nicolson submitted a memorandum to Sir Eyre Crowe in which he outlined a possible compromise solution in which Greece would undertake mandates for the disputed territories in northern Epirus and Asia Minor, with the exception of the sanjak of Smyrna, which would be annexed directly. Even the Americans, Nicolson argued, recognized that the Greeks held an absolute popular majority in the Smyrna sanjak and so could not oppose its reunification with Greece. Subsequently, on the basis of instructions from Balfour, Hardinge asked Nicolson to undertake personal negotiations with Mezes, who as early as March 16 had evidenced great eagerness to reconcile all differences.[15] Nicolson's diary gives an account of these negotiations:

March 24, . . . Go down and see Mezes, who is a titular head of their delegation. We agree about Asia Minor—a semicircle from Aivali to the north of Scala Nova. That is something. . . .

March 25, . . . Continue my discussion with Mezes. Deal with Northern Epirus. I suggest autonomy under League of Nations, with mandate for Greece. This frightens him considerably. . . .

March 26, Work out in detail scheme for partition of Turkey. . . .

March 27, Work out scheme for an autonomous Epirus. Venizelos . . . says that Col. House has hinted to him that the United States will accept the Franco-British line in Asia Minor. He was pleased. . . .

March 28, With Arnold Toynbee to the American Delegation. We discuss the future of Turkey. We agree upon a frontier for the future Armenian State. We also finally agree on a joint line for the Greek Zone in Asia Minor, subject to some alteration if Italy is given a mandate in the same regions. As regards the Constantinople zone, we want to bring the Turks down to the Marmora at Panderma, but the Yanks want to exclude them completely.[16]

This agreement was never specifically considered by the Greek Committee. Instead, the Central Territorial Committee formally approved the original report, with the addition of draft boundary articles for the Bulgarian peace treaty, and submitted it to the Council of Ten on March 30. However, the covering report of the Central Territorial Committee indicated, though not openly, the change that had actually taken place. In it the American delegate Mezes contented himself with a single reservation to the effect that he believed the Central Committee could not "consider itself authorized to make recommendations on the subject of Greek claims" in either Europe or Asia Minor, "for this would be to make assumptions regarding the Turkish State, whereas, by its decision of March 11, the Supreme Council has reserved the question of the formation of that State." [17] This reservation pointedly took no notice of the position of the American delegates on the Greek Committee, who had totally opposed the recognition of Greek claims in Asia Minor. Instead, it left the door open for American acceptance of these claims should its delegates to the Council of Ten so desire. It also indicated that, depending on what happened to Constantinople and the Straits, the United States might well repudiate its previous acceptance in the Greek Committee of Greece's claim to eastern and western Thrace.[18]

That the Greek Committee's report was not officially altered was apparently due initially to consideration for the opinion of William Westermann, the American expert on Asia Minor and a member of the Greek Committee. Westermann, who remained vehemently opposed to granting Greek claims in Asia Minor, was asked by Mezes if he wanted the committee's report changed to conform to the new American policy. Westermann replied negatively, stating that he would prefer to have the report stand and be subsequently overridden. Mezes readily agreed.[19] From a tactical point of view, this procedure also made good sense. The Anglo-American agreement had been negotiated without Italian knowledge and had been achieved through private negotiations outside the formal structure of the Peace Conference. Moreover, it impinged directly on Italian claims. Since the Council of Ten would not be bound in any case to observe the recommendations of the Greek Committee, there was little sense in making public an agreement that would result in indignant and justified Italian charges regarding secret diplomacy and failure to negotiate fairly the question of Italian claims. Moreover, until agreement on the disposition of European Turkey, the Straits, and the rest of Asia Minor had been obtained, it was in the interest of all three concurring parties not to appear to be forcing a fait accompli upon the Italians.

An agreement that brought the United States into line with Britain and France regarding Greek claims in Asia Minor had nevertheless been attained. Behind this fact lie a good many questions, all leading to the crucial one: Why did the United States's position regarding Asia Minor change so suddenly and so completely within the course of a few days?

Was it because the American delegates on the Greek Committee, Day and Westermann, were the only Americans who opposed the Greek claims?[20] This was hardly the case. The intelligence report of January 21 had opposed any Greek zone in Asia Minor.[21] On

March 4, during a discussion among the American Commissioners Plenipotentiary, both Lansing and Bliss agreed that America's "general view was that no Hinterland can properly be separated from the Coast." [22] On March 7, Miller told Mezes that he was "wholly opposed to the Greek claims." [23] In a report written two days later, Mezes expressed his own doubts as to the economic and ethnological justification of the Greek demands. He recommended instead that "a guarantee to this area of generous autonomy within Turkey, with the direct appeal to the Court of the League, might well best meet the needs of the population, if not the very natural ambitions of Greece." [24] Finally, on March 12, the American commissioner at Constantinople, Lewis Heck, warned against giving Smyrna to the Greeks. [25]

What, then, prompted the American change? On the day that the Nicolson-Mezes discussions began, Mezes sent a message to Colonel House which indicated that in return for agreeing to the Greek claims for the Dodecanese, the Smyrna region, and the Enos-Midia line northwest of the Straits, he was demanding the acceptance of the American line in northern Epirus, which would give Greece some, but not all, of the territory it claimed. [26] This would indicate that Mezes envisioned a compromise, however unequal it might be. He did not achieve it. The most to which Nicolson would agree was Nicolson's own scheme for an autonomous northern Epirus under a Greek mandate, a solution that remained unacceptable to the Americans long after the agreement on Asia Minor had become an established fact. [27]

Actually, Mezes' scheme was not so much a compromise plan as it was an attempt to salvage at least one of the recommendations of the American delegates on the Greek Committee. The basic decision to accept the British and French position regarding Greek claims in Asia Minor was imposed on Mezes rather than taken by him. On March 25, Westermann, a long-time opponent of Greek claims, wrote to Mezes:

The impression which I gained from our conversation last evening was that the American commissioners, either President Wilson and Colonel House or Colonel House alone, had accepted the British-French proposal to grant to the Greeks a certain district in Asia Minor about Smyrna. Neither the name of President Wilson nor that of Colonel House was definitely mentioned; but the phrase "higherups" used in the conversation seems to justify me in the conclusion.

This decision overrides the stand taken by the American delegates on the Commission upon the Greek claims. The reasons for the reversal of our decision, as I gained it from our conversation were: (1) the necessities of the international political situation; and (2) the obvious one that there are distinctly two sides to the question of the Greek claims in Asia Minor and that the members of our commission believed more strongly in the Greek side than I did.[28]

This contention that the decision had been taken by "higherups" would seem to be substantiated by the fact that Mezes had tended personally to side with the anti-Greek faction. His sudden eagerness to reach a settlement so opposed to his own views coincided closely with Wilson's resumption of personal control of the negotiations upon his return to Paris on March 14. Two days later Wilson sent a rather cryptic note to Mezes.

I have gone over these articles twice and find that I have nothing essential to suggest. I hope that they may be ready for final consideration by the "Four" as soon as Mr. Lloyd George returns. He has had a special interest in this matter.[29]

It seems likely, though not certain, that the subject of this communication was the question of Greek claims in Asia Minor. Certainly Lloyd George had always been the strongest proponent of Greek claims in this area. Since the report of the Greek Committee was then under discussion in the Central Territorial Committee, it is logical to assume that Mezes had sought Wilson's comments regarding the proposals. It would hardly seem coincidental that on the same day Wilson sent him this note Mezes suddenly evidenced a strong desire to reconcile the differences reflected in the report.[30]

Moreover, Lloyd George states in his memoirs that Wilson personally

overruled the recommendation of his representative on the Commission and fell in with the proposals of the British and French experts as to the best settlement of the Greek demands. He was through the whole of our discussion a stout advocate of the Greek claim to Smyrna.[31]

Subsequently, when the Supreme Council began discussion of the future of Anatolia, it would be Wilson who proposed "to unite to Greece in full sovereignty Smyrna and the surrounding district, as proposed in the report of the Greek Commission (as subsequently modified by agreement between the British and American experts . . .), and in addition to give Greece a mandate over the larger area claimed by M. Venizelos."[32]

It is highly unlikely that Colonel House had anything to do with this decision. During Wilson's absence from Paris, House had secretly committed the United States to accept mandates in Turkey. On March 1 Sir Maurice Hankey wrote Lloyd George, "Colonel House has told me privately that America would take a Mandate in Turkey and I rather gathered that they would like to take one for Armenia and Constantinople, although they have not committed themselves."[33] House, Hankey related, had gone on to say that though he could not openly undertake to accept a mandate, "he could work on a private understanding that they could do so." [34] On March 7, it appears House told Lloyd George and Clemenceau in a private conversation that the United States would assume "some sort of general supervision over Anatolia." [35] This being the case, it was only logical for the American delegation to follow the policy originally recommended by the intelligence section that Greek claims in Asia Minor should be opposed.[36] House did not inform Wilson that he had taken this stand. In his cable to Wilson on March 7, he mentioned only the mandates for Armenia and Constantinople, stating that he had said he thought the United States "would be willing."[37] However, in his diary he also noted: "We decided many other things that I did not put in my cable because too much explanation would have been needed." [38]

Wilson undoubtedly learned what House had done as soon as he returned to Paris, and this probably was one of the factors that led to a sudden cooling of relations between Wilson and House. Having a much more realistic approach than House as to the possibility of America's accepting any mandates at all, Wilson certainly realized that America could not accept one in Anatolian Turkey. The city of Smyrna was unquestionably Greek, and there were indications that Venizelos would be willing to accept any additional territory as a League mandate rather than annexing it directly.[39] Moreover, reports were being received ever more frequently telling of Turkish plans against the Greeks or reciting tales of atrocities already committed.[40] These reports must have played a role in influencing a person with such high moral convictions as those repeatedly expressed by Wilson.

Wilson's attitude also may well have been affected by the problems of the European settlement. Although the Adriatic crisis had not reached the proportions it was later to assume, it was already of sizable scope and import. Wilson's attitude toward Italy already was not the most cordial, and there were repeated reports of Italian troop landings along the southern coast of Anatolia. He must have recognized that if Greece did not get the territory, Italy probably would.

The biggest issue in the Council of Four immediately after Wilson returned was the question of reparations. Wilson continually urged a more moderate attitude toward Germany, and it was at about this time that Lloyd George began to associate himself decisively with the American position.[41] In return, Wilson may well have been willing to take a more favorable view toward the British position on Greek claims. It is interesting to note that the French, with whom both Wilson and Lloyd George were becoming increasingly annoyed, did not share in the discussions that led to the United States's adoption of the British viewpoint on Greek claims. Equally interesting is the fact that opposition within the British delegation to Greek claims in Asia Minor remained strong, led by the military and the India Office and supported by many within the diplomatic section. In fact, so great was the opposition that Robert Vansittart noted on April 8 that he had not seen the name of anyone well acquainted with the Near East who thought Smyrna should go to Greece.[42] Thus, Nicolson's willingness to substitute a Greek mandate for direct annexation of all but the Sandjak of Smyrna may well have been motivated as much by dissension within the British government as by a desire to conciliate the Americans. In any case, the minority view prevailed, championed chiefly by Nicolson, Crowe, and, above all, Lloyd George.

Greek Occupation of Smyrna

The Italian Threat in Asia Minor

The decision of the Council of Ten to form the Committee on Greek and Albanian Affairs prompted Italy to continue its efforts to reach a separate agreement with Greece.[43] However, it soon became obvious that the breach between the two nations was complete. Venizelos complained bitterly to the Peace Conference concerning Italian actions everywhere from Albania to Adalia. He claimed that in Bulgaria the Italians had formed an Italo-Bulgarian league, that they were preventing any Greek contact with the inhabitants of the Dodecanese, were subsidizing the Turkish press, and were encouraging the Turks in Smyrna to oppose a Greek occupation by force of arms.[44]

As the Peace Conference wore on, the Italians became more and more disturbed over the fact that they still had not been allowed to occupy the area in Anatolia promised them in the secret treaties. As tension among the Allies over Italy's claim to Fiume became increasingly severe, the Italians became ever more convinced that the other powers, in collusion with Greece, were determined to limit Italy's actions in Anatolia as much as possible. By the beginning of May, Sonnino was commenting bitterly that Italy was unlikely to obtain any real settlement of its territorial aspirations because of the ill-feeling among the powers.[45] The result was Italian initiatives in two directions.

Starting in mid-March, Italian troops landed periodically at Adalia for the purpose of "maintaining order," but always reembarked. These spot landings and withdrawals continued throughout April, and by May 5, the Italians had troops on a more or less permanent basis at both Adalia and Marmaris. It was obvious that the Italians were on the verge of occupying the territory they regarded as being rightfully theirs.[46]

At the same time, the Italian high commissioner in Constantinople, Count Carlo Sforza, began actively to solicit Turkish friendship and support. Sforza was convinced that a partition of Anatolia would be disastrous for Italian economic interests there, since a fragmented

Turkey would assure the predominance of British and French influence in the Near East. Therefore, with what he assumed was the tacit consent of the Italian Foreign Office, Sforza consistently posed as a friend to the Turkish government, and he sought to minimize the negative impact of Italy's territorial occupation by successfully urging Rome that the number of occupying troops be kept small. He was aided in his policy by Turkish recognition that the alternative to an Italian sphere of influence would all too likely be an extensive one for Turkey's archenemy Greece. Thus, while physically staking out their territorial claims in order to strengthen Italy's position at the negotiating table, the Italians also sought to win Turkish sympathy by indicating Italy's willingness to oppose an even harsher settlement.[47]

Decision for Greek Occupation

The intransigence of the Italian delegation over Italy's right to Fiume led President Wilson to issue a public statement on April 23 that was designed to rally pro-Wilsonian elements in Italy. His hope was that these groups could in turn exert domestic political pressure on the government for a more moderate attitude regarding Italy's territorial claims. The result, however, was the withdrawal of the Italian delegation from the Peace Conference on April 24, and Orlando's return to Rome where he met with overwhelming support from all segments of the population.[48] Clemenceau, Lloyd George, and Wilson continued to meet in Paris, and as it became evident that the Italians were not going to return to Paris immediately, the anti-Italian attitude of the three leaders reached ever-greater heights. On May 2, events took a sudden and dramatic turn. Incensed by the fact that Italy had sent several ships to Smyrna, Wilson offered to do likewise. "If I do it, it should bring results—and far be it from me to want this to be war. But the attitude of Italy is undoubtedly aggressive; she is creating a menace to peace, even in the middle of a conference of Peace." [49] In reply, Lloyd George stated that Venizelos had requested the sending of an Allied ship to Smyrna, and added that he thought all three nations should be represented. This was quickly agreed to, causing Clemenceau to remark, "What a beginning for the League of Nations! " [50]

Three days later, on May 5, anti-Italian sentiment among the Big Three reached fever pitch. Wilson wrathfully recounted tales of Italian atrocities on Rhodes, while Lloyd George expounded on Italy's "grand plan of action in the Eastern Mediterranean." [51] Referring to the Italian occupation of Marmaris and Adalia, he expressed the fear that the other Allies might soon find Italy occupying half of Anatolia. He thought it might be well to reconsider the old plan for redistributing the temporary forces of occupation in the Ottoman Empire. As part of this they could allow Greek forces to occupy Smyrna, "since their compatriots were actually being massacred at the present time and there was no one to help them." [52]

Since the Italians had announced that they would return to the Peace Conference for the presentation of the draft treaty to the Germans on May 7, it was imperative that any formal decision involving Greek occupation of Smyrna should be made quickly. Therefore, the following day Lloyd George reiterated his proposal and suggested that Greece send two or three divisions to the area but that they should be retained on shipboard and be allowed to land only if there were "a menace of trouble or massacres." [53] Wilson, however, asked "why they should not be landed at once? The men did not keep in good condition on board ship." [54] Both Lloyd George and Clemenceau were in accord. When Clemenceau asked if Italy should be warned, Lloyd George brusquely replied, "Not in my opinion." [55] With these few words the decision was made.

The Landing at Smyrna

After the return of the Italians to the Peace Conference, discussion concerning the Smyrna landing continued only at sessions of the Big Three from which the Italians were absent. The negotiations were carried on in the utmost secrecy, so much so that the members of the American delegation, with the exception of General Bliss, knew nothing about the plan. The whole process of dispatching Greek troops to Smyrna provides one of the most striking examples of the lack of communication within the American delegation and Wilson's tendency to "go it alone."

The first step was to consult Venizelos. Naturally he was delighted with the proposal and stated that he could send two divisions that were then in Macedonia, one of which was ready to go. It was decided that British Admiral Calthorpe should be in command of the Allied ships and the landing procedure. This, it was hoped, would intimidate the commander of the Italian ships then anchored in the harbor at Smyrna. It was also decided that the Turks should hand over the forts to an initial landing party composed entirely of French troops, which would in turn be relieved by Greek forces. This would avoid the "mixing up of nationalities," [56] and thus give the Italians less of an excuse for taking any action. Also, there would be less chance of an outbreak of Turkish-Greek hostilities if the French acted as intermediaries in the transfer of the forts.

The biggest problem was that of devising a system by which Italy and Turkey could be warned of the impending action early enough to prevent a sudden, overt reaction on the part of their troops on the scene. At the same time it was necessary to delay the news long enough to ensure the acceptance of the scheme as a fait accompli. [57] Wilson in particular was opposed to informing them before the last possible minute, stating that it was "important to keep all this business as secret as possible." [58] The Greek troops were due to arrive on the morning of May 14. It was decided that the Italian representatives in Paris would be informed on the afternoon of May 12, and that Constantinople would be told thirty-six hours in advance that Smyrna must be turned over to the Greeks, though the actual time of the landing would be given the Turks only twelve hours before it occurred.

On May 11, all plans had to be changed. The news had leaked out at Constantinople, apparently from an English source. Wilson and Venizelos were ready to land first and then make an agreement with the Italians before the Greeks took over. However, Clemenceau opposed this, and Balfour backed him up. "We may be forced to a conflict, but unless you desire to provoke it yourself, do what M. Clemenceau asks, speak first to the Italians." [59] Therefore, it was decided to postpone the landing for twenty-four hours. Italy would be told that while the Italians were away from the Peace Conference, news of disturbances at Smyrna had made it necessary to decide to occupy it, but that Italy was welcome to join Britain and France in providing detachments for the initial landing. [60]

The following day Orlando was informed of the proposed landing.

The Turks were firing on the Greeks, Lloyd George stated, and it was only logical to send Greek troops to protect Greeks. Although Orlando protested that the British, French, and Italian detachments should remain in order to give the occupation an international character, he gave in upon receiving assurances that "the landing was without prejudice to the ultimate disposal of Smyrna in the Treaty of Peace." [61]

The landing took place on May 15. The French, British, and Italian contingents met with no opposition, but when the Greek troops landed in order to take over, rioting and violence broke out.[62] Subsequent investigation would show that there had been no real danger of violence at Smyrna prior to the landing. The disturbances that occurred at the time of the landing and those which followed were products of the landing itself, for the Greek officers in charge made little effort to keep either their troops or local Greek civilians from acts of violence against the Turkish residents of Smyrna.[63]

Italian and Turkish Reaction to the Landing

Public opinion in Italy regarded the Greek occupation of Smyrna with outrage and bitterness. Official reaction was swift. Two days after the landing took place, the Italians, without consulting any of the other powers, landed troops at Scalanuova and established control over the customs house there. Subsequently, they claimed that this and other landings were necessary because the security of the area was in jeopardy.[64] A. H. Lybyer's scornful comment that the "only security menace was of their own future hold upon that neighborhood," best summarizes the attitude of the other powers.[65] Apparently it never occurred to them that this might hold equally well for the Greek occupation of Smyrna.

The initial reaction in Constantinople was a conviction that the Allies intended to partition all of Anatolia and leave nothing to Turkey.[66] In the interior, a small anti-Greek movement appeared, led by a Turkish general Mustapha Kemal. The disarmament of the Turkish army, which had been proceeding quietly under British supervision, stopped; the Turks seized all the ammunition dumps in which they had been discarding their weapons, and British officers were driven out of the interior. Though the Turks subsequently protested mildly against the Italian occupations, they also sought Italian help, both militarily and diplomatically, in opposing Greek territorial ambitions.[67]

The dispatch of Greek troops to Smyrna was by far the most important single decision concerning the Near East taken during the first six months of the Peace Conference. It was criticized by many at the time and by almost everyone in later years.[68] Both the British War Office and Foreign Office offered "serious warning and protests" prior to the landing.[69] This may indicate why Lloyd George would have been content initially to leave the Greek troops on shipboard in the harbor. Winston Churchill commented later, "I cannot understand to this day how these eminent statesmen in Paris, Wilson, Lloyd George, Clemenceau and Venizelos, whose wisdom and prudence and address had raised them under the severest tests so much above their fellows, could have been betrayed into so rash and fatal a step." [70] A partial, though biased, answer was provided by A. H. Lybyer two years after the Peace Conference.

The pleasant insinuating ways of Venizelos more and more obscured the facts that his position even in Greece rested upon Allied bayonets, and that the people were not the heroes and philosophers of classic lore, but a modern group of very mixed descent, given to trading and shipping, inept in administration, cruel and dishonest on occasion to an equality with Byzantinized Turks, and no more civilized all things considered, than the neighbors and enemies whom they despised and belittled.[71]

Two false arguments, both seeking to justify the Greek occupation, have been advanced. It has been maintained that the decision was taken at a time when the Greek occupation was merely part of a larger overall plan that included having the Italians in Adalia, the French in Cilicia, the United States in Armenia, and an international zone at Constantinople.[72] This was hardly the case. Although several plans had been proposed, at the time the decision was made the United States opposed French control of Cilicia, and the only matters the Big Three were agreed on regarding Anatolia was that Greece should have a zone around Smyrna and that ideally they would like to keep Italy completely out of Asia Minor. The second argument is that at the time of the landing opinion in Paris had shifted in favor of leaving the Turks in Constantinople, that there was therefore a good possibility that Greece might not obtain eastern Thrace, and that this would necessitate compensation elsewhere.[73] This is not correct. The idea of leaving the sultan as resident, though not sovereign, in Constantinople was first broached by Lloyd George on May 14, and was not considered seriously until well after the Greek landing had taken place. Moreover, in the Greek Committee, the United States, France, and Britain had all agreed in principle to the cession of eastern Thrace to Greece. Although the United States maintained that no final decision could be taken until the fate of Constantinople was definitely decided, there is no indication that it ever questioned the basic recommendation of the committee until the summer of 1919. The subject of Thrace was never discussed either in the Council of Ten or the Council of Four.[74]

The decision to send Greek troops to Smyrna followed logically from the aims, attitudes, and prejudices of the Big Three. The overwhelmingly favorable impression that Venizelos made on them, plus their fear that his government might fall if he did not get what he had promised his people, undoubtedly helped to determine their stand. Other interests also played a part. Lloyd George, quite apart from his strong, emotional philhellenism, envisioned Greece as Britain's future agent in exerting control over the Aegean.[75] Clemenceau wanted British and American cooperation on European issues; he also had no desire to see Italy strengthened. More important, France had no major interest in the area involved. Here Clemenceau could afford to be accommodating; on Syrian affairs he could not. Wilson consistently took an anti-Turkish attitude; moreover, he apparently felt that Greek ethnological claims were justified in Smyrna. Yet in agreeing to this action (in fact, being the first to suggest the *immediate* landing of troops), Wilson was accepting an occupation and administration of new (and enemy) territory by a nation that claimed it as its own. This was to be done totally outside of the authority and control of the League of Nations and before any final decision as to ultimate disposal of the area had been reached. It was obvious that such an occupation would be taken by the Greeks as implicit recognition of their claims; in accepting it Wilson was in effect agreeing to the type of partition outside of League auspices that he hitherto had opposed.

Important as all of these factors may have been, it is clear that none of them constitutes the chief reason for the Big Three's decision to support a Greek occupation of Smyrna. That they did so was due primarily to their annoyance with Italy over its claims in the Adriatic. This anti-Italian feeling reached such a pitch when the Italians left the Peace Conference that it became, particularly for Wilson, an obsession. Over and above all other issues, far over-shadowing any consideration of Turkish or Greek rights or concern over possible massacres, was the single consideration that Italy must not be allowed to gain control of Smyrna. The alternative to Italian control was Greek occupation.

On balance, it would seem that in order to prevent one outcome, the powers sanctioned another that was equally unjustified. By this action they greatly intensified a problem that had been difficult from the start. The Greeks assumed that this action meant that all of Turkey would be divided, with shares for everyone, and that they had merely been granted immediate control of one part of their eventual share.[76] In this conclusion they were justified, for in spite of assurances to Italy that the issue was not prejudged, it is evident that from that time on Clemenceau, Lloyd George, and Wilson assumed that Smyrna, plus an additional undefined region, would be annexed by Greece.[77] Turkish resistance to this decision would ultimately thwart many of the Allied plans in Anatolia.

---

1. Hurewitz, *Diplomacy,* 2:11. See also above Chapter 1.

2. *U.S. Doc., P.P.C.,* 11:50–51, American Commissioners Plenipotentiary, 2/18/19; Miller, *Diary,* 17:105–6, 3/1/19; Foreign Office, F.O. 608/93/362-1-1/1512, Balfour to Imperiali, 11/26/18; 414, Rodd to Balfour, 12/10/18; Cabinet Papers, Cab. 24/66, G.T. 5955, Draft memorandum, Cecil to Pichon, 10/8/18; *Br. Doc.,* 7:259–60, For. Min., 2/26/20, n. 4, Imperiali to Balfour, 11/16/18. Balfour made little effort to conceal his dismay that Lloyd George had ever negotiated the Saint Jean de Maurienne Agreement, commenting that it had been done without his knowledge while he had been in Washington in 1917, although Lloyd George must have had "worthwhile reasons, no doubt." Mantoux, *Conseil des Quatre,* 2:40, 5/11/19.

3. For the text of the report see Miller, *Diary,* 10:284–310, 3/8/19; House Papers, Dr. 23, fols. 119 A-B, 120; Cabinet Papers, Cab. 29/11, W.C.P. 401. For a comment, see Nicolson, *Peacemaking,* p. 280, 3/8/19. The *procès verbal* of the meetings of the committee may be found in Cabinet Papers, Cab. 29/8, W.C.P. 111, 141, 145, 192, 198; 29/9, W.C.P. 226, 234, 244. The minutes of the meetings are in House Papers, Dr. 23, fols. 118, A-M; Foreign Office, F.O. 608/37/92-1-4. For published bulletins pertaining to the committee meetings, see Miller, *Diary,* 17:17–18, 25, 72, 91, 95–96, 112, 149. Nicolson's comments on the committee's work are in *Peacemaking,* p. 266, 2/21/19; p. 274, 3/1/19; p. 277, 3/4/19.

4. Nicolson, *Peacemaking*, p. 276, 3/6/19; p. 283, 3/12/19; pp. 311–12, 4/14/19.

5. Ibid., p. 276, 3/3/19; Foreign Office, F.O. 608/38/97-1-1/479, Italian actions in Albania, January 1919. On the question of the southern boundary of Albania as established by the powers in 1913–14, and on Greek claims to Epirus, see E. C. Helmreich, *The Diplomacy of the Balkan Wars, 1912–1913*, pp. 334–39.

6. Miller, *Diary*, 10:288. Upon reading the report, Albert Lybyer of the American delegation submitted a report completely opposing the cession of western Thrace to Greece. See House Papers, Dr. 23, fol. 119, 3/22/19.

7. Miller, *Diary*, 10:291.

8. Ibid. See also Nicolson, *Peacemaking*, p. 274, 3/1/19.

9. Miller, *Diary*, 10:291.

10. Ibid., pp. 300–301. See also Lloyd George Papers, F 23/4/22, Hankey to Lloyd George, 2/23/19.

11. On March 11, the Council of Ten had accepted Lloyd George's recommendation that discussion of the constitution of a Turkish state should be adjourned until President Wilson returned to Paris. This was the basis for Mezes' refusal to consider the Greek Committee's report, although both Tardieu and Crowe pointed out that the report dealt only with recommendations regarding Greek claims. *U.S. Doc., P.P.C.,* 4:325–26, C. of Ten, 3/11/19; Cabinet Papers, Cab. 29/10, W.C.P., 370, Minute, Central Committee on Territorial Questions, 3/17/19; Miller, *Diary*, 17:228–29; J. T. Shotwell Papers, Box 3, Central Territorial Committee minutes, 3/17/19.

12. See p. 92.

13. Nicolson, *Peacemaking*, pp. 284–85, 3/16/19; p. 285, 3/17/19.

14. Ibid., p. 281, 3/9/19; *U.S. Doc., P.P.C.,* 4:195, C. of Ten, 3/5/19; p. 214, 3/6/19.

15. Foreign Office, F.O. 608/37/92-1-1/4392, Nicolson to Crowe, 3/15/19; F.O., 608/111/385-1-11/8163. Comments of British delegation on Clemenceau's proposals of March 22, 3/23/19; Nicolson, *Peacemaking*, pp. 284–85, 3/16/19. See also House Papers, Dr. 29, fol. 180, Nicolson to Wiseman, 3/15/19; Nicolson to Mezes, 3/28/19.

16. Nicolson, *Peacemaking*, pp. 288–91, 3/24/19–3/28/19.

17. Cabinet Papers, Cab. 29/11, W.C.P. 416, Report of the Central Committee on Territorial Questions," (n.d.).

18. House Papers, Dr. 30, fol. 199, Summary report of Central Territorial Committee, 3/28/19; Dr. 23, fols. 118L, 120A, Final report of Greek Committee, 3/30/19; Cabinet Papers, 29/11, W.C.P. 416, Report of Central Committee on Territorial Questions, (n.d.); W.C.P. 498, Minute, Central Territorial Committee meeting, 3/28/19; also in Shotwell Papers, Box 3; Nicolson, *Peacemaking*, p. 287, 3/21/19; *U.S. Doc., P.P.C.,* 4:716, n. 1 Council of Foreign Ministers, 5/16/19.

19. Westermann, Diary, 3/25/19. When Nicolson asked Westermann during the Anglo-British negotiations if he had changed his mind about Smyrna, Westermann replied that he had not, but rather was working under specific orders. Ibid.

20. For a further discussion of these problems as they were interpreted by the American delegates on the Greek Committee, see *U.S. Doc., P.P.C.,* 11:525, Day and Westermann to Grew, 3/13/19. In opposing a Greek zone at Smyrna, Day had taken the opposite point of view from that ascribed to him by Nicolson on January 7 and 9. See *Peacemaking*, pp. 226–29; also above, Chapter 2. But apparently by March 24 Day had again come around to his original outlook. E. Seymour, *Letters from the Paris Peace Conference*, p. 186.

21. See above, Chapter 2.

22. *U.S. Doc., P.P.C.,* 11:91, American Commissioners Plenipotentiary, 3/4/19.

23. Miller, *Diary*, 1:156–57, 3/7/19.

24. Ibid., 6:284, 3/9/19.

25. Woodrow Wilson Papers, V-A, Box 15, Heck to Paris Peace Conference, 3/12/19.

26. Miller, *Diary*, 7:152, Mezes to House, 3/24/19.

27. Nicolson, *Peacemaking*, pp. 312–13, 4/15/19.

28. Miller, *Diary*, 7:167, Westermann to Mezes, 3/25/19; House Papers, Dr. 29, fol. 195; State Dept., A.C.N.P. 185.5122/13. In the same letter Westermann indicated his willingness to continue work even though it would be "on the basis of a decision in which my own knowledge does not allow me to concur." He went on to say that he "assumed the principle comes from Col. House." However, in his diary Westermann, who disliked and distrusted Mezes, indicated that he had sent a copy of the letter to House, "because I think he [Mezes] may have lied about the orders from the 'higherups'." Westermann, Diary, 3/25/19. See also Yale Papers, II-8; State Dept., A.C.N.P., 185.5135/25A, Westermann(?) to Cappo, 5/3/19. In his diary, House makes no mention of having discussed the issue with anyone at any time.

29. Woodrow Wilson Papers, V-A, Box 16, Wilson to Mezes, 3/16/19.

30. Nicolson, *Peacemaking*, p. 285, 3/16/19.

31. Lloyd George, *Truth*, p. 1249. It is easy to believe that Wilson was responsible for the shift in American policy. It is less easy to accept the statement that this was done "with the help of his advisors." It is clear that Westermann was in no way consulted; yet in any consultation of advisors he would have been the most logical one to turn to, since he was both a member of the Greek Committee and the designated American expert on Western Asia. Mezes apparently was not consulted, but rather told directly by Wilson to come to an understanding. For statements regarding Wilson's well-known general failure to consult his advisors, see Lansing, *Big Four*, pp. 40–45; and Evans, *U.S. and Partition*, pp. 172–73.

32. *U.S. Doc.*, *P.P.C.*, 5:586, C. of Four, 5/13/19. See also below, Chapter 5.

33. Lloyd George Papers, F 23/4/28, Hankey to Lloyd George, 3/1/19.

34. Ibid.

35. Lloyd George, *Truth*, p. 288.

36. Westermann commented in his diary on February 21 that he was opposing French and British proposals to give land in Asia Minor to Greece because Turkey was to be a mandatory, and to partition it in this way would hinder the work of the mandatory power.

37. House Papers, Dr. 49, fol. 12; Seymour, *House Papers*, 4:358–59.

38. House Papers, Diary, 3/7/19.

39. Nicolson, *Peacemaking*, p. 284, 3/16/19. The day of Wilson's return to Paris, Venizelos sent him a personal memorandum regarding Greek claims in Asia Minor. Woodrow Wilson Papers, V-A, Box 15, Venizelos to Wilson, 3/14/19. Wilson met privately for three hours with Clemenceau and Lloyd George that afternoon. F. L. Polk Papers, Sterling Memorial Library, Yale University, New Haven, Connecticut, Dr. 78, fol. 9, Lansing to Polk, 3/15/19. Permission to reprint from the F. L. Polk Papers granted by Yale University Library.

40. Woodrow Wilson Papers, V-A, Box 15, Venizelos to Wilson, 3/13/19; *Current History* 9 (March, 1919):549–52.

41. Mantoux, *Conseil des Quatre*, 1:13–104, 3/24/19–3/31/19.

42. Foreign Office, F.O. 608/102/378-3-2/6484, Ryan to Mallet, 3/16/19, Vansittart minute, 4/8/19; F.O. 608/103/383-1-1; F.O. 608/103/383-1-3/4400; 4523; 4940; 4943, March, 1919; F.O. 608/103/383-1-5/6102, Toynbee minute, 4/3/19; F.O. 406/41/37, Curzon memorandum, 4/18/19; Cabinet Papers, Cab. 29/11, W.C.P. 427, Memorandum, India delegation, 4/1/19; W.C.P. 459, Montagu memorandum, 4/3/19; Cab. 29/28, Minutes, British Empire delegation, 4/3/19; H. Nicolson, *Curzon: The Last Phase, 1919–1925*, p. 94; Beer, Diary, 3/7/19.

43. Foreign Office, F.O. 608/93/362-1-1/1512, Martino to Hardinge, 2/6/19; Hardinge to Martino, 2/11/19; Nicolson, *Peacemaking*, p. 259, 2/7/19; p. 260, 2/9/19.

44. Woodrow Wilson Papers, V-A, Box 11, H. White memorandum, 1/31/19; Foreign Office,

F.O. 608/83/342-8-5/5169, Venizelos to British delegation, 3/12/19; F.O. 608/94/362-1-3/4122, Nicolson memorandum, 3/12/19; Balfour to Curzon, 3/14/19; 4553, Crowe minute, 3/18/19; F.O. 608/103/383-1-5/8158, Venizelos to Peace Conference, 4/22/19; Nicolson, *Peacemaking*, p. 283, 3/12/19; Lloyd George, *Truth*, pp. 1246–48. At this time the Greeks were alone in advocating an immediate occupation of Smyrna; they had, in fact, been urging such a step since the previous October. See R. Poincaré, *Au Service de la France: neuf années de souvenirs*, 10:371, 10/2/18; Foreign Office, F.O. 608/103/383-1-3/5024, Webb to Foreign Office, 3/15/19; F.O. 608/94/362-1-3/4740, Nicolson minute, 3/20/19.

45. Orlando repeatedly expressed fear for the fate of his government unless he could give the Italian Chamber tangible evidence that Italian interests in the Near East were being safeguarded. Foreign Office, F.O. 608/93/362-1-2/2473, Balfour to Curzon, 2/17/19; 2539, Curzon to Balfour, 2/20/19; 3185, 2/28/19; 3548, Balfour to Curzon, 3/9/19; F.O. 608/83/342-8-3/5104, "Conversation between British and Italian Delegates Regarding the future of Asia Minor," 3/21/19; Nicolson, *Peacemaking*, p. 283, 3/12/19, Sonnino Papers, Reel 26, no. 954, Biancheri to Sonnino, 4/11/19; no. 1150, Sonnino to Paris, 5/2/19.

46. Sonnino Papers, Reel 26, no. 432, Caviglia to Sonnino, 3/2/19; no. 797, Biancheri to Sonnino, 3/30/19; Reel 46, no. 314, Sonnino to London, Paris, and Cospoli, 3/23/19; no. 386, Sonnino to Rome, Paris, 4/7/19; Reel 44, no. 85, Biancheri to Paris, 4/18/19; France, *Bulletin périodique de la presse Italienne*, no. 108; Foreign Office, F.O. 608/93/362-1-2/3548 ff; United States, Department of State, Papers Relating to the Internal Affairs of Turkey, 1910–1929 (hereafter cited as Turkey), 867.00/862, Heck to Sec. State, 4/1/19; Adm. Mark Bristol Papers, Library of Congress, Box 16, Diary, 4/27/19; Mantoux, *Conseil des Quatre*, 1:485, 5/5/19; *U.S. Doc., P.P.C.*, 5:466, C. of Four, 5/5/19; R. S. Baker, *Woodrow Wilson and World Settlement*, 2:191; Frangulis, *Crise Mondiale*, 2:61–62, Greek Admiral of the eastern Mediterranean to Venizelos, 4/12/19; Sachar, "U.S. and Turkey," p. 108; *Times* (London), 4/4/19. Permission to reprint from the Mark Bristol Papers granted by Children's Hospital of the District of Columbia.

47. Sonnino Papers, Reel 26, no. 581, Sforza to Sonnino, 3/10/19; no. 625, Biancheri to Sonnino, 3/19/19; nos. 852, 854, Sforza to Sonnino, 3/30/19; no. 882, 4/5/19; Reel 46, no. 368, Sonnino to Sforza, 4/3/19; no. 409, Sonnino to Italian military authorities, 4/12/19; no. 600, Sonnino to Italian military command, 5/28/19; Sforza, *Diplomatic Europe*, pp. 52–53; C. Sforza, *Makers of Modern Europe*, pp. 358–62; Foreign Office, F.O. 608/114/385-1-23, Randall to Headlam-Morley, 3/1/19; F.O. 608/103/383-1-1/5021, Webb to Foreign Office, 3/13/19; F.O. 608/94/362-1-3/7578, Deedes to War Office, 4/4/19; State Dept., Turkey, 867.00/859, Heck to Sec. State, 3/11/19; Kinross, *Ataturk*, p. 167; Pech, *Alliés et Turquie*, p. 45, 3/30/19.

48. For an excellent discussion of Wilson's statement and its impact on the Peace Conference, see Mayer, *Politics of Peacemaking*, chap. 20. See also *D.R.F.P., Allied Press Supplement*, 6:5/14/19; Seton-Watson, *Italy*, pp. 529–30.

49. Mantoux, *Conseil des Quatre*, 1:455, 5/2/19; Foreign Office, F.O. 608/94/362-1-4/8946, Derby to Hardinge, 5/2/19; Woodrow Wilson Papers, V-A, Box 27, Benson to Bristol, 5/2/19; Benson to OPNAU (Washington), 5/2/19.

50. Mantoux, *Conseil des Quatre*, 1:450–56, 5/2/19; *U.S.Doc., P.P.C.*, 5:407–13, 422, C. of Four, 5/2/19.

51. Mantoux, *Conseil des Quatre*, 1:485, 5/5/19.

52. *U.S. Doc., P.P.C.*, 5:466–67, C. of Four, 5/5/19. See also Mantoux, *Conseil des Quatre*, 1:485-86, 5/5/19.

53. Mantoux, *Conseil des Quatre*, 1:499, 5/6/19.

54. *U.S. Doc., P.P.C.*, 5:484, C. of Four, 5/6/19.

55. Mantoux, *Conseil des Quatre*, 1:499, 5/6/19.

56. *U.S. Doc., P.P.C.*, 5:558, C. of Four, 5/10/19. Bliss, who was present along with the British military representatives, records that he and his colleagues believed that sending a

Greek force would cause trouble, "but we were not asked to express an opinion." Bliss Papers, Box 65, Diary, 7/13/19.

57. Wilson remarked that since the Greeks had the council's permission and the Italians did not, the Italians could not land without provoking a grave incident. Just what would be done if the incident did occur did not seem to concern any of the Big Three, *U.S. Doc., P.P.C.,* 5:558, C. of Four, 5/10/19.

58. Mantoux, *Conseil des Quatre,* 1:512, 5/7/19. See also *U.S. Doc., P.P.C.,* 5:504, C. of Four, 5/7/19. Regarding this failure to tell the Italians immediately, the chief of the British Imperial General Staff, General Sir Henry Wilson, commented in his diary, "What rotten behavior to a friend and ally." C. E. Callwell, *Field-Marshal Sir Henry Wilson, His Life and Diaries,* 2:191. General Bliss agreed wholeheartedly. Bliss Papers, Box 65, Diary, 5/6/19. See also, State Department, A.C.N.P., 185.5134/2, Conference, Venizelos and Military Committee, 5/6/19.

59. Mantoux, *Conseil des Quatre,* 2:43, 5/11/19.

60. Ibid., p. 44.

61. *U.S. Doc., P.P.C.,* 5:577, C. of Four, 5/12/19. See also pp. 570–71, 578; Mantoux, *Conseil des Quatre,* 2:49–52, 5/12/19. The Italians had suspected that such a decision might be taken ever since Orlando's return to Paris. See S. Crespi, *Alla Difesa d'Italia in Guerra e a Versailles Diario, 1917–1919,* p. 532, 5/7/19; Sonnino Papers, Reel 26, no. 1202, Romano to Sonnino, 5/7/19.

62. Foreign Office, F.O. 608/104/383-1-6/10126, Webb to Foreign Office, 5/14/19; 5/15/19; 10251, Calthorpe to Foreign Office, 5/17/19; 12973, Admiralty report regarding Greek occupation of Smyrna; Bristol Papers, Box 16, Diary, report for week ending 5/18/19.

63. See below, Chapter 7.

64. *U.S. Doc., P.P.C.,* 5:668–69, C. of Four, 5/17/19; p. 726, 5/19/19, App. I; Cabinet Papers, Cab. 29/24, M. 168, Orlando to Supreme Council, 5/18/19; Foreign Office, F.O. 608/39/97-1-5/10444, Rodd to Balfour, 5/19/19. See also File 97-1-5, passim; Balfour Papers, MSS 49745, Rodd to Balfour, 5/26/19; Sonnino Papers, Reel 46, no. 508, Sonnino to Constantinople, 5/8/19; no. 528, Sonnino to Navy Ministry, Rome, 5/15/19; no. 543, Sonnino to Biancheri, 5/18/19; *Bulletin périodique de la presse Italienne,* no. 112; *D.R.F.P.:Allied Press Supplement,* 6:5/28/19.

65. A. H. Lybyer, "Turkey Under the Armistice," p. 465.

66. Pech, *Alliés et Turquie,* pp. 53–54, 5/16/19; Foreign Office, F.O. 608/111/385-1-14/11128, Calthorpe to Balfour, 5/27/19; Bristol Papers, Box 27, Bristol to Paris, 5/20/19; 5/21/19; State Department, Turkey, 867.00/876, Ravndal to Sec. State, 5/20/19; 867.00/877, 5/21/19. See also Adivar, *The Turkish Ordeal,* pp. 22–27.

67. Sonnino Papers, Reel 25, no. 1774, Indelli to Sonnino, 5/15/19; no. 1789, Elia to Sonnino, 5/18/19; Reel 26, Sforza to Sonnino, 5/19/19; Reel 25, no. 1870, Elia to Sonnino, 5/30/19; Reel 46, no. 524, Sonnino to Italian mission in Adalia, 5/14/19; Foreign Office, F.O., 608/104/383-1-6/11045, Calthorpe to Balfour, 5/26/19; Sforza, *Modern Europe,* pp. 361–62; W. S. Churchill, *The World Crisis: The Aftermath, 1918–1928,* p. 389; C. Price, *The Rebirth of Turkey,* p. 141; Lybyer, "Turkey Under the Armistice," p. 466; Evans, *U.S. and Partition,* pp. 173–76; Adivar, *Ordeal,* p. 46.

68. General Sir Henry Wilson noted that he and the other members of the Military Committee all thought at the time that the Smyrna expedition was "stupid." Callwell, *Henry Wilson,* p. 190, 5/6/19; p. 192, 5/10/19. See also Bliss Papers, Box 65, Diary, 7/13/19. É. Driault and M. Lheretier state that Admiral Calthorpe, who was in charge of the landing, expressed his opposition to it. *Histoire diplomatique de la Grèce de 1821 à nos jours,* 5:368–69. His American counterpart, Admiral Bristol, called the occupation "a most unfortunate occurrence. It is a great surprise to everyone that it was done." Bristol Papers, Box 16, report for week ending May 18, 1919. See also, G. Gaillard, *The Turks and Europe,* p. 50; Great Britain, *Parliamentary Debates,* (Commons), 5 ser., 116; col. 813; Meinertzhagen, *Diary,* p. 23, 6/26/19; Pallis,

Anatolian Venture, pp. 7, 62–66, 106; Price, *Rebirth,* p. 141; A. Ryan, *The Last of the Dragomans,* p. 128; Ronaldshay, *The Life of Lord Curzon,* 3:265–66; 4/18/19; Nicolson, *Curzon,* pp. 91-97; Hankey, *The Supreme Control at the Paris Peace Conference, 1919: A Commentary,* pp. 162–63; R. Vansittart, *The Mist Procession: the Autobiography of Lord Vansittart,* pp. 217–18.

69. Even Nicolson, a strong supporter of Greek claims, noted on March 20 that it would be absolutely foolish and stupid to send Greek troops to Smyrna at that time. Foreign Office, F.O. 608/94/362-1-3/4740. See also F.O. 608/103/383-1-3/6339, Curzon to Balfour, 4/3/19; Churchill, *Aftermath,* p. 388; Nicolson, *Curzon,* p. 94.

70. Churchill, *Aftermath,* p. 390.

71. Lybyer, "Turkey Under the Armistice," p. 456.

72. Nicolson, *Curzon,* pp. 92–93.

73. Ibid., p. 103; Pallis, *Anatolian Venture,* p. 66.

74. For a detailed examination of the Anatolian and Straits problems, see below, Chapter 5.

75. Regarding Lloyd George's personal attachment to Greece and Venizelos, see Nicolson, *Curzon,* pp. 95–96; Churchill, *Aftermath,* p. 415.

76. Sachar, "U.S. and Turkey," p. 112; Pallis, *Anatolian Venture,* p. 66. Venizelos told Nicolson on May 24 that he had received a letter from Wilson agreeing to a Greek mandate over the vilayet of Aidin and Greek sovereignty in the sanjaks of Smyrna and the caza of Aivali. This was not correct. Though the Council of Three had indeed agreed to part of these claims, Wilson in his letter stated only that he agreed "entirely" with Venizelos's views concerning the invalidity of Italian claims in Asia Minor. See Nicolson, *Peacemaking,* pp. 347–48, 5/24/19; Polk Papers, Dr. 74, fol. 124, Wilson to Venizelos, 5/21/19.

77. Mantoux, *Conseil des Quatre,* 2:41, 5/11/19; *U.S. Doc., P.P.C.,* 5:584–86, 5/13/19; pp. 614–16, 622–23, 5/14/19; Cabinet Papers, Cab. 29/24, M. 152, Big Three agreement regarding Asia Minor, 5/14/19.

V ❀ ANATOLIA AND CONSTANTINOPLE: THE QUESTION OF MANDATES

I N THE PERIOD between the signing of the armistice at Mudros and the end of the first phase of the Paris Peace Conference in June, 1919, conditions in Turkey were far from static. Despite the resignation and flight of the leaders of the Young Turk party and the formation of a cabinet from which its members were excluded, the party itself (known as the Committee of Union and Progress, or C.U.P.), which had governed Turkey before and during the war, had in no sense been destroyed. A *Times* correspondent reported that the C.U.P. existed "almost intact and . . . is the only efficient thing Turkey has produced," [1] while American Commissioner Heck warned Ambassador Sharp in Paris that the cabinet had "no real hold on the country, the great majority of officials being still members of the C.U.P. organization." [2]

The Constantinople Government and the C.U.P.

In an effort to break the hold of the party, Sultan Mehmed VI dissolved the C.U.P.-dominated legislature on December 21, 1918. Although the Turkish constitution required new elections within three months, the sultan announced that, owing to the turmoil of the times, elections would not be held again until four months after the signing of the peace treaty. [3] This attempt to silence the C.U.P. merely forced the organization to go underground. A new Turkish

National Defense Committee appeared and was generally conceded to be an offshoot of the C.U.P. Its aims were the retention of as much Turkish territory as possible and the freeing of C.U.P. leaders who were under arrest. This new organization constituted a serious threat to the Allies and the existing government, and led to an intensified Allied campaign of arrests and court martials of C.U.P. members.[4]

Although the British and French were agreed on the policy followed toward the C.U.P., it was at this time that their rivalry over dominance in the Near East became publicly evident. The arrival in Constantinople of the new Allied commander in chief of European Turkey, French General Louis Franchet d'Esperey, was the signal for an increase in Anglo-French tension. British diplomats, at least those at the Peace Conference, suddenly became much more willing to accept anything that the Armenians and Greeks said as true, while the French in Constantinople became increasingly open in their support of the established Turkish regime, which they regarded as both cooperative and docile.[5]

The Turkish government watched eagerly for signs of such antagonism. Since it was apparent that the Ottoman Empire had been written off by those powers whose policy, until then, had been to preserve it, it seemed Turkey's only hope was to pursue the time-honored practice of exploiting differences between the victors. Thus the Turks approached representatives of Britain, the United States, France, and Italy, in each case suggesting a clear preference for guidance by that representative's nation. In both the British and American cases, these advances met with a clear rebuff; the French and Italian reaction was a good bit warmer. The Italian government, embittered by the decision to land Greek troops at Smyrna, instructed its emissaries that "the Italian government has held and will hold itself completely free to deal directly with Turkey on any questions not involving directly the political or other interests of the Allied Powers."[6] Even more important, the Turkish government came to believe that if the Franco-British alignment could be disrupted, Turkey would be likely to retain the support of France because of the large French commercial investments in the Ottoman Empire and the threat that a disruption of Turkish political and economic stability would pose to the security of Ottoman Debt bonds, the majority of which were in French hands. While quite willing to join with the Allies in punitive measures against the C.U.P., the Constantinople government did not hesitate to encourage as best it could any incipient discord within the victorious coalition.[7]

The Turkish Delegation to the Peace Conference

Despite the fact that a draft peace treaty had not yet been formulated, a Turkish delegation was granted permission to come before the Council of Ten on June 17, 1919. The delegation was headed by the sultan's brother-in-law Damad Ferid Pasha who had been appointed grand vizier on March 4. In a prepared statement that was aggressive rather than humble in tone, Damad Ferid maintained that the Turkish people had not been responsible for Turkey's entrance into the war or for atrocities committed against the Armenians and Greeks; in fact, the Turkish people had always been pro-British and pro-French, and heartily deplored the persecutions. Nor was the sultan at fault. The whole blame rested squarely on the few leaders of the C.U.P., who, through their alliance with Germany and their control of the army, had terrorized the rest of Turkey into submission. Not only had Christians been persecuted, but three million Moslems had felt the terror of the C.U.P. as well. Basing his claim on the common religion of the majority, he asked that all of the Ottoman Empire be kept together, for any disruption of this "compact bloc. . . . would be detrimental to the peace and tranquility of the East." [8] He promised that a written memorandum of specific proposals would follow.

This memorandum turned out to be even more belligerent in tone than Damad Ferid's statement to the Council of Ten. Stating bluntly that the Ottoman government would not accept "the dismemberment of the Empire or its division under different mandates," [9] the memorandum went on to enumerate what the government would be willing to accept. In Thrace, in order to protect Adrianople, a return to the boundaries of the 1878 Congress of Berlin was necessary. The coastal islands and all territory extending to the Russian and Persian borders, including Mosul, must belong to Turkey. If the Allies recognized the existing Russian Armenian state, the Turks would be willing to negotiate with it regarding their common frontier. The various Arab provinces must remain under the religious control of the caliphate at Constantinople. Although they would be granted a considerable degree of local autonomy, all governors must be appointed by the sultan, with the exception of the Hedjaz, which could organize its own form of administration. Finally, Turkey would be willing to negotiate with Britain on both the Egyptian and Cyprus questions.[10]

The reaction of the Council of Ten was one of incredulous amazement. Wilson commented that he had "never seen anything more stupid," while Lloyd George called the delegation and its memorandum "good jokes" and commented that such a showing was "the best proof of the political incapacity of the Turks."[11] Rejecting the concept of the nonresponsibility of the Turkish people, the council stated in a written reply that "a nation must be judged by the Government which rules it."[12] Refusing equally to accept an appeal that Turkey should be judged not by the recent past but by the beneficent treatment of minorities exhibited in earlier Turkish history, the council commented:

> History tells us of many Turkish successes and many Turkish defeats.
> . . . Yet in all these changes there is no case to be found, either in Europe
> or Asia or Africa, in which the establishment of Turkish rule in any country
> has not been followed by a diminution of material prosperity and a fall
> in the level of culture; nor is there any case to be found in which the
> withdrawal of Turkish rule has not been followed by a growth in material
> prosperity and a rise in the level of culture. Neither among the Christians
> of Europe, nor among the Moslems of Syria, Arabia, and Africa, has the
> Turk done other than destroy wherever he has conquered; never has he
> shown himself able to develop in peace what he has won in war.[13]

As to the question of religious unity, the council noted that during the war members of the Moslem faith had fought on both sides, and since the armistice

> nothing touching religion has been altered, except the security with which
> it may be practiced: and this, wherever Allied control exists, has certainly
> been altered for the better. . . . To thinking Moslems throughout the world,
> the modern history of the Government enthroned at Constantinople can
> be no source of pleasure or pride.[14]

Finally, regarding the Turks' stated intention of bringing about "an intensive economic and intellectual culture," the council replied that "no change could be more startling or impressive; none could be more beneficial." [15] Certainly the Turkish delegation had hurt, rather than helped, Turkey's position at the Peace Conference.

Decision to Partition Anatolia

The question of Anatolia was not discussed to any extent by either the Council of Ten or the Council of Four until the beginning of May. This does not mean that no thought had been given to it or that no general agreements had been made.[16] On March 7, Colonel House had promised Lloyd George and Clemenceau that America would assume mandates over Constantinople, the Straits and Armenia, as well as some form of "general supervision over Anatolia." [17] On April 1, as a result of Wilson's apparent disavowal of House's promise concerning Anatolia and the president's acceptance of the Greek Committee's proposal for a Greek zone in Asia Minor, the Council of Four agreed to a new set of general principles. It was decided that in the peace treaty Turkey would need to know only what territories it would not retain, and that the boundaries of the Greek zone would be "extended beyond strictly ethnographic limits, in order to open the ports of the western coast." [18] Turkey would be required to agree in advance to accept whatever arrangements the powers eventually decided upon for Anatolia. If it were not to be independent, it would be placed under a different mandate from that of Constantinople and the Straits.

Nonetheless, the question of Italian claims made it virtually impossible to postpone indefinitely all decisions regarding the future of Asia Minor. No longer able to fall back on the alternative solution of an American mandate for Anatolia, Britain and France were faced with the task of fulfilling their pledges of equal compensation for Italy in any Near East settlement, a problem that was further complicated by the situation in the Adriatic.[19]

In the debates in Paris, much emphasis was being placed on the fact that Italian demands for Fiume were nowhere encompassed in the 1915 Treaty of London. This made it all the more difficult for Britain and France to go back on the territorial pledges that *had* been made in that treaty. Recognizing that some sort of Near East settlement that included Italy would have to be made, and anxious to find a solution to the Fiume imbroglio that would prevent the Italians from leaving the Peace Conference, Lloyd George suggested to Wilson and Clemenceau on April 21 that perhaps Italy could be "induced to agree" to give up Fiume if, in addition to Adriatic concessions already offered, some sort of territorial adjustment favorable to Italy were made in Asia Minor. Clemenceau, with whom Lloyd George had previously consulted, thereupon produced a map that allocated the southern half of Anatolia, less the Greek zone, to Italy as a mandate. A separate state would be constituted at the Straits. The remaining portion of Anatolia would be a French mandate. To Wilson's objection that Italy lacked colonial administrative experience, Lloyd George observed that the Romans had been very good colonial governors. To this Wilson replied dryly, "Unfortunately, the modern Italians are not the Romans." [20] He was also fearful of difficulties with Italy if America had a mandate next to an Italian one, presumably referring here to Armenia.

However, when Lloyd George subsequently asked if he could, in an effort to placate the Italians, say to them that if Asia Minor were divided into spheres of economic influence Italy would get a large share, Wilson reluctantly agreed, as long as it was under a League mandate. He still believed that it was necessary for the Turks to have some sort of government, and "one ought not, from this point of view, to divide their territory." [21] The implication that perhaps an Italian mandate over all Anatolia would be politically preferable to partition was not lost on Lloyd George. He protested sharply that it would be quite a job to govern all Anatolia, whereupon Wilson remarked that partition "presented great difficulties," too. [22] Thus, the situation was more muddled than before. The one clear point was that Wilson, despite his acquiescence to Lloyd George's proposal, was averse to both the idea of partitioning the Turkish area of Anatolia and of dividing it into nonmandated economic spheres of influence. In any case, the plan came to naught, for the Italians steadfastly refused to consider any settlement that did not allow satisfaction of their annexationist claims to Fiume.

The departure of Orlando from the Peace Conference on April 24 turned the other members of the Council totally against Italy, and it was in this atmosphere that the Big Three decided to send Greek troops to Smyrna. Yet it was the decision in favor of the Greek occupation that again brought the matter of Italian claims to the fore, for when the Italians returned to the conference on May 7, they became more insistent than ever upon a final decision regarding the territorial distribution in Asia Minor. As a result, Lloyd George returned again to his scheme for settling the Adriatic crisis by providing the Italians with suitable compensation elsewhere. To further this idea the British delegation met separately with Orlando and Sonnino on the morning of May 13. Nicolson's account of the meeting gives an insight into the methods by which the problems of the world were sometimes solved at Paris.

I spread out my big map on the dinner table and they all gather round. LG, AJB, Milner, Henry Wilson, Mallet and myself. LG explains that Orlando and Sonnino are due in a few minutes and he wants to know what he can offer them. I suggest the Adalia Zone with the rest of Asia Minor to France. Milner, Mallet and H. Wilson oppose it: AJB neutral.

We are still discussing when the flabby Orlando and the sturdy Sonnino are shown into the dining room. They all sit round the map. The appearance of a pie about to be distributed is thus enhanced. LG shows them what he suggests. They ask for Scala Nova as well. "Oh no," says LG, "you can't have that—it's full of Greeks!" He goes on to point out that there are further Greeks at Makri, and a whole wedge of them along the coast towards Alexandretta. "Oh no," I whisper to him, "there are not many Greeks there." "But yes," he answers, "don't you see it's coloured green?" I then realized that he mistakes my map for an ethnological map, and thinks the green means Greek instead of valleys, and the brown means Turks instead of mountains. LG takes this correction with great good humour. He is as quick as a king-fisher. Meanwhile Orlando and Sonnino chatter to themselves in Italian. They ask for the coal-mines at Eregli. LG, who really knows something about his subject by now, says, "But it's rotten coal, and not much of it in any case." Sonnino translates this remark to Orlando. "*Si, Si,*" replies the latter, "*Ma, l'effetto morale, sa!*"

Finally they appear ready to accept a mandate over the Adalia region, but it is not quite clear whether in return for this they will abandon Fiume and Rhodes. We get out the League Covenant regarding Mandates. We observe (I think it was Milner who observed) that this article provides for "the consent and wishes of the people concerned." They find that phrase very amusing. How they all laugh! Orlando's white cheeks wobble with laughter and his puffy eyes fill with tears of mirth.[23]

That afternoon, Lloyd George presented his plan to Clemenceau and Wilson.[24] Admittedly anxious for an Adriatic settlement, he defended the Italian claims and proposed the creation of an Italian mandate for the southern half of Anatolia. The Italians had every right to be disgruntled, he maintained, for everyone except Italy had been asked to accept mandates, including the United States, which did not really want any. Clemenceau made no effort to conceal his dislike for the Italians, but agreed to accept Lloyd George's plan. His acceptance was undoubtedly helped by the fact that this plan was similar to the one proposed three weeks earlier, in that the northern half of Anatolia would be given to France as a mandate.

In contrast, Wilson suddenly became the great defender of Greek claims. Not only should Greece be given full sovereignty over the territory recommended by the Greek Committee, but Venizelos's claim to a "mandate outside the purely Greek zone" should be accepted. He felt that Greece should be "taken into the family of nations," and if given this job the Greeks "would rise to the occasion." [25] This stand by Wilson must have greatly pleased and secretly amused Lloyd George, for the prime minister long had been a supporter of Venizelos's demands and had generally met with American opposition to any extension beyond purely Greek areas. He therefore readily accepted Wilson's suggestion and, in doing so, used this "concession" to bring Wilson around to his point of view on the rest of his plan.

Nicolson was instructed to draw up resolutions incorporating these proposals, which he did with evident distaste. Although a confirmed supporter of Venizelos, he was moved to comment in his diary, "It is immoral and impracticable. . . . The Greeks are getting too much." [26]

These resolutions were accepted the next day, with only minor changes, as part of a comprehensive proposal to be made to Italy. Incorporated into the scheme was a formal resolution agreed to by all three statesmen to the effect that the United States, subject to

Senate approval, would accept mandates for Armenia, Constantinople, and the Straits area.[27] Yet the debate showed that the Big Three were far from agreement as to the nature of the mandates themselves.[28] Wilson maintained that being a mandatory power gave no special economic rights of any kind, since any hint of a partition of spoils had, above all, to be avoided. Moreover, it would be impossible for the Anatolian mandates to exist if they were not completely separated politically. Southern Anatolia should be "a self-governing unit, to elect its own Governor-General, with Konia as its capital. Otherwise, there would be the difficulty of a single capital in which the representatives of both Mandatories would live." [29] Thus, Wilson who previously had indicated preference for a single mandate over all of Anatolia, had adopted the opposite viewpoint and now supported a complete political division between the north and south.[30] In this he was supported by Clemenceau. Although the latter did not subscribe to Wilson's viewpoint regarding special economic rights, he recognized that any other political solution would lead to a great deal of Franco-Italian friction and rivalry. Clemenceau even went so far as to assert that he "would prefer that all of Anatolia should become an independent state rather than to see it become a source of perpetual quarrels between the Italians and us." [31]

Lloyd George was not at all happy with this suggestion. He openly admitted that he regarded the proposed mandates system as really a continuation of the type of economic control through foreign advisors that had existed in Turkey before the war. The mandate would entitle the nation assigned to it to have priority in naming these advisors. Complete political separation of the various mandates meant the destruction of Turkey altogether. This was something Lloyd George did not wish to see happen. Moreover, if the sultan were moved from Constantinople to Brusa as had been planned, he would come completely under French domination. Another possible solution was that the sultan should stay at Constantinople, outside the territorial boundaries of the new Turkish state. From there he could exercise nominal supervision over the whole of Turkey. "France would then overlook one part of Anatolia, Italy another part, Greece a third, while the United States overlooked the Sultan." [32]

No final decision was reached. However, at Wilson's suggestion, the Big Three did agree to the division of Turkish Anatolia into two separate political units, leaving the method of implementation "for further consideration." [33]

Decision Not to Partition Anatolia

It seemed for a time as if a settlement of sorts had been obtained. Lloyd George, however, had overextended himself, and he shortly found himself the victim of a rising tide of opposition from within his own government. In April, Lloyd George and Clemenceau's original partition scheme had drawn strong protests from British experts, who branded the scheme "unworkable from the financial and economic point of view," and maintained that it "would cause such intense and justified indignation throughout the Moslem world that the British Empire could not afford to consent to it, even if it were militarily possible to carry it out." [34] The decision to send Greek troops to Smyrna met with equally great criticism in military and diplomatic circles. With the revival of the Anatolian partition plan following the landing, the British cabinet itself became agitated. Threats of resignation came from Montagu, Curzon, and even Balfour. [35] Balfour in particular, though willing to accept Turkish expulsion from Constantinople, emphatically opposed any partitioning of Turkish Anatolia. In a memorandum that Lloyd George presented to the Council of Four on the morning of May 17, Balfour stated:

> We are all most anxious to avoid as far as possible placing reluctant populations under alien rule. . . . Is it a greater crime to join together those who wish to be separated than to divide those who wish to be united? And if the Anatolian Turks say they desire to remain a single people under a single sovereign, to what principle are we going to make appeal when we refuse to grant their request? [36]

Balfour therefore proposed that Turkey should constitute a single, undivided state with no mandate, the capital to be at Brusa or Konia. This would be coupled with direct and indirect control of finances and police by the Allies, a system to which the Turks were well accustomed. Recognizing that "the Italians must somehow be mollified," [37] Balfour suggested that Italy should be given the right of first refusal on all economic concessions within the area around Adalia. Italy would not have a mandate, but would have a sphere of economic influence.

> This is designed to do two things; to maintain something resembling an independent Turkish Government, ruling over a homogeneous population; the other is to find a position for the Italians within this Turkish state which will make a sufficient appeal to the ambitions of the Italian Government. From every other point of view the plan is, I admit, a bad one; but from this point of view—which is the one at the moment chiefly occupying our thoughts—I still think it worthy of serious consideration. [38]

In other words, Balfour was returning to the traditional concept of spheres of influence that Lloyd George had favored earlier in the Council of Four debates.

Strong oppositition to the separation of Constantinople from the Turkish state had also developed within the British government. On the afternoon of May 17 the Council of Four received a delegation of the Government of India.[39] Headed by Edwin Montagu, M.P., secretary of state for India, the delegation asked for the retention of an independent Turkish state, which should include Asia Minor, Constantinople, and Thrace and which would be admitted to the League of Nations. Emphasizing the religious role of the sultan as caliph, they pointed out that there were seventy million Moslems in India, many of whom had fought in the Near East and all of whom desired to keep the caliph in Constantinople. In addition, the delegation appealed to historic British-French colonial ties with Islam and to the Fourteen Points.[40]

Upon the delegation's withdrawal from the council chamber, Lloyd George announced that to him the problems of partitioning seemed too great. The unrest that would be caused in the Mohammedan world would be tremendous and would make it impossible for any Western nation successfully to administer a mandate in any Moslem area. Therefore, he was firmly in favor of finding a way to leave the sultan in Constantinople as the religious head of Islam. Of course, the Straits would be taken away, but some method would have to be found to keep up the appearance that the sultan was being left in possession of the capital at Constantinople. A speech made on January 5, 1918, in which Lloyd George had said that the capital would be left with the Turks,[41] suddenly became a sacred bond, and he earnestly argued that Britain was pledged to that statement. This was a sharp about-face for a man who four days before had declared, "The Turk when he has the least amount of power is a brute. Whatever the difficulties which we shall encounter from the Moslems of India, it is necessary that we should finish with the Turkish regime."[42] Indeed, just two days earlier, Lloyd George had been the leading advocate of an Italian mandate in southern Anatolia.

Why this sudden change? The answers are varied. There is no question but that Lloyd George was disturbed by the interpretation of political independence that Wilson and Clemenceau attached to the concept of the two mandates in Anatolia. Second, news of the unauthorized Italian landings at Scalanuova had just reached Paris. This upset all the Big Three, and particularly Wilson, who suggested that unless Orlando's explanations were satisfactory, all discussion of Italian claims should be suspended.[43] Third, Lloyd George finally had become aware that he had agreed to things on which he did not have the backing of many members of his government. Mounting opposition at home to his partition scheme made Lloyd George's plan for arranging an Adriatic settlement impossible. He needed a way out. The combination of the Indian deposition and the general indignation at illegal Italian moves seemed tailor-made for the occasion.[44] Consequently, he maintained that "if the Italians continued on their present lines, it might be better to have only one mandate for Anatolia," to which Clemenceau replied that "for his part he did not want it." [45]

The next day, May 18, events took a dramatic turn. Orlando called on Lloyd George and asked him to support an Italian mandate over all of Anatolia.[46] When Lloyd George refused point-blank, Orlando hinted that Asia Minor would be important only if Italy were refused Fiume. As Lloyd George recalled the conversation, "I asked him, 'You prefer Fiume to a mandate in Asia Minor?' He answered, 'Yes.' 'And you would abandon all claims to Asia Minor if you could have Fiume?' 'Eventually.' And then he indicated his willingness to have Italy build a new port for the Yugoslavs." [47]

Lloyd George hastened to inform Wilson and Clemenceau of this conversation, and added: "Frankly he had changed his mind about dividing Anatolia. He thought that it would be a mistake to tear up this purely Turkish province." [48] Moreover, Turks and Moslems everywhere hated the Italians even though they respected the British, French, and Americans. An Italian mandate, consequently, would create difficulties for the other Allies in their mandates. A week ago he had advocated concessions in Asia Minor in order to obtain a settlement in the Adriatic. Now he had changed his mind. "If the Italians could be gotten out of Asia Minor altogether it would, in his opinion, be worth giving them something they were specially concerned in, even if it involved the Allies swallowing their words." [49] He admitted that he was vacillating, but said this was the way he felt.

Wilson immediately rejoined that "he did not in the least mind vacillating, provided the solution reached was the right one." [50] He had been much impressed by the representations of the Indian delegation. Both he and Lloyd George had forgotten that they had promised not to destroy Turkish sovereignty. He had promised it in the Fourteen Points, and these principles could not be violated. Therefore it might well be advisable to avoid any partitioning of Turkish Anatolia, though certainly the Turks could not retain control over Constantinople and the Straits. Perhaps the sultan could remain, if he wished, at Constantinople in circumstances similar to those of the pope in the Vatican. Although the sultan would have no sovereignty there, he would "be separated from his Kingdom merely by a narrow strip of water and territory." [51] As far as the new Turkish state was concerned, Wilson proposed that it should be required to accept the counsel and advice of a power such as France on certain specific issues, such as financial and economic matters.

What he was suggesting was in effect to give a mandate to France without calling it a mandate. That is to say, France would not be responsible to the League of Nations, she would be in a similar position as an independent friendly country advising the Turkish Government under treaty stipulations. [52]

Both Clemenceau and Lloyd George readily agreed to the plan, although Lloyd George stated that "if France took a position of this kind towards the whole of Asia Minor, which would be a very important trust, he would have to ask for a re-examination of the whole question of mandates in the Turkish Empire." [53]

As to the plan for buying off the Italians with Fiume, Wilson at first violently objected; but when Lloyd George explained his scheme for the building of a second port for Yugoslavia, Wilson agreed, subject to a plebiscite in which the people of Fiume indicated their desire to be united to Italy. This condition was in reality an insurmountable stumbling block, for the Italians were quite aware that they were unlikely to win a plebiscite in that area. Though concrete evidence is lacking, it is impossible to believe that Orlando ever seriously considered such a solution, especially when one notes that Wilson insisted that the plebiscite should be held after, not before, the Italians had invested large sums to build a second port for Yugoslavia.[54]

Be that as it may, the Anatolian part of the scheme met its downfall from another source. Two days later Lloyd George was forced to disavow the plan for an unofficial French mandate in Anatolia. The reason soon became apparent. On May 18, members of the British cabinet had arrived in Paris for top-level discussions with the British peace delegation. Only Curzon and Balfour supported the taking of Constantinople from the Turks, and they joined the others in opposing a French sphere of influence in Anatolia. Lloyd George had no choice but to repudiate his previous agreement on this matter.[55]

Meeting with Clemenceau and Wilson on May 21, Lloyd George presented a new comprehensive plan for settlement of the Near East question. This called for a "full" United States mandate over Constantinople and the Straits, Armenia, and Cilicia, and a "light" mandate over all of Anatolia. If the United States refused this light mandate, there should be none at all. If America took the Anatolian mandate, the sultan would remain at Constantinople; otherwise, Lloyd George was of the opinion that he should leave. In any case, the Turkish state should be assured access to the Black Sea, the Mediterranean, and the Sea of Marmara. Greece would be allowed to annex the area proposed by the Greek Committee but should not have a mandate over any other territory. France would have a provisional mandate over Syria, and Britain over Mesopotamia and Palestine, pending the report of the Commission of Inquiry. Arabia would be independent, the Moslems would retain control of their Holy Places, and the question of the location of the caliphate would be left to them.[56]

In presenting this new plan to Clemenceau and Wilson, Lloyd George emphasized that after the removal of Armenia, Constantinople, and Smyrna, the rest of Anatolia would be ninety-five percent Turkish. It was also necessary to remember the views of the seventy million Moslems in the British Empire, one million of whom had fought in the war, mostly on the Turkish front. "The more he thought the matter over, the less was he . . . willing to agree to the partition of Asia Minor." [57] He stated that he had discussed this question for the past two days with the British cabinet and that a "formal decision" against it had been made.[58]

Regarding a mandate for Anatolia as a whole, Lloyd George hoped America would take it, as the United States was the only nation for which the Turks had respect, chiefly because it had had no past dealings with the Moslems. The Turks hated both the British and the French. Lloyd George was particularly opposed to a French mandate over all Anatolia, because the Turks were "honestly afraid lest the Algerian experiment should be tried in Turkey, involving the complete subservience of Mohammedans to Christians." [59] Also, if France were given the mandate, Italy would have a right to demand compensation under the terms of the Treaty of London. Italy could not be allowed to have an Anatolian mandate, but to give it to France would "make the position of Italy impossible," especially since the basis of all Italian claims was fear "lest France should regard herself as the only Mediterranean Power." Here again, his views "had been prepared in consultation with his colleagues." [60]

Thus, Lloyd George maintained, if the United States would not take an Anatolian mandate, the Turks should be left alone. They would only be governing themselves rather than subject peoples, and could be kept under close indirect supervision through American pressure from Constantinople and Armenia, and French influence from Syria. By keeping control of the Ottoman Debt Council and retaining the public works concessions, the powers would also be able to achieve effective financial control of the area. As to the loss of economic spheres of influence, none of the nations other than the United States had the capital available to invest heavily in Anatolia in any case.

It was at this point that Wilson suddenly informed the council that he intended to send his commission delegates to Syria the following Monday. Clemenceau, as has been seen, refused to send his delegates and warned that he would never accept a settlement that was done "contre moi." [61] He claimed that France had made a series of concessions involving Mosul, Cilicia, and the British railroad rights from Mosul to the Mediterranean, and had received nothing but broken promises in return. Not only was he bitter at what he regarded as Britain's failure to live up to its promises in Syria but he was also extremely incensed at British attempts to deprive France of a mandate in Anatolia, a mandate that Lloyd George had suggested in one form and agreed to in another during the past week. Emotionally citing centuries of tradition, Clemenceau claimed that France had more of an interest in Turkey than had any other power. Although he would not leave the Peace Conference if matters were decided against French claims in the Near East, he might well have to leave the government, and he added, "Think what you are doing to us and think about it twice." [62]

Although this attitude was understandable, it should be remembered that when a single Anatolian mandate had first been proposed on May 17, Clemenceau had stated categorically that he wanted no part of it. His attitude had changed only when Wilson proposed that the mandate be outside the control of the League of Nations. It would appear that it was this provision that made the project seem worthwhile to Clemenceau.

For his part, Wilson was quick to assert categorically that the United States could not take an Anatolian mandate because of lack of American interest or investment in the area. Although he thought that the United States would take the Armenian mandate and perhaps Constantinople, he was positive that he would be unable to persuade Congress to take a mandate over all Anatolia. However, he believed that if it were at all possible the sultan should be left in Constantinople. Wilson then reverted to his former suggestion that France be given an unofficial mandate over all Anatolia. Since France already was the chief advisor to Turkey on matters relative to the Ottoman Debt, it could easily take over other functions such as commerce and the police.[63]

Thus the powers seemed hopelessly deadlocked, and their relations had become so strained that discussion of the whole problem of Turkey was adjourned by tacit consent.[64]

A month later one more attempt was made to reach a settlement before Wilson left Paris.[65] The only notable change in position occurred when Wilson indicated that he now was of the opinion that the sultan and his government should not be allowed to remain in Constantinople. "He had studied the question of the Turks in Europe for a long time, and every year confirmed his opinion that they ought to be cleared out." [66] In this he was seconded by Clemenceau, though Lloyd George, by now fully aware of the tremendous split within his government, refused to commit himself. Wilson again proposed that there should be no official mandate over Turkey, but that some power should be allowed a "firm hand" in the general overseeing of Turkish administration. Ultimately, Clemenceau suggested that the council take no final action, because it had no available means to enforce any decision relative to Anatolia or the Straits, and the participation of the United States could not begin until the Senate gave its consent. The others agreed, and the discussion ended.

What had been accomplished? In the long run very little. Twice the Big Three had seemed on the verge of an agreement. Twice Lloyd George, under pressure from a cabinet that opposed the partition of Anatolia and any Italian or French predominance in it, had been forced to disavow his previous commitments. Anxious and willing to achieve a settlement in Anatolia, Lloyd George found himself at the mercy of a cabinet whose members, though opposing the desires of others, could not agree among themselves on the policy they wanted to follow in regard to the Turkish state.[67]

Clemenceau, extremely passive in the earlier stages of the negotiations, had become increasingly truculent as Britain refused to allow French occupation of Syria and made and withdrew offers of territory in Anatolia. Once the German treaty was finished and the Anglo-

American commitment to aid France in the case of a German attack
had been obtained, Clemenceau no longer had to soft-pedal French
pretensions in the Near East in hopes of achieving a European
settlement more favorable to France.[68]

Orlando found himself in the unfortunate position of representing
the one power whose Near Eastern claims Wilson, Lloyd George,
and Clemenceau were unanimous in opposing. Excluded after the
middle of April from the majority of the Near East negotiations,
Orlando made demands in Asia Minor that remained consistent and
generally in line with the provisions of the wartime secret agreements.
Though at one point he did indicate privately a willingness to give
up these claims, it was only in return for the guaranteed right to
Fiume, something Wilson was unwilling to grant. Moreover, Sonnino,
Orlando's foreign minister, was intensely anti-American and had
developed a deep dislike for Wilson.[69] He was convinced that by
remaining firm Italy could obtain both Fiume and its share of Anatolia. It is unlikely that Sonnino would have accepted any compromise agreed to by Orlando, and his failure to do so would have
in all likelihood created a major domestic political crisis for Orlando.
One must therefore conclude that even if the British cabinet had
supported Lloyd George's scheme, that Italians would not have
accepted permanently any solution that denied them equal compensation with the other powers in a Near East settlement.

Wilson's role in the Anatolian debate was complex and contradictory. The day before he left Paris, Wilson asserted in a press
conference that he had made no mandate promises in Turkey "as
I have no right to promise anything of that kind." [70] However, he
stated that he thought the American people would accept an Armenian mandate because of America's long interest there. "I have
felt," he continued, "that there would be a certain advantage in
our being at Constantinople, in that it would keep it out of European
politics." [71]

It is true that Wilson technically had not promised that America
would take mandates in Armenia and Constantinople, for the one
formal commitment that Wilson had made to this effect had been
part of a planned proposal to the Italians that was subsequently
nullified by Lloyd George's renunciation of the scheme.[72] But in

the discussions of the Council of Four he had expressed great confidence that America would indeed become a mandatory power. All plans as to the allotment of mandates and the treatment of Turkey had been built on the assumption that the United States would accept the Armenian and Straits mandates, a premise that Wilson had done nothing to discourage and much to encourage. Whatever doubts Lloyd George and Clemenceau may have had, they publicly accepted the position that it would be worthwhile to postpone any further discussion of the Turkish treaty until approval for the assumption of mandates was voted by the United States Senate.[73]

In the discussions themselves, Wilson evidenced a high degree of deviousness and indecision. Upholding shiny ideals on the one hand, he compromised to the point of reversing himself on the other. He did not seem to know his own mind on many issues, vacillating on the partitioning of Anatolia and the expulsion of the Turks from Constantinople without any of the justifiable reasons that Lloyd George had for doing so. Only on the question of the ultimate disposition of Smyrna was Wilson reasonably consistent. He always held, in opposition to many in his delegation, the belief that Smyrna should go to Greece for ethnic reasons. As the Peace Conference progressed, this was reinforced by his ever-increasing opposition to Italian claims. Although it was Lloyd George who suggested the dispatch of Greek troops to Smyrna, Wilson, far from being reluctant, was the one who suggested that they land immediately rather than remain, at least initially, on shipboard as Lloyd George originally had proposed. All in all, Wilson must bear the responsibility on an equal basis with Lloyd George for the Greek landing in Asia Minor. Later, Wilson deviated from his premise of ethnic justification when he became an advocate of a large Greek mandate "outside the purely Greek zone."[74]

Even more serious was the fanaticism with which Wilson opposed Italian claims, a backlash, at least partially, from the Fiume controversy. His proposal, made not once but several times, that Anatolia be left as a single unit under the guidance of France, was prompted in great part by the fact that this solution would, as he himself observed, "leave the Italians out entirely."[75] This French guidance, moreover, would be similar to a mandate in terms of the influence of the supervising power, but it would not be called one and would not be under the supervision of the League of Nations. There would be no need, therefore, of compensating anyone, because Turkey technically would be completely independent though bound by treaty to accept the supervision and advice of an outside power.

The mandate principle was fundamental to Wilson's whole conception of the League of Nations. He had fought long and bitterly at Paris to bring the mandate scheme into existence and to prevent any final apportionment of mandates outside League auspices. In his proposal for unsupervised French authority in Turkish Anatolia, Wilson violated this concept as well as the doctrine of League supervision over former enemy territory, and thus disregarded two of the basic premises upon which he earlier had sought to justify the very existence of the League of Nations. Here, then, was a betrayal of an institution that Wilson regarded as the most important achievement of the Peace Conference, and the establishment of which had served as the motivation for the majority of his actions at Paris.

1. *Times* (London), 1/1/19.

2. *U.S. Doc., P.P.C.*, 2:280–81, Heck to Sharp, 1/4/19. See also the *Times* (London), 11/2/18, 1/9/19; Foreign Office, F.O. 608/83/342-8-4/8514, Curzon memorandum, enclosure 2, 4/18/19.

3. *Times* (London), 1/13/19; *Le Temps*, 1/22/19. Mehmed VI (Vahideddin) succeeded to the throne in July, 1918. He was deposed by the Nationalist government of Mustapha Kemal Pasha (Ataturk) in November, 1922. As a ruler he was without influence; the offices of sultan and caliph remained important only inasmuch as they represented the culmination in one individual of the religious and secular governing arms of the traditional Ottoman state.

4. *Times* (London), 2/1/19; 2/10/19; 4/22/19; Kinross, *Ataturk*, pp. 167–70.

5. *U.S. Doc., P.P.C.*, 6:215–16, C. of Four, 6/6/19; pp. 217–18, App. 2; pp. 232–33, 6/7/19; Mantoux, *Conseil des Quatre*, 2:327–28, 6/6/19; p. 334, 6/7/19; Sonnino Papers, Reel 26, no. 204, Sforza to Rome, 2/7/19; Lloyd George Papers, F8/3/23, Churchill to Balfour, 3/1/19; Foreign Office, F.O. 608/108/385-1-1/10891, Calthorpe to F.O., 5/7/19; F.O. 608/104/383-1-6/12765, Calthorpe to F.O., 5/19/19; F.O. 608/112/385-1-14/10295, Webb to F.O., 4/24/19; F.O. 608/112/385-1-15-15968, Calthorpe to F.O., 6/6/19; F.O. 608/114/385-1-23/12966, Calthorpe to F.O., 6/18/19; 13538, 6/11/19; Cabinet Papers, Cab. 29/25, M. 237, Calthorpe to Balfour, 6/4/19; Bristol Papers, Box 27, Bristol to Paris, 5/11/19; State Dept., Turkey, 867.00/885, Ravndal to Sec. State, 6/6/19; Pech, *Alliés et Turquie*, p. 27, 2/9/19; pp. 62–64, 5/30/19–5/31/19. At the same time the French press gradually became more and more pro-Turk. R. Puaux, *Constantinople et la Question d'Orient*, passim; *Correspondance d'Orient*, 5/30/19; F.O. 608/104-383-1-6/10386, Derby to Curzon, 5/18/19; *Times* (London), 4/5/19; P. Loti, "The Turks: A Plea for Justice," pp. 65–67; J. Bardoux, *De Paris à Spa*, p. 324; Pichon, *Partage*, p. 163; *D.R.F.P.: Allied Press Supplement*, 5:2/5/19; 6:6/4/19.

6. Sonnino Papers, Reel 46, no. 522, Sonnino to London, 5/14/19. See also *Bulletin périodique de la presse Italienne,* no. 113.

7. *U.S. Doc., P.P.C.,* 2:282, Heck to Sharp, 1/4/19; State Dept., Turkey, 867.00/867, Heck to Sec. State, 4/29/19; 894, Ravndal to Sec. State, 7/1/19; Bristol Papers, Box 27, Bristol to Paris, 5/26/19, 5/31/19; Foreign Office, F.O. 608/111/385-1-11, passim; Sonnino Papers, Reel 26, no. 83, Sforza to Sonnino, 1/25/19; Reel 46, no. 785, DeMartino to Rome, 6/25/19; Pech, *Alliés et Turquie,* pp. 34–35, 2/25/19; pp. 55–56, 5/20/19.

8. *U.S. Doc., P.P.C.,* 4:511, C. of Ten, 6/17/19. See also ibid., pp. 509–11; 6:116, C. of Four, 5/30/19; Mantoux, *Conseil des Quatre,* 2:257, 5/30/19; Cabinet Papers, Cab. 29/16, W.C.P. 937, Request of Turkish grand vizier to come to Paris, 5/22/19; Bristol Papers, Box 27, Bristol to Paris, 6/4/19, 6/5/19, 6/8/19.

9. *U.S. Doc., P.P.C.,* 6:694, C. of Four, 6/25/19, App. 10.

10. Ibid., pp. 691–94; Mantoux, *Conseil des Quatre,* 2:519–20, 6/25/19; *Br. Doc.,* 4:647–51; M. Paillarès, *Le Kémalisme devant les Alliés,* pp. 37–41.

11. Mantoux, *Conseil des Quatre,* 2:520, 6/25/19. See also *Le Temps,* 7/3/19; *New York Times,* 6/19/19, 6/28/19.

12. *U.S. Doc., P.P.C.,* 6:689, C. of Four, 6/25/19, App. 9.

13. Ibid. As a comment on Turkish history this statement hardly was justified, especially considering the history of Western Europe in relation to religious toleration and the treatment of minorities.

14. Ibid., p. 690.

15. Ibid., p. 691. The tone of this document, which was officially transmitted by Clemenceau in his role as president of the Supreme Council, did much to dampen the growing Turkish sentiment in Constantinople favorable to a French mandate. See State Dept., Turkey, 867.00/894, Ravndal to Sec. State, 7/1/19; *Le Temps* 7/3/19. For the initial draft by Balfour, see Cabinet Papers, Cab. 29/17, W.C.P. 1044, 6/23/19. For the polite reply of the Turkish delegation, see F.O. 608/118/385-3-5/14116, 6/30/19.

16. Miller, *Diary,* 6:285, 3/9/19; p. 320, 3/11/19; 1:251, 4/14/19; Foreign Office, F.O. 406/41/20, Curzon to Derby 3/5/19; F.O. 608/114/385-1-20/4476, Curzon to Derby, 3/12/19; F.O. 608/83/342-8-3/5104, Conversation between British and Italian delegates regarding the future of Asia Minor, 3/21/19.

17. Lloyd George, *Truth,* p. 288. See also above, pp. 86–87.

18. Mantoux, *Conseil des Quatre,* 1:114, 4/1/19.

19. Neither the British nor the French were disposed favorably toward Italy. At one point Clemenceau commented that "public opinion in France had been antagonized a good deal by d'Annunzio's boasts that Italy had won the war, and he was by no means disposed to discuss favorably Italian claims anywhere," Lloyd George, *Truth,* pp. 289–90, 3/7/19.

20. Mantoux, *Conseil des Quatre,* 1:308, 4/21/19. See also ibid., pp. 301–6, a meeting on the morning of the same day; *U.S. Doc., P.P.C.,* 5:106–7, C. of Four, 4/21/19.

21. Mantoux, *Conseil des Quatre,* 1:309, 4/21/19.

22. Ibid., p. 310.

23. Nicolson, *Peacemaking,* pp. 332–34, 5/13/19. On May 1, the British experts had submitted a memorandum regarding an Italian settlement. This involved a succession of hypothetically possible concessions, the last and most extreme of which was an Italian mandate for all of Anatolia, minus the Greek zone. This scheme was never seriously taken up by Lloyd George. Cabinet Papers, Cab. 29/14, W.C.P., 755, Memorandum by southeastern European section of British delegation, 5/1/19. See also Nicolson, *Peacemaking,* pp. 316–17, 4/27/19; p. 318, 4/30/19.

24. *U.S. Doc., P.P.C.,* 5:581–86, C. of Four, 5/13/19; Mantoux, *Conseil des Quatre,* 2:57–62, 5/13/19; Lloyd George Papers, F206/2/5, Notes of the views of the British delegation on the future of Anatolia, 5/13/19.

25. *U.S. Doc.*, *P.P.C.*, 5:584, C. of Four, 5/13/19.

26. Nicolson, *Peacemaking*, p. 335, 5/13/19.

27. *U.S. Doc.*, *P.P.C.*, 5:622, C. of Four, 5/14/19, Apps. 1 and 2 to C.F. 13A; Cabinet Papers, Cab. 29/24, M. 151. See also Lloyd George Papers, F205/2/1; Westermann, Diary, 5/16/19. According to Nicolson, the resolutions would have been far more severe had he not done "a clever thing. I watered everything down. I tried to introduce at least the elements of sanity into their decisions." He thought this might well get him into trouble but felt he must try and save them from themselves; for "their decisions are immoral and impracticable." Just how and what he actually did, if anything, is not clear. Nicolson, *Peacemaking*, p. 337, 5/14/19.

28. *U.S.Doc.*, *P.P.C.*, 5:618-20, C. of Four, 5/14/19; Mantoux, *Conseil des Quatre*, 2:72-77, 5/14/19.

29. *U.S. Doc.*, *P.P.C.*, 5:619, C. of Four, 5/14/19.

30. Wilson's reasons for doing so are unclear. H. Sachar maintains that Wilson suddenly became fearful at his heavy involvement in Near East affairs, and saw this as a means of escape. "U.S. and Turkey," p. 109.

31. Mantoux, *Conseil des Quatre*, 2:76, 5/14/19.

32. *U.S. Doc.*, *P.P.C.*, 5:619, C. of Four, 5/14/19.

33. Ibid., p. 620. This plan, supposedly very secret, was discussed fully in *Le Temps* on May 18 and 19. This is a good example of the continued appearance of "secret" material in the French press, which infuriated Lloyd George and particularly Wilson. See also, *D.R.F.P., Allied Press Supplement*, 5/28/19.

34. Foreign Office, F.O. 608/111/385-1-11/8163, Memorandum regarding Clemenceau's proposal of April 22 [*sic*], 4/23/19.

35. Nicolson, *Peacemaking*, p. 340, 5/16/19; pp. 341-42, 5/17/19.

36. *U.S. Doc.*, *P.P.C.*, 5:670, C. of Four, 5/17/19, Appendix; Baker, *Wilson and World Settlement*, 3:303-7; Cabinet Papers, Cab. 29/24, M. 162; Balfour Papers, MSS 49752, "The Problem of Italy and Turkey in Anatolia," 5/16/19. For the drafting of this memorandum see ibid., "Notes on Asia Minor Proposals," 5/15/19, and Nicolson, *Peacemaking*, pp. 334-41, 5/13/19-5/17/19.

37. *U.S. Doc.*, *P.P.C.*, 5:671, C. of Four, 5/17/19, Appendix.

38. Ibid., p. 672.

39. Indian Moslem pressure continually had been growing stronger. At one protest meeting the speaker had gone so far as to say, "Our feelings at the moment against the British and her [*sic*] type are very much akin to those which the British people had against Germany when the war broke out." *Times* (London), 5/13/19. See also Pech, *Alliés et Turquie*, p. 57, 5/22/19; *Parliamentary Debates* (Commons), 5th ser., 113:2378, 3/20/19; *Times* (London), 3/25/19, 4/19/19, 5/16/19, 5/26/19, 5/30/19, 5/31/19, 6/2/19, 6/6/19, 6/13/19; M. H. Kidwal of Gadia, "Sultan of Turkey and Constantinople," p. 632; Foreign Office, F.O. 608/109/385-1-6/8923, Synopsis of memoranda by India Government officials, 4/30/19.

40. *U.S. Doc.*, *P.P.C.*, 5:690-701, C. of Four, 5/17/19. Mantoux, *Conseil des Quatre*, 2:98-104, 5/17/19.

41. Dickenson, *Documents*, pp. 109, 113; Lloyd George, *War Memoirs*, 5:62, 65. According to Sir Maurice Hankey, who was in a position to know, this statement had been made only as an "invitation to the Turks to come out of the war." Since Turkey did not, the statement had no subsequent validity. T. Jones, *Whitehall Diary*, 1:93, Hankey to Jones, 8/28/19.

42. Mantoux, *Conseil des Quatre*, 2:60, 5/13/19. The *New York Times* bitterly attacked Lloyd George for his apparent change on the Constantinople issue (5/21/19).

43. The Italian desire for Scalanuova and the powers' unhappiness at the occupation stemmed from the same fact. As soon as a spur line connecting it with the Smyrna-Aidin railroad

was built, Scalanuova, located at the mouth of the Menderes River valley, would take over Smyrna's preeminent trading position. All trade with any section of Anatolia other than the Black Sea littoral could be carried through Scalanuova faster and cheaper than through Smyrna. See Gaillard, *Turks and Europe*, p. 46.

44. R. S. Baker, suggests that the appearance of the Indian delegation before the Council of Four was actually planned by Lloyd George as a means of extricating himself from his earlier promises. This may well be true; certainly the delegation could not have appeared had Lloyd George really opposed its doing so. Baker, *Wilson and World Settlement*, 2:197. See also F.O. 608/82/342-6-1/8261, Ramsay to Mallet, and Vansittart minute, 4/21/19.

45. *U.S. Doc., P.P.C.*, 5:669, C. of Four, 5/17/19. See also Mantoux, *Conseil des Quatre*, 2:88, 5/17/19.

46. Lloyd George Papers, F206/2/3, Italian Mandate Claims and Proposals for Asia Minor, 5/13/19. Two days before, the Italian government had sent a memorandum to the American delegation requesting the same thing. Miller, *Diary*, 9:373, 5/16/19; Crespi, *Alla Difesa*, p. 560, 5/13/19.

47. Mantoux, *Conseil des Quatre*, 2:110, 5/19/19. See also *U.S. Doc., P.P.C.*, 5:707, C. of Four, 5/19/19. For an account based on an Italian source see M. Macartney and P. Cremona, *Italy's Foreign and Colonial Policy, 1914-1937*, p. 63.

48. *U.S. Doc., P.P.C.*, 5:708, C. of Four, 5/19/19.

49. Ibid., p. 710.

50. Ibid., p. 708.

51. Ibid., p. 709.

52. Ibid.

53. Ibid., For another account of this meeting see Mantoux, *Conseil des Quatre*, 2:111-14, 5/19/19. Also Baker, *Wilson and World Settlement*, 2:199-200.

54. *U.S. Doc., P.P.C.*, 5:710, C. of Four, 5/19/19; p. 759, 5/21/19; pp. 769-70, App. 1; 6:51, 5/26/19; Mantoux, *Conseil des Quatre*, 2:113, 5/19/19. In a May 21 memorandum regarding Italian territorial claims, De Martino specifically rejected any solution that did not grant Italy a sizeable mandate in Anatolia. Sonnino Papers, Reel 51.

55. Nicolson, *Peacemaking*, p. 343, 5/19/19. See also ibid., p. 346, 5/21/19; Nicolson, *Curzon*, pp. 106-7; Lloyd George Papers, F8/3/53, Churchill to Lloyd George, 5/14/19; F40/2/55, Montagu to Lloyd George, 6/22/19; S. D. Waley, *Edwin Montagu, A Memoir and an Account of his Visits to India*, p. 243. Subsequent letters from Montagu to Lloyd George protested Lloyd George's continued support of expelling the Turks from Constantinople when only "a minority or two" favored such a policy. See Sir D. Waley, "Life of the Hon. Edwin Samuel Montagu," pp. 281-84. Also, Callwell, *Henry Wilson*, 2:167-68, 2/1/19; p. 193, 5/15/19.

56. *U.S. Doc., P.P.C.*, 5:760, C. of Four, 5/21/19; pp. 770-71, App. 3.

57. Ibid., p. 756.

58. Mantoux, *Conseil des Quatre*, 2:133, 5/21/19; *U.S. Doc., P.P.C.*, 5:756, C. of Four, 5/21/19.

59. *U.S. Doc., P.P.C.*, 5:757, C. of Four, 5/21/19.

60. Ibid., p. 758.

61. Mantoux, *Conseil des Quatre*, 2:137, 5/21/19. See also above, Chapter 3.

62. Ibid., 2:140, 5/21/19. Lloyd George's reaction was to ridicule both France's sudden concern in Turkish affairs and its claims to be a dominant interest in Turkey.

63. Ibid., p. 143; *U.S. Doc., P.P.C.*, 5:755-56, C. of Four, 5/21/19. In a meeting with Magie and Westermann on May 22, Wilson informed them of his proposal regarding French dominance in Anatolia. Two days later the two experts responded favorably, though they expressed a preference for single American mandate for Constantinople, Anatolia, and Ar-

menia. State Dept., A.C.N.P. 185.5136/31, Wilson interview with Magie and Westermann, 5/22/19; 185.5136/32 Magie and Westermann to Wilson, 5/24/19; Westermann, Diary, 5/22/19; W. L. Buckler Papers, Dr. 21, fol. 25, Letter to Mrs. Buckler, 5/22/19. For other American opinions favoring an American mandate in Anatolia, see Bristol Papers, Box 9, Lybyer memorandum, 5/20/19; Woodrow Wilson Papers, V-A, Box 27, Memorandum by King and Crane, 5/1/19.

64. Baker, *Wilson and World Settlement*, 2:203. An important side result of this angry disagreement was the abrupt disavowal by Lloyd George and Clemenceau of an agreement regarding the division of oil resources in the Near East that had been negotiated by Mr. Walter Long for the British and Senator Berenger for the French. For details concerning the negotiation and cancellation of this agreement, see below, Chapter 9.

65. *U.S. Doc., P.P.C.*, 6:675–76, C. of Four, 6/25/19; pp. 711–13, 6/26/19; Mantoux, *Conseil des Quatre*, 2:516–20, 6/25/19; pp. 530–40, 6/26/19; Balfour Papers, MSS 49752, Balfour memorandum for Lloyd George, 6/26/19.

66. *U.S. Doc., P.P.C.*, 6:676, C. of Four, 6/25/19; See also Mantoux, *Conseil des Quatre*, 2:518, 6/25/19.

67. Nicolson, commenting on the cabinet meeting in Paris on May 19, clearly indicated this split: "I am summoned to the Rue Nitot, but not asked to attend the meeting. I sit outside, but as there is only a glass partition between me and the Cabinet I hear what they say. Curzon presses for ejection of Turk from Europe, and accepts Greek zone at Smyrna although with deep regret. Montagu and Milner are all against disturbing the Turk still further. Winston wants to leave him as he is, but to give America the mandate over Constantinople and the Straits, with a zone extending as far as Trebizond. AJB wants Constantinople under an American mandate, Smyrna to Greece and the rest of Turkey as an independent kingdom, supervised by foreign 'advisors.' Lloyd George is non-commital. No decision come to in so far, as through the glass darkly, I can ascertain." Nicolson, *Peacemaking*, p. 343, 5/19/19.

68. Cambon, in London was bitterly critical of what he regarded as Clemenceau's softness on Near Eastern affairs. He wrote to his son concerning this matter on April 15: "All this to assure an American and British alliance [with France], but neither Lloyd George nor Wilson has the right to contract these alliances and in reality they are giving nothing." How prophetic Cambon's words were even he could hardly have realized. Cambon, *Correspondance*, 3:323, 4/15/19. For a similar attitude see Pech, *Alliés et Turquie*, p. 49, 4/17/19.

69. See above, Chapter 1; also Mayer, *Politics of Peacemaking*, pp. 679–80.

70. Thompson, *Peace Conference Day by Day*, p. 406, 6/27/19.

71. Ibid.

72. *U.S. Doc., P.P.C.*, 5:622, C. of Four, 5/14/19, App. 1, CF-13A; also Cabinet Papers, Cab. 29/24, M. 151. See above, pp. 114–15.

73. *U.S. Doc., P.P.C.*, 6:729, C. of Four, 6/27/19.

74. Ibid., 5:584, C. of Four, 5/13/19.

75. Ibid., p. 709, 5/19/19.

VI ❋ THE BRITISH EVACUATION
OF ARMENIA AND SYRIA

F<small>ROM</small> July through November, 1919, the Peace Conference put aside the problem of a peace treaty with the Ottoman Empire, for the European powers were agreed that little of a constructive nature could be achieved until America's position on the Armenian and Constantinople mandates was known. In this five-month period the efforts of the Peace Conference relative to Near Eastern affairs centered chiefly on three problems. These were the reallocation of occupying forces in Armenia and Syria, the delimitation of "provisional" zones of Italian and Greek occupation in Asia Minor, and the settlement of Bulgarian boundaries in Thrace.

Only the discussion regarding Thrace resulted in a definite settlement. All other action taken on these matters was of a provisional nature aimed at achieving some form of immediate, if temporary and precarious, stability. Yet in the long run the events of this period were highly influential in determining both the terms of the final treaty and its subsequent failure.

Britain Withdraws from Armenia

In the summer of 1919 there was growing danger of complete anarchy in Armenia and the Caucasus. Armenian troops were facing attacks by Kurdish and Tartar forces from the north, east, and south. A growing Turkish nationalist movement in the interior of Anatolia posed an ever-increasing threat to the successful creation of any Armenian state. Although the Turkish government in Constantinople signified its willingness to accept an Armenian state on former Russian territory, it supported all groups that opposed the inclusion of Ottoman soil in such a state. As winter approached and hundreds of repatriated Armenians had nowhere to go, relief problems became severe.[1]

By the middle of the summer it had become clear that a great deal of opposition existed in the United States to American acceptance of the Armenian mandate. The feeling was widespread that expensive, miserable, and unprofitable mandates were being foisted on the United States while other nations obtained easy, lucrative ones. In the light of this criticism, Wilson decided on August 1 to send a separate American political commission to Armenia to study the problem of repatriation and the economic, military, and political problems that a mandatory nation would encounter. Despite a recommendation by the American delegation in Paris that ten thousand American troops be sent to Armenia immediately, it was evident that no American decision would be forthcoming for some time, and there was much to indicate that the ultimate answer would be negative.[2]

This left Britain in an awkward position. Since January the British government had been anxious to withdraw its troops from the Caucasus region. For a time, plans for redistributing occupation forces in the Near East had called for Italy to take over this area as a possible alternative to occupation of southern Anatolia, and in private discussions with the British the Italians had indicated their willingness to replace British troops and ultimately to accept a Caucasus mandate.[3] The mandate per se would include Georgia and Azerbaijan, though we know today that the Italians secretly considered the possibility of an Armenian mandate as well. However, when domestic issues precipitated a cabinet crisis leading to the fall of the Orlando-Sonnino government in June, 1919, the new Nitti-Tittoni government quickly dispelled any notions that Italy might act in the Caucasus. The resurgence of anti-Bolshevik forces under General Denikin in the spring and summer of 1919 had led Italian experts to doubt the long-term efficacy of a Caucasus mandate, since Denikin openly insisted on the eventual reincorporation of the new splinter states into Greater Russia. Disillusioned as well by Italy's failure to obtain any satisfaction for its claims in Anatolia, the new government wanted no part of any involvement in the Caucasus, for it was determined to accept nothing that might allow the other powers to assert that Italy had received enough compensation without a mandate over southern Anatolia. Conversely, this decision actually pleased all the Allies, even the British, for the unauthorized Italian occupation of the Adalia region had removed any justification for compensation in the Caucasus.[4]

However, the Italian decision left the British without a replacement force. The withdrawal of troops under these circumstances might well lead to an outbreak of rioting and massacres. The British delegation in Paris, many members of Parliament, and most newspapers therefore opposed withdrawal before some substitute occupation force was found. Popular support for an Armenian mandate was widespread in Britain; even the influential *Times* favored it, both for humanitarian reasons and because of Armenia's key position in relation to India and Russia.[5] Nevertheless, although the scheduled evacuation date was postponed from June 15 to August 15, the British government persisted in its plan to get out of the Caucasus.

At the same time Britain increased its pressure upon America to take some definite action. In response to American protests against the forthcoming British withdrawal, Curzon bluntly told United States Ambassador John Davis that the British would stay only if the United States indicated a willingness to take over eventually and agreed to pay the occupation costs until some decision was reached. Although the State Department was cordial to the idea, it could only refuse, for funds were not available unless Congress appropriated them. The political turmoil over the ratification of the German peace treaty was such that the State Department recognized that any request which seemed to suggest American acceptance of any foreign commitments would only infuriate many in the Senate and hinder the realization of the long-range program of the administration. Ambassador Davis had to content himself with appeals to Britain's humanitarian spirit and former commitments to the Armenians, along with warnings of the dangerous effect that anti-British feeling in the United States, engendered by the withdrawal of British troops, would have on the ratification prospects of the German treaty.[6]

Nevertheless, Britain stood firm, and the evacuation, which would take until October to complete, began as scheduled on August 15. The one concession was an announcement that Britain would study the possibility of leaving political missions in various key cities with a small guard of either British or native troops. Although this was better than nothing, all reports indicated that it was far from enough.[7]

The evacuation greatly annoyed Clemenceau, who long had been anxious for a similar withdrawal from Syria. On August 25, he climaxed several days of anti-British jibing by stating:

As to saving the Armenians he didn't know what could be done. There were no American troops. British troops were employed elsewhere. The French were not allowed by the British to play any part in Asia Minor. The Italians, it was true, had gone to Asia Minor in spite of the British, but they declined to replace the British in the Caucasus. As to the Turks, they were themselves powerless, as they could not control their own troops. He did not see from what quarter the Armenians could expect any assistance.[8]

Balfour, seeing an opening, seized upon Clemenceau's statement that Britain would not allow France "to play any part in Asia Minor" and made it clear that Britain would have no objection whatsoever to France's sending troops to Armenia. Clemenceau agreed to consult with his military staff and four days later offered to send ten to twelve thousand men.[9]

Both the British and the Americans regarded this offer with deep suspicion, believing that it was merely a French scheme to gain a foothold in the section of Asia Minor that had been promised to them in the Sykes-Picot Agreement. No one believed that it emanated from a genuine desire to assist the Armenians. Yet there was little to do but go along with the plan. No other nation was willing to take on the chore, and from the British point of view it was worthwhile to accept any proposed solution, however unpalatable, that would spare Britain the charge of having abandoned the Armenians.[10]

That British and American scepticism was well founded became evident when Clemenceau refused to send French troops by the most obvious route via the Black Sea to Batum and thence by rail to Erivan. Instead, he insisted on an approach from the Mediterranean by way of Alexandretta and Mersina, which meant sending supplies and horses by a long circuitous route, partly by rail but much of the way over roads that the Americans and British considered impassable despite French assurances to the contrary. In terms of reaching the trouble spots quickly and easily, this route made little sense. However, it had the advantage to the French of necessitating a prior occupation of Cilicia and southern Armenia. This was all that really interested Clemenceau. A month later, when France received the right to occupy this territory as part of a general Syrian agreement, Clemenceau immediately gave up any pretense of sending troops to the rest of Armenia.[11]

The final result was that France occupied only the southern area (where the threat of disturbances had never been great), while Britain, despite protests from all sides and the tearful plea of the Armenian prime minister, withdrew all its troops from the Caucasus by the end of September, with the exception of a garrison at Batum. The Armenian situation had reached its darkest point since the end of the war.[12]

Why, in the face of tremendous opposition at home and abroad, did the British government persist in this policy?[13] The cost of the occupation was a very important factor, although the reason given publicly was that Britain was doing the lion's share of work in the Near East and that the troops in the Caucasus were draftees long overdue for demobilization. Although the government could not admit publicly that money was the chief concern, the actual unimportance of the draftees issue can be seen in that Lloyd George had originally planned to transfer them to Constantinople to augment the garrison there rather than bring them home.[14] Equally significant was Curzon's stated willingness to keep the troops where they were if the United States paid the bill.

Underneath the financial reasons, however, lay a deeper concern. The British had been in occupation of Armenian territory since the end of the war. The government was only too aware that an Armenian mandate would be costly in money and men, with little possibility of any significant compensation in return. They also realized that the presence of British troops in the area over a long-term period could result very easily in a de facto mandate, all protestations to the contrary. The ever increasing evidence in the summer and fall of 1919 that the United States might refuse the Armenian mandate made it imperative that the British withdraw, not so much to increase pressure on America to accept as to get Britain out of a bad position if it did not. If an American refusal should come when British troops were still in occupation, Britain would from then on be held responsible for any subsequent horrors that might occur. This would be true whether British troops remained or were withdrawn. This eventuality the British were determined to avoid.[15]

French Occupation of Syria

Syria was the most serious source of Anglo-French discord regarding the Near East. The divergence of views during the first months of the Peace Conference had been so great that negotiations, even concerning the reallocation of temporary occupation forces, had completely broken down. Discussion on these matters were not officially reopened by the Supreme Council until the middle of September; even then it was only because the situation, far from remaining static, had deteriorated to such a degree that some form of immediate settlement was imperative.

The King-Crane Commission

During the summer of 1919, the Syrian problem was complicated by the presence in the Near East of the American section of what had originally been planned as an inter-Allied commission of inquiry. This group, headed by Henry King and Charles Crane, arrived in the Levant in early June and remained until the end of July. Although their instructions called for a general investigation of the wishes of all the peoples of the Ottoman Empire, they correctly understood that the chief area of their investigation was intended to be Syria and Palestine; and the majority of their time and effort was spent in this region.

The news that an international commission was being sent had been greeted joyously by Feisal, but his disillusionment and suspicion were equally great when he found out that only the American section was actually coming. This discovery, coupled with insistent rumors that Britain was going to evacuate Syria and turn it over to France, led Feisal to suspect the existence of an Anglo-French agreement. His suspicion was enhanced by French statements that the fate of Syria had been decided and that the investigating commission was nothing more than a front to keep the Arabs quiet until final Franco-British arrangements could be made.[16]

All of this led Feisal to adopt two new tactics. He publicly placed all his faith in whatever recommendations the King-Crane Commission might make, and he refused to accept blunt declarations by the British that under no circumstances would Britain accept a mandate for the area. Nevertheless, his confidence was shaken enough for him to instruct his followers to opt first for an American mandate, and only secondly for a British one. Although not yet regarded as "perfidious," there is no doubt that "Albion" was suspect.[17]

At the same time, Feisal gave tacit recognition to a growing movement for total independence that had appeared in the area around Damascus during the summer of 1919. There is little to indicate that he took this movement seriously. Rather, he saw in it a useful weapon of threat and intimidation, for if this movement ever received his full support it would mean that an all-out war would have to be fought by whatever power finally accepted the Syrian mandate.[18]

Upon its return to Paris, the King-Crane Commission reported that the great majority of the inhabitants opposed the separation of Syria and Palestine and the creation of a Zionist Jewish national home. It also stated that, with the exception of the Christian population concentrated in Lebanon, the delegations interviewed and the petitions received overwhelmingly favored the United States as the mandatory power for the area, with Great Britain the second choice. The same majority was unalterably opposed to any form of French control, no matter how slight.[19]

The report was never considered by the Supreme Council, and the text was not made public until December, 1922.[20] Therefore, the King-Crane Commission and its report played no official role in the formulation of the Turkish treaty, especially since it became clear soon afterward that the United States would not play an active role in administering, or even negotiating, the Turkish peace.[21] Nevertheless, the general outline, if not the specific details, of the report was well known to the press;[22] and unofficially the influence of the commission was great, for by its very presence in the Near East it provoked a crisis in Anglo-French relations.

French Grievances Increase

During the course of the summer, the French press became highly critical of alleged methods by which the British, and the Arabs supported by the British, made sure that the commission heard only select witnesses and testimony. The French government did nothing to stop this newspaper attack, and the British ambassador came away from an interview with Pichon convinced that the Quai d'Orsay fully concurred with the charges of a rigged investigation. In fact, the French government even went so far as formally to accuse the British of arresting those who testified in favor of France before the King-Crane Commission.[23] The French attitude was that the Syrian question had been settled in 1916 and all that remained was to implement agreed-on terms. Moreover, since Britain had declared its lack of interest in the Syrian mandate, the French could not understand why British nationals in the Near East were so active in opposing French claims to the territory.[24]

How justified was this bitter attitude? First of all, in terms of the apportionment of mandates by the Peace Conference, the Commission of Inquiry was nothing more than a false front, though its members did not recognize it as such. Britain had repeatedly stated it would not take the mandate; Wilson admitted the United States could not; therefore, it made little difference what the people wanted, for France was going to be the mandatory power. However, many British officers in the Near East, naturally prejudiced in favor of the Arabs, refused to accept this fact. If it were true, they asked, why send the commission? And their doubts were transmitted, perhaps unintentionally, to the Arabs, for whom they remained both a source of hope and discord.[25] The government in London had hoped that by announcing a policy of abstention in Syria the Arabs would be pushed into working out an agreement with the French. The presence of the King-Crane Commission in the Near East made this impossible.

Second, there is little question that such things as the manipulation of witnesses and the organization of declarations to the commission did occur. The British in London, though denying it publicly, admitted it privately.[26] The French were not in a position to corral witnesses, much as they might have wished to. At the same time it should be pointed out that the commission was well aware that this organized lobbying was taking place, and its members did their best to take this into account in formulating the final report.[27] Certainly, with the exception of the Christian population, Arab hostility to the French had been well attested for many years from so many sources that it is impossible to question the commission's findings on that score.

It is true that the commission raised all sorts of false hopes, promoted intrigue everywhere in the Near East, aroused passions in France and Britain, and effectively hindered any possible Franco-Arab reconciliation. In this sense the judgment of Gertrude Bell, in October, 1919, that the sending of the commission was a criminal deception was eminently justified.[28] Yet to a great extent it was the increase in Anglo-French tension created by the work of the commission that forced each side, particularly the British, to begin anew efforts to reach a settlement on the occupation question.

Britain Decides to Seek a Settlement

Both the British government and public were genuinely shocked at the depth of French hostility to Britain evidenced in the French press. The immediate and widespread reaction was that Franco-British friendship was all important. A solution must be reached, if necessary at the expense of the Arabs. Popular pressure, expressed through Parliament and the press, demanded a settlement.[29]

Chief among those desiring a rapprochement was Balfour. The weariness and frustration brought on by working with a prime minister with whom he agreed less and less, and who rarely consulted him or allowed him a free hand in the negotiations, was beginning to become unbearable.[30] Moreover, his disgust with the moralistic tone of British policy appears to have increased daily. A man who sincerely believed that the Zionist aspirations were right, he was honest enough to admit that implementation of their program would be in complete opposition to all the principles of self-determination so often subscribed to by the Allies, and for which the Commission of Inquiry had been sent to the Levant. In a memorandum dated August 11, he stated:

In short, so far as Palestine is concerned, the Powers have made no statement of fact which is not admittedly wrong, and no declaration of policy which, at least in the letter, they have not always intended to violate.[31]

The same criticism, Balfour admitted, could be made to a lesser degree of Britain's wartime policy of joining France in a partition of the Near East, while at the same time promising independence and self-determination to the Arabs. Any state, mandated or not, that was forced to accept the protection and advice of a specified foreign nation could not be truly independent. Since France was the only nation interested in Syria, that was what was going to happen, commission or no commission.[32]

It was while the crisis over Syria was building that the issue of the British evacuation of the Caucasus came to the fore. Britain, as has been seen, regarded the offer by France to send troops into the area as a suspect but welcome gift, one that removed Britain from the horns of an awkward moral dilemma. This contemplated occupation, however, made it all the more imperative that a general solution should be reached. To allow French troops to occupy neighboring Cilicia and Armenia but keep them out of Syria proper would create an extremely explosive situation. Moreover, the British fully realized that in offering to send troops to Armenia, the French had created an excellent weapon with which to blackmail Britain. The ever-present possibility of a French renunciation of its offer constituted an undeclared threat at a time when the British government was using this offer as a welcome cover for its own withdrawal. The French government, without saying a word, had greatly increased its pressure on the British for a settlement.[33]

All of this public and undercover agitation put Lloyd George in a position where there was nothing to do but yield. The problem was how to do it with as little loss of face as possible. Hopefully, a protective guarantee for the Arabs could be obtained along with fulfillment of most of the promises that had been made to them. But the basic necessity was to create a settlement.

The September Agreement

Thus, Lloyd George's decision to vacation at Deauville in northern France in early September was not a purely personal whim. Nor was the calling of Field Marshall Allenby from Cairo to meet with him a matter of routine report and consultation. After discussing the matter with Allenby and others (among whom were neither Balfour nor Curzon), an *aide mémoire* on the Syrian question was drafted, and it was decided that Lloyd George should stop in Paris on the way home to meet with Clemenceau.[34]

Upon his arrival in Paris, Lloyd George showed the *mémoire* to the chief American delegate at the Peace Conference, Frank Polk. According to a British memorandum, Polk received it with no "adverse comment." [35] Drawn up as a draft agreement, the *mémoire* called for the withdrawal of British troops from Syria and Cilicia, beginning on November 1, 1919. The area east of the Sykes-Picot line would be turned over to the Arabs; the area to the west would go to the French. Until the final boundary between Palestine and Syria was determined, the British would continue to occupy outposts in accordance with the boundary they claimed. Britain was ready to discuss the final boundaries at any time, and would readily "submit the question to the arbitration of a referee appointed by President Wilson," should this be necessary. The French were to allow Britain to build a railroad and an oil pipeline from Haifa to Mesopotamia. Should Britain and France fail to agree on a route, the question would be submitted to arbitration. Finally, France would formally accept the duty of protecting the Armenian people, and would be given permission to send troops via Alexandretta to the Caucasus.[36]

This was what the British wanted. What did they get? Despite two private conversations between Lloyd George and Clemenceau, in the Supreme Council meeting on September 15, Clemenceau agreed only that French troops should replace British troops in the area defined, and did so specifically on condition that this should not be regarded as French acceptance of any of the other provisions of the *aide mémoire*. He maintained that though he was willing to discuss these issues, they could not be agreed upon hastily. This was especially true because the question of Syrian boundaries could only be decided within the framework of the whole Turkish settlement (i.e., possible Anatolian concessions). "When the question of Turkey was considered as a whole, it might be possible to grant what could not be granted when the question of Syria was considered in isolation." [37] As for Armenia, Clemenceau's enthusiasm for the venture suddenly waned. It would cost a lot of money and be a very grave responsibility. He had

offered to send French troops to Armenia because the Armenians were threatened with massacre, in order to render a service to the Conference. This offer, however, could not constitute a provision of an agreement since France was not desirous of going to Armenia and it would involve an enormous burden.[38]

Despite his disappointment at the rejection of most of his proposals, Lloyd George accepted the French conditions. At Clemenceau's insistence, he agreed to inform Feisal of the agreement, and also undertook to persuade Feisal to accept half his subsidy from France and to let token contingents of French troops stationed in Damascus remain. Much to Lloyd George's disappointment, Clemenceau refused to meet with Feisal until this was accomplished.[39]

Thus France had obtained the desired occupation of western Syria and Cilicia without fulfilling any of the conditions so adamantly insisted upon by the British four months before. In May the British had refused to withdraw their troops from any part of Syria unless the French accepted a permanent territorial revision that would place the proposed rail line from Mosul to the Mediterranean within the British Palestinian mandate. Now, not only had France obtained the right to occupy all but the disputed territory, but Britain had formally recognized that the southern boundary was provisional and temporary for military occupation purposes only. Moreover, the British evacuation was to take place prior, not subsequent, to a formal agreement between France and the Arabs. This again was the opposite of what the British had demanded initially as the price for their military withdrawal from Syria. Although the evacuation of British troops from the Arab sector could conceivably open the way for the creation of a truly independent Arab state, it also would give the French the opportunity to extend their influence into this area.

Britain did manage to save some face by retaining its forces in the disputed southern zone and by obtaining French agreement not to send troops into Arab territory east of the Sykes-Picot line. Yet in every sense of the term this was a substantial diplomatic victory for France, one that had not been achieved by accident. Conceding little or nothing in return, France had obtained the transfer of military and political dominance in Syria and Cilicia from British to French hands. The skillful manipulation of the Armenian and King-Crane Commission affairs, coupled with the use of the press to publicize French grievances, had forced Britain publicly to demonstrate its friendship for France, and to do so with no strings attached.[40]

Attempts to Revoke the September Agreement

The Yale Plan

Although Polk had not objected to the provisions of the September Agreement, many Americans did. Among them was a member of the American delegation, Captain William Yale, who had been a member of the King-Crane Commission. In a report dated October 21, he stated:

The Arabs will not accept this agreement, there will be conflict with the French along the coast and the shadowy border between the Syrian Hinterland and the Syrian Littoral. There will be serious danger of a massacre of native Catholics of Damascus, Homs, Hameh and Aleppo. All competent

observers are agreed that this conflict would spread to Mesopotamia; it
is believed that the Arabs would then throw in their lot with the Turkish
rebels and that in a short time the entire Near East would be engaged
in a conflict with the Allies.[41]

On September 27, Yale went to London "on orders from the
American Commissioners to learn what was happening." [42] At the
same time he undertook, apparently on his own initiative, to act
as a mediator in reaching a Near East settlement that would be
acceptable to Feisal as well as to the British and French. At the
suggestion of H. Wickham Steed, editor of the *Times,* Yale sent
an anonymous letter containing a plan for a Syrian settlement to
the *Times,* which printed it on October 8. This plan was based on
the premise that it was politically impossible for any of the four
interested parties in the Near East—British, French, Arab, or Zionist—to put forward a compromise scheme in the general interest.
Therefore, any solution would have to come from and be imposed
on all by an outside force.

The plan called for Mesopotamia to be divided into two sections,
with the northern half an independent state under a supervisory
British mandate and the southern half under a direct British mandate
or administration, with a certain amount of autonomy allowed in
local government. Syria would likewise be partitioned. Syria proper
(the area of the four cities) would be independent under an advisory
French mandate. Lebanon would be under direct French administration and control. Palestine would have a general British mandate,
and the Zionists would be allowed to carry forward their plans.[43]
It was suggested that the United States should be used in the negotiation and promotion of this scheme.

The plan had much to be said for it. Realizing that the French
would accept no less a position in Syria than that held by Britain
in Mesopotamia, Yale's proposition established a quid pro quo by
which Britain's basic pledges to the Arabs could be fulfilled in return
for certain British concessions in Mesopotamia. Moreover, though
it was not mentioned, this plan implied the possibility of an eventual
joining together of the two independent areas with the new kingdom
of the Hedjaz. This would form the confederation of Arab states
so dear to the hearts of the Arab nationalists. Thus the plan provided

a solution that would enable every group to achieve its major aim, yet without any loss of prestige because the compromises had been imposed by an outside force.

What grounds did Yale have to hope that such a solution would meet with a favorable reception? Apparently he had been in touch with certain Frenchmen, of whom the most important was Philippe Berthelot, and had been led to believe some such solution might be possible.[44] Yale reported that Robert de Caix, author of some extremely violent anti-British articles, had told him that "if the British would give up Mesopotamia, France would only be too glad to give up Syria, thus leaving intact the Ottoman Empire." [45] De Caix was a person of some importance. He had been the chief French negotiator in the conversations with Feisal during the previous spring, and on October 9 he was appointed personal secretary to the new French high commissioner for Syria, General Henri Gouraud.[46] What authority he had to make this statement is unknown. In any case, perhaps because Yale had had similar assurances from other French officials, he based his whole scheme on the idea of the equal status of both the Mesopotamian and Syrian mandates.

In London, Yale's plan was widely acclaimed by the press, and in Paris, "Pertinax" gave his approval. Yale discussed the plan with many persons and obtained the support of several top British officials including Allenby, Hogarth, McMahon, Lawrence, Cornwallis, and Stirling. Among the Arabs, Nuri Said and Rustum Haidor approved the scheme and Feisal, though officially opposing any compromise, told Yale that he would accept any solution imposed on him by the Americans.[47]

Yale later claimed that the plan was accepted by the British cabinet, but it would appear that in fact such was not the case.[48] He returned to Paris intending to present the scheme formally to the French, but never had a chance to do so. Yale had advanced his proposal on his own initiative, and now felt he must obtain the consent of his superiors, especially if the United States was to serve as the mediator and "proponent" of the plan. On October 27, the American commissioners forwarded Yale's plan to the State Department, which refused permission for Yale to proceed.[49] According to David Garnett, this was extremely unfortunate, because "all the

parties to a deadlock were prepared to agree to a solution which
had been formulated—provided it was imposed on them from the
outside." [50] The claim that "all parties" were agreed is a gross over-
statement. Even so, it is true that a proposal that had seemed to
offer a solution that might be acceptable to all was never allowed
serious consideration, due to American refusal to become involved
in the dispute, even in the role of neutral arbiter. [51]

Feisal

Feisal had been summoned from the Near East by Lloyd George
prior to the latter's meetings with Clemenceau. He arrived in London
on September 18, and was informed of the new agreement the next
day. As was expected, he protested bitterly. He even claimed that
a formal treaty had been signed between the Arabs and the British.
Although Curzon went to some lengths to prove this was untrue,
British promises had been made often enough and clearly enough
to provide a good deal of moral justification for the Arab contention.
Feisal recognized that the September 15 pact in effect partitioned
Syria in accordance with the Sykes-Picot Agreement, and he strongly
urged its cancellation. He asked that a final solution should be sought
immediately by the Peace Conference. [52] The tone of his protests gave
eloquent witness to the fact that he saw his own doom in the proposed
settlement. As leader of a revolt against his religious leader (the
sultan-caliph in Constantinople), Feisal had put himself in a precarious position, and he was well aware of what might be in store for
him if he could not deliver the unified state he had promised. [53]

Despite all his efforts, Feisal was unable to bring about the dissolution of the agreement. He then suggested the creation of an
inter-Allied board that would negotiate the terms of the military occupation as well as the actual detailed boundary between the French
and Arab zones of occupation. This proposal was acceptable to Lloyd
George, but was refused by Clemenceau. [54] As long as France had
been excluded from Syria, Clemenceau had been reluctant to
negotiate directly with Feisal. [55] Now he took the position that this
was a purely Franco-Arab issue. Moreover, he explicitly stated that

the September agreement in no way committed France to accept the independence of an Arab state. Rather, Clemenceau regarded the whole area as being within a single French sphere. He maintained that all the agreement implied was that France would be willing to accept Arab occupation and government in part of this area as long as law and order were preserved. France's right to intervene in the area was not open to question. As far as he was concerned, negotiations could only take place regarding the prerequisites for French intervention, and this would have to be settled with no British or American participation or interference of any type.[56]

This stand provoked some bitter correspondence between Lloyd George and Clemenceau, each charging the other with bad faith. Eventually, however, the British gave in.[57] Feisal had no choice but to go to Paris in late October, 1919, where he commenced protracted negotiations with Clemenceau that were to stretch into 1920 before an agreement was finally reached.

Thus, by the end of November when the British finished the evacuation, Clemenceau had scored a complete victory for France's Syrian policy. Except for Mosul and some territory along the unsettled Palestine-Syrian border, British troops had evacuated not only the zone of direct control that had been allotted to France in the Sykes-Picot Agreement, but also the area in which France had been given exclusive rights of influence. Moreover, this had been done without securing either a guarantee from the French regarding permanent Arab rights in the area of the four cities or a final settlement of the Palestine-Syrian border issue. The British subsidy to Feisal had been cut in half (£75,000), and he had been told that if he wanted the rest he would have to get it from the French. Finally, France's right to deal directly with the Arabs in the area of the four cities, without any outside interference, had been recognized tacitly by the British. Though there would still be much talk, some violence, and a great deal more Franco-British hostility, by November, 1919, the territorial settlement in the Arab portion of the Ottoman Empire, marked by British abandonment of the Arabs in Syria, was to all intents and purposes complete.

1. In an effort to coordinate the extensive relief measures, the Peace Conference appointed a high commissioner for Armenia. Since most of the aid came from America, it was only natural that an American, Col. William Haskell, was appointed to the post. *U.S. Doc., P.P.C.,* 6:741, Supreme Council (hereafter referred to as S.C.), 6/28/19; 7:28, 7/5/19; p. 41, 7/7/19; pp. 647-48, 8/11/19; *Br. Doc.,* 1:22, S.C., 7/5/19; p. 31, 7/7/19; p. 389, 8/11/19; *U.S. Doc., 1919,* 2:827, American mission to Washington, 7/5/19; State Dept., Turkey, 867.00/878, Ravndal to Sec. State, 5/24/19; Bristol papers, Box 9, Doolittle (Tiflis) to Paris, 7/17/19, 7/19/19; 7/24/19; Cabinet Papers, Cab. 29/18, W.C.P. 1145, Hoover memorandum, 7/16/19; Foreign Office, F.O. 608/95/365-1-3/13201, Cairo to War Office, 6/6/19; F.O. 608/82/342-5-4/14901, Boghos Nubar Pacha to Balfour, 7/8/19; Crowe to Boghos Nubar Pacha, 7/12/19; F.O. 608/78/342-1-6/17550, File on conditions in Armenia; Pech, *Alliés et Turquie,* pp. 78-80, 8/18/19; *Times* (London), 5/6/19, 7/15/19, 7/22/19, 8/11/19, 8/16/19, 8/21/19; Howard, *King-Crane Commission,* pp. 239-40.

2. On May 5, General Bliss told Sir Henry Wilson that Congress would never allow American troops to go to Constantinople and Armenia. Callwell, *Henry Wilson,* 2:188. See also F. Palmer, *The Life and Letters of Tasker Bliss,* p. 413, 6/28/19; *Br. Doc.,* 1:131, S.C., 7/18/19, Telegram from Wilson; 3:480-81, Curzon to Lindsay, 8/11/19; *U.S. Doc., P.P.C.,* 11:261-64, American Commissioners Plenipotentiary. 6/30/19; *U.S. Doc., 1919,* 2:825-26, American mission to Washington, 7/3/19 (2); p. 827, 7/5/19; p. 828, Lansing to Paris, 8/11/19; Miller, *Diary,* 20:375-76, 7/31/19; *Times* (London), 8/2/19, 8/12/19; Howard, *King-Crane Commission,* p. 241; Gidney, *Mandate,* pp. 196-97.

3. Foreign Office, F.O. 608/83/342-8-3/5104, Conversation between British and Italian delegates regarding the future of Asia Minor, 3/21/19; F.O. 406/41/97, Curzon to Balfour, 9/11/19; F.O. 406/42/15, Curzon to Calthorpe, 4/11/19; Lloyd George Papers, F12/2/20, Lloyd George to Curzon, n.d.; F47/8/12, Henry Wilson to Lloyd George, 5/9/19; Sonnino Papers, Reel 23, no. 82, Sonnino to Rome, 3/22/19; Reel 46, no. 314, Sonnino to London, Paris and Cospoli, 3/23/19, Reel 46, no. 423 Sonnino to Sforza, 4/17/19; no. 633, Sonnino to Cospoli, 6/2/19; Reel 27, no. 1640, Sforza to Sonnino, 6/5/19.

4. *U.S. Doc., P.P.C.,* 5:467-68, C. of Four, 5/5/19; 8:648, S.C., 8/11/19; *Br. Doc.,* 1:289, S.C., 8/11/19; 3:478-79, Balfour to Lloyd George, 8/9/19; Lloyd George Papers, F47/8/14, Henry Wilson to Lloyd George, 5/14/19; Foreign Office, F.O. 406/41/97, Curzon to Balfour, 9/11/19; F.O. 608/85/347-1-6, File on British evacuation of the Caucasus; R. Ullman, *Anglo-Soviet relations, 1917-1921,* 2:219-31; F. Nitti, *The Wreck of Europe,* pp. 149-51; Sonnino Papers, Reel 26, no. 97, Biancheri to Sonnino, 1/28/19; Reel 44, no. 48, 2/18/19; Reel 51, DeMartino memorandum, "Relazione," 5/21/19; Reel 27, no. 1437, Sforza to Sonnino, 5/23/19. For a discussion of the fall of the Orlando government, see Mayer, *Politics of Peacemaking,* pp. 783-86. Curzon hailed the Italian decision not to go to the Caucasus as the one Italian "belated and solitary act of prudence." *Br. Doc.,* 4:12, n. 5, Four Power Meeting, 7/3/19.

5. *Times,* (London), 5/2/19; Hovannisian, *Armenia,* pp. 247-49.

6. *U.S. Doc., 1919,* 2:828, Lansing to Davis, 8/9/19; 8/11/19; pp. 830-31, Davis to Lansing, 8/15/19; pp. 833-34, 8/20/19; pp. 834-35, Lansing to Davis, 8/23/19; pp. 835-37, 8/26/19; Polk Papers, Dr. 82, fol. 4, Haskell to Polk, 10/28[23?]/19; Bristol Papers, Box 9, Doolittle (Tiflis) to Bristol, 7/30/19, 7/31/19; *New York Times,* 8/28/19; *Br. Doc.,* 3:478-79, Balfour to Lloyd George, 8/9/19; pp. 480-81, Curzon to Lindsay, 8/11/19; pp. 482-84, Curzon to Balfour, 8/12/19; 4:741, Nabakoff to Graham, 8/26/19; pp. 743-44, Balfour to Curzon, 8/29/19; 1:574, S.C., 8/29/19, App. A, Haskell to Peace Conference; Cabinet Papers, Cab. 24/86, G.T. 7949, Memorandum by Balfour and Lloyd George, 8/9/19; *Times* (London) 8/5/19, 8/12/19, 8/13/19, 8/16/19; Sachar, "U.S. and Turkey," pp. 132-33; Kazemzadeh, *Transcaucasia,* pp. 259-60; Howard, *King-Crane Commission,* pp. 244-48.

7. *U.S. Doc., 1919,* 2:830-31, Davis to Lansing, 8/15/19; p. 837, 8/26/19; *Times,* (London), 8/19/19; Callwell, *Henry Wilson,* 2:211, 9/2/19. The United States had one more string to

its bow. On August 22, Admiral Bristol, under instructions from Washington, warned the Turkish government that if any massacres occurred as a result of the withdrawal of British forces, Turkey would forfeit any rights to sovereignty guaranteed by the Fourteen Points, and threatened a "complete dissolution of the Turkish Empire." The Turks mildly replied that they were not allowed enough police and troops to enforce quiet. However, the American action infuriated the other members of the Supreme Council. They plainly indicated their irritation at unilateral action by the one power that was not officially at war with Turkey, and noted that the punishment threatened was one that only the Peace Conference as a whole could impose. *Br. Doc.,* 4:736–38, Webb to Curzon, 8/22/19, and Foreign Office minutes found in F.O. 608/385/1/1/18325; *Times* (London), 8/25/19; *U.S. Doc., 1919,* 2:831–32, Lansing to Paris, 8/16/19; Bristol Papers, Box 27, Paris to Constantinople, 8/20/19, Bristol to Paris, 8/21/19, 8/22/19; Bristol to Paris and Washington, 8/25/19; *U.S. Doc., P.P.C.,* 7:839–40, 858–59, S.C., 8/25/19; State Department, Turkey, 867.00/914 Ravndal to Sec. State, 8/25/19; 924, Bristol to Sec. State, 9/13/19.

8. *Br. Doc.,* 1:508, S.C., 8/25/19; *U.S. Doc., P.P.C.,* 7:839–40, S.C., 8/25/19.

9. *Br. Doc.,* 1:569, 574, S.C., 8/29/19; *U.S. Doc., P.P.C.,* 8:5, 11, S.C., 8/29/19; Foreign Office, F.O., 608/78/342-1-6/18473, French delegation note regarding the sending of troops to Armenia, 8/29/19.

10. *U.S. Doc., 1919,* 2:838, American mission to Lansing, 8/30/19; pp. 838–39, Lansing to American mission, 9/2/19; Polk Papers, Dr. 88, fol. 18, Diary, 8/29/19; 9/1/19; Cabinet Papers, Cab. 23/12, W.C. 621, 9/2/19; *Br. Doc.,* 4:743, Balfour to Curzon, 8/29/19; p. 745, 8/31/19; p. 747, Curzon to Balfour, 9/2/19; p. 748, Balfour to Curzon, 9/3/19; p. 756, Curzon to Campbell, 9/8/19; p. 761, Robeck to Curzon, 9/15/19; Lloyd George Papers, F12/1/39, letter, Curzon to Lloyd George, 9/2/19; Curzon to Lloyd George, 9/17/19; A. Bonar Law Papers,101/3/142, Bonar Law to Balfour, 9/4/19; Callwell, *Henry Wilson,* 2:211, 9/2/19.

11. *Br. Doc.,* 1:569, 574, S.C., 8/29/19; *U.S. Doc., P.P.C.,* 8:5, 11, S.C., 3/29/19; U.S. Doc., *1919,* 2:840–41, American mission to Lansing, 9/22/19. Bonar Law expressed the predominant British view regarding the route the French troops planned to take when he wrote Lloyd George, "If they . . . let us get away, though this is a rather cynical thing to say, I would not much care if they propose to help them from Mars instead of Alexandretta." Lloyd George papers, F31/1/9, 9/5/19.

12. Cabinet papers, Cab. 23/12, W.C. 622, 9/18/19; Foreign Office, F.O. 406/42/52, Tilley to Churchill, 9/17/19, and Curzon minute; *Br. Doc.,* 3:548–49, Wardrop to Curzon, 9/12/19; p. 663, Tilley to de Fleuriau, 11/26/19; Foreign Office, F.O., 608/78/342-1-6/19095, F.O. to de Robeck, 12/1/19; *Times* (London), 9/20/19.

13. The Labour Party was the only group that openly opposed the British occupation of the Caucasus. *Times* (London), 8/25/19.

14. *U.S. Doc., P.P.C.,* 5:468, C. of Four, 5/5/19; Foreign Office, F.O. 406/41/97, Curzon to Balfour, 9/11/19.

15. *Br. Doc.,* 3:478–79, Balfour to Llyod George, 8/9/19; pp. 480–81, Curzon to Lindsay, 8/11/19; pp. 511–12, 8/18/19; 4:738, Lindsay to Curzon, 8/25/19; p. 742, Hohler to Kerr, 8/27/19; *Times* (London), 8/26/19, 8/30/19, 9/1/19.

16. Kedourie, *England and the Middle East,* p. 143; *Br. Doc.,* 4:263, Clayton to Curzon, 6/1/19; p. 279, Memorandum by Cornwallis (n.d.); p. 374, Cheetham to Curzon, 9/9/19; pp. 297–98, C. of Four, 6/25/19.

17. *Br. Doc.,* 4:274–75, Curzon to Derby, 6/11/19; pp. 275–76, Allenby to Curzon, 6/12/19; p. 277, Clayton to Curzon, 6/15/19; Balfour to Curzon, 6/16/19; p. 298, Balfour to Allenby, 6/26/19; pp. 365–66, French to Curzon, 8/29/19.

18. Ibid., p. 265, Clayton to Curzon, 6/5/19; pp. 286–94; 6/23/19; p. 299, French to Curzon, 6/26/19; pp. 311–13, 7/10/19; pp. 360–65, 8/26/19; p. 370, Meinertzhagen to Curzon, 9/3/19; Kedourie, *England and the Middle East,* pp. 145–46; Antonius, *Arab Awakening,* p. 293.

19. For the text of the report, see *U.S. Doc., P.P.C.*, 12:751–63, or *Editor and Publisher* 55 (December 2, 1922): 1–27. See also, Baker, *Wilson and World Settlement*, 2:210–18; *Br. Doc.*, 4:285–86, Clayton to Curzon, 6/20/19; p. 210, French to Curzon, 7/7/19.

20. The Americans never gave copies to their allies, recognizing that it might well provoke a "fight," though they did allow members of the British delegation to read it. *U.S. Doc., P.P.C.*, 11:432–33, American commissioners and technical advisors, 9/24/19.

21. *Br. Doc.*, 4:315–16, French to Curzon, 7/19/19.

22. For example, see the *Times*, (London), 7/28/19; Howard, *King-Crane Commission*, p. 219; Gidney, *Mandate*, p. 164.

23. The British emphatically denied this charge. *Br. Doc.*, 4:321–23, Balfour to Curzon, 7/28/19; pp. 327–28, Curzon to Balfour, 8/1/19; pp. 371–72, Curzon to Cambon, 9/6/19.

24. The British government formally protested the French press statements to the French Foreign Office. Moreover, there was some feeling that it was more than a mere coincidence that the only pro-French area visited by the commission was also the one area militarily occupied by the French. Gontaut-Biron, *Comment*, chap. 13, *Times* (London), 9/1/19, 9/2/19, 9/3/19. R. de Caix, "The Question of Syria," pp. 145–49; pp. 169–74; *Le Figaro*, as quoted by the *Times* (London), 8/11/19; *Le Temps*, 7/7/19, 8/19/19, 8/23/19, 9/8/19, 9/15/19; *D.R.F.P., Allied Press Supplement*, 6:7/9/19; Lloyd George Papers, F89/4/13, Kerr to Lloyd George, 8/20/19; Foreign Office, F.O. 608/107/384-1-3/16945, Cambon to Foreign Office, 7/28/19; 18421, Curzon to Cambon, 8/25/19; F.O. 608/107/384-1-7/15855, Derby to Curzon, 7/20/19; 16735, Grahame to Curzon, 7/30/19; 16824, 8/1/19; 17275, 8/5/19; 17690, 8/9/19; 17832, 8/12/19; F.O. 608/114/385-1-23/14211, Derby to Curzon, 7/1/19; *Br. Doc.*, 4:309–10, Derby to Curzon, 7/7/19; pp. 318–20, Grahame to Curzon, 7/26/19; pp. 320–21, 7/27/19; pp. 335–37, Curzon to Grahame, 8/8/19; pp. 349–51, Grahame to Curzon, 8/12/19; pp. 353–43, 8/18/19; pp. 355–59, Curzon to Balfour, 8/25/19; pp. 367–69, French to Curzon, 8/30/19; A Fabre-Luce, *La Crise des Alliances*, p. 53, Zeine, *Arab Independence*, pp. 101–5.

25. *Br. Doc.*, 4:342, Balfour memorandum, 8/11/19; Kedourie, *England and the Middle East*, pp. 143–44.

26. *Br. Doc.*, 4:342, Balfour memorandum, 8/11/19.

27. *U.S. Doc., P.P.C.*, 12:848–50, Report of the King-Crane Commission, Confidential Appendix, "The Interference of the Occupying Governments with the Commission's Inquiry"; Kedourie, *England and the Middle East*, pp. 145–46.

28. Kedourie, *England and the Middle East*, p. 147. Miss Bell was a noted author who had travelled widely in the Near East. From 1916 until 1926 she served as the assistant political officer and Oriental secretary in the British administration at Baghdad. The validity of the King-Crane Report itself, particularly in the light of subsequent historical developments, is another matter completely. See Howard, *King-Crane Commission*, pp. 320–24.

29. This conciliatory attitude was warmly received in the French press. *Times* (London), 8/21/19, 8/23/19, 9/4/19, 9/6/19, 9/10/19, 9/11/19; *Le Temps*, 8/19/19, 8/23/19/ 9/8/19; *Br. Doc.*, 4:377–78, Grahame to Curzon, 9/10/19; Garnett, *Lawrence Letters*, p. 282; Meinertzhagen, *Diary*, p. 26, 7/3/19.

30. Cambon, *Correspondance*, 3:353–54, 9/4/19.

31. *Br. Doc.*, 4:345, Balfour memorandum, 8/11/19. See also his memorandum to Lloyd George, 2/19/19, in Lloyd George Papers, F3/4/12. Also, the *Times* (London), 9/16/19.

32. *Br. Doc.*, 4:343–45, Balfour memorandum, 8/11/19.

33. Balfour clearly recognized what the French were doing. See Balfour Papers, MSS 49752, Balfour to Foreign Office, for War Office, 8/31/19. In a message to Lloyd George, Clemenceau implicitly, but clearly, linked the offer of French troops for the Caucasus with the desirability of achieving an agreement concerning Syria. Lloyd George Papers, F51/1/37, Kerr to Lloyd George (message from Clemenceau), 9/11/19.

34. Cabinet Papers, Cab. 21/153, Notes of three meetings held at Hennequeville, Trouville, 9/9/19, 9/10/19, 9/11/19. *Br. Doc.*, 4:379–80, Lloyd George to Clemenceau, 9/11/19. Lloyd George wanted to negotitate the Syrian affair directly with Clemenceau. He considered Balfour as being too soft on this issue and had discouraged Clemenceau's earlier suggestions that Balfour and Clemenceau work out an arrangement. Lloyd George Papers, F89/4/9, Davies (for Lloyd George) to Kerr, 8/15/19.

35. *Br. Doc.*, 4:384, Summary of the Paris negotiations, 9/17/19; Yale Papers, IV-8; Polk Papers, Dr. 78. fol. 53, Memorandum of conversation with Lloyd George, Allenby, Bonar Law, and Churchill, Paris, September, 1919.

36. *Br. Doc.*, 1:690–93, S.C., 9/15/19; pp. 700–701, App. B; *U.S. Doc., P.P.C.*, 8:205–8, S.C., 9/15/19; pp. 216–17, App. B. See also Temperley, *Peace Conference*, 6:152.

37. *Br. Doc.*, 1:693, S.C., 9/15/19; 4:380, Clemenceau to Lloyd George, 9/11/19. See also Lloyd George Papers, F51/1/40, Unsigned note describing interview with Clemenceau, 9/12/19.

38. *Br. Doc.*, 1:692, S.C., 9/15/19.

39. Ibid., pp. 685–86; 4:384–85, Summary of Paris negotiations, 9/17/19; *U.S. Doc., P.P.C.*, 8:200–201, S.C., 9/15/19, British Treasury officials had been asking the government for some time to begin a gradual reduction in the sudsidy to Feisal in September, 1919. Foreign Office, F.O., 608/93/360-1-2/18627, Treasury letter, 8/23/19.

40. The agreement was generally welcomed in France. Only a few openly opposed it maintaining that Mosul should be included in the French zone. British Cabinet approval was obtained on September 18. The *Times* (London) hailed the settlement with unmitigated enthusiasm and urged an immediate effort to reach a permanent solution. Gontaut-Biron, *Comment*, pp. 314–22; *Journal des Débats*, pp. 511–12 Saint Brice, "L'Accord Syrien," pp. 145–52; *Le Temps*, 9/18/19; Cabinet Papers, Cab. 21/153, War Cabinet, 9/18/19; Cabinet Committee meeting, 9/22/19; G.T. 8176, Telegram to Allenby, n.d.; *Times* (London), 9/17/19, 9/18/19, 9/19/19; *Br. Doc.*, 4:392–94, Grahame to Curzon, 9/18/19.

41. Garnett, *Lawrence Letters*, p. 284; Yale Papers, VI-42, fol. 112.

42. Manuel, *American Palestine Relations*, p. 253. Yale was concerned about the problems of Mesopotamian oil. He was known to have been an agent for the Standard Oil Company before the war and was suspected of still being so by both the British and French. In any case, in his conversations with British authorities he made it clear that he thought the United States would never accept a monopoly by any one country of the oil fields in Mesopotamia. *Br. Doc.*, 4:278; Clayton to Hardinge, 6/17/19; Gontaut-Biron, *Comment*, p. 266–67; Garnett, *Lawrence Letters*, p. 285; Howard, *King-Crane Commission*, pp. 268–70.

43. *Times* (London), 10/8/19; Yale Papers, VI-42, fols. 112, 114; Howard, *King-Crane Commission*, p. 267.

44. Yale Papers, VI-42, fol. 115, Garnett, *Lawrence Letters*, p. 287; *U.S. Doc., P.P.C.*, 11:427, American Commissioners Plenipotentiary, 9/23/19.

45. Yale Papers, VI-42, fol. 112; Kedourie, *England and the Middle East*, p. 133.

46. *Br. Doc.*, 4:464–65, Derby to Curzon, 10/13/19; Gontaut-Biron, *Comment*, pp. 331–32; Cambon, *Correspondance*, 3:360; 10/11/19; *Times* (London), 10/12/19.

47. Yale Papers, VI-42, fols. 112, 115; Polk Papers, Dr. 82, fol. 14, Polk to Lansing, 10/20/19; *Times* (London), 10/8/19, 10/10/19; Garnett, *Lawrence Letters*, pp. 284–86; Kedourie, *England and the Middle East*, p. 164; Howard, *King-Crane Commission*, p. 265.

48. Garnett, *Lawrence Letters*, pp. 286–87; Manuel, *American Palestine Relations*, p. 254. The cabinet meeting was supposed to have been held on October 13, 1919, but neither the editors of the *Documents on British Foreign Policy, 1919–1939*, nor the author of this study could find any record of such a discussion. See *Br. Doc.*, 4:422, n. 2. Yale's own account of his meeting with a Colonel Watson, who supposedly told him of the cabinet approval, does not bear out his contention of cabinet support, nor does a subsequent letter from Watson

to Yale dated October 28, 1919. Yale Papers, VI-42, fols. 112, 113, 115; Polk Papers, Dr. 78, fol. 63, Yale report to Polk of interviews in London.

49. Manuel, *American Palestine Relations,* p. 254, Evans, *U.S. and Partition,* pp. 224–26. Garnett says that the commissioners themselves refused Yale because "President Wilson on his final return to the United States had left them without authority to make any decision or to take any action." Garnett, *Lawrence Letters,* p. 288. In his report, Yale stated that upon his arrival in London he apprised American Ambassador John Davis of his intended course of action, and had received "advice and encouragement." Yale did state that Davis had told him that he could give him no letters of introduction or take any official notice of Yale's actions. Davis, on the other hand, wrote Polk that Yale had told him of his plans and actions only just prior to Yale's return to Paris, and Davis expressed strong disapproval of what Yale had done. Polk replied that he had been "horrified" to learn of Yale's doings in London, and had told him that he should mind his own business. "I think he was quite surprised to find that he really had not been doing a real service for humanity." Yale Papers, VI-42, fols. 113, 115; Polk Papers, Dr. 73, fol. 120, Davis to Polk, 10/14/19; Polk to Davis, 10/19/19; Buckler Papers, Dr. 51, fol. 25, letter to Mrs. Buckler, 10/15/19.

50. Garnett, *Lawrence Letters,* p. 288.

51. This view, with which the author concurs, was expressed to him by Professor Yale during an interview in April, 1960.

52. Cabinet Papers, Cab. 21/153, Hussein to Feisal, text of purported British-Arab agreement, n.d. (September, 1919); *Br. Doc.,* 4:395–404, Feisal-Lloyd George meeting, 9/19/19; pp. 406–9, Feisal to Lloyd George, 9/21/19; pp. 413–19, Feisal-Lloyd George meeting, 9/23/19; pp. 440–42, Feisal-Hussein correspondence, 9/22/19–10/4/19; pp. 444–49, Curzon to Feisal, 10/9/19; pp. 443–44, Feisal to Lloyd George, 10/9/19; pp. 455–56. Cornwallis memorandum, 10/11/19; the *Times* (London), 10/24/19.

53. This point has been brought out by Kedourie, *England and the Middle East,* p. 149.

54. *Br. Doc.,* 4:421–22, Cornwallis-Feisal conversation, 9/25/19; pp. 443–44, Feisal to Lloyd George, 10/9/19; p. 451, Lloyd George to Feisal, 10/10/19; pp. 458–62, Feisal-Lloyd George meeting, 10/13/19; State Department, Turkey, 867.00/967, Polk to Sec. State, 10/21/19; 970, Polk to Sec. State, 10/24/19; Polk Papers, Dr. 88, fol. 18, Diary, 10/17/19, 10/22/19; Buckler Papers, Dr. 51, fol. 25, Letters to Mrs. Buckler, 10/17/19, 10/22/19; Cabinet Papers, Cab. 24/93, C.P. 114, Clemenceau to Feisal, 11/2/19; Feisal to Clemenceau, 11/5/19; *Times* (London), 10/20/19.

55. For his most recent refusals, see *Br. Doc.,* 4:380, Clemenceau to Lloyd George, 9/11/19; 1:685–86, S.C. 9/15/19.

56. Ibid., 4:452–54, Clemenceau to Curzon, 10/11/19; pp. 468–69, Clemenceau to Derby, 10/14/19; pp. 490–92, Derby to Curzon, 10/20/19.

57. This acrimonious interchange provoked some sharp comments from Cambon who railed against "Clemenceau and Lloyd George who try to settle matters directly, get angry, say bad things, and send nasty telegrams . . . [all because they] have forgotten the methods of diplomacy." Cambon, *Correspondance,* 3:361–62, 10/19/19. The *Times* (London) of October 21 advocated that the question be settled through open discussions by teams of negotiators, rather than in secret by two "over-wrought and over-worked Prime Ministers." See also *Br. Doc.,* 4:463, Curzon to Derby, 10/13/19; pp. 468–69, Clemenceau to Derby, 10/14/19; p. 473, Curzon to Derby, 10/15/19; pp. 474–76, 10/16/19; pp. 479–89, 10/18/19; pp. 495–97, 10/22/19.

VII ❀ FRONTIERS IN THRACE AND OCCUPATION ZONES IN ASIA MINOR

ALTHOUGH the Supreme Council had agreed to postpone discussion of the Turkish treaty until the American position on mandates was known, one issue could not be put aside. This was the southern frontier of Bulgaria, which had to be settled in order to complete the Bulgarian peace treaty. This in turn involved Allied agreement on the disposition of Thrace.

Partial Solution in Thrace

The Thracian question was discussed at length by the Central Territorial Committee during July, 1919. Whereas the attitude of Britain and France remained consistent with the earlier report of the Greek Committee,[1] the viewpoint of the United States altered considerably. As a result, two diametrically opposed positions appeared.

The position taken by the French and British delegates was that Bulgaria was a defeated nation and must be shown that this was the case. They therefore supported Venizelos's claims to eastern and western Thrace. They maintained that any forced population shifts that had taken place after Bulgaria had gained control of western Thrace in 1913 should not be considered in determining national majorities.[2] They also pointed out that the proposed internationalization of the Straits would give Bulgaria an open and unrestricted outlet to the sea, which along with a free port on the Aegean would satisfy all of Bulgaria's economic needs. Finally, they argued that the cession of western Thrace to Greece was necessary in order to link eastern Thrace, with its large Greek population, directly to Greece.[3]

These arguments had led the American delegates on the Greek Committee to accept the British and French point of view in early March. However, it should be remembered that the American delegate on the Central Territorial Committee, Sidney Mezes, had subsequently added a reservation stipulating that the United States would neither support nor reject the recommendations of the Greek Committee, on the grounds that Greek claims could only be adjudicated in conjunction with decisions regarding the future of the Turkish state, a subject that the Council of Ten had reserved for itself.[4] At the time he made this reservation the British and French assumed that it was designed to provide the necessary leeway for American acceptance of a Greek zone in Asia Minor, something the Americans on the Greek Committee had strenuously opposed. In this assumption they were undoubtedly correct, yet from a Wilsonian point of view the extension of this reservation to include Thrace made good sense. It was assumed that the United States would undertake the Constantinople mandate, and therefore the Americans were particularly concerned that the territorial limits be such as to ensure the economic viability and easy administration of the mandate. Moreover, western Thrace had an overwhelmingly predominant Turkish population. Therefore, the very ethnic grounds that helped justify for Wilson his pro-Greek stand on Smyrna mitigated against Greek claims in this area.

As a result of all these factors, in early July the United States delegates on the Central Territorial Committee specifically repudiated the agreement reached by the Greek Committee and refused to agree to the cession of western or eastern Thrace to Greece. Instead they insisted that the prewar boundaries should be retained (with the possible exception of territory given to the new international state at the Straits). The territory had many more Bulgarians than Greeks, they argued, and the purported preference of the predominantly Bulgarian-speaking Moslem population for Greek rather than Bulgarian rule was highly questionable. Moreover, Greece had voluntarily concurred in the cession of the territory to Bulgaria in 1913. Direct Bulgarian access to the Mediterranean was an economic necessity, and a free port in Greek territory would not be the same thing. Bulgarian cession of this territory would create a basis for the renewal of Balkan strife in the future. Therefore, the American delegates maintained that "ethnographical, economic, and political arguments, as well as possession supported by valid claims, all favor the maintenance of the Bulgarian boundaries as they are at the present time." [5]

President Wilson, however, when informed of the stand taken by his own delegation, did not agree. Although determined "that Greece should not be given Bulgarian Thrace," [6] he was equally convinced that Bulgaria had no real ethnic or other claim to the territory either. Therefore, on July 25 he sent a telegram to the American delegation in Paris urging that they insist that both eastern and western Thrace become part of the new international state at Constantinople. Bliss, White, and Polk were horrified. Although they were agreed that western Thrace should under no circumstances be given to Greece, they were also convinced that the inclusion of all the territory in the international state would be regarded as American greediness, since the United States was slated to undertake the mandate at Constantinople. Therefore, they agreed to seek a solution, if possible, that would allow at least western Thrace to remain in Bulgaria. [7]

Events in Asia Minor undoubtedly had much to do with the strengthened American determination not to give in on the subject of western Thrace. It is evident that the Americans felt both guilt and embarrassment at the violence that the Smyrna landings had produced. Bliss noted in his diary: "We all believe that to give Western Thrace to Greece will result in even worse conditions than have resulted by giving Smyrna to Greece." [8] Polk commented in a similar vein before the Supreme Council on August 7. [9]

Italy, in line with its long-standing opposition to Greek claims, continued its opposition to Greek ambitions in Thrace. Nonetheless, during the first part of July, Tittoni, with the consent of the others, met with Venizelos in an effort to obtain Greek consent to a compromise. On July 21, he reported to the Supreme Council that Venizelos refused to withdraw or reduce his claims to all of western and eastern Thrace. Thus it was obvious that a settlement would have to be imposed on both Greeks and Bulgarians, a settlement that neither would accept voluntarily.[10]

When the problem finally came before the Supreme Council on July 31, the American and Italian delegates offered proposals that differed from the position taken by their nations in the sessions of the Central Territorial Committee. Henry White, in accordance with Wilson's instructions, suggested that all of Bulgarian Thrace be transferred to the Constantinople international state and that a clause signifying this intention be inserted in the Bulgarian treaty. Tittoni, in turn, proposed that eastern Thrace be divided along strictly ethnological lines between Bulgaria and Greece, a policy that would clearly favor Greek claims. This considerable softening of Italy's previous hard-line position was taken by the others as an indication that Greece and Italy had worked out their differences privately, a possibility that Wilson, for one, found very irritating to contemplate, for it would leave the United States isolated in its policy conflict with the other powers.[11]

However, it was soon discovered that Tittoni's suggestion was unworkable, for it failed to provide for Bulgarian access to the Aegean. The same objection was made to a Greek proposal that Thrace be an autonomous state under Greek sovereignty. The American proposal that the whole territory be given to the new international state, albeit with guarantees allowing Bulgaria access to the Aegean, was opposed, particularly by Clemenceau, who maintained that it would be impossible to agree on a mandatory power for Constantinople if the territory of the state were so greatly increased. As a compromise solution, André Tardieu proposed that while sovereignty over eastern and western Thrace should be granted to Greece, the port of Dedeagatch on the Aegean should be made a free city. It, along with railroad connections to Bulgaria, should be administered by an international commission.[12]

Polk refused to accept this solution. "His instructions from President Wilson were very clear that a large Bulgarian population was not to be handed over to Greece."[13] However, adopting the basic French concept, Polk proposed that an international state be created that would include not only Dedeagatch and the railroad, but Adrianople and the Bulgarian area of western Thrace as well. The rest of eastern Thrace and a small section of western Thrace then could be given in full sovereignty to Greece. Although both the British and French were willing to accept this, the French continued to protest that their solution gave guarantees enough to Bulgaria and was far more workable than having two international states with a segment of Greece in the middle. Venizelos accepted both plans, although expressing a decided preference for Tardieu's.[14]

Polk agreed to submit both plans to Wilson. Much to his distress, that very day he received a cable from Lansing stating Wilson's determination that either all Thrace should become part of the international state, or western Thrace should be returned to Bulgaria. Nevertheless, Polk submitted the new compromise schemes to Washington. In a telegram to Colonel House on August 20, he commented:

We almost made a compromise on the Thracian situation after a hard fight against the whole "bunch" and were then told by Washington that they would not listen to any compromise whatever, but wanted Eastern and Western Thrace in an International State. That of course is out of the question, for as long as it is not known who is to have the mandate for Constantinople neither the British nor French would be willing to run the chance of the other getting all the territory along the Aegean. I have telegraphed again to Washington and am waiting anxiously to see whether I am going to get "spanked" or whether we can close up the Bulgarian treaty.[15]

On August 28, Lansing reiterated Wilson's rejection of both the French scheme and Polk's own proposal. Therefore, on September 1, when the matter finally came before the Supreme Council again, Polk was forced to revert to the original Wilsonian proposal that all Thrace should be incorporated into the Constantinople state. The one concession he was able to offer was that the small portion of western Thrace that had a predominantly Greek population should go to Greece. He met, as he obviously knew he would, complete hostility. The French refused even to consider this solution. Balfour did not express a final opinion but instead suggested that since no agreement was possible, the Bulgarian frontier should be delineated and Bulgaria directed to turn over all the area south of this line to the Allied and Associated Powers for eventual disposition. The territory would be occupied by Allied troops, with Greek forces being allowed to move into the area of western Thrace attributed to Greece by all the nations. Bulgaria would be assured eventual access to an Aegean port in the treaty. This scheme appealed to the Americans who saw the occupation as a likely first step toward the plan for a single international state. As Polk told the American commissioners, "Eastern Thrace is tied up with Constantinople by the International body that is there. . . . We can make no objection to their sending in troops other than Greek troops into Western Thrace, if they offer to." [16]

By the following day the Central Territorial Committee had drawn the boundary line and the council accepted it unanimously.[17] Thus, for the purposes of the Bulgarian treaty, the issue was solved, but with respect to a Turkish settlement, only one decision had been made. This was that Bulgaria would not be given a territorial outlet to the Aegean Sea. The permanent disposition of Thrace was far from decided. Again, this time due to Wilson's personal intransigence, the council had failed in an attempt to reach a definitive settlement on at least one of the many Turkish problems facing it.

Despite this display of seeming strength, the general American position relative to a Near Eastern settlement had been weakened. In accepting the final solution, Polk was forced to state that the United States could not participate in the occupation of the territory that had been taken over from Bulgaria by the Allies. This was despite the fact that America was slated to assume the Constantinople mandate of which this territory would be a part if Wilson's own recommendations were followed. Moreover, this decision came on the heels of a communique from Wilson stating that it would be a long time before America would be able to make any commitment regarding its participation in the Near East mandatory system. It had become all too clear that though the United States might insist on a continuing role in negotiating the Near East peace settlement, the likelihood of its participating actively in enforcing that settlement was dwindling fast.[18]

Greek and Italian Zones of Occupation in Asia Minor

Another problem with which the Supreme Council had to deal in the summer and fall of 1919 was that of the Italian and Greek forces in Asia Minor. Not only were both expanding the territory under their control at a rapid rate, but the Italian action had been taken completely without the sanction of the Peace Conference. The Greeks had long since exceeded the limits of the zone of occupation prescribed for them in Paris. It appeared that Italian and Greek troops would soon meet, and there was great fear that this might in turn provoke armed hostilities between the two.[19]

Attitude of the New Italian Government

On June 19, 1919, under attack regarding foreign policy from the right and domestic policy from the left, the Orlando government was forced to resign. Orlando was succeeded as prime minister by Francesco Nitti, who selected as his foreign minister Tommaso Tittoni, a person regarded as much less nationalistic and imperialistic than his predecessor, Sidney Sonnino. The representatives of the new Italian government arrived in Paris on June 28 for the signing of the German treaty and were presented shortly thereafter with an Allied statement protesting the Italian intervention in Anatolia. The Italians were warned that there was little chance of Italian claims being discussed at Paris as long as the occupation continued. If Italy maintained this policy it would lose "all claim to assistance or aid from those who were once proud to be her associates." [20]

Instead of reacting in a hostile manner Tittoni did his best to reestablish cordial relations. Balfour recorded that in a private meeting with Tittoni on July 1, the latter was "in the highest degree friendly and conciliatory, and he expressed in quite unmistakable language his earnest desire for a complete and friendly understanding with England and France." [21] Two days later, at an informal meeting of the representatives of the four powers, Tittoni "made it clear that he disapproved of the policy of his predecessors in sending troops to Asia Minor. . . . Coal and raw materials were Italy's real needs, not fresh territorial responsibilities." [22] However, although he was willing to recognize that the occupation did not prejudge the final territorial distribution and to pledge that no further advance would take place, he refused to withdraw the troops, on the grounds that this could not be done without jeopardizing his government's position, for it would be a public humiliation for Italy. In other words, although the new Nitti government showed signs of being more tactful and friendly, in reality little other than the atmosphere of the negotiations had changed.

On July 7, in a formal reply to the note of June 28, Tittoni justified, as Orlando had before him, the Italian landings in Anatolia as having been necessary to maintain public order. He claimed that the Greek landings at Smyrna had created great popular unrest and had also menaced Italy's position in the area. Scalanuova was the only good port outside Smyrna, and Italy's right to occupy it was based on Article 9 of the Treaty of London. Moreover, he asserted that the Italian occupation had been peaceful, unlike the Greek, and that the people had actually welcomed them.[23]

Although the other three powers refused to accept these arguments, it was clear that the Italian occupation had been mainly a reaction to the Greek landing at Smyrna and that the two issues would have to be treated and settled jointly. The Greek question, therefore, constituted a major topic of discussion in the Supreme Council during the summer months.

The Greeks in Smyrna

Ever since the Greek troops had landed at Smyrna, reports had been received that indicated considerable Turkish military resistance to the Greek occupation of territory outside the city. Unlike the Italians, the Greeks encountered heavy resistance from the Turks. This opposition continued to stiffen throughout June, and it was rumored that Turkish officers were leaving Constantinople for central Anatolia to organize further resistance to the Greeks. It appeared that, far from preventing disturbances, the presence of Greek troops was causing them.[24]

The European community at Smyrna, with the exception of the Greeks, publicly voiced its opposition to the cession of the city to Greece, and a *Times* correspondent pointedly emphasized that Greeks constituted only 35 percent of the total population of the Aidin vilayet. In the House of Commons, Foreign Office spokesman

Cecil Harmsworth was forced on two occasions to admit that Greeks had massacred Turks in Smyrna and that this had occurred within sight of the Allied ships in the harbor. The correspondent for the *Times* recommended that the occupying forces should be put under British and French command.[25]

The British representatives at Constantinople did not hesitate to lay the blame for the strife and the renewed Turkish resistance directly upon the Greeks. They criticized the Peace Conference for authorizing the landing of Greek troops and for failing to make a definite statement of the intent, purpose, and territorial limitations of the occupation. As Admiral Webb put it: "We do our best to create a situation which sets them at each other's throats . . . . Up to the time of the Smyrna landing we were getting on quite well. . . . Now things are quite changed." [26] The British high commissioner, Admiral Calthorpe, made no attempt to hide his belief that the fault for the unrest lay chiefly with the Greeks:

The cause [of the unrest] is indefiniteness which has characterized whole situation in Aidin Vilayet during and subsequent to occupation of Smyrna. The Turks as you are aware accepted fact of occupation with ill grace [but as *a*] *fait accompli* on condition that occupation was well defined in limits and conducted with some measure of decency. Information so far received appears to show that neither of these conditions have [*sic*] been fulfilled. . . . Territory at present occupied by Greeks is merely a prelude to further advance and events on the spot have fully borne out this conjecture. This constant menace of invasion which Turks ascribe not to decisions of Paris Conference but to exorbitant ambitions of Athens politicians coupled with contemplation of Greek behavior in areas occupied by them has roused the Turks of all classes from attitude of passive surliness to one of active hostility.[27]

The senior Allied naval officer at Smyrna, British Commodore Fitzmaurice recommended that "the sole prospect of peace in Aidin Vilayet is to withdraw Greek troops into Smyrna Sanjak." [28] Similarly, American High Commissioner Admiral Mark Bristol commented bitterly to Washington that "if allowed to have his way he [Venizelos] will utterly destroy possibility of decent settlement either in Balkans or in Asia Minor." [29] Time and time again, Bristol recommended that the Greeks not be allowed to stay in Smyrna. Both the British and American authorities on the scene believed that if the Greeks were allowed to remain permanently in Asia Minor, the interior provinces would revolt against the authority of Constantinople, and a peaceful settlement would be impossible.[30]

The fighting between the Greeks and the Turks centered in the town of Aidin, which was captured, lost, and recaptured by the Greeks, with the victors each time committing brutal atrocities against the civilians of the opposing nationality in the town. Though Aidin was well beyond the limits of the coastal zone the Allies had allotted to Greece, Venizelos maintained that the Greek advance had been necessary to halt the enemy and to prevent the concentration of Turkish troops. He admitted this had been done without consulting the Peace Conference, but he pleaded that there had been little choice, due to the slowness of communications between Smyrna and Paris. Yet, it soon became evident that the reoccupation of Aidin had taken place on explicit orders from Venizelos in Paris, and the Greek high commissioner in Smyrna openly acknowledged that the action should not have taken place without the permission of the Supreme Council.[31]

Definition of an Italian-Greek Boundary

On July 10, the long awaited clash between Italian and Greek troops took place. A dispatch from Smyrna reported that in defiance of the British commodore's orders, "Greek troops have crossed the river south of Aidin. . . . Shells fired by Greek artillery fell inside Italian lines." [32] The Italians protested the Greek action to the Supreme Council. In a message to Clemenceau, Tittoni asked for the creation of a buffer zone between the two forces, which would be occupied by French and British troops. Clemenceau reacted by scornfully asking in the council meeting how the Italians, who did not have permission to be in Asia Minor at all, could protest the action of those who did, at least, have the right to be there. He did not see how blame could be placed on the Greeks.[33]

Venizelos, in turn, charged that the Turks were being encouraged by the Italians to resist and that the Italian zone was being used as a base for Turkish operations against the Greeks.[34] In an appearance before the Supreme Council on July 16, he maintained that it was necessary to stop the Italian advance and that the sanjak of Smyrna alone could not be defended from the Turks because the railroads in the sanjak all had a center outside the territory. He asked that the council either give him a final definite line of demarcation or complete freedom of action. If a line of demarcation were established, he suggested that a small inter-Allied force be sent to occupy a zone between the Greeks and the Turks.[35]

Balfour immediately took up the idea of a delineation of the zones of occupation, and suggested that Allenby's staff work out the boundaries. At the same time, he obtained the explicit recognition of both the Greeks and the Italians that the armed occupation would in no way prejudge the final territorial settlement.[36]

The Italians were not at all happy about having Allenby's staff work out the boundaries of the Greek and Italian zones, for they regarded the British as being extremely pro-Greek. Although this was correct so far as Lloyd George was concerned, many within the British government and practically all of the British administration in Turkey opposed the Greek claims. The Italians, however, were not convinced that these groups could be effective, and so, in an effort to avoid a decision that they were certain would favor Greece, Tittoni suggested that Italy and Greece be given a chance to work out the problem directly.[37]

Two days later Tittoni and Venizelos reported agreement on the boundary between the Greek and Italian zones. Control of the Aidin-Smyrna railroad was to be given to Greece, but the Meander (Menderes) River would remain in the hands of the Italians. The council approved this scheme and also decided that all Allied troops, British, Greek, or Italian, in the area would be placed under the command of the Allied commander in chief, Field Marshal Allenby. This was not done without a bitter comment from Clemenceau that Allenby was really "a British officer receiving orders from the British Government rather than . . . Allied Commander in Chief." [38] Balfour reacted sharply to this criticism, but pointed out that the actual person in charge would be General Milne, who would have the job of fixing the limits of the Greek and Italian advance against the

Turks. It was decided that Turkey should be informed of this decision and required to withdraw all its forces from the area immediately. At the same time, formal assurances would be given that the limiting lines would in no way affect any final territorial settlement.

The crisis was suddenly over. Italy and Greece had worked out their joint boundary and had agreed to defer to the decision of an outsider in regard to the other limits of their zone of occupation. Balfour and Clemenceau were extremely relieved at this turn of events. Neither of them appeared, at least publicly, to be suspicious of the overnight change in attitude which the agreement reflected. Actually, the sudden settlement of this small, but thorny, boundary problem had occurred in the process of Italian-Greek negotiations leading to a much wider secret agreement on all points of discord between the two nations.

The Tittoni-Venizelos Agreement

On July 29, the Tittoni-Venizelos Agreement was signed.[39] In it the Italians promised to support Greek claims to southern Albania and Thrace in return for Greek support of Italy's desires for an Albanian mandate. Italy also agreed to cede to Greece all the Aegean islands save Rhodes. Provided its claims in Albania and Thrace were fulfilled, Greece promised to accept the provisional line between the two zones of military occupation in Asia Minor as the final territorial boundary. Italy would not develop Scalanuova, but rather would use Smyrna as a free port with no customs charges on Italian imports shipped out of the city by rail. Both nations reserved the right to "full freedom of action" if Italy did not obtain full satisfaction of its demands in Asia Minor or Greece did not realize its ambitions in Thrace and Albania. Any points on which the two nations were agreed that were not mentioned in the final peace treaty would be put into a special convention between the two powers.

In the agreement it was emphasized that this was in no sense a treaty; rather it was a definition and recognition of each nation's aims and aspirations. This distinction was made in order to keep the agreement secret, and it enabled the two states legally to bypass national regulations concerning ratification of treaties and the new League of Nations requirement that all treaties be made public. In actuality, Venizelos privately informed Clemenceau and Balfour of the negotiations on July 24. Subsequently, he consulted continually with the British, but apparently not with the French and Americans. As early as August 1, Balfour was able to inform London of the main provisions of the agreement, and Polk could report to Washington that Tittoni had admitted that a Greek-Italian agreement did exist.[40]

The Tittoni-Venizelos Agreement was taken far more seriously by Venizelos than it was by the Italians, because for him it was the first concrete written recognition of his many claims.[41] For Italy, it fulfilled its purpose when the boundary line between the Greek and Italian zones was recognized by the Supreme Council, for despite protests to the contrary, this in effect constituted a recognition by the Supreme Council of the Italian zone as a fait accompli.[42] Moreover, since the boundary was based on a negotiated agreement with Greek forces, which were in Asia Minor under the direct mandate of the Peace Conference, an aura of legitimacy for the Italian position was created.

Dispatch of a Commission of Inquiry to Smyrna

On July 18, the same day the Supreme Council approved the Italian-Greek boundary settlement, it considered Turkish complaints that charged the Greeks with massacres and with driving more than 150,000 Moslems from their homes. Clemenceau, supported by Tittoni, urged that a commission of inquiry should be sent to investigate the charges, for it was necessary to assure the Turks that the Allies had not sent the Greeks to Smyrna "merely to commit atrocities." [43] Balfour was more reticent, doubting whether the commission would do any good, although he admitted that Venizelos had told him that Greek troops had been guilty of atrocities. Nevertheless, realizing that opposition to an inquiry could produce a real issue at home, for the British government was being severely questioned in the House of Commons on the matter of Greek atrocities, Balfour acquiesced; and a commission consisting of one delegate from each of the four great powers was sent to Smyrna. Though the Greeks and Turks were allowed to send observers, these men were not permitted to be present at the actual meetings of the commission.This restriction was imposed so that witnesses would not feel intimidated while testifying. Instead, the commission was instructed that "all necessary data" should be given the observers, presumably the record of the testimony minus the names of those testifying.[44]

The reaction of the Turkish government both to the decision to limit the zones of occupation and to the sending of a commission of inquiry was favorable. Although maintaining that Greece and Italy had no rightful claim to any territory whatsoever, the grand vizier declared that the temporary stabilization of the situation would greatly increase the authority of his government, and an official Turkish communiqué stated: "Without doubt the humanitarian decision of the Peace Conference will fill everyone with gratitude."[45]

Thus, during the late summer and early fall of 1919, the Supreme Council had two authorized groups working to bring the Smyrna issue under control. The first of these was the commission under General Milne whose job was to determine the limits of the Italian and Greek zones of occupation. The second was the commission [of inquiry] that had been sent to investigate the reported Greek atrocities in Smyrna.

Report of the Milne Commission

On October 2, General Milne submitted a report to London concerning the delimitation of the Turco-Greek frontier. No mention was made of the Italian zone. In the report he pointed out that the Greeks had occupied purely Turkish territory, and he also recognized that the Turks would not be satisfied with a partial withdrawal. "Guerrilla warfare," he asserted, "will continue as long as Greek troops remain in [the] Sanjak, and any further advance will tend to create further difficulties."[46] Thus, Milne recommended that the best of a bad situation would be for the Greeks to stop where they were, adopting the best tactical line available in any given area.

The one exception to this recommendation concerned the line in the area of Aidin and the Menderes River valley. Milne noted that anti-Greek feeling was extremely high in the area and pointed out that if the current boundary were adhered to, it would mean the Greeks would have to defend Aidin on three sides against the Turks. He therefore presented two alternatives. Either the Greeks should be allowed to advance far enough to obtain a defensible frontier, or they should withdraw from the whole area and confine their occupation to the Smyrna sanjak, whereupon the abandoned territory would be occupied by an inter-Allied force. Milne advocated the latter solution: first, because any advance would be a further Greek intrusion into Turkish territory and would thus meet with fierce resistance; second, because the Greeks were in Aidin in defiance of the expressed will of the Supreme Council.[47]

The idea of an inter-Allied force at first met with a favorable reception. However, the British and Americans soon balked at Italian participation, on the familiar grounds that this could constitute a sanctioning of the Italian occupation in Asia Minor. Sir Eyre Crowe, who had replaced Lord Balfour as the British delegate to the Supreme Council, also stated that Venizelos was willing to accept the solution only if the inter-Allied force were composed of British, French, and Greek troops. To place both Italian and Greek troops in the same force, Crowe stated, would create "new difficulties." In the face of this opposition, Vittorio Scialoja, who had succeeded Tittoni at the conference table, decided to give in and reap whatever reward might be forthcoming from what Crowe praised as his "conciliatory attitude." [48]

Even so, the proposed inter-Allied force never materialized, for the French eventually decided that they could not send troops. The British, who had agreed to participate despite serious War Office reservations, immediately followed suit, whereupon the Supreme Council voted on November 12 to void the previous resolution and allow the Greeks to continue in sole occupation of the territory. At the same time the council refused, despite British protests, to allow Greek troops to undertake the strategic advances that Milne had felt were absolutely necessary if the Greeks were to remain in Aidin at all. Thus, the final solution was precisely the one that General Milne had stated should be avoided at all costs.[49]

The reasons for the failure to organize an inter-Allied force were twofold. The French, in particular, were worried about what such an occupation might eventually involve. The report of the Smyrna Commission had just been received, and one of its recommendations was the replacement of all Greek troops in Asia Minor by an inter-Allied military force. It was all too clear that participation in the small border force recommended by Milne might develop quickly into a commitment of a very different nature. The anti-Greek findings of the Smyrna Commission undoubtedly influenced the sudden French decision that "they had no troops to spare." Clemenceau commented that an inter-Allied occupation force would find itself "protecting the Greeks from attacks which they had brought on themselves." [50]

Second, disagreement over the position of General Milne generated a great amount of ill will between Britain and France in the fall and winter of 1919–20. Milne was the official commander of the forces at Constantinople. The French maintained he could no longer keep this position since he had recently been appointed commander of Anatolian Turkey. They asserted that the commander in chief of Allied Forces in the Balkans and European Turkey, General Franchet d'Esperey, was free to appoint a new Constantinople chief. Since the British did not want a Frenchman to make this appointment, they argued that Milne could designate one of his officers to "hold the fort" in Constantinople. Behind this controversy lay the fact that in Asia Minor Milne was technically subordinate to Allenby, while in Constantinople he and his troops were under Franchet d'Esperey's command.[51]

The French regarded both Allenby and Milne as British officers controlled by the British government rather than impartial Allied commanders. The British in turn made no secret of their dislike for Franchet d'Esperey and what they considered to be his pro-French, pro-Turkish, and anti-Greek efforts in the area stretching from Albania to Constantinople. The result was an effort by each side to have the other's general removed. Needless to say, neither Milne nor Franchet d'Esperey was replaced.[52]

Report of the Smyrna Commission

The report of the commission investigating the claims of Greek atrocities at Smyrna was completed on October 13 and presented to the Supreme Council on November 8.[53] It proved to be a severe indictment, not only of Greek actions, but of the decision of the Council of Four to send troops to Smyrna in the first place:

Fears of massacres of Christians were not justified. . . . The conditions of security in the Vilayet of Aidin and at Smyrna, in particular, did not at all justify the occupation of the Smyrna forts. . . . The internal situation in the Vilayet did not call for the landing of Allied troops at Smyrna. On the contrary, since the Greek landing, the situation is troubled because of the state of war existing between the Greek troops and the Turkish irregulars.[54]

The commission placed most, if not all, of the blame for the disorders and atrocities on the Greek officers' failure to control either the Greek civilians or the behavior of their own men. It did recognize that action against some of the responsible parties had been taken after the fact.

If the Peace Conference intended ultimately to cede the territory to the Greeks, the commission recommended that the latter should be given a free hand. The commission opposed this solution, however, because of the overwhelming Turkish popular majority in all the cities except Smyrna and Aivali. Instead, it recommended the replacement of Greek troops with a much smaller inter-Allied force, which might or might not have a Greek contingent. Even this force should be temporary, and the Turkish gendarmerie should be reconstituted under the command of Allied officers so that the inter-Allied force could be withdrawn as soon as possible.

The Greek observer attached to the commission, Colonel Mazarakis, took vehement exception to these recommendations. He asserted that the occupation had been necessary due to the possibility of massacres, that all incidents had taken place only after Turkish attacks on Greek military personnel, that these attacks were unexpected since the Turks were supposed to have been disarmed by the terms of the armistice, and that within the zone occupied by the Greeks perfect order existed whereas "outside of this zone there is complete anarchy." [55] Moreover, he complained that despite the instruction of the Supreme Council, he had not been allowed to see the record of all testimony given to the commission.[56]

When Venizelos was called before the Supreme Council to answer the charges formulated in the report, he was even more emphatic in denouncing the work of the commission. He protested that the Greek army had been condemned without being allowed to see the testimony or defend itself. Charging that the commission had refused to hear witnesses proposed by Colonel Mazarakis, he maintained that it had heard only one side of the story.[57]

In the Supreme Council discussion the Greek position was championed unreservedly by the British representative, Sir Eyre Crowe. Crowe deeply resented the fact that the commission technically had gone beyond the limits of its instructions and examined the justification of the presence of troops in the Smyrna area.[58] Here his colleagues were in agreement with him. One can sense in the minutes of these meetings an irritation at the commission for reviving an issue about which the powers had since come to have a good many doubts, and one that they would have preferred to bury as far as possible from the light of public display. What the commission had failed to take into account, perhaps because it was unaware of it, was that the chief reason for sending troops to Smyrna was the determination of Wilson, Clemenceau, and Lloyd George to prevent a threatened Italian occupation of the same area. Concern that the Greek population might be in danger had not been the real motivating factor; it had been, however, the official reason given to the Italians and announced to the world at large. The council hardly cared to have its public excuse exposed as a fake, especially when revealing the real reason would bring not only a charge of bad faith from the Italians but also cries of "power politics," "secret diplomacy," and "old-fashioned intrigue" from all advocates of the vaunted Wilsonian "open diplomacy." Finally, knowledge of Wilson's part in such a decision would give his enemies in America valuable ammunition in their campaign to keep the United States from joining the League of Nations, a campaign that already showed signs of being successful.

Crowe also was adamant in his insistence that had the commission heard the Greek side of the story the result would have been far different. He pointed out that the Greeks had admitted certain errors, were punishing those responsible, and that peace now reigned in the area, except for the front lines. "He felt that the Greeks had done their best and on the whole had succeeded rather well." [59]

The Supreme Council nevertheless accepted the conclusions of the commission regarding "the excesses and acts of violence committed by the Greek troops, although it apologized to Venizelos for some of the Commission's secret tactics." [60] In a note to the Greek prime minister, the council affirmed the commission's contention that the majority of blame for the disturbances rested with the Greek military authorities. The council did recognize that punitive action against some offenders had been taken. At the same time, permission was granted for Greece to remain in occupation of all the territory it had already taken, although the council specifically stated that this action must in no way be considered as prejudging a final settlement. [61]

Venizelos chose to make no further protest against the commission's findings. Rather, he registered a specific reservation on another matter. Taking issue with the stipulation regarding the council's free hand in the disposition of Smyrna, Venizelos claimed that the fact that Greek troops had occupied the territory strengthened Greece's right to it.

May I point out that, whatever be the reasons for the decision to send Greek troops to Smyrna, the Supreme Council could not be mistaken as to the interpretation given it, with good reasons, by the Greek Government and people. The Greek claims on Smyrna and the neighboring regions were not only well-known, but they had been officially formulated to the Conference, defended at length before the Supreme Council, and frankly approved by the Committee on Greek Territorial Claims. In occupying Smyrna, Greece knew that if she were not yet legally, she was at least morally, entitled to it. She did not simply send her troops as executive instruments to a foreign country. . . . Therefore, although the occupation of Smyrna did not constitute, from a strictly juridical point of view, a new right to the benefit of Greece, in fact, it has created a new situation which should not be disregarded. It does not extend the rights which Greece previously had in Smyrna, and already recognized by the Committee on Greek Affairs, but at least it corroborates them and strengthens the legitimate confidence of the Greek nation in the final decision of the Peace Conference.[62]

In a private letter to Crowe, Venizelos was even more explicit:

I do not, of course, infer that the occupation intrusted to Greece is equal to a definite recognition of her sovereignty over the occupied area. But I desire to state that when Greece was asked to proceed to this occupation, not only was there no mention made to me of its being temporary, but on the contrary, the very decision implied—though tacitly—that this occupation was the first step towards giving Greece part of western Asia Minor. Mr. Lloyd George can testify as to the correctness of my impression.[63]

Why Venizelos chose to refer specifically to Lloyd George is not altogether clear. It is quite possible that Lloyd George had notified Venizelos unofficially of the Council of Four's sentiments when the decision to send Greek troops to Smyrna was made in May. Certainly, Venizelos knew that Lloyd George would adopt as strong a pro-Greek position as possible. In any case, Venizelos was right in his assertions. It was only when the Italians were informed of the landing that the provisional restriction was made for the first time, and Venizelos's claim that he personally was not made aware of this clause until after the occupation took place was thoroughly justified.[64] Equally correct was Venizelos's impression that at the time of the landing the Allies were agreed that Greece should be given part of Asia Minor.[65]

Britain Stands by Greece

With the acceptance of the Smyrna Commission's report, the situation rested. The Greeks remained in total control of the occupied area, carrying on little more than skirmishes with the Turkish irregulars who opposed them. Within the zone they tightened their control of the administration to the point of setting up their own board of censorship. This and other actions prompted the Allied high commissioners at Constantinople to protest that the Greek high commissioner in Smyrna was acting in a completely arbitrary and unilateral fashion. This remonstrance elicited from Crowe the comment that after all, those at Smyrna knew the situation much better than those at Constantinople. Britain was making it clear that it intended to back the Greeks to the hilt.[66]

In doing this, Britain was leaving itself in a vulnerable position. It was evident by November, 1919, that it was most unlikely that the United States would accept the Constantinople mandate. This opened the possibility, at least, that the city might revert in one way or another to the Turkish state, for neither Britain nor France would permit the other to control it. If this happened, the position of favorite with the sultan would again be desirable. In committing itself to full-fledged support of Greek ambitions in Asia Minor, Britain was gambling that Greece would permanently supplant Turkey as the dominant local force in the eastern Mediterranean area. Ever more openly the British government was following what best can be described as a modified version of Catherine the Great's "Grand Scheme" of a re-created Byzantine Empire, a concept that, if unrealistic, had in Venizelos a spokesman whose power over others had been admitted by all who knew him.

The British evacuation of Armenia and Syria, the question of Thrace, and the delimitation of zones of occupation in Asia Minor were the main issues relating to the Near East that confronted the Peace Conference between July 1 and the end of November, 1919. There were, of course, other developments of importance, but they did not reach a crisis point or generate much discussion among the powers. They may, therefore, safely be left for consideration in the next two chapters when an account of the Franco-British discussions in London during December, 1919 and January, 1920, will afford an opportunity for examination of the whole range of questions that still remained to be settled.

With the opening of these London meetings, the months of stalemate and stagnation would end, and the process of formulating a peace with Turkey would again be examined in earnest and with certain sense of desperation. Certainly, the situation had deteriorated greatly in the preceding twelve months. The failure of the United States to ratify the Versailles treaty indicated that ultimately the United States would probably have to renounce any active part in the administration of a Near East settlement.[67] This opened a host of new problems for the other powers. In addition, Turkish opposition was rising in Anatolia, brought on by the Greek occupation of Smyrna. This was coupled with the powers' growing awareness of their own military weakness (especially in the face of domestic pressures for demobilization and cuts in military expenditure).[68] In November, 1919, enforcement of an eventual peace treaty seemed much more problematical than it had a year before, when a completely beaten and prostrate Turkey had signed the Armistice of Mudros.

1. See above, Chapter 4.

2. This argument was hardly justified, for Bulgaria had acquired the territory legally, and the boundaries had received full international recognition.

3. Foreign Office, F.O. 608/55/120-6-1/15321, Nicolson minute to Crowe, 7/11/19; 15322, Nicolson memorandum and Crowe minute, 7/15/19, 7/16/19; F.O. 608/33/81-1-14/16105, Frontier of Bulgaria, Report of Central Territorial Commission, 7/24/19; *Br. Doc.*, 1:173–74, S.C., 7/21/19, App. A; *U.S. Doc., P.P.C.,* 7:247–48, S.C., 7/21/19, App. A.

4. See above, pp. 86–87.

5. *U.S. Doc., P.P.C.*, 11:279, American Commissioners Plenipotentiary, 7/8/19; 7:243–46, S.C., 7/21/19, App. A; Polk Papers, Dr. 74, fol. 125, Johnson to White, 7/21/19; *Br. Doc.*, 1:169–72, S.C., 7/21/19, App. A; C. Haskins and R. Lord, *Some Problems of the Peace Conference*, pp. 283–85. For the Greek rebuttal, see *U.S. Doc., P.P.C.*; 7:378–80, 396–98, S.C., 7/29/19; *Br. Doc.*, 1:241–47, S.C., 7/29/19; "The Question of Thrace, an Official Greek View," pp. 134–37. For the Bulgarian position, see Cabinet Papers, Cab. 29/18, W.C.P. 1209, Bulgarian delegation to Peace Conference, 8/1/19; also 1235, 1237, 8/8/19; 1270, 8/23/19; 1298, 9/10/19.

6. Letter, Wilson to Lansing, 8/4/19, quoted in Evans, *U.S. and Partition*, p. 200.

7. Polk Papers, Dr. 74, fol. 126, Wilson to White, 7/25/19; fol. 127, Polk to Wilson, 7/31/19; Bliss Papers, Box 65, Diary, 7/28/19; 7/29/19.

8. Bliss Papers, Box 65, Diary, 7/28/19.

9. *U.S. Doc., P.P.C.*, 7:610, S.C., 8/7/19; *Br. Doc.*, 1:362–63, S.C., 8/7/19.

10. *U.S. Doc., P.P.C.*, 7:136–37, S.C., 7/15/19; p. 234, 7/21/19; *Br. Doc.*, 1:93, S.C., 7/15/19; p. 162, 7/21/19.

11. *U.S. Doc., P.P.C.*, 7:434–42, S.C., 7/31/19; *Br. Doc.*, 1:258–66, S.C., 7/31/19; Evans, *U.S. and Partition*, pp. 198–200. In fact an Italian-Greek agreement had been reached. See below, pp. 163–65.

12. *U.S. Doc., P.P.C.*, 7:607–11, S.C., 8/7/19; *Br. Doc.*, 1:361–64, S.C., 8/7/19.

13. *U.S. Doc., P.P.C.*, 7:610, S.C., 8/7/19; *Br. Doc.*, 1:363, S.C., 8/7/19. See also Evans, *U.S. and Partition*, pp. 199–200.

14. *U.S. Doc., P.P.C.*, 7:607–11, S.C., 8/7/19; pp. 671–72, 8/12/19; 8:48–49, 9/1/19, App. B.; Polk Papers, Dr. 74, fol. 130, Memorandum of British-American agreement, 8/7/19; fol. 131, Draft telegram, Polk to Sec. State, 8/9/19(?); fol. 136, Polk to Lansing, 8/28/19; *Br. Doc.*, 1:361–64, S.C., 8/7/19; pp. 399–402, 8/12/19; p. 593, 9/1/19, App. B; 7:748–51, map opposite p. 750, Balfour to Curzon, 9/6/19; Cabinet Papers, Cab. 23/11, W.C. 615, 8/14/19.

15. *U.S. Doc., P.P.C.*, 11:634, Polk to House (London), 8/20/19; See also ibid., 7:672, S.C., 8/12/19; Polk Papers, Dr. 74, fol. 132, Lansing to Polk, 8/12/19; Polk to Lansing (3), 8/15/19; fol. 134, Polk to Lansing, 8/19/19; fol. 136, Polk to Lansing, 8/23/19; 8/25/19.

16. *U.S. Doc., P.P.C.*, 11:409, American Commissioners Plenipotentiary, 9/3/19; 8:35–37, S.C., 9/1/19; pp. 50–51, App. C; Polk Papers, Dr. 74, fol. 136, Lansing to Polk, 8/28/19; Dr. 78, fol. 13, Letter, Polk to Lansing, 8/30/19; *Br. Doc.*, 1:589–91, S.C., 9/1/19; pp. 594–95, App. C.

17. *U.S. Doc., P.P.C.*, 8:55–57, 63–67, S.C., 9/2/19; *Br. Doc.*, 1:597–98, 603–4, S.C., 9/2/19; Foreign Office, F.O., 608/55/120-6-3/18656, Norman to Curzon, 9/6/19.

18. *U.S. Doc., P.P.C.*, 7:193, S.C., 7/18/19; 11:425–26, Polk to American commissioners, 9/23/19.

19. Nicolson, *Peacemaking*, p. 343, 5/19/19; *U.S. Doc., P.P.C.*, 5:723, C. of Four, 5/19/19; 6:712–14, 6/26/19; Mantoux, *Conseil des Quatre*, 2:532–34, 6/26/19; Foreign Office, F.O., 608/93/362-1-2/15338, Calthorpe to Balfour, 7/13/19; Sonnino Papers, Reel 46, no. 628, Sonnino to military section of Italian Peace delegation, 6/1/19; no. 666, Sonnino to Paris, London, Athens and Peace delegation, 6/7/19.

20. *Br. Doc.*, 4:4–6, S.C., 6/28/19, App. 1. The British ambassador to Rome, Sir Rennell Rodd, was extremely apprehensive of the new Nitti government, which he regarded as anti-British and rather pro-German. By July 2, however, he had changed his mind completely. Balfour Papers, MSS 49745, Rodd to Balfour, 6/19/19, 6/23/19, 7/2/19. For a discussion of the Orlando government's demise, see Mayer, *Politics of Peacemaking*, pp. 783–86.

21. Foreign Office, F.O. 608/39/97-1-5/14807, Balfour to Curzon, 7/1/19. See also *Br. Doc.*, 4:10, Four Power Meeting, 7/3/19, n.3.

22. *Br. Doc.*, 4:10, Four Power Meeting, 7/3/19. Lansing's account of this meeting makes no mention of such an Italian attitude. Compare ibid., pp. 10–12, with *U.S. Doc., P.P.C.*, 7:17–19, Four Power meeting, 7/3/19. See also T. Tittoni and V. Scialoja, *L'Italia alla Conferenza della Pace, Discorsi et Documenti*, p. 40, Tittoni to the Italian Chamber of Deputies, 9/27/19; K. Ziemke, *Die neue Türkei, 1914–1929*, p. 121.

23. *Br. Doc.*, 4:16–26, Tittoni to Lloyd George, 7/7/19. See also ibid., p. 11, n. 10; 1:84, S.C., 7/12/19, n. 8; Tittoni and Scialoja, *Italia alla Conferenza*, pp. 119–23, 7/7/19.

24. State Department, Turkey, 867.00/887, Ravndal to Sec. State, 6/10/19; 867.00/891, Ravndal to Sec. State, 6/28/19; Miller, *Diary*, 18:514–18, 6/21/19; *Times* (London), 6/6/19, 6/20/19, 6/24/19, 7/2/19; Sonnino Papers, Reel 27, no. 1612, Biancheri to Italian Peace delegation, 6/4/19. For a discussion of the Turkish resistance movement, see below, Chapter 10.

25. Foreign Office, F.O. 608/104/383-1-6/12352 (n.d.); 11984, 6/6/19. These files contain reports from Canadian, Swedish, and American sources all attesting to Greek atrocities at Smyrna. Ronaldshay, *Curzon*, 3:267–68, Curzon to Balfour, 6/20/19; *Times* (London), 6/27/19, 7/5/19, 7/11/19, 8/27/19, 9/19/19; Bristol Papers, Box 16, Report for week of July 20, 1919. *Parliamentary Debates* (Commons), 5th ser., 116:1996, 6/4/19; 118:303–4, 6/26/19.

26. *Br. Doc.*, 4:655–56, Webb to Curzon, 6/28/19. See also ibid., p. 657, Calthorpe to Curzon, 6/29/19.

27. Ibid., pp. 658–59, Calthorpe to Balfour, 7/1/19; *Times* (London), 7/1/19.

28. *Br. Doc.*, 4:659–60, Calthorpe to Balfour, 7/4/19.

29. Bristol Papers, Box 27, Bristol to Paris, 7/30/19.

30. Ibid., Box 16, Diary, Reports for weeks of 6/1/19, 6/22/19; 6/29/19; Box 27, Bristol to Paris, 8/5/19; State Department, Turkey, 867.00/916, Bristol to Sec. State, 8/28/19; Foreign Office, F.O. 608/111/385-1-14/11128, Calthorpe to Balfour, 5/27/19; Lloyd George Papers, F 46/10/7, General Staff memorandum regarding Greeks in Asia Minor, 7/10/19. See also *Br. Doc.*, 4:680–81, 682–83, 684–86, 730–32, 733–34, 751–53, 765, 781, 792, 809, 870–71, 873–76.

31. *Br. Doc.*, 4:658, Balfour to Curzon, 6/29/19; p. 665, Calthorpe to Balfour, 7/5/19, and n.2; p. 666, Calthorpe to Curzon, 7/7/19, and n.1; p. 862, Crowe to Curzon, 11/10/19, enclosure 2; *Times* (London), 7/3/19, 7/8/19; H. Luke, *Cities and Men: An Autobiography,* 2:58.

32. *Br. Doc.*, 4:680, Calthorpe to Curzon, 7/10/19.

33. Foreign Office, F.O. 608/93/362-1-2/15541, French representatives to Clemenceau, transmitting message from Rome, 7/12/19; *Br. Doc.*, 1:83–84, S.C., 7/12/19; pp. 86–87, App. D; *U.S. Doc., P.P.C.*, 8:121–22, S.C., 7/12/19; p. 128, App. D.

34. There was some basis for this. In the summer of 1919, the Turkish grand vizier sought out the Italian high commissioner, Count Carlo Sforza, and asked him to have Italy provoke a plebiscite in Smyrna, which would then vote overwhelmingly for an Italian occupation. When the leaders of the new Turkish resistance heard of this, they asked Sforza not to, for they stated that if Italy took over Smyrna, the Turkish resistance would have to fight Italy, and this they did not want to do. In turn, Sforza apparently offered to support Mustapha Kemal in opposing Greeks in Smyrna. As early as February, 1919, Sforza purportedly told Kemal: "You may be sure that if you are in trouble this embassy is at your disposal." Kinross, *Ataturk,* p. 167; Sforza, *Modern Europe,* p. 362; Foreign Office, F.O. 608/115/385-1-28/16138, Calthorpe to F.O., 6/26/19.

35. *Br. Doc.*, 1:105, S.C., 7/15/19; App. H., p. 106, 7/16/19; 4:680–82, Balfour to Calthorpe, 7/11/19; *U.S. Doc., P.P.C.*, 7:152–53, S.C., 7/15/19, App. H; pp. 154–55, 7/16/19; G. Bourdon, "The Italians in the Ottoman Empire." For earlier correspondence of Venizelos with the Peace Conference on this problem, see Frangulis, *Crise Mondiale,* 2:70, Venizelos to P.C., 6/18/19; p. 73, 6/20/19; p. 75, 6/23/19; p. 77, 7/10/19.

36. *Br. Doc.*, 1:107–8, S.C., 7/16/19; *U.S. Doc., P.P.C.*, 7:155–56, 7/16/19; Balfour Papers, MSS 49752, Suggestions as to procedure with regard to troops in Asia Minor, 7/17/19.

37. *Br. Doc.*, 1:108–9, S.C., 7/16/19; 4:686–88, Balfour to Curzon, 7/16/19; *U.S. Doc., P.P.C.*, 7:156–58, S.C., 7/16/19.

38. *Br. Doc.*, 1:132–36, S.C., 7/18/19; 4:691–92, Balfour to Curzon, 7/21/19 and n.3; pp. 717–19; Calthorpe to Curzon, 8/5/19; pp. 719–20, Curzon to Balfour, 8/7/19; Balfour Papers, MSS 49752, Balfour to C.I.G.S., 7/24/19; *U.S. Doc., P.P.C.*, 7:194–98, S.C., 7/18/19; Frangulis, *Crise Mondiale,* 2:82; *Times* (London), 8/9/19.

39. For the text, see Giannini, *Documenti per la Storia,* p. 17.

40. Balfour Papers, MSS 49750, Notes of a private conversation between M. Clemenceau, M. Venizelos, and myself, 7/24/19; State Department, A.C.N.P., 185,5134/17A, White to Sec. State, 7/29/19; Foreign Office, F.O. 608/54/120-3-12/17010, Balfour to Curzon, 8/1/19; Lloyd George Papers, F 89/3/20, Kerr to Lloyd George, 8/4/19; Polk Papers, Dr. 74, fol. 128, Polk to Wilson and Lansing, 8/1/19, 8/5/19.

41. For a pro-Greek interpretation see Frangulis, *Crise Mondiale,* 2:93–98, 102–3.

42. *Br. Doc.*, 1:135, S.C., 7/18/19.

43. Ibid., pp. 130–31; *U.S. Doc., P.P.C.*, 7:191–92, S.C., 7/18/19.

44. Foreign Office, F.O. 608/86/399-1-6, File relating to Inter-Allied Commission to Smyrna; Cabinet Papers, Cab. 29/27, M. 467, de France to S.C., 8/11/19; *Parliamentary Debates*

(Commons), 5th ser., 117:741, 7/1/19; col. 1133, 7/3/19; *Times* (London), 7/3/19, 7/4/19; *Br. Doc.*, 4:652, Curzon to Balfour, 6/26/19; p. 654, Balfour to Curzon, 6/28/19, also nn. 2,3; 1:130–32, 138–39, 142, S.C., 7/18/19; p. 165, 7/21/19; p. 188, 7/25/19; p. 413, 418, 8/14/19; p. 446, 8/20/19; *U.S. Doc., P.P.C.*, 7:191–92, 200–201, 207, S.C., 7/18/19; pp. 238–39, 249–50, 7/21/19; pp. 687–88, 693, 8/14/19; p. 730, 8/20/19; H. C. Woods, "Sèvres, Before and After," p. 548.

45. *Br. Doc.*, 1:343, S.C., 8/6/19; 4:718, Calthorpe to Curzon, 8/5/19; Pech, *Alliés et Turquie*, p. 76, 8/4/19.

46. *Br. Doc.*, 1:879, S.C., 10/7/19, App. H.

47. Ibid., pp. 879–80; *U.S. Doc., P.P.C.*, 8:531–33, S.C., 10/7/19.

48. *Br. Doc.*, 1:868–72, S.C., 10/17/19; *U.S. Doc., P.P.C.*, 8:512–17, S.C., 10/7/19. The Turkish reaction to the Milne line was essentially negative. The government at Constantinople indicated that it expected Turkish resistance to continue. Foreign Office, F.O. 608/271/10/136, Milne to Djemal Pasha, 11/3/19; Djemal Pasha to Milne, 11/5/19, 11/15/19.

49. *Br. Doc.*, 4:827, Curzon to Crowe, 10/18/19; pp. 833–34, Crowe to Curzon, 10/20/19; p. 852, Curzon to Crowe, 11/3/19; p. 856, Crowe to Curzon, 11/5/19; p. 877, 11/12/19; 2:264– 67, S.C., 11/10/19; pp. 287–89, 295–96, 11/12/19; Cabinet Papers, Cab. 24/90, G.T. 8396, Churchill memorandum, 10/23/19; *U.S. Doc., P.P.C.*, 9:78–84, S.C., 11/10/19; pp. 121–24, 131–33, 11/12/19.

50. *Br. Doc.*, 2:267, S.C., 11/10/19.

51. In the Supreme Council on July 16, Clemenceau tried unsuccessfully to maintain that Allenby's command included Syria and Mesopotamia but not Anatolia. Ibid., p. 108, 7/16/19; *U.S. Doc., P.P.C.*, 8:157, S.C., 7/16/19.

52. Of course, the real issue at stake was the question of influence over the Turkish government at Constantinople. For documents pertaining to this matter, see Cabinet Papers, Cab. 23/42, I.W.C., 41, 12/3/18; Cab. 24/88, G.T. 8179A, Lloyd George to Clemenceau, 9/16/19; Foreign Office, F.O. 608/108/385-1-1, General file on Franchet d'Esperey affair, 1919; *Br. Doc.*, 2:129–30; 4:255; 719–20, 728–29, 766, 768–71, 775–77, 783, 827, 834, 835, 856, 871, 873; 7:458–62; Callwell, *Henry Wilson*, 2:171, 2/28/19; Azan, *Franchet d'Esperey*, p. 248; Adkisson, *Britain and the Kemalist Movement*, pp. 82–83.

53. The text of the report in the original French may be found in *Br. Doc.*, 2:237–58, S.C., 11/8/19. An English translation is in *U.S. Doc., P.P.C.*, 9:44–73, S.C., 11/8/19. The report may also be found in the Bristol Papers, Box 27. For a discussion of the commission's work and of the report, see P. Buzanski, "The Interallied Investigation of the Greek Invasion of Smyrna, 1919," pp. 325–43.

54. *U.S. Doc., P.P.C.*, 9:47, S.C., 11/8/19.

55. Ibid., p. 68; *Br. Doc.*, 2:255, S.C., 11/8/19.

56. The commission had been instructed originally to provide the observers with a record of all testimony taken by the commission, but it refused to do so on the grounds that much of the testimony was given only on specific promise that it would be kept secret. The Supreme Council reluctantly backed up this decision, declaring that it could not contradict a promise given by the commission. *Br. Doc.*, 1:837, S.C., 9/30/19; 2:7, 10/16/19; *U.S. Doc., P.P.C.*, 8:463–64, S.C., 9/30/19; 9:68, 10/16/19. Foreign Office file F.O. 608/86/349-1-6 contains protests from both Greeks and Turks regarding the role of the observers. Lloyd George believed that the Greeks, as one of the Allied powers, should have been allowed to participate in all commission meetings and to cross examine all witnesses. Cabinet Papers, Cab. 21/174, Hankey to Crowe, 9/17/19.

57. *Br. Doc.*, 2:231–34, S.C., 11/8/19; *U.S. Doc., P.P.C.*, 9:38–42, S.C., 11/8/19.

58. *Br. Doc.*, 1:837, S.C., 9/30/19; 2:262–67, 11/10/19; 4:857–69, Crowe to Curzon, 11/10/19, and enclosures 1–4; *U.S. Doc., P.P.C.*, 8:463–64, S.C., 9/20/19; 9:37–38, 78–84, 11/10/19.

59. *Br. Doc.*, 2:263–64, S.C., 11/10/19; *U.S. Doc., P.P.C.*, 9:79–80, S.C., 11/10/19.

60. *Br. Doc.*, 2:295, S.C., 11/12/19; *U.S. Doc., P.P.C.*, 9:132, S.C., 11/12/19.

61. *Br. Doc.*, 2:287–89, 295–96, S.C., 11/12/19; *U.S. Doc., P.P.C.*, 9:121–24, 131–33, S.C., 11/12/19.

62. *Br. Doc.*, 2:352–53, S.C., 11/18/19, App. B.

63. Ibid., 4:904–5, Crowe to Curzon, 11/26/19, enclosure. See also the *Times* (London), 12/4/19; Frangulis, *Crise Mondiale*, 2:84; *Current History* 10 (August, 1919):247.

64. *Br. Doc.*, 4:204, Curzon to Crowe, 11/26/19.

65. See above, Chapters 4 and 5.

66. This was done over the protests of Sir Henry Wilson, who records that he told Curzon that "if the Foreign Office goes on backing Greece against Turkey, we shall be in trouble all over the Near East." Callwell, *Henry Wilson*, 2:214, 11/7/19; Foreign Office, F.O. 608/103/383-1-3/20213, Greek delegation to Clemenceau, 11/4/19; 21120, Greek administration at Smyrna, report from Constantinople, 12/10/19; *Br. Doc.*, 4:857, Robeck to Curzon, 11/7/19; 2:275, S.C., 11/11/19; pp. 296–98, 11/12/19; p. 378, 11/21/19, n. 1; *U.S. Doc., P.P.C.*, 9:95, S.C., 11/11/19; p. 133, 11/12/19.

67. The Senate failed to ratify the Versailles treaty in a vote taken on November 19, 1919. On November 16, Lansing cabled Polk that the "present state of the public mind" made it impossible to conceive of American acceptance of any mandate anywhere. Polk Papers, Dr. 78, fol. 16, Lansing to Polk, 11/17/19. For a good, brief account of the ratification conflict, see D. M. Smith, *The Great Departure; The United States and World War I, 1914–1920*, chap. 10.

68. For a summary of these pressures in various Allied countries, see T. Williams, "America's Duty to Turkey," pp. 215–16.

VIII ❊ ANGLO-FRENCH PRIVATE NEGOTIATIONS

O N NOVEMBER 10, 1919, President Raymond Poincaré of France, accompanied by his foreign minister, Stéphen Pichon, paid a four-day visit to Britain. According to Curzon, "Within the hour of the arrival of the French Presidential party in London, M. Pichon attended, by appointment, to see me in the Foreign Office." [1] Pichon proposed that private British-French discussions should be initiated immediately regarding the Turkish peace settlement:

America having disappeared from the scene as a factor in the settlement of the East, and all chance of an American mandate for any portion of the Turkish Empire having, in his opinion, vanished, there remained only two parties whose interests had seriously to be considered and reconciled, namely, Great Britain and France. . . . Conversations must take place, and an understanding must be arrived at, before the Peace Conference addressed itself to the Turkish question.[2]

To all of this Curzon agreed "with gratification," [3] and it was decided to hold the discussions in London during December.

Both the French and the English regarded Turkish affairs with increasing anxiety. Curzon expressed this sense of urgency when he told Pichon:

By next spring, . . . there might very likely be no Turkish Government to deal with at all. It was more than possible that there would be no one to accept the sort of treaty which the Allies would desire to impose. It was even conceivable that the defeated Turks, who would then be one of the few parties on the scene with a serious force available, would declare war upon the Allies, and dare them to enforce their terms. If this were the case, I did not see how we were to conquer Asia Minor, or who was to do it; and the ignominious result might be that the weakest and most abject of our foes would end by achieving triumph.[4]

The evident deterioration of the authority of the government at Constantinople, and the rising power of resistance elements in Anatolia, now known as the Nationalist movement, meant that the longer a peace treaty was delayed, the more difficult it would be to institute and enforce.[5]

Anglo-French Tensions

The Anglo-French conversations on the Near East settlement took place in an atmosphere of surface cordiality. In reality, at the time they began, on no other issue were the relations of the two allies so strained. Each suspected the other of entering into secret consultations and negotiations with the Turks. It was increasingly evident that the interests of the various European nations in Turkey were tending to create just the split among them for which the Turks had so long hoped.[6]

Much of the difficulty stemmed from the pro-British manifestations of the Turkish government at Constantinople. Despite the fact that Turkey had suffered defeat mainly at the hands of British troops, and despite Britain's open and staunch support of Greek and Armenian ambitions, the Turkish government remained eager to establish close relations with Britain. As early as March 30, 1919, the grand vizier told Admiral Calthorpe that Turkey would submit "to England, but to England alone."[7] At that time he proposed a rough draft for a treaty of alliance between the two nations. No response was made by the British. During the course of the summer, reports from British agents in Turkey continually stressed that the Turks would "willingly accept" only a British mandate, or if that were impossible, an American one.[8]

The Secret Anglo-Turk Treaty

Much uncertainty has existed about Anglo-Turkish negotiations in the late summer of 1919. According to subsequent accounts, the Turkish advances were well received by the British. On September 12, 1919, a three-man British delegation negotiated a secret treaty of alliance with the Turkish grand vizier, Damad Ferid Pasha. In it the British purportedly agreed to guarantee the territorial integrity of the new Turkey and to sustain its requests before the Peace Conference. Constantinople would remain in Turkish hands and would be the seat of the caliphate. Britain would furnish a strong military force to protect minorities and crush all revolutionary movements. In return, Turkey supposedly agreed to the establishment of an independent Kurdistan and relinquished all rights in Egypt and Cyprus. The sultan would use the spiritual powers of the caliphate to create acceptance of British authority in Syria, Mesopotamia, and elsewhere. Finally, the Straits were to be under British surveillance.[9]

In the past, credence has generally been given to accounts of this treaty;[10] now it seems highly unlikely that it ever really was negotiated and signed. It is true that rumors were widespread in Constantinople in August, 1919, that the British were about to come to an agreement with the sultan.[11] It is also clear that the Turkish government would have welcomed such an event. On September 8, the grand vizier complained to Admiral Webb that failure to reach a peace settlement was creating great difficulties:

. . . the only way by which it seemed to him [the grand vizier] it might be possible to shorten it would be by coming to a secret understanding with Great Britain. I [Webb] at once replied that such an idea was quite out of the question, we would never dream of taking any step except in conjunction with our Allies, and what would they say if they found that His Majesty's Government had indulged in any conversation with the Turkish Government.[12]

The British remained constant in this attitude, and official approval of this policy was given by Curzon on September 23.[13] This would indicate that a secret agreement, though proposed by the Turks, was never considered seriously by the British. Since later accounts of the treaty all emanated from Turkish sources, it is possible that the Turkish government, while officially denying the existence of such a treaty, planted false information in an attempt to create a split between France and England.

Both the American and French high commissioners in Constantinople obtained summaries of the terms of the alleged agreement by December, 1919, and the French newspaper *Eclair* published the purported text on February 11, 1920. News of the agreement confounded the Foreign Office, which launched a full scale investigation during the latter part of January. This investigation disclosed that not only were no two accounts in agreement as to whom the British agents had been, but that no authorization had been granted by anyone for the conclusion of such an arrangement. The Foreign Office refused to credit the document as anything more than a forgery aimed at creating trouble between the British and the French.[14]

Another factor puts the existence of this secret treaty in doubt. Historians have maintained that from September on the British were no longer anxious to expel the Turks from Constantinople and that therefore this treaty was in complete agreement with British foreign policy at that time.[15] This is not the case. The Anglo-Turk agreement would have gone against all that the chief architects of British foreign policy were attempting to do. Throughout the latter half of 1919, Lloyd George and Curzon constantly advocated the expulsion of the Turks from Europe. In this they were so successful that the French were finally persuaded to agree in the December conversations. It was not until January 6, 1920, that Britain abandoned this policy of excluding Turkey from Europe and then only because of its defeat in a cabinet meeting despite the vehement support given it by Curzon and Lloyd George.[16] It is impossible to believe that these men would have worked so hard to convince the French in December, thus opening themselves to such a thoroughly humiliating defeat at home, had they intended as far back as September to agree ultimately to leave the Turks in Constantinople.

The Picot-Kemal Conversations

To the French, even before they became aware of the supposed existence of an Anglo-Turkish treaty, the pro-British attitude of the government in Constantinople was obvious. One can hardly blame the French for assuming that this was reciprocated by the British.[17] Partly for this reason, but also because of the exposed position of French forces occupying Cilicia, Georges Picot, who had just been relieved as high commissioner in Syria, returned to France by way of Sivas where he met with the leader of the Nationalist movement, Mustapha Kemal Pasha, on December 5 and 6.[18]

In these discussions Kemal stated his willingness to accept a French economic mandate over all of Anatolia. He also reiterated statements previously made to the Harbord Commission indicating his readiness to accept American aid if it were available.[19] He categorically refused to consider help from Britain, but made it clear that what he sought was the assistance of a single power, preferably France. With great delight Picot agreed that French advisors should be part of the Interior, Finance, and Justice Departments, that they might even be Turks chosen by the French, and that certainly they would be there not "to control, but to collaborate." [20]

However, when Picot brought up the subject of Cilicia, the discussion was not nearly so amicable. Kemal refused to renounce his claim to it, describing Cilicia as a "piece of our body." [21] Picot then conceded France's willingness to withdraw its troops provided three conditions were fulfilled. These consisted of the right of supervision of local administration and protection of minorities, reorganization of the police under French supervision, and Franco-Turkish economic collaboration with a French monopoly of all economic concessions. Of these, Kemal agreed only to the police reorganization; as to administrative supervision, he would admit only that French consuls should have a special interest and influence in the area. Even for these concessions he demanded a unilateral French guarantee of the integrity of the Ottoman Empire against possible depredations by the British and Italians.[22]

To this, of course, the French could not agree and the issue was dropped. Kemal probably had hoped that his conciliatory attitude regarding French preeminence in Anatolia would lead the French to reciprocate in Cilicia. The French, however, were not willing to concede something they had for something so tentative, especially when any Anatolian "mandate" would depend on the success of Kemal's movement and the consent of the other Allied powers. Until this came about, France would evacuate Cilicia only with guarantees of its future position there, which Kemal was quite unwilling to give.[23]

Nevertheless, the conversations did ease tensions relative to Cilicia, and for over two months after these meetings Nationalist protests regarding French behavior in Cilicia, which until that time had been a regular occurrence, ceased.[24] It is interesting to note that the last of these protests, sent a week before Kemal's meeting with Picot, was not read by the British Foreign Office until December 31, at which time it received the following notations:

M. Picot's visit to Mustafa Kemal at Sivas, of which the W[ar] O[ffice] have now received sure confirmation, does not seem to have been very effective.
We can well afford, I think, to encourage French penetration in Asia Minor. It is likely to keep their hands very full and may compel them to slacken their more objectionable activities elsewhere.
                                                      G. Kidston, Dec. 31/19
                                                      J.A.C. Tilley, 31/19
They do not realize what they are in for.[25]
                                                      C. 1/1

It is not clear what the basis was for an interpretation that the Picot-Kemal conversations had failed. Certainly it could not be drawn from reading a document that had originated a week before the meeting took place. Evidence that the French felt very differently can be found in the record of the December negotiations.

The December Discussions

When the Anglo-French negotiations opened in December, it seemed as if an Anglo-French split had occurred. The British, well aware that discussions of some sort between Kemal and Picot had taken place, tended to interpret it as evidence "that French policy in [the] Near East is now to win over Arabs and Turks with the view of throwing [the] combination against British influence and interests." [26] The French, in turn, were extremely suspicious of Britain's pro-Greek attitude, as well as of what they took to be signs of a rapprochement between Britain and the government at Constantinople. The haste and urgency evidenced by the representatives of the two nations regarding a Near East settlement was due not so much to fears of Turkish collapse as to anxiety for the future of Anglo-French relations. It was imperative that the rupture be healed before it became incurable by becoming public. [27]

Clemenceau's brief visit to London had been brought about by a desire on the part of the two prime ministers to examine the general state of European affairs in the light of the American Senate's refusal to ratify the Treaty of Versailles.[28] Therefore, only one of the meetings with Lloyd George had to do with the problems of the Near East. Almost without exception, the two leaders referred matters to Curzon and Philippe Berthelot, chief secretary of political and commercial affairs at the Quai d'Orsay.[29] These two were instructed to "examine various questions connected with Turkey and prepare alternative drafts for consideration." [30] It was in their meetings that agreement on various topics was achieved.

Anatolian Mandates

Immediately after his arrival in London on the morning of December 11, Clemenceau met privately and informally with Lloyd George. Their discussion, covering a wide range of topics, was communicated by Lloyd George to a conference of British ministers held at 1:00 p.m.[31] Thus, when the conversations officially opened at 3:00 p.m. that afternoon, agreement on certain issues was almost instantaneous. As soon as the meeting got underway, Clemenceau announced:

To start with, the system of mandates should be renounced so far as Asia Minor is concerned. When he spoke of renouncing the system of mandates for Turkey, he did not wish to include the Arab part of the former Turkish Empire. In discussing the question from a Turkish point of view, however, he felt that he ought not to include Cilicia as part of Syria, since the Turks did not admit that it was part of Syria. He, therefore, asked whether Mr. Lloyd George agreed with him in abandoning the system of mandates for Turkish Asia, excluding the portions inhabited by Arabs.[32]

Lloyd George was only too happy to agree to this proposal, although it undoubtedly had come as a surprise, for as late as November 24, Lloyd George had told Polk that "the French are anxious to keep Constantinople and Asia Minor intact, and rather hope for a mandate themselves."[33]

By making this seemingly casual agreement, the statesmen were taking a rather definite stand not only on the future of the Turkish state but also on the problem of Greek and Italian ambitions in Asia Minor. The reasons are apparent from Lloyd George's account of their private conversation that morning. Now that it was clear that the United States would not play an active role in carrying out either the European or Near Eastern peace treaties, neither Clemenceau nor Lloyd George had any compunctions about negotiating a settlement that would be completely favorable to his nation. Both men were thoroughly out of patience with Italy, chiefly because of its intransigence over the Adriatic question. Lloyd George undoubtedly felt that French willingness to give up the "unofficial" French mandate scheme, which France had supported ever since Wilson had proposed it the previous spring, far outweighed the blow a renunciation of mandates would give to Venizelos's ambitions in Asia Minor. In any case, this decision did not preclude out-and-out annexation of territory by Greece, and an agreement that prevented extended Greek control in Asia Minor would be greeted enthusiastically by many within the British government who had long been critical of Lloyd George's support of Greek ambitions in Asia Minor. In addition, and this must have been very important to Lloyd George: "It further appeared that he [Clemenceau] did not really care whether the Sultan was allowed to remain in CONSTANTINOPLE or to be kept out of it: he would however prefer to have him there, with a joint Anglo-French control of the Turkish Empire."[34] It was clear that Clemenceau had come to London in a conciliatory mood regarding Constantinople.

Two factors probably had much to do with Clemenceau's cooperative attitude. The first was his concern for British support in enforcing
the European settlement, especially in the area of reparations, where
the issue of proportionate national shares of German payments
remained to be solved. The apparent failure by the United States
to accept its role in previously negotiated guarantees of French
territorial boundaries against German aggression had also released
Britain from any obligations under this agreement. This was highly
upsetting to Clemenceau, who was determined that the Anglo-French
alliance should be preserved. Speaking to Lloyd George, he commented that "he realized that, owing to America's defection, everything now depended on Great Britain. He anticipated a revolution
in Italy, as there was no one there with any authority at all . . . ;
[he] thought that Italy would drop out of the Alliance." [35]

Second, until this time, the French had been making a rather
unsuccessful effort to gain favor with the sultan. Now, however, Picot
had just completed his meetings with Mustapha Kemal, in which
a virtual French economic mandate in Anatolia had been promised.
It would be logical to assume that this had much to do with Clemenceau's change of mind. Also, the same explanation would account
for his statement to Lloyd George regarding Cilicia. Although somewhat ambiguous, it appears that Clemenceau was renouncing a
mandate over this area because the Turks claimed it as rightfully
theirs. This seemingly incomprehensible position becomes more understandable, however, if it is looked at in the light of the Picot-
Kemal discussions concerning an Anatolian economic mandate and
Cilicia. The French policy change during December and January
was more than likely due, at least in part, to considerations unknown
to the British.

Greek, Italian, and French Claims to Asia Minor

The decision to do away with mandates in Anatolia made it imperative that France and Britain should agree on the disposition of
Greek and Italian claims in that area. The report of the Smyrna
Commission, plus Britain's support of Greek ambitions, had turned
the French completely against the Greeks, and Clemenceau told

Lloyd George that he believed it had been a mistake to send Greek troops to Smyrna. The Greeks should be required to leave before they were driven out by the Turks. Suitable compensation could be arranged for in Thrace.[36] Even the British, despite Crowe's impassioned backing of Venizelos in the Supreme Council debates, were beginning to have second thoughts. A memorandum from the Foreign Office on December 12, stated that "the problem would no doubt have been simplified if the Greek occupation of the Smyrna area had not been sanctioned by the Supreme Council, at any rate at a date so long before the final Turkish settlement." [37] This view had long been held by Lord Curzon and Winston Churchill, who had opposed the Smyrna landings from the start. Therefore, in the December meetings the British suggested that Smyrna be returned to Turkish sovereignty, but with guarantees to ensure almost complete autonomy and self-government by the local Greek population. The governor of the area would have to be Greek. To this Berthelot readily agreed.[38]

This move was a complete reversal of the original British position relative to Smyrna. Yet in no way did it signify a lessening of the pro-Greek attitude on the part of Britain. Hand in hand with this agreement went the condition that all Thrace up to the Enos-Midia line should be ceded to Greece. This would include Adrianople, where reverse guarantees similar to those at Smyrna would protect the Turkish population. Both Curzon and Berthelot felt that a compromise of this sort would be acceptable to Venizelos.[39]

That this alternative solution was suggested and accepted is evidence of British and French lack of concern for the position and desires of President Wilson. Wilson had been the chief opponent of Greek annexation in Thrace, and because of his protests the matter had been held in abeyance. Now it was evident that his opposition was no longer thought to be of any real significance.

The two powers obviously recognized that it would be difficult to allow Greece either territorial annexations or a mandate in Asia Minor if similar privileges were to be denied to Italy. Yet, both Clemenceau and Lloyd George believed that Italy was not that anxious to maintain a physical presence in Anatolia. In fact, Clemenceau stated, he thought "that the Italians were ready to clear out of Asia Minor if the Greeks did the same." [40] Thus, by forcing a Greek withdrawal, all of Anatolia could be returned to at least the nominal control of the sultan. At the same time, in order to meet what both the British and French admitted were legitimate Italian claims in Asia Minor, the French accepted a British suggestion that Italy be accorded a sphere of economic priority in southern Anatolia. This would not prevent other nations from investing in the area, but would give the Italians first option on any economic investment proposed.[41]

As to Cilicia, the French, while stating their intention of maintaining control over the forts in the Taurus mountains, declared they would try to arrive at a plan whereby the French could remain in Cilicia under some form of nominal Turkish sovereignty.[42] This corresponded directly with the stand taken by Picot in his conversations with Kemal, and it is evident that the French regarded the issue as open to negotiation. These negotiations, moreover, would be with Kemal, for there is no indication that the French ever broached the matter to the government at Constantinople.

Constantinople and the Straits

The question of Constantinople and the Straits had purposely been held in abeyance during the preceding months while the European powers waited hopefully for the United States to take the mandate for the proposed international state. The European states had agreed to the American mandate chiefly because it seemed an easy way to solve a complicated problem. By December, 1919, when it had become obvious that American participation would not be forthcoming, all the old religious, political, and commercial issues reappeared in a more intensified form. Constantinople had always been a bone of contention between the British and the French. Now that a third power could not be called in, it was necessary to face the issue.

The central question was whether the Turks should be left in Constantinople or forced completely out of Europe, with the capital reestablished at Brusa. In June, both Clemenceau and Wilson had supported the latter scheme on the assumption that America would undertake the Constantinople mandate. Lloyd George, though personally in agreement, was forced because of dissension within the British cabinet to take a noncommittal, if acquiescent, position.[43] However, with America's defection, attitudes changed. In December Clemenceau sought to leave the Turks in Constantinople while Lloyd George and Curzon were much more insistent that the Turkish government should wield no political power on the European side of the Straits. Fundamental to this clash was the fact that both the British and the French recognized that France would be the nation most likely to exert a preponderant influence in the new Turkish state because of its prewar monopoly of industrial and monetary investment within Turkey. Consequently, France sought to expand the scope of the Turkish state in order to strengthen it, whereas Britain wished to restrict its authority wherever possible.[44]

The desire to push the Turks from Constantinople was consistent with Britain's pro-Greek policy. Any lessening of Turkish power would automatically increase Greek prestige and authority in the eastern Mediterranean. Britain, as the largest naval power, stood to have the greatest authority on any Straits commission. Should an international control commission ever cease to function, with the Turks out of the city it would be possible to turn the area over to Greece. Either way, Britain could continue to wield the inexpensive, indirect control over the Straits that it had so long achieved through a similar policy with the Ottoman government.

Why should Britain pursue this policy when the government at the Porte openly manifested its preference for British control and supervision? The answer would seem to be twofold. First, the British, already committed to their Greek scheme, realized that it would be impossible to pose as the principal friend of both Greece and Turkey for very long. Second, by December, 1919, the British command in Constantinople had very little use for the sultan or his regime. They recognized that the government was unable to control Anatolia and were convinced that it could not last. This opinion was conveyed to the Foreign Office and was reflected by Lord Curzon in his conversation with Pichon on November 10.[45] To accept the proferred position of advisor would be to place a bet on a dying horse.

The British authorities in Constantinople, both military and political, vehemently favored expelling the Turks from Constantinople. Calthorpe, de Robeck, Ryan, and Hohler all took this attitude.[46] Many at home in Britain considered the Turk as no more than a barbarian, particularly because of Turkish treatment of the Armenians. This was the same attitude that had been expressed by the Liberals in Gladstone's day, and it still carried political overtones, with the Liberal and Labour groups generally favoring expulsion and the Conservatives tending to be more pro-Turkish in their attitude.[47] Mixed with this was the age-old religious antagonism toward the infidel. This attitude had found a specific cause in the demand for the return of Santa Sophia to the Greek Orthodox. A mounting campaign in the press, the formation of organizations, public rallies, and so forth testified to the popular emotional appeal of this issue. In general, public opinion seemed to favor the expulsion of the Turks from Constantinople.[48]

On December 10, a conference of six ministers met with Lloyd George for the purpose of establishing the policy lines the prime minister should follow in his conversations with Clemenceau the following day. During the discussion Lloyd George, Curzon, and Balfour strongly supported Turkish expulsion from Constantinople. However, both Lloyd George and Curzon indicated a willingness to allow the sultan to remain in Constantinople in his position as caliph. The result would be to create a situation analogous to that of the pope at the Vatican in Rome. Montagu and Churchill who, in their roles as secretary of state for India and secretary of state for war and air respectively, had opposed forcing the Turk out of Constantinople, appeared somewhat mollified. Montagu indicated that he was willing to accept the internationalization of Constantinople and the transferring of the Turkish government across the Straits to Brusa as long as the sultan would have the power to reside in Constantinople. Churchill, indicating that "it would be wise, in his opinion, to keep him [the sultan] in Constantinople, under our eye," added that "however, he was quite prepared to support anything that was agreed upon by the Prime Minister and M. Clemenceau." [49]

As a result of this conference, Lloyd George and Curzon clearly thought that a consensus had been reached that would enable them

to seek an agreement with Clemenceau based upon the abrogation
of any Turkish political sovereignty and authority in the area of
Constantinople and the Straits. In reality this was not the case, for,
as Herbert Fisher, president of the Board of Education, pointed out
just before the meeting adjourned, there remained "a difference of
opinion as to the extent of the nominal power to be vested in the
Sultan." [50]

In the meeting of the two prime ministers the next day, the future
of the Straits and Constantinople was discussed thoroughly:

M. CLEMENCEAU . . . He would say at the outset . . . that in his view
the Straits must be kept in the hands of an Allied force and taken altogether
out of the hands of Turkey. Should the Straits include Constantinople?
. . . His opinion was that it would be a mistake to take the Turks out
of Constantinople. He would consider Constantinople as separate from the
Straits. . . . If the idea of cutting up Asia Minor was abandoned, it was
our interest to leave a certain amount of prestige to the head of the State
of Asia Minor. . . . If the Sultan was to govern in our interest, the more
responsibility we could give him the better. It would be easier to govern
through the Sultan as an intermediary, and for this reason it would be
better to leave him in Constantinople. . . .

MR. LLOYD GEORGE . . . The British Government felt that complete
control of the Straits would not be assured unless Constantinople also was
in the hands of some international force. . . . The Straits ought to be
made self-supporting, but this could not be done without Constantinople.
In the port and the city . . . it should be possible to raise sufficient taxes
and dues to pay for the troops. . . . The fact was he did not want to include
a big sum in his budget for maintaining troops for the Straits. . . . If
the Sultan was in Constantinople, his Ministers and Administration would
also be there, and there would be constant intrigues, etc. He would attempt
to divide the Powers and play one off against the other. . . . An alternative
which had been suggested, he thought first by M. Venizelos, was that the
Sultan should be established in a sort of Vatican at Constantinople. . . .

LORD CURZON . . . Another point which had to be borne in mind was
that the Turkish policy of the Future would be strongly nationalist. . . .
If the Sultan at Constantinople was in control of such a party with all
the memories and prestige of the past, and strongly nationalist in sentiment,
there must inevitably be trouble which would react on the French in Tunis
and Tripoli and Algeria no less than on the British in Egypt and India.
The Mahometan would say that the Turk had never been beaten at all,
and to prove it they would point to the fact that he was still in possession

of Constantinople and Adrianople, from which place he continued to exercise his full powers as Khalif. . . .

M. CLEMENCEAU . . . He, himself, was opposed to the creation of a new Pope in the East. It was quite bad enough to have one Pope in the West, and as to establishing a holy place in Constantinople, it must be recalled that the Mahometan already had Mecca. . . . He admitted that if the Sultan was left at Constantinople there would be danger of the Mahometans saying that the Turks had never been beaten, and that the Allies had not dared to remove him from Constantinople. . . . The Turks had shown that they were not fit for self-government, and there must be some form of supervision and some form of control over their military organization over the Dardanelles and Bosphorus with a strip of territory behind. He preferred the system he had proposed, though he realized the objections to it. Nevertheless, he would range himself alongside of the British plan if some of the difficulties which he foresaw could be removed. The great necessity was to avoid Anglo-French friction. . . . He realized that the logical solution was to join Constantinople to the Dardanelles and Bosphorus under single inter-allied European authority.[51]

What had happened was that Lloyd George and Curzon, while mentioning the compromise solution arrived upon at the Conference of Ministers the day before, had in essence strongly urged the complete expulsion of the Turk from Europe and had received Clemenceau's assent. The next day, the French accepted the British plan with a minimum of protest. Berthelot, for one, was pleased. He noted in the memorandum that contained the French acceptance of the British scheme:

From a moral and historical point of view, the eviction from Europe of a state based on the right of conquest and the oppression of different races and superior civilizations represents a triumph of *Droit*. The loss of Constantinople will mark the final eclipse of the mysterious powers over the Moslem population in areas under British and French jurisdiction [control] which its possession had conferred upon the descendants of Osman. The taking of Constantinople by the Turks marked the end of the middle ages. Their exodus will mark the beginning of a new period.[52]

Thus the main British position was accepted. Given Clemenceau's vehement opposition to the so-called Vatican proposal, Curzon and Lloyd George, who had never really favored the scheme, were only too glad to omit any such provision in the final agreement.[53] Constantinople and the Straits would be taken from the Turks and established as a separate political and territorial entity governed by an international commission. The sultan and his government would have to relocate in Asia Minor. Therefore, subsequent discussion between Curzon and Berthelot centered on the technical problems of organization, administration, and control of the new Constantinople state as well as its future relations to the Turkish state in Anatolia. Agreement was reached on almost all major points, though questions involving the transfer of authority and sources of revenue for the new state were deferred for examination by the expert committees of the Peace Conference at Paris.[54]

Control of the Anatolian Turkish State

Once decisions were made concerning European mandates in Asia Minor and the future of Constantinople and the Straits, the remaining problem was that of the formation and administration of the Turkish state in Asia Minor. Here the primary question was the type and extent of control that the Allies would hold over the Turkish government. It was agreed that the best way, both of protecting European financial investments and of controlling the actions and policies of the Turkish government, would be to work through supervision of government finances. This matter had been thoroughly discussed by British and French financial experts, and all were agreed that any organizational structure involved should be arranged so as to be totally separate from the groups administering the Constantinople state. Therefore, while the prewar Ottoman Debt Council would continue to exist in a revised form and for the time being would work out of Constantinople, a new Financial Commission made up only of the great powers would be constituted upon establishment of the new Anatolian state. The staff and machinery of the old Debt Council that had been "all over the Turkish Empire . . . could now be put, with all its experience and efficiency at the disposal of the Financial Commission. All the new machinery would not therefore have to be created afresh and the Turkish Government were already used to this large measure of European interference and control." [55]

Lord Curzon expressed great fear that world public opinion would react unfavorably to this system, "if, as he understood, the Financial Commission were practically to impose every year a budget which the Legislative Assembly would have to accept." [56] He was particularly concerned that the Moslem world would charge the Allies with preventing the development of democratic self-government, "however unlikely such a development might be in practice." [57] He therefore proposed a specific statement that such control would end with the repayment of the prewar Ottoman debt, after which the question would be submitted to the League of Nations. To this everyone readily assented, as well they might, for it was hardly likely that the Turkish government would be able to do any more than meet the interest payments, irrespective of repaying the principal, in the foreseeable future.[58]

The decision to exclude Turkey from Constantinople constituted a complete victory for the policies of Lloyd George and Curzon. In accepting this scheme, Clemenceau in effect abandoned his position of supporting the sultan's regime, for as he himself had pointed out, if the powers really intended to rule through the sultan, it was imperative that the sultan be made as strong as possible.[59] Clemenceau's acceptance of the British viewpoint indicated that the French, like the British, were beginning to regard the Constantinople government as collapsing and incapable of survival. Under these conditions, both British and French interests dictated that they should gain firm control of Constantinople and the Straits.

The mere fact that the French sent Picot to see Kemal is indicative of their loss of confidence in the Constantinople regime. Kemal's expressed preference for French advice and economic assistance in Anatolia cannot but have had its effect on the Quai d'Orsay. Just as Britain had sought and found a new force to champion in Greece, so now it would seem the French were beginning to regard Kemal as the man of the hour and were considering the possibility of working with him.

It may be argued that the extensive French and British planning regarding Allied financial control in Anatolia hardly indicated an intention on the part of either power to abandon the sultan's government. Actually, other considerations were involved. Through this plan, the commercial, industrial, and investment interests of the Allies could be preserved, either in the faint possibility that the old government could survive and regain authority and control, or be transferred subsequently to a new Anatolian regime if that were possible. There is little to indicate that either France or Britain entertained much hope for the sultan's government or were in any way prepared to defend it. Had either power been truly concerned about maintaining a strong Turkish government, it would have insisted on the retention of Constantinople by the royal regime. The new plan for Anatolia would cost the Allies nothing and require few men. If the sultan's regime did survive, the British and French would dominate most of Asia Minor; if not, they would still control that area which counted most, Constantinople and the Straits.

One final note of interest remains. During the course of the discussions, Berthelot pointedly stated:

The French Government had originally not favored the policy of expelling the Turks from Europe, ... but they had deferred to the superior arguments of the British Government. They presumed, therefore, that the British Government were determined to carry through this policy and would not go back on it or them.[60]

To this Curzon replied that though he, Lloyd George, and Balfour all favored this policy, it had not come before the full cabinet, and all decisions were "subject to revision or confirmation by both the British and French Governments." [61]

It was almost as if Berthelot had a premonition of impending trouble. Nevertheless, it appeared that the thorniest of the Turkish peace problems had been swiftly, completely, and amicably solved.

1. *Br. Doc.*, 4:878, Curzon memorandum, 11/12/19. Curzon had replaced Balfour as Foreign Secretary on October 24, 1919.

2. Ibid., p. 879. The British had been convinced for some time that no United States action regarding mandates was likely. This was confirmed on November 23 by Viscount Grey who was in Washington at the time. Grey advised immediate resumption of negotiations. See Foreign Office, F.O. 608/111/385-1-11/17992, Balfour to Curzon, 8/18/19; Balfour Papers, MSS 49734, Curzon to Balfour, 10/13/19; Cabinet Papers, Cab. 23/12, W.C. 617, 618, Cabinet

conclusions, 8/19/19; W.C. 619, Cabinet conclusions 8/20/19; Cab. 23/18, C.1 (19), Appendix, minutes of Conference of Ministers, 10/31/19; *Br. Doc.*, 4:901, Grey to Curzon, 11/23/19. Also, *U.S. Doc., P.P.C.*, 11:675-76, American mission to Sec. State, 11/29/19; Bristol Papers, Box 27, Memorandum on United States policy relative to the treaty with Turkey, 11/26/19; *Times* (London), 10/21/19; 11/13/19; 12/19/19; 1/9/20; *Parliamentary Debates* (Commons), 5th ser., 123:768-69, 12/18/19.

3. *Br. Doc.*, 4:879, Curzon memorandum 11/12/19.

4. Ibid., p. 880. Curzon had long been concerned about the problem of enforcing a Turkish peace treaty, and time and again had warned against the drafting of an unenforceable peace treaty. Cabinet Papers, Cab. 24/77, G.T. 7037, Curzon to Cabinet, 3/25/19; Foreign Office, F.O. 608/108/385-1-1/7102, Curzon to Balfour, 4/12/19; Polk Papers, Dr 78, fol. 121, Davis to Polk, 11/11/19.

5. The rise of the Nationalist movement and its relation to the British-French negotiations in December–January, 1919-20 will be discussed in Chapter 10.

6. State Department, Turkey, 867.00/945, Bristol to Sec. State, 10/1/19; Foreign Office, F.O. 608/111/385-1-11/17992, Graham to Curzon, (5), 8/31/19-9/28/19; F.O. 608/272/41/41, Robeck to Curzon, 12/22/19; Pech, *Alliés et Turquie*, pp. 73-75, 7/28/19; pp. 80-81, 8/28/19; *Br. Doc.*, 4:895, Robeck to Curzon, 11/18/19. Both the French and British had heard rumors that the Italians were on the verge of negotiating a pact with the Nationalist group. It was also widely reported that the Italians were providing arms and ammunition to the Turkish forces that were opposing the Greeks around Smyrna. Ibid., pp. 831-33, Robeck to Curzon, 10/20/19. Since then, Count Carlo Sforza, Italian high commissioner in Constantinople, has admitted to having been in constant contact with the Kemalist movement from the moment of its inception. Sforza, *Modern Europe*, p. 357. Turkish newspaper correspondent Ahmed Emin Yalmin commented: "The Italians were viewed by us as the only reliable participants in the Inter-Allied occupation of Turkey. They were well controlled and they tried to be just." A. E. Yalmin, *Turkey in My Time*, p. 72. See also *Br. Doc.* 4:839-40, Meinertzhagen to Curzon, 10/22/19; Sforza, *Diplomatic Europe*, p. 53; Pallis, *Anatolian Venture*, pp. 123, 134-35.

7. *Br. Doc.*, 4:754, Webb to Curzon, 9/8/19, n. 3.

8. Ibid., p. 753, 9/7/19. See also ibid., n. 4. Actually the Turks had started approaching the British about a British mandate for Turkey in December, 1918. Foreign Office, F.O. 608/108/385-1-1/988, Webb to Balfour, 12/31/18. See also F.O. 406/41/34, Calthorpe to Curzon, 4/3/19. File 608/111/385-1-11 covers several Turkish approaches in February and March, 1919. See also *Br. Doc.*, 4:711, Calthorpe to Curzon, 7/31/19; p, 725, Webb to Curzon, 8/9/19; p. 742, 8/27/19; Sonnino Papers, Reel 46, no. 414, Sonnino to Constantinople, 4/13/19; Reel 27, no. 1424, Sforza to Sonnino, 5/22/19.

9. P. Loti, *La Mort de Notre Chère France en Orient*, pp. 153-54, Copy of secret agreement between Turkey and England, 9/12/19; Bristol Papers, Box 27, Bristol to Sec. State, 12/12/19. See also Pech, *Alliés et Turquie*, p. 125, 4/8/20, n. 1.

10. Howard, *Partition*, pp. 241-42; Cumming, *Franco-British Rivalry*, p. 91; Gaillard, *Turks and Europe*, p. 178; Frangulis, *Crise Mondiale*, 2:118; Gontaut-Biron, *D'Angora à Lausanne*, p. 12; Pichon, *Partage*, p. 203; W. Yale, *The Near East, a Modern History*, p. 281.

11. State Department, Turkey, 867.00/915 Ravndal to Sec. State, 8/2/19.

12. *Br. Doc.*, 4:753, Webb to Curzon, 9/8/19.

13. Ibid., pp. 781-82, Curzon to Robeck, 9/23/19.

14. Bristol Papers, Box 27, Bristol to Sec. State, 12/12/19, 12/18/19; State Dept, Turkey, 867.00/1166, Bristol to Sec. State, 2/2/20; Foreign Office, F.O. 371/4241/173042 and 174587, Derby to Foreign Office and Curzon minute, 1/23/20; Phipps to Derby, 1/24/20; Edmonds minute, 1/24/20; Robeck to F.O. 1/28/20 and Edmonds minute, 1/30/20; Hardinge to Curzon, 1/29/20; F.O. 371/5117/E 260-83-44, Robeck to Curzon, 2/3/20; E 83-83-44, Graham to

Curzon, 2/11/20. Both the British and Turkish governments officially denied the existence of the treaty in April, 1920. Foreign Office, F.O. 371-5117/E 4401-83-44, Webb to Foreign Office, 4/21/20; Loti, *Mort de France,* pp. 154–55; Pech, *Alliés et Turquie,* pp. 124–25, 4/8/20; *Correspondance d'Orient* (May 15, 1920), pp. 413–14.

15. Howard, *Partition,* pp. 241–42, 455, n. 88; Cumming, *Franco-British Rivalry,* p. 91.

16. See below, Chapter 9.

17. Frangulis, *Crise Mondiale,* 2:134; Pech, *Alliés et Turquie,* pp. 77–79, 8/14/19.

18. State Department, Turkey, 867.00/1038, Bristol to Sec. State, 12/10/19; Pech, *Alliés et Turquie,* pp. 96–97, 11/15/19; p. 99, 12/7/19; Pichon, *Partage,* p. 203; Yale, *Near East,* p. 281.

19. Led by Lieutenant General James Harbord, this commission had been sent by President Wilson to Armenia in the fall of 1919 for the purpose of ascertaining the problems a mandatory nation would encounter there. See above, p. 132. According to the commission's report, Kemal had indicated a preference for an American mandate. *U.S. Doc., 1919,* 2:858–59, Harbord Report, 10/10/19. For an extensive account of the Harbord Commission's journey, see a series of twelve articles on the American military mission to Armenia in *The Armenian Review,* (1949–50).

20. Gontaut-Biron, *Comment,* pp. 1338–40; Gontaut-Biron, *D'Angora à Lausanne,* p. 12; Frangulis, *Crise Mondiale,* 2:134; R. Davison, "Turkish Diplomacy from Mudros to Lausanne," p. 178; *Times,* (London), 10/25/19.

21. Gontaut-Biron, *Comment,* p. 338. See also Kinross, *Ataturk,* p. 234.

22. Gontaut-Biron, *Comment,* pp. 338–40.

23. Interpreting these discussions on Anatolia and Cilicia as two separate topics makes it easier to explain the outbreak of hostilities between the Nationalist and French forces in Cilicia early in 1920. See below, pp. 252–53.

24. *Br. Doc.,* 4:538, Robeck to Curzon, and enclosures, 11/19/19. See also Pech, *Alliés et Turquie,* pp. 95–97, 11/15/19.

25. *Br. Doc.,* 4:587–88, Robeck to Curzon, 12/12/19, and enclosure, Dispatch from Mustapha Kemal Pasha, 11/28/19, n. 2. American Intelligence at Constantinople also reported that the Picot mission had failed. State Department, Turkey, 867.00/1085, American Mission (Constantinople) to Sec. State, 12/20/19.

26. *Br. Doc.,* 4:560, Meinertzhagen to Curzon, 12/29/19.

27. Both sides recognized that a rapprochement was overdue. Cabinet papers, Cab. 21/158, Notes of a conversation between the prime minister and M. Loucheur at 10 Downing Street, 12/3/19.

28. Lloyd George Papers, F12/2/8, Negotiations concerning Clemenceau's visit to London in December, 1919, F12/2/9, Curzon to Lloyd George, with enclosures; Cabinet Papers, Cab. 23/18, C. 12(19), 12/10/19, App. 6, Draft conclusions of Conference of Ministers, 12/6/19; Cab. 23/35, S-5, Conference of Ministers, 12/11/19.

29. Pichon, who had been ill for some time, had recently suffered a stroke resulting in partial paralysis. Berthelot had been carrying on Pichon's work, and was well equipped to carry on the negotiations. Cambon, *Correspondance,* 3:364, 11/22/19; p. 367, 12/14/19.

30. *Br. Doc.,* 2:784, Clemenceau-Lloyd George conversations, 12/11/19-12/13/19, Text of Resolutions.

31. Cabinet Papers, Cab. 23/35, S-5, Conference of Ministers, 12/11/19.

32. *Br. Doc.,* 2:727, Clemenceau-Lloyd George conversations, 12/11/19.

33. *U.S. Doc., P.P.C.,* 11:675, American commission to Sec. State, 11/29/19. See also Miller, *Diary,* 20:416–19, Polk to Lansing, 9/11/19.

34. Cabinet Papers, Cab. 23/35, S-5, Conference of Ministers, 12/11/19.

35. Ibid. See also *Br. Doc.*, 2;748–49, Anglo-French Conference, 12/12/19; pp. 761–64, 12/13/19; F. S. Northedge, *The Troubled Giant: Britain Among the Great Powers, 1916–1939*, pp. 160–61.

36. *Br. Doc.*, 2:733, Clemenceau-Lloyd George conversations, 12/11/19; Cabinet Papers, Cab. 23/35, S-5, Conference of Ministers, 12/11/19.

37. *Br. Doc.*, 4:950, Berthelot memorandum and British notes, 12/12/19.

38. Ibid., pp. 950–51; pp. 962, 964–65, Curzon-Berthelot second meeting, 12/22/19; p. 998, Curzon memorandum, 1/4/20; Churchill, *Aftermath*, pp. 388–90; L. Mosley, *The Glorious Fault; The Life of Lord Curzon*, p. 236; Nicolson, *Curzon*, p. 107; Ronaldshay, *Curzon*, 3:265–69.

39. *Br. Doc.*, 4:951, Berthelot memorandum and British notes, 12/12/19; pp. 962, 964–65, Curzon-Berthelot second meeting, 12/22/19.

40. Ibid., 2:733, Clemenceau-Lloyd George conversations, 12/11/19.

41. Ibid., 4:949, Berthelot memorandum and British notes, 12/12/19; p. 961, Curzon-Berthelot second meeting, 12/22/19. In their private conversation before the conference officially opened, Clemenceau had indicated to Lloyd George that he would be willing to grant some economic concessions to Italy in Asia Minor. Cabinet Papers, Cab. 23/35, S-5, Conference of Ministers, 12/11/19.

42. *Br. Doc.*, 4:942. Berthelot memorandum and British notes, 12/12/19; pp. 961-62, Curzon-Berthelot second meeting, 12/22/19.

43. See above, p. 123.

44. Foreign Office, F.O. 608/109/385-1-6/16827, Draft mandate (British) for Constantinople and the Straits; State Department, A.C.N.P., 185.513/33, Clemenceau to Polk, 8/22/19; *Le Temps*, 10/8/19; *A Review of the Foreign Press: Political Review* (London) (hereafter cited as *R.F.P.: Political Review*), 1/16/20, 1/23/20, 1/30/20, 2/13/20; "Un Diplomate," *Paul Cambon, Ambassadeur de France, 1843–1924*, p. 307; J. Bardoux, *Lloyd George et la France*, p. 218; A. Mandelstam, *La société des nations, et les puissances devant le problème arménien*, pp. 143–51; Gaillard, *Turks and Europe*, pp. 74–83.

45. See above, pp. 179–80.

46. *Br. Doc.*, 4:853–54, Robeck to Curzon, 11/4/19; p. 997, Curzon memorandum, 1/4/20.

47. P. Graves, *Briton and Turk*, p. 199; Churchill, *Aftermath*, p. 395, Gaillard, *Turks and Europe*, p. 114.

48. Gaillard, *Turks and Europe*, pp. 99–101; Toynbee, *Western Question*, pp. 90–91; *Times* (London) 12/29/19; 1/8/20; "The Future of Turkey," pp. 40–41; *The Near East* (February, 1920): 177; Lord Bryce, "The Settlement of the Eastern Question," pp. 1–9; House Papers, Dr. 31, fol. 243, Memorandum of Resident members of the University of Oxford.

49. Cabinet Papers, Cab. 23/35, S-4, Conference of Ministers, 12/10/19. Polk had recognized this aspect of French policy as early as September, 1919. Polk Papers, Dr. 78, fol. 14, Letter, Polk to Lansing, 9/22/19.

50. Cabinet Papers, Cab. 23/35, S-4, Conference of Ministers, 12/10/19.

51. *Br. Doc.*, 2:728-31, Clemenceau-Lloyd George conversations, 12/11/19.

52. Ibid., 4:947, Berthelot memorandum, 12/12/19.

53. Ibid., pp. 993–94, Curzon memorandum, 1/4/20.

54. Regarding the religious use of Santa Sophia, it was decided that "if any differential treatment were thought necessary . . . it might be treated as an ancient monument in which all denominations and creeds would have an equal interest, but which should not be used for purposes of religious worship by any particular faith." All other mosques would

continue as Moslem places of worship. *Br. Doc.*, 4:941, Curzon-Berthelot first meeting, 12/22/19.

55. Ibid., pp. 960–61, Curzon-Berthelot second meeting, 12/22/19; p. 948, Berthelot memorandum and British notes, 12/12/19; Cabinet Papers, Cab. 24/95, C.P. 391, no. 4, British Peace delegation draft proposals for financial conditions of peace with Turkey.

56. *Br. Doc.*, 4:963, Curzon-Berthelot second meeting, 12/22/19.

57. Ibid.

58. The Ottoman Debt in 1914 stood at £140,000,000.

59. See above, 192.

60. *Br. Doc.*, 4:940, Curzon-Berthelot first meeting, 12/22/19.

61. Ibid.

IX ❀ FURTHER ANGLO-FRENCH
DISCUSSIONS

Ｉｎ THE COURSE of the December Anglo-French meetings a variety of questions relating to the non-Turkish peoples and areas of the former Ottoman Empire were discussed. Agreement, at least in general terms, was reached on almost all the topics involved.

Armenia

The Armenian question was dealt with in a surprisingly summary fashion. Britain and France had eagerly sought an American mandate, and were distressed at the apparent unwillingness of the United States to take this troubled area off their hands.[1] Both governments realized that Armenian claims for a large state stretching from Trebizond to Cilicia were impractical and unrealistic. Instead, at Curzon's suggestion, a much smaller, completely landlocked area was decided on, extending westward just far enough to include the town of Erzerum. This territory, which had formerly been in Turkey, would be joined to the existing Republic of Armenia that had been in existence since the collapse of Tzarist Russia. A commercial outlet to the Black Sea would be provided through the free port of Batum.[2]

It was recognized that the Armenians would constitute a distinct minority even in this smaller state and that the hardest problem would be that of enforcing order. The Armenians had been requesting arms, ammunition, and officers from the Allies since the previous September.[3] A complicating factor was the Allies' general distrust of the Armenians; as George Kidston of the British Foreign Office put it, "I fear that there is not the slightest doubt that the Armenian is at least as good a hand at massacring as his Moslem neighbor."[4] Consequently, there was no agreement as to the number or type of troops that would be required to pacify the area. Estimates ranged from a French figure of 20,000 European troops down to a few officers in an advisory capacity, which some British seemed to think would be enough.[5]

Further complicating the question of enforcement, though no one would admit it directly, was the growing conviction on the part of all the powers that Bolshevik forces would shortly triumph in the civil war then being waged in Russia. In fact, on December 12, the British cabinet decided that Britain would not enter into any more commitments to aid the anti-Bolshevik forces in Russia, though it would continue to sell them military goods if they wished to buy.[6] The decision was presented to representatives of the other major powers on December 13 and was immediately accepted by Clemenceau, while the American, Italian, and Japanese representatives greeted it sympathetically. In addition, the powers agreed to a British suggestion that "as regards the border communities with non-Russian populations which have been struggling for freedom and self-government, the Allies will give them such assistance in defending their liberties as may be found desirable in the circumstances of each case as it arises."[7] The implications that this statement held for the future of the new Armenian state could hardly have been worse.

What it all ultimately came down to was the fact that Britain and France were fully committed to support the creation of an Armenian state, yet neither had the will, men, or money actively to promulgate the solution. Kidston put the British dilemma clearly:

With regard to the Eastern Vilayets, I do not believe there is any possibility of any sort of mandate, international or otherwise, or of dividing the country up into Kurdish or Armenian zones without a military force sufficiently strong to keep the Turk and C.U.P. influence out and to impose respect of the divergent internal elements. And this, I venture to suggest, is the crux of the difficulty, not only here but everywhere and the C.U.P. knows it. The War Office contemplates having to hand over the Anatolian Railway to the Turks from sheer lack of a sufficiency of men to hold it. In Mesopotamia, Egypt, Palestine, Asia Minor, not to speak of India, our forces are necessarily being demobilized, and from all these places there is a constant shout for more men and fresh drafts which are not forthcoming. Nor is there money to pay for more.[8]

Clemenceau expressed similar views in his conversation with Lloyd George on December 11:

. . . The Armenians were a dangerous people to get mixed up with. They required a great deal of money and gave very little satisfaction. He was in favor of letting them have a republic, or whatever else they wanted. France was unwilling to spend any money in Armenia.[9]

No agreement on the enforcement question was reached, and the matter was referred for further consideration to the Allied Military Mission in Paris. At the same time, Berthelot agreed that a "British suggestion as to confiding to the Council of the League of Nations the task of helping Armenia with men and money might well be adopted, if the French, British, and Italian Governments found later, after examination by experts, that they could not supply the necessary resources alone." [10]

Kurdistan

"The term Kurdistan," wrote Sir Arnold Wilson, "is a loose term without any generally accepted geographical significance." [11] Living in valleys lying between vast mountain ranges in the area where the present day Syrian, Turkish, and Iraqian borders meet, the Kurds possessed little sense of unity or loyalty other than to the particular tribe to which they belonged. It was estimated that about half of the population of the Mosul vilayet was Kurdish, with elements also to the north and east.[12] In the Sykes-Picot Agreement most of this area had been confided to France. The cession of Mosul to Britain had altered this, and British forces had been in nominal occupation of the territory since the close of the war. The Kurds were violently anti-Arab and for centuries had carried on a vendetta with the

Armenians. They had little liking for the Turkish government at Constantinople. The British maintained that what the Kurds really wanted was a British protectorate over the whole region, and they evolved a tentative plan for the establishment of an "Arab province of Mosul fringed by autonomous Kurdish States under Kurdish Chiefs who will be advised by British Political Officers."[13] None of this was particularly pleasing to the French.[14]

During the summer of 1919 the British dispatched Major Edward Noel on a fact-finding mission to Kurdistan in an effort to establish how qualified the people were to receive the privilege of self-determination. This expedition was undertaken enthusiastically by Noel who was described by a British political advisor at Constantinople as a "fanatic" and "an out and out Kurd." His views on Kurdistan reflected this bias.[15] The mission generated a great deal of hostility between the Turkish government and the British, for the Turks claimed that the Kurdistan question was an internal affair and accused Noel of fomenting separatist feeling among the Kurds.[16]

Attempts at creating the proposed federation of tribes under Sheikh Mahmud ended in an abortive rebellion against British authority by the sheikh himself.[17] During the spring, summer, and fall of 1919, several British military and civilian agents in Kurdistan were ambushed and murdered. Three distinct uprisings occurred, all of which necessitated large-scale retaliatory action by British Indian forces. These campaigns, however successful from the military standpoint, brought only partial political success. Although British administration was securely established in central and southern Kurdistan, by December, 1919, their administrative control over the mountainous borders of northern Kurdistan had ended. Considering that British control was so tenuous and that three separate revolts had occurred in the space of eight months, the British were hardly justified in maintaining that the Kurds desired British supervision and control.[18]

Undoubtedly reacting to these problems, the British Foreign Office indicated to the French in December a new conviction that it could not undertake direction of the area outside the Mosul vilayet. The problem was to prevent this area from coming under French jurisdiction as had been called for originally in the Sykes-Picot Agreement. To return it unconditionally to the Turks was deemed impossible, for that would create a "tongue" of Turkish land stretching down from Asia Minor that would separate the proposed Armenian state from Syria and Mesopotamia and would serve as a perfect outlet for Turkish intrigue in all three areas. Neither the British nor the French wanted this. Therefore, Berthelot proposed that the Kurdish territory should indeed be returned to Turkish sovereignty, but given a great deal of local autonomy under joint Anglo-French supervision and control. To this Curzon countered with the suggestion that the area should be separated from Turkey and left entirely on its own, guaranteed against Turkish aggression but without any "formally appointed advisors, whether British or French." [19]

One must infer from this that the British (and the French as well, for Berthelot accepted this scheme) sought to wash their hands of the problem by ignoring it. It was assumed that the Kurds would be unable to interfere outside their mountain valleys and that therefore the best solution would be to leave them to their own tribal rivalries. This attitude was strengthened by news of a Kurdish-Armenian agreement in which each recognized the other's claims and both asked for the creation of two separate states under a single mandate. This show of amicability between the two traditionally antagonistic groups eased the situation considerably and made it easier for Curzon and Berthelot to agree that the Kurd should be left to his own devices.[20]

Mosul

Although Curzon and Berthelot had agreed on the general terms of a Kurdish settlement, delineation of the geographical limits of the Kurdish state had to await a decision on the Mosul vilayet boundaries, for this vilayet was to remain under British direction and control.

Mosul had been awarded to France in the Sykes-Picot Agreement because of Lord Kitchener's aversion to having territory controlled by Britain bounded by land allotted to Russia.[21] Under the original plans for Turkish partition, this would have been the case had Britain held Mosul. This cession to France had been a serious mistake, for the Turkish Petroleum Company, in which Great Britain held the controlling interest, had obtained a concession to all oil exploitation in the Mosul vilayet just prior to the outbreak of the war. To cover this, the French had agreed that any British concessions obtained before the war from the Turks would not be prejudiced even if they fell within the French sphere of influence. However, to have any territory under British economic development and French political control would create a highly volatile situation, and both governments realized this. When Clemenceau visited London in December, 1918, Lloyd George immediately broached this subject, and received Clemenceau's consent to the attachment of Mosul to the British sphere in Mesopotamia.[22]

The French subsequently asserted that Clemenceau had agreed to the Mosul cession only on the condition that France would have a share in developing the oil resources, that Britain would support the remaining provisions of the Sykes-Picot Agreement in the face of American opposition, and that France would receive mandates to all the territory assigned to it in the Sykes-Picot Agreement, including the four interior cities.[23] The British maintained, however, that no promises other than a broad one that Syria should be in the French sphere had been made and that any concession regarding a French share in the exploitation of Mosul oil would be granted only in return for additional British rail and pipeline rights.[24]

The truth on the question of promises is not easily ascertainable. Both sides were agreed that Britain should have Mosul. It is hard to believe that the British, with their pro-Arab policy, would have consented in December, 1918, to French conditions that so thoroughly limited Arab claims. Yet it is even more inconceivable that Clemenceau would have made such a gift without obtaining concessions of some sort in return. Certainly, beginning in January, 1919, the French contended otherwise. Later, Clemenceau stated: "I cannot admit that I consented without an equivalent to the extension of the British mandate to Mosul and Palestine. It would have been unprecedented that such concessions should have been made without any precise definition on paper, all the advantage being on the one side." [25] Or, as Berthelot put it in February, 1920: "M. Clemenceau in London had, no doubt, made certain general statements out of the generosity of his heart; but he at present only had a very vague recollection of any promises which he may have made, and those promises did not constitute any sound basis for claiming concessions." [26] This sums up the question nicely. Regardless of what was said in December, 1918, the agreement was purely verbal. No written memorandum of the conversation had been made, and, therefore, the question for all intents and purposes remained as open as before.[27]

Oil Rights

In December, 1918, the French started pressing for an Anglo-French agreement regarding the division of oil resources in the Near East and Mediterranean regions. Although the British Petroleum Executive was eager to open negotiations out of fear that refusal would lead to a Franco-American agreement to which Britain would be forced to subscribe, the Foreign Office, led by Lord Curzon, objected to any such undertaking. Curzon consistently maintained that no discussions should be held until a territorial settlement had been decided on by the Peace Conference. It was decided, nevertheless, that the British government should indicate its willingness to cooperate with the French and to grant them some share in the Turkish Petroleum Company, but that "no scheme could be agreed to in detail until after the Peace Conference." [28] Despite this stand, at an interdepartmental conference held in Paris on February 1, it was decided that France should be offered a 25 percent share in the Turkish Petroleum Company. A memorandum to this effect was sent Balfour asking for his approval, which was subsequently received. Sir John Cadman of the Petroleum Executive was entrusted with the negotiations, with a maximum of 30 percent set as the highest allowable French share.[29]

Meanwhile Lord Curzon had become aware of what was happening in Paris and had sent a disapproving dispatch asking for information.[30] This request was never answered. Sir Louis Mallet, Balfour's private secretary, noted that Cadman had taken to London the document initialed by Balfour approving the specific proposals because "he wanted to have this to show to Lord Curzon, so that I hardly think this requires an answer."[31] Curzon, however, was not satisfied by Cadman's explanations and again wrote Balfour asking if he had indeed consented to negotiations then underway in London. On March 17, Balfour, unaware of the specific course the negotiations were taking, replied that although it was imperative that the French understand that Britain accepted their participation in the Turkish Petroleum Company, it would be better not to negotiate on details until the territorial settlement had been decided on by the Peace Conference.[32] Thus, while the Petroleum Executive believed it was proceeding with Balfour's approval, to the Foreign Office this hardly seemed to be the case.

Cadman, in the meantime, had negotiated an agreement with Senator Henry Berenger, the French commissioner general of petroleum products, who had come to London specifically for this purpose. A draft was submitted to various British departmental offices on March 13.[33] This document, which became known as the Long-Berenger Agreement, spelled out in detail the terms of a settlement governing the distribution of oil rights in the Near East. France and Britain agreed to split evenly all rights obtained by either nation in Russia, Rumania, and Galicia. France would obtain 34 percent of all "disposable" oil in the British Crown colonies; Britain would receive the same concession from France. France would obtain the 25 percent share in the Turkish Petroleum Company previously held by Germany, but would have to reserve 5 percent of this holding for native government investment should this be desired. Finally, Britain would have the right to build two pipelines across territory mandated to France from Mosul to the Mediterranean.[34]

Despite the fact that Curzon remained dubious as to the authorization behind the scheme, the British government approved the agreement, contingent upon the successful conclusion of negotiations that would give the British government control of the Royal Dutch Shell Combine and thus a 75 percent interest in the Turkish Petroleum Company. This was achieved and approved on May 8, and the way was cleared for the formal British confirmation of the Long-Berenger Agreement on May 16, 1919.[35]

The most interesting fact concerning the Long-Berenger negotiations, however, was that until May 21 apparently neither Lloyd

George nor Clemenceau knew that they had taken place or that an agreement existed. Information regarding the agreement reached them at the worst possible moment, for it was on May 21 and 22 that the crisis over Clemenceau's refusal to send delegates with the investigatory commission to Syria reached its peak.[36] Neither Clemenceau nor Lloyd George professed to know anything about the agreement, nor was either in a mood to recognize any sort of cooperation between their two nations. The result was that on May 21, Lloyd George angrily wrote Clemenceau canceling all arrangements regarding pipe and railroad lines from Mosul to the Mediterranean.[37] Although it is not at all clear that his original intent also involved the abrogation of the Long-Berenger arrangements concerning oil, the next day the discussion in the Council of Four became so acrimonious that Lloyd George indicated that he regarded his letter as applying to that agreement as well. To this Clemenceau curtly assented.[38]

In the aftermath of these events, Lloyd George set out to find out who was responsible for the Cadman-Berenger negotiations. From this investigation two interesting facts emerged. The first was that neither Long nor Cadman, nor anyone in the Petroleum Executive, was aware of Lloyd George's conversation about Mosul with Clemenceau the previous December. Nor did the political and economic sections of the Foreign Office have any record of it.[39] The second was the interesting position taken by the prime minister regarding the general question of an agreement regarding oil rights. In a memorandum dated July 10, 1919 he noted:

I knew nothing about this Oil agreement until it was casually mentioned to me, by someone not connected with the Foreign Office, in the course of a conversation in Paris. I heard of it with great surprise. As the negotiations with the French government on the Syrian question were in my hands, I certainly thought I ought to have been informed of an agreement which had been negotiated which directly affected the position. On merits I am against entering into any arrangement about oil with the French until we have first of all determined the boundaries. The proposed agreement seemed to me to place us entirely in the hands of the French and unless we have direct access to the Mediterranean that will always be the case. That is, therefore, the first question to determine and until it is decided these negotiations ought not to be proceeded with.

I have another objection to these negotiations. I feel strongly that the discussions between France and ourselves on important questions of policy ought not to be mixed up with arrangements about oil in which private companies are involved.[40]

This attitude reflected traditional concepts regarding the separation of business and politics, the corollary of which was the wartime slogan "business as usual." The British, free traders by nature, clung to this concept long after it had been abandoned by others. True, the principles had often been violated during the war, but that had been a matter of necessity not of right. Also, since the British occupied the area in question, they held the upper hand and clearly saw no reason to commit themselves until the territorial issue was definitely settled. In any case, the British position prevailed, and during the summer of 1919 was reiterated time and again. American requests for information regarding the agreement brought only the reply that the matter was being held in abeyance.[41]

All requests by representatives of private companies to undertake work on previous concessions or to reconnoiter the territory for possible new ones were refused. Two Zionist geologists were allowed to scout in Palestine; on one other occasion a private company agent did slip into Mesopotamia, much to the dismay of the British Foreign Office. The only sanctioned exploration in areas occupied by British troops was by British government agents. This policy was defended by the contention that these were agents of the government and not of private companies. Considering the British government's interest in both the Anglo-Persian and the Royal Dutch Shell companies, this hardly served as much of a reassurance to the Americans and French. To make matters worse, Curzon bluntly told the American ambassador that "this is an investigation on behalf of H. M. Government whose intentions for the present are to take all necessary measures to utilize oil products discovered in occupied territory to their own advantage."[42] It is obvious that the British stand was not taken purely on the high moral grounds of separation of business and politics that Lloyd George so assiduously professed.[43]

From August 12, when the final correspondence concerning the abrogation of the Long-Berenger Agreement took place,[44] until the Lloyd George-Clemenceau conversations of December 11, no discussion concerning oil occurred between the British and the French on any level. Nor was there any public concern about the problem. During the fall of 1919 a great debate raged in the pages of the *Times* as to whether Mesopotamia was worth retaining, even as a mandate. Yet in the whole discussion no mention was made of oil, even by those favoring its retention. In the same way, Sir Arnold Wilson gives no impression that oil was considered a particularly vital factor. Later, in 1924, Curzon was to assert in a letter to the *Times:* "During my tenure in the Foreign Office . . . oil had not the remotest connexion with my attitude or with that of His Majesty's government on the Mosul question, or the Iraq question, or the Eastern question in any aspect." [45] This statement, though overdrawn, may describe the general attitude of the Foreign Office and the prime minister, but it hardly reflects the position of all concerned. Certainly there was growing anxiety within certain government offices that failure to renegotiate the agreement might result in the breaking down of the Royal Dutch Shell Agreement which, as Sir Hamar Greenwood, the new minister of petroleum affairs, pointed out, was "closely connected with satisfactory arrangements being arrived at with the French." [46] Considerable fear existed also that France might associate with Standard Oil instead of becoming a junior partner with British oil interests.[47]

Lloyd George, upon the advice of the cabinet, agreed to "bear in mind" the unanimous recommendation of the departments in favor of the agreement when he met with Clemenceau on December 11. "If the conversations took a turn justifying him in resuscitating the Agreement, he would not neglect to do so."[48] However, when the meeting took place Lloyd George was given no opportunity to discuss the issue. Instead, Berthelot handed Lord Curzon a memorandum concerning the French position on oil. The British were charged with attempting to create an oil monopoly "from Egypt to Burma and from Circassia to the Persian Gulf."[49] French participation in the development of oil concessions everywhere in the Near East, including Persia, was demanded. In a subsequent memorandum, Berthelot defined the issue even more clearly:

The Mosul concession in so far as France is concerned entails, as an essential compensation demanded alike by industry and by the French Parliament, strict equality in the exploitation of petroleum in Mesopotamia and Kurdestan. This point carries great importance, by reason of the absolute lack of petroleum in France and her needs. Like iron and coal, petroleum has assumed a vital part in the independence and "self-defense" of all the nations of the world. The willingness of France and England to arrive at an agreement, in order to ensure peace, must be clearly manifested in the industrial as well as in other spheres. The principle once admitted, the conditions regarding the passage and freedom of the pipelines will be easy to regulate.[50]

The contention that France should be given a share in the Anglo-Persian Oil Company or that the oil reserves of Mosul and Kurdistan should be shared equally was rejected out of hand by the British. Berthelot and Berenger accepted this refusal calmly, for both were convinced that the 25 percent which had been allotted in the Long-Berenger Agreement was equitable. They had told this to Clemenceau, but had been instructed to ask for an even division, and they had done so without enthusiasm or conviction.[51]

Therefore, when Sir John Cadman met with Senator Berenger and concluded a new agreement regarding oil resources, it followed almost exactly the terms of the Long-Berenger pact. In addition, France agreed to a provision calling for two railways to the Mediterranean paralleling the pipelines previously agreed upon.[52] This agreement was accepted by Curzon and Berthelot as a basis of settlement in a meeting on December 23, 1919. Curzon stated that he believed Lloyd George had already signified his approval, but Berthelot was careful to qualify French acceptance as being dependent on approval by Clemenceau. Once this question was settled, Curzon and Berthelot found little difficulty in reaching an agreement on the Syria-Mosul boundary line.[53]

Here matters rested. The two powers were almost exactly where they had been the previous April regarding Mosul and the question of oil. The British, however, had succeeded in their policy of putting wraps on the whole question until the political and territorial settlement in the Near East had become more clearly defined. Nor was the question raised again until the Peace Conference reconvened in London in the middle of February, 1920. It is clear that during 1919 and the first month of 1920, the terms of an oil settlement per se caused minimal friction. Moreover, the petroleum question in general was considered far less important than other matters by the statesmen primarily responsible for the making of peace with Turkey.[54]

Syria and Palestine

The replacement of British by French troops in Syria, which was completed by December 10, left two major problems still unsolved. The first was the question of the relationship between the French and the Arabs; the second involved the Anglo-French dispute over the Syrian-Palestine border.

France and the Arabs

In accordance with the September agreement, the British turned over control of Damascus, Homs, Hama, Aleppo, and the surrounding territory to the Arabs, while the western portion of Syria was occupied by the French. The exact boundary between the French and Arab controlled zones was left open for negotiation between Feisal and Clemenceau, and the British went to great lengths to persuade Feisal that an agreement with Clemenceau was needed.[55]

In late November a temporary arrangement was agreed upon by Feisal and Clemenceau. France would not occupy the contested area of occupation for three months while negotiations between the two leaders continued. In turn, the Arabs withdrew their troops, and control of the area was vested in a six-man Arab-French commission headed by the French military commander in Syria, General Henri Gouraud. This solution hardly served to pacify the area, for during the next few months repeated Arab-French skirmishes took place and rumors of French intentions to march into the territory circulated widely.[56]

On January 7, 1920, Feisal left Paris for Syria. He took with him an unsigned agreement with Clemenceau, for which he maintained he needed to gain support at home before making it official. This draft agreement called for Arab recognition of a French mandate over all of Syria and Lebanon. In return, France would recognize an Arab state in the area of the four cities, which would be ruled by Feisal with the assistance of French political, economic, and military advisors. French troops would be concentrated on the Cilician border and would only be called into the Syrian interior upon the joint request of the Arab head of state and the French high commissioner. The boundary line between this state and a separate Lebanon was left for future decision. Thus, although a long-range settlement seemed to have been reached, a no-man's-land continued to exist, which could and did provide fuel for an ever-increasing hostility between the two groups.[57]

The Syrian-Palestine Frontier

The question of the Palestine-Syrian border was one of the issues on which not even a tentative agreement was reached in the Anglo-French December meetings. Here the French based their position on the Sykes-Picot Agreement. Berthelot stated that Clemenceau believed he had conceded enough in agreeing to a British, rather than an international, mandate for Palestine. France would be willing to guarantee 33 percent of the waters flowing from Syrian mountain ranges into Palestine for the use of the Zionists, but it would not accept any boundary revisions. The British demanded with equal vigor the extension northward of the Palestine frontier so as to include a part of the Litani River valley and the streams flowing south from Mount Hermon into the Jordan River. At the same time the British indicated that they were willing to drop their insistence that territory should be given Britain in order to allow a Mosul-Mediterranean railway to pass through British territory. They announced that they were studying the feasibility of including the railway within the territory originally allotted to Britain in the Sykes-Picot Agreement. If this proved impossible, the French guarantees given in the Greenwood-Berenger Agreement would suffice.[58]

The discussion, therefore, was carried on solely in terms of Zionist needs. Nevertheless, the fact that Britain would have the Palestine mandate and France the Syrian helped to stiffen resistance on each side. For the British, there was the feeling that Clemenceau was holding out only in order to receive compensation elsewhere. It was widely rumored that France wanted British consent to a French attempt to obtain Spanish Tangier through direct negotiation with Spain. The British, however, had no intention of conceding anything. The French Foreign Office, in turn, was disgruntled over previous French concessions without a quid pro quo and was determined to have no more of it. The upshot was that Curzon and Berthelot agreed to disagree and referred the whole matter back to their respective prime ministers.[59]

New Anglo-French Complications Appear

Despite failure to agree on the Palestine and Syrian border questions and the problem of military aid to Armenia, the Franco-British conversations had brought general concurrence on solutions for most of the other problems connected with the formulation of a Turkish peace treaty. The Anglo-French alliance seemed to have met the test in the Middle East and emerged stronger than ever. It appeared that little remained to be done, other than to hold formal drafting sessions and to "inform" the Italians of the decisions that had been made. Yet by the time the Peace Conference did reconvene in London in February of 1920, much of the December work had been completely undone and relations between the French and British had reached a state of high tension. This was due to three developments: the refusal of the British Cabinet to sanction the Constantinople policy agreed upon in December; the defeat of Clemenceau in his candidacy for the French presidency and the creation of a new French government headed by Alexandre Millerand; and French reluctance to hold formal peace discussions anywhere but in Paris.

British Repudiation of the Constantinople Agreement

Once the December discussions were concluded, it was necessary to present the arrangements to the British and French cabinets for approval. No sooner were they brought before the full British cabinet than one of the key issues on which many other agreements were based was completely repudiated. On January 6, the plan to exclude Turkey from Europe was rejected "by a considerable majority," despite its having the support of Lloyd George and Curzon.[60] Although the written conclusions of this meeting avoid linking departments or individuals to the arguments presented, it would appear that the Foreign Office stood almost alone in support of the scheme. Winston Churchill has described the conflict as follows:

In these controversies Lord Curzon, mounted upon the Foreign Office, rode full tilt against Mr. Edwin Montagu, whose chariot was drawn by the public opinion of India, the sensibilities of the Mohammedan world, the pro-Turkish propensities of the Conservative Party, and the voluminous memoranda of the India Office.[61]

Certainly, the India Office, led by the secretary of state for India, Edwin Montagu, vehemently opposed the taking of Constantinople from the Turks. Montagu regarded the results of the Anglo-French conversations as a betrayal of the conclusions reached at the Conference of Ministers on December 11, which he thought had accepted the concept of nominal Turkish sovereignty, if not governmental authority, over Constantinople and the Straits.[62] Numerous letters to British newspapers and personal telegrams to the prime minister from Moslem sources sought to buttress Montagu's stand regarding Constantinople. Much of this came from an organized lobby known as the Central Islamic Society, which had its headquarters in Great Britain. Support was also forthcoming from several members of Parliament.[63]

Not only were Moslems within the British Empire keenly concerned about the possible loss of the holy city of Constantinople, the traditional seat of the caliphate, but the Hindu *Swarajists*, led by Mohandas Gandhi, joined with them in this cause. On November 23, a pan-Indian conference comprising both groups called for the preservation of the Ottoman Empire, the maintenance of the caliphate at Constantinople, and the assurance that the control of the Holy Places in the Hedjaz would be under Arab jurisdiction. The Hindu concern was not religious but political. The Moslems in India constituted the single strongest group that supported the British and opposed independence. By supporting the Moslem cause, the Hindu nationalists sought not only to increase the immediate Anglo-Moslem rift but to set themselves up as defenders of Moslem rights in the hopes of ultimately obtaining cooperation in the drive for independence. If, despite their efforts, the last great city of the Moslem world was lost, the resulting Moslem-British rift would serve equally well to encourage Moslem support of the nationalist cause.[64]

One of the issues that greatly concerned the British cabinet, but on which there was no agreement, was the long-term danger of Russian ambitions to control Constantinople and the Straits. Though in the discussions in the cabinet meetings and ministerial conferences the term "bolshevism" was often used, it was always clear that this was regarded as being synonymous with the Russian national state. Should the Bolsheviks triumph in the Russian civil war, as the British and French were agreed was now likely, it would mean a hostile rather than friendly government permanently established in power. In any case, the British cabinet assumed that General Denikin's forces in southern Russia would be destroyed shortly and that Russian Bolshevik forces would soon control at least all territory up to the newly established independent Caucasus states. The incentives for subsequent joint Russian-Turkish action in the Caucasus were obvious. Those members of the cabinet who favored retaining the Turk in Constantinople argued that to expel him would be to invite an alliance between the sultan's government and Russia. On the other hand supporters of the Curzon-Berthelot agreement argued that "a victorious Bolshevist Russia would be infinitely more powerful with the Turk at Constantinople," [65] for the Turks would then be able to close the Straits in case of war between Russia and Britain. Thus it would be far better to have them out of the area completely, for a Russo-Turkish alliance would be far less of a threat if Turkish sovereignty were limited to Asia Minor.[66]

In the cabinet decision, however, none of these factors was as important as the opposition of the War Office to the expulsion of the Turks from Europe.[67] This opposition was not based on any ethical, emotional, political, or religious grounds, but rather on the issue of practical expediency. As Churchill later put it, "We had not got any soldiers and how could you drive and keep the Turks out of Constantinople without soldiers? . . . As long as the Dardanelles could be kept open for the free passage of ships . . . we were content."[68] This could be done, the War Office believed, far more economically by leaving the Turks in political control. A small international force under the direction of a supervisory commission could concern itself solely with the running of the Straits. Thus, the government, administration, policing, and defense of an international state, a state whose inhabitants opposed its very existence, would be avoided. An independent state would require a defense system and garrison capable of beating back any Turkish attempt to regain control. This would be extremely costly both in men and materials, particularly because both sides of the Straits would have to be defended. It was also maintained that if any Allied supervision in Anatolia were contemplated, it could be achieved far more easily through control over the sultan and his government at Constantinople than by having separate systems of authority for Constantinople and Asia Minor. These arguments, touching particularly on the critical problem of size and financing of the armed services, must have had a tremendous impact on the other members of the cabinet, considering the antimilitaristic attitude of the general populace and the admittedly strained economic conditions that had been partially responsible for British withdrawal from the Caucasus.[69]

Finally, there was the fact that the vast majority of British troops in Near Eastern areas other than Palestine were Indian, many of them Moslem.[70] If the home draftees were withdrawn their replacements would likely be Indian, and certainly any additional strength would have to be. This brought the issue full circle and put the religious question in a new light, for it would be difficult to ask Indian soldiers to enforce a solution to which so many were completely opposed.[71]

Curzon was extremely bitter about the cabinet defeat, regarding it as almost a personal insult, and he vigorously protested the decision. He was convinced that the Turks could not be managed simply by allowing them to remain in Constantinople and then indirectly controlling that city. The powers would ultimately be forced to bring the Turkish state under relatively close international supervision;

the Allies were letting themselves in for a system that "when produced, . . . may cause some surprise." [72]

This does not mean that Curzon opposed financial and administrative supervision of the Turkish government. Far from it. He had willingly assented to French schemes on this matter. But by separating all European territory from the Turkish state it would always be possible, if necessary, to sever all connections with Turkey and still retain what was most important, control of Constantinople and the Straits. By returning Constantinople, the Allies were binding themselves inextricably to involvement in Turkish affairs anywhere, at any time, and in any form. This is what Curzon most wished to avoid and constituted a danger that the supporters of a Turkish Constantinople failed to see.

In an obvious effort to pin the blame for an unpopular decision upon the British (where it rightfully belonged), the French had let the press know at the end of December that Constantinople would be taken from the Turks, although no official announcement had been made. [73] The French action complicated matters, for it made it much harder to reverse positions. Nonetheless, the move had to be made. On January 8, Lloyd George and Curzon journeyed to Paris for the closing sessions of the Supreme Council. Although no discussion of the Constantinople problem took place in the council meetings, it is probable that Lloyd George and Curzon informed the French of the change in Britain's attitude as soon as they arrived in Paris. [74]

On January 11, Berthelot submitted a memorandum to the British in which the arguments for both Constantinople solutions were summarized and a plan of organization for each was included. [75] This memorandum caused a crisis of its own within the British government. Montagu and the Foreign Office each prepared draft replies; neither was accepted by the full cabinet, which regarded the former as too lenient and the latter too severe. [76] Lloyd George took the highly irregular step of showing Montagu's draft to Venizelos and asking for his comments. Venizelos, as might be expected, protested against allowing the Turks to cross the Straits and supported a boundary at the Chataljah lines. He further argued that this concession should ensure the outright cession of Smyrna to Greece, a concept that Montagu, of course, did not at all accept. The pro-Greek commitment on the part of Lloyd George was never more clearly indicated. Recognizing that Venizelos's recommendations could only bolster the minority position, Lloyd George sought to bring an outside influence to bear on what was essentially an internal split on policy questions within the British cabinet.[77]

A third draft, based on reluctant consultations between Montagu and Curzon, was ultimately prepared. It called for acceptance of the Chataljah lines as the western boundary, but at the same time waived claims for reparations and limited Allied control over Turkish finances specifically to sources of revenue needed to meet military occupation expenses, along with service and payments on the prewar debt. Smyrna would be returned to Turkish suzerainty with provisions for Greek control of the local government; in Adrianople the reverse situation would exist. This draft was circulated to members of the cabinet, much to Curzon's displeasure; for as he told Lloyd George, "Once the principle (retention or expulsion) is decided I think it is the business of the Foreign Office and no other office to draw up the scheme." [78] Though Curzon asked for authorization to give a copy of the draft to Berthelot, it is not clear whether this permission was granted. What is evident is that even after the decision on Constantinople there was still a great amount of dissension within the British cabinet as to the implementation of the major policy decisions that had been taken.[79]

The Defeat of Clemenceau

The confusion within the British cabinet on Turkish policy was more than matched by that arising within France by the defeat of Clemenceau in the presidential election in January, 1920. Parliamentary elections had been held in November, 1919, under a new electoral law that allowed proportional representation in a given district only if no party received an absolute majority of the vote. This system in turn had led to the election of a right-of-center parliament, nationalistic and imperialistic in outlook, more than 50 percent of whose members were practicing Catholics.

In general, the election results indicated popular support for Clemenceau's hard-line policy regarding a stern peace with Germany, and constituted a repudiation of the more moderate Wilsonian position taken by left-of-center groups. However, though there was little question of Clemenceau's personal popularity in the nation at large, this was not reflected in the Senate and Chamber of Deputies where Clemenceau, with his barbed tongue, vehement anticlericalism, and rough-and-ready parliamentary tactics had alienated to a greater or lesser degree a majority of the legislators. There was also the realization that Clemenceau hardly would be willing to play the role of public figurehead that was traditional for a French president. Clemenceau later confirmed this when he told Jean Martet in June, 1928:

I shouldn't have remained in office three months. What they wanted was someone who would let them alone. I shouldn't have waited a week before going off the deep end. You must realize that if I had agreed to take over that job, it wouldn't have been for the purpose of opening Horticultural Exhibitions. I should have done or tried to do something.[80]

Even so, had Clemenceau actively campaigned or sought the position, the legislators would probably never have dared to flaunt public opinion. Instead, he allowed his name to be placed on the ballot by friends, without ever announcing his candidacy. This vagueness left the door open for his enemies to coalesce and unite behind former Speaker of the Chamber of Deputies Paul Deschanel. When a preliminary straw vote on January 16, indicated that in all probability he would be defeated, Clemenceau withdrew his name and two days later submitted his resignation as premier.[81] Perhaps the soundest comment on his defeat was made by Paul Cambon:

I do not say that Clemenceau would have made a good President, but his designation would have been the fulfillment of the last elections, the condemnation of the socialists and radicals, an act of recognition for the man who saved the war. From this viewpoint, his defeat has a serious portent.[82]

Clemenceau was succeeded as premier by Alexandre Millerand, who at that time was serving as commissioner general of Strasbourg in charge of the administration of Alsace and Lorraine. A man with long parliamentary experience, he had started as a member of the Radical Socialist group, but had become increasingly conservative since the turn of the century. He had held various portfolios in the government and was a veteran of parliamentary affairs. Although his cabinet was approved, it was a dubious confirmation and one that many thought would last only until the shifting of presidents on February 18.[83] Millerand took the Foreign Affairs portfolio himself; Berthelot, who would be named permanent secretary-general of the Quai d'Orsay in September, 1920, became for all intents and purposes his second in command and closest advisor.

Location of the Peace Conference

The change in French governments brought about a new crisis that for a time threatened to stall all negotiations on the Turkish settlement. The issue itself was so trivial as to be both amusing and ridiculous. The French balked at any suggestion that any of the formal work of the Peace Conference, including drafting of the Turkish treaty, should be done in London. Instead they envisaged the forthcoming London conference scheduled for February as another general discussion of principles. The British, however, refused to continue negotiations on the ministerial level in Paris, which meant that although some of the expert commissions might remain there, the main drafting of the treaty would have to be done in London. After much acrimonious discussion, it was agreed that the receiving of Turkish delegations and the signing and ratification of the treaty should take place in Paris, but that any other discussions which necessitated the presence of British ministers would take place in London. The French interpreted this to mean Lloyd George alone; the British extended it to include all those of ministerial rank. As it turned out, once the conference began the French never raised the issue in other than a theoretical sense, and the Conference of London met and worked with no dissension over this particular issue.[84]

Thus the stage was finally set for the Peace Conference to begin serious discussion of the Turkish peace terms. Although agreement on a wide variety of issues had tentatively been reached between the French and British, others remained to be settled. The reversal of British policy regarding the Turkish evacuation of Constantinople had not been completely worked out within the ranks of the British cabinet; moreover, this had an unsettling effect on many other areas of agreement. The Italians, of course, had to be informed of the decisions that had been made, and in such a manner as to avoid too severe an injury to Italian pride.[85]

The terms of agreement, though sketched in broad outlines in the Anglo-French discussions, remained muddled and lacking in precise definition. Two things, however, were apparent from the December-January meetings. Both Britain and France were becoming increasingly concerned about the Turkish settlement, and they were determined that the solution should be worked out in accordance with their own wishes. Italy was regarded as a necessary nuisance, while neither Britain nor France any longer felt obliged to consider seriously the wishes of the United States. At the same time, there was a growing realization of the ever-declining strength, not only of the sultan's government, but of the British and French position in the Near East. This was partly due to domestic, economic and military conditions, but it was also the result of the growing strength of the new Nationalist movement under Mustapha Kemal, a factor the European governments were only then beginning to recognize. It is to a brief examination of the influence that this movement had on the peace negotiations up to the opening of the London conference in February, 1920, that we now turn.

1. See above, Chapter 8, note 2; also *Current History* 11 (October, 1919):65; *Times* (London), 10/4/19.

2. *Br. Doc.,* 4:952-56, Berthelot memorandum and British notes, 12/12/19; p. 962, Curzon-Berthelot second meeting, 12/22/19.

3. The British hotly debated whether such aid should be given; the Foreign Office and the peace delegation supported it, the War and India Offices opposed. Ibid., 3:556, Curzon to Wardrop, 9/17/19; pp. 600-601, Wardrop to Curzon, 10/19/19; 1:574, S.C., 8/29/19; 4:777-79, Dutasta to Norman, 9/22/19; p. 797, Grey to Curzon, 10/7/19; *Times* (London), 9/29/19.

4. *Br. Doc.*, 4:907, Kidston to Crowe, 11/28/19; State Dept., Turkey, 867.00/1191, Bristol to Sec. State, 4/1/20. Kazemzadeh agrees: "During the Russian occupation of Turkish Armenia the Armenians looted and massacred the Turks to their hearts content." Kazemzadeh, *Transcausasia*, p. 256. See also, Gidney, *Mandate*, p. 176. On November 18, the Turkish government asked for American military protection against Armenian attacks on Moslems in Cilicia. State Department, Turkey, 867.00/1076, Bristol to Sec. State, 12/11/19.

5. *Br. Doc.*, 4:965–66, Curzon-Berthelot second meeting, Appendix, 12/22/19.

6. Cabinet Papers, Cab. 23/18, C. 13(19), 12/12/19; Cab. 23/20, S-12, Conference of Ministers (Paris), 1/19/20.

7. *Br. Doc.*, 2:782, Text of Resolutions, Allied Conference, 12/11/19–12/13/19. See also, ibid., pp. 744-48, Allied Conference, 12/12/19; pp. 764-65, 773, Clemenceau-Lloyd George conversations, 12/13/19; pp. 776–78, Allied Conference, 12/13/19. France and Britain accepted this clause immediately, the representatives of the other three powers did so with the reservation that their home governments must be consulted.

8. Ibid., 4:910, Kidston to Crowe, 11/28/19. See the *Times* (London), 10/24/19.

9. *Br. Doc.*, 2:734, Clemenceau-Lloyd George Conversations, 12/11/19.

10. Ibid., 4:962, Curzon-Berthelot second meeting, 12/22/19.

11. Wilson, *Loyalties*, 2:127.

12. Ibid. See also Foreign Office, *Handbooks*, no. 57, "Mohammedan History."

13. Wilson, *Loyalties*, 2:123, Instructions to Wilson, 5/10/19. See also ibid., p. 116.

14. Ibid., pp. 127-32, 134, 143-44; *Times.* (London), 10/29/19. The Kurds at the Peace Conference claimed they wanted a British protectorate. *Br. Doc.*, 4:679, Calthorpe to Curzon, 7/10/19, also n. 6; pp. 704-5, 7/29/19; p. 813, Crowe to Curzon, 10/12/19; Pech, *Alliés et Turquie*, pp. 94–95, 11/13/19.

15. *Br. Doc.*, 4:693-95, Hohler to Tilley, 7/21/19. Noel was assistant to the British political resident in the Persian Gulf.

16. Foreign Office, F.O. 608/95/365-1-4/4250, Baghdad to Balfour, 3/12/19; 16343, Noel Diary, 4/7-23/19; F.O. 608/95/365-1-1, General file regarding Noel Enquiry Mission, see especially 18689, Calthorpe to Curzon, 7/23/19, which has copies of Noel's report. F.O. 608/273/75/208, General review, situation in Kurdistan, 1/8/20; *Br. Doc.*, 4:693-98, Hohler to Tilley, 7/21/19; p. 782, Meinertzhagen to Curzon, 9/27/19, pp. 821-23, Robeck to Curzon, 10/18/19, enclosure 1; p. 920, 12/4/19; pp. 921-23, enclosure 1; Wilson, *Loyalties*, 2:134; Ryan, *Dragomans*, pp. 140-41. For documents outlining the Turkish point of view on Kurdistan, see Turquie, *Ministère des affaires étrangéres, Le livre rouge. La Question de Mossoul de la signature du traité d'armistice de Moudros, (30 Octobre 1918 au 1 Mars, 1925)*, nos. 43, 50, 51, 59-65, 67.

17. Foreign Office, F.O. 608/95/365-1-2/1539, Noel memorandum, 12/8/18; F.O. 608/95/365-1-3/11144, G.O.C., Mespot, to War Office, 5/25/19; 11239, Wilson to India Office, 5/25/19; 11863, G.O.C., Mespot to War Office, 7/5/19; Wilson, *Loyalties*, 2:136-39; C. Edmonds, *Kurds, Turks and Arabs*, pp. 29-31, 45-52; *Times* (London), 7/11/19.

18. Wilson, *Loyalties*, 2:136-40, 144-46, 147-53; *Times* (London), 8/15/19, 10/4/19, 11/19/19, 12/15/19.

19. *Br. Doc.*, 4:966-67, Curzon-Berthelot third meeting, 12/23/19; also pp. 967-70, French note on Kurdistan. See also F.O. 608/95/365-1-1/20991, Curzon to Wilson, 11/22/19; Wilson to Curzon, 11/27/19.

20. State Department, A.C.N.P., 185.5133/7, Representatives of Kurdistan and Armenia to Clemenceau, 11/20/19; *Br. Doc.*, 4:742-43, Hohler to Kerr, 8/27/19; pp. 821-23, Robeck to Curzon, 10/18/19, enclosure 1; pp. 925-27, 12/9/19; p. 928, Curzon to Robeck, 12/10/19; Wilson, *Loyalties*, 2:142, India Office to Wilson, 8/24/19; *Times* (London), 11/11/19; 11/18/19.

21. Balfour noted later, "I remember agreeing with him." *Br. Doc.*, 4:373-74, Balfour memorandum, 9/9/19.

22. *Br. Doc.*, 4:244, Grey to Cambon, 5/15/19; pp. 244-45, Cambon to Grey, 5/15/19; A. Tardieu, "Mossoul et le pétrole"; B. Shwadran, *The Middle East, Oil and the Great Powers*, pp. 193-97; Lloyd George, *Truth*, p. 1038. See also above, Chapter 1.

23. Foreign Office, 608/107/384-1-3/2983, Curzon to Balfour, 2/21/19; (regarding Cambon-Graham meeting, 1/30/19); F.O. 608/107/384-1-6/1562, French draft of proposed New Anglo-French agreement regarding Syria, 2/5/19. Tardieu, "Mossoul"; Temperley, *Peace Conference*, 6:182-83; *U.S. Doc., P.P.C.*, 5:3, C. of Four, 3/20/19.

24. F.O. 608/231/1371-1-4/2642, Mallet to Balfour, 2/3/19; 2633, Memorandum by Petroleum Executive and Foreign Office, 2/20/19; *U.S. Doc., P.P.C.*, 5:763, C. of Four, 5/21/19; *Br. Doc.*, 4:340-49, Balfour memorandum, 8/11/19; p. 446, Crowe to Curzon, 10/13/19, enclosure; p. 483, Lloyd George to Clemenceau, 10/18/19; Wilson, *Loyalties*, 2:124; R. de Gontaut-Biron, *La France et la question de Mossoul*, pp. 11, 15.

25. *Br. Doc.*, 4:521, Clemenceau to Lloyd George, 11/9/19. However, in a statement in the Council of Four sessions of May 21, Clemenceau gave an interpretation that generally sustantiates the British "no concession" view. *U.S. Doc., P.P.C.*, 5:760, C. of Four, 5/21/19.

26. *Br. Doc.*, 7:108, S.C., 2/17/20.

27. Lloyd George, *Truth*, p. 1038.

28. *Br. Doc.*, 4:1093, Clerk to Kerr, 6/17/19, enclosure; Lloyd George Papers, F92/14/3, Cadman-Berenger meeting, 12/17/18; de Fleuriau to Balfour (Curzon), 1/6/19; Memorandum on Admiralty meeting, 1/15/19; F.O. 608/231/1371-1-4/2633; Statement on the French proposal for participation in Oil concessions in Mesopotamia and Persia, 2/20/19.

29. Lloyd George Papers, F92/14/3, Notes of interdepartmental meeting, Paris, 2/1/19; Foreign Office, F.O. 608/231/1371-1-4/2642, Mallet minutes with Balfour initials, 2/3/19.

30. Foreign Office, F.O. 608/221/840-1-1/1370, Curzon to Balfour, 2/4/19.

31. Ibid., Mallet minutes.

32. Ibid., F.O. 608/231/1371-1-4/2896, Curzon to Balfour, 2/22/19, and Mallet minutes; Balfour to Curzon, 3/17/19.

33. Ibid., F.O. 608/75/203-1-4/4628, Cadman to Board of Trade, 3/13/19; Cabinet Papers, Cab. 24/92, C.P. 59, Long memorandum, 11/4/19.

34. Walter Long was first lord of the Admiralty and minister in charge of petroleum affairs. Although Cadman did the negotiating for Great Britain the agreement was signed by Long, who officially ranked as Berenger's counterpart. *Br. Doc.*, 4:1089-92, Long-Berenger Agreement, 4/8/19; Temperley, *Peace Conference*, 6:182.

35. Foreign Office, F.O. 608/231-1-4/6336, Curzon to Balfour, 4/2/19; 2630, Petroleum Executive to War Cabinet, n.d. (February, 1919); F.O. 608/75/203-1-4/10821, Minutes of interdepartmental conference, 4/29/19; F.O. 608/75/203-1-4/10822, Wellesley to Cambon, 5/16/19; Lloyd George Papers, F92/14/1, Kidston to Tufton, 5/5/19; Cabinet Papers, Cab. 24/76, G.T. 6961, Petroleum Executive to War Cabinet, 2/22/19; Cab. 23/10, W.C. 564, 5/8/19.

36. See above, Chapter 3.

37. Lloyd George Papers, F51/1/26, Lloyd George to Clemenceau, 5/21/19; Foreign Office, F.O. 608/102/378-1-1/11027, Kerr to Curzon, 5/21/19 and minutes; *Br. Doc.*, 4:1092, Clerk to Kerr, 6/17/19, n. 2; *U.S. Doc., P.P.C.*, 5:756-66, C. of Four, 5/21/19.

38. *U.S. Doc., P.P.C.*, 5:807-11, C. of Four, 5/22/19; Mantoux, *Counseil des Quatre*, 2:159-63, 5/22/19. Lloyd George Papers, F92/14/2, Percy to Kerr, 5/29/19; Foreign Office, F.O. 608/102/378-1-1/11027, Kerr to Curzon, 5/21/19, Percy minute to Tufton, 5/30/19.

39. *Br. Doc.*, 4:1092, Clerk to Kerr, 6/17/19, Foreign Office, F.O. 608/102/378-1-1/11027, Kerr to Curzon, 5/21/19; Marginal notations made in London on copy of letter sent by Lloyd George to Clemenceau, 5/21/19; Lloyd George Papers, F33/2/66, Cadman to Davies, 7/24/19.

40. Lloyd George Papers, F12/1/55, Lloyd George memorandum, 7/10/19. This memorandum was changed to the third person singular by Lloyd George's private secretary, J. T. Davies, and sent to Lord Curzon. See *Br. Doc.*, 4:1100, Davies to Curzon, 7/11/19.

41. Miller, *Diary*, 9:429, 5/21/19; *Br. Doc.*, 4:1095–96, Balfour to Curzon, 6/26/19; p. 1097, Curzon to Balfour, 7/8/19; p. 1099, Balfour to Curzon, 7/25/19, enclosure; Polk Papers, Dr. 73, fol. 121, 11/1/19. For a general description of American policy relating to oil in this period see J. A. de Novo, "The Movement for an Aggressive American Oil Policy Abroad," pp. 854–76 and *American Interests and Policies in the Middle East, 1900–1939*, pp. 169–76; Evans, *U.S. and Partition*, pp. 292–308.

42. *Br. Doc.*, 4:629, Hardinge to Allenby, 1/26/20. See also Bristol Papers, Box 17, Diary, 1/3/20. The British were well aware of the tremendous sulphur and oil potential of the Mosul fields. Foreign Office, F.O. 608/231/1371-1-3/3073, Baghdad to India Office, and Foreign Office, 2/19/19; Cabinet Papers, Cab. 21/1919, Petroleum situation in the British Empire and Mesopotamia, 1918.

43. *Br. Doc.*, 4:277–78, Balfour to Clayton, 6/16/19; p. 280, Clayton to Curzon, 6/19/19; p. 352, French to Curzon, 8/13/19; p. 366, Curzon to French, 8/30/19; p. 382, Meinertzhagen to Curzon, 9/12/19; p. 406, Curzon to Meinertzhagen, 9/20/19; p. 501, Curzon to Grey, 10/30/19; p. 503, Davis to Curzon, 10/31/19; p. 541, Curzon to Davis, 11/21/19; p. 627, Allenby to Curzon, 1/18/20, and n. 2.

44. For details of the formal cancellation, see ibid., p. 1092, Clerk to Kerr, 6/17/19; pp. 1096–97, 7/4/19; p. 1101, Curzon to Cambon, 7/22/19; p. 1110, French Chargé d'Affaires to Curzon, 8/12/19.

45. *Times* (London), 8/2/24. See also Wilson, *Loyalties*, vol 2, passim; Kedourie, *England and the Middle East*, pp. 193–94; Edmonds, *Kurds*, p. 398; E. Monroe, *Britain's Moment in the Middle East, 1914–1956*, p. 103; *Times* (London), 8/14/19, 9/23/19, 10/23/19, 11/8/19, 11/10/19, 11/13/19, 12/13/19.

46. Cabinet Papers, Cab. 24/94, C.P. 259, Greenwood memorandum 12/6/19.

47. Ibid., Cab. 24/92, C.P. 59, Long memorandum, 11/4/19; Cab. 24/93, C.P. 115, Long memorandum, 11/11/19; Cab. 23/18, C. 10(19), 12/3/19, and App. 2, Conclusions of Conference of Ministers, 11/19/19.

48. Ibid., Cab. 23/18, C. 12(19), 12/10/19.

49. *Br. Doc.*, 4:1112, Weakly memorandum, 12/13/19. See also ibid., 2:735, Clemenceau-Lloyd George conversations, 12/11/19.

50. Lloyd George, *Truth*, p. 1100–1101, 12/12/19. Original French text in *Br. Doc.*, 4:583, Berthelot memorandum and British notes, 12/12/19.

51. *Br. Doc.*, 4:597, Curzon-Berthelot third meeting, 12/23/19; p. 1113, Cadman-Berenger conversation, 12/18/19.

52. For the text, see ibid., pp. 1114–17. Also Cabinet Papers, Cab. 23/18, C. 14(19), 12/15/19; Lloyd George Papers, F19/2/2, Greenwood to Lloyd George, 12/23/19, and enclosure, Cadman to Greenwood, 12/23/19. As had been the case with Mr. Long the previous April, the agreement was signed by Greenwood as the appropriate political authority, rather than Cadman.

53. The British acceded to the French request that the basin of the Khabur River should be included in the Syrian French zone. See *Br. Doc.*, 4:596–97, Curzon-Berthelot third meeting, 12/23/19; p. 602, fourth meeting, 12/23/19.

54. Both Donald Bishop and Max Beloff have pointed out in their writings the "indifference with which the Foreign Office treated economic problems." D. G. Bishop, *The Administration of British Foreign Relations*, p. 226. As Beloff comments in discussing the work of the Foreign Office: "The promotion of British business was . . . not given the priority that some people would have wished to see in the new competitive world." Beloff, *Imperial Sunset*, p. 354.

55. *Br. Doc.*, 4:463, Curzon to Derby, 10/13/19; pp. 468–69, Clemenceau to Derby, 10/14/19; p. 473, Curzon to Derby, 10/15/19; pp. 474–76, 10/16/19; pp. 479–89, 10/18/19; pp. 495–97,

10/22/19; Cabinet Papers, Cab. 24/93, C.P. 165, Feisal to Lloyd George, 11/6/19; *Times* (London), 12/16/19.

56. *Br. Doc.*, 4:533, Meinertzhagen to Curzon, 11/17/19; pp. 555–58, Feisal to Curzon, 11/28/19, enclosures; pp. 559–68, Hardinge-Cambon conversation, 11/29/19; p. 590, Curzon to Derby, 12/17/19, enclosure; pp. 591–92, Feisal to Curzon, 12/19/19; pp. 613–15, Meinertzhagen to Curzon, 1/13/20; Polk Papers, Dr. 78, fol. 72, Conversation with General Haddad, and enclosures, 12/1/19; *Times* (London), 12/29/19, 12/30/19, 12/31/19, 1/9/20, 1/19/20, 1/20/20; Longrigg, *Syria and Lebanon*, p. 96.

57. *Br. Doc.*, 4:592–95, Derby to Curzon, 12/20/19, and n. 2; pp. 611–12, 1/8/20; pp. 612–13, Forbes-Adams to Young, 1/12/20; p. 615, Meinertzhagen to Curzon, 1/13/20; pp. 625–27, Vansittart to Curzon, 1/17/20, enclosures, 1,2; 7:103–7, S.C., 2/17/20; pp. 113, 117–18, 2/18/20; State Department, Turkey, 867.00/1102, Bristol to Sec. State, 1/24/20; W. E. Hocking, *The Spirit of World Politics, with Special Studies of the Near East*, p. 257; Antonius, *Arab Awakening*, p. 301; *Correspondance d'Orient*, pp. 64–66, 1/30/20; Zeine, *Arab Independence*, pp. 120–30.

58. *Br. Doc.*, 4:454, Crowe to Curzon, Clemenceau memorandum, 10/10/19; pp. 578–79, Berthelot memorandum and British notes, 12/12/19, pp. 597–98, Curzon-Berthelot third meeting, 12/23/19; pp. 599–602, fourth meeting, 12/23/19; pp. 604–5, Derby to Curzon, 12/27/19, enclosure; p. 610, Curzon to Derby, 1/8/20; p. 631, Derby to Curzon, 1/2/20, enclosure. Not all departments within the British government agreed. On December 30, the Board of Trade issued a memorandum stating: "It is of great importance that the frontier between French and British spheres should be so defined as to secure a route entirely in the British zone." F.O. 608/271/7/7.

59. *Br. Doc.*, 4:466–67, Crowe to Curzon, 10/13/19, enclosure; pp. 492–95, Peterson to Forbes-Adam, 10/20/19, enclosure and n. 5; pp. 599–603, Curzon-Berthelot fourth meeting, 12/23/19; pp. 607–9, Forbes-Adam memorandum, 12/30/19. The rumor concerning Tangier proved ultimately to be correct, though France never tied this to the negotiations over oil rights. See below, Chapters 12, 13.

60. Balfour, who also supported the scheme, was not present. Cabinet Papers, Cab. 23/20, C. 1(20), and App. 4, Curzon memorandum, 1/7/20; Cab. 23/37, Conference of Ministers, 1/5/20; *Br. Doc.*, 4:992–1000, Curzon memorandum, 1/4/20.

61. Churchill, *Aftermath*, p. 395. See also ibid., p. 396; Cumming, *Franco-British Rivalry*, p. 92–95; Nicolson, *Curzon*, p. 112–15; Ronaldshay, *Curzon*, 3:270; Cambon, *Correspondance*, 3:375–76, 2/18/20.

62. Cabinet Papers, Cab. 24/95, C.P. 382, Montagu memorandum, 1/1/20. See also ibid., C.P. 326, Montagu memorandum, 12/18/19; Lloyd George Papers F 40/2/64, Montagu to Lloyd George, 12/13/19; Waley, *Montagu*, p. 243.

63. Foreign Office F.O. 608/112/385-1-14/16727 a,b, Dispatches from Indian Moslems, 8/29/19–12/12/19; F.O. 608/273/63, Moslem deputations regarding future of Constantinople; F.O. 608/272/25/32, Aga Khan to Montagu, 1/8/20; Cabinet Papers, Cab. 24/96, C.P. 432, Montagu memorandum and dispatches, 1/6/20; Cab. 24/97, C.P. 590, 1/19/20; 590a, 2/5/20, Dispatches from India and so forth; *Br. Doc.*, 4:847, Curzon to Crowe, 10/30/19; *Times* (London), 8/2/19, 9/10/19, 10/28/19, 11/8/19, 12/20/19, 12/24/19, 1/9/20, 1/14/20, 1/17/20.

64. Cabinet Papers, Cab. 24/95, C.P. 326, Montagu memorandum, 12/18/19; Cab. 23/37, Conference of Ministers, 1/5/20; Cab. 24/96, C.P. 432, Montagu memorandum, 1/6/20, (Government of India telegram, 5/18/19); India, Superintendent of Government Printing, *India in 1919*, pp. 23,47; idem, *India in 1921–1922*, p. 36; Pichon, *Partage*, pp. 202–3; Graves, *Briton and Turk*, p. 199; Gaillard, *Turks and Europe*, pp. 121–24; Adkisson, *Britain and the Kemalist Movement*, pp. 260–61.

65. Cabinet Papers, Cab. 23/37, Conference of Ministers, 1/5/20; also in Cab. 23/20 C.1(20), App. 1.

66. Ibid., Cab. 23/20, C.1(20), and Apps. 1,2,3; Gaillard, *Turks and Europe*, pp. 95–97; *Times*, (London), 1/7/20.

67. It is interesting to note that the military representatives in Constantinople had long ago given up the idea that it would be desirable to have a Nationalist government in Constantinople or that such a government could be controlled by the Allies. They had therefore become strong advocates of Turkish expulsion from the city. The War Office at home, however, refused to accept this advice and remained a staunch supporter of the plan to retain the Turks in Constantinople. See above, Chapter 8; and Cabinet Papers, Cab. 23/37, Conference of Ministers, 1/5/20.

68. Churchill, *Aftermath*, p. 395.

69. Cabinet Papers, Cab. 24/95, C.P. 342, General Staff memorandum, 12/24/19; Cab. 24/96, C.P. 410, Churchill memorandum, 1/6/20; Cab. 23/37, Conference of Ministers, 1/5/20; Cab. 23/20, C.1(20), 1/6/20; Callwell, *Henry Wilson*, 2:218, 12/30/19; p. 221, (n.d.); *Times* (London), 2/19/20; *Parliamentary Debates* (Commons), 5th ser., 125:1026, 2/19/20; Churchill, *Aftermath*, pp. 392–96.

70. At the end of September, 1919, there were 21,000 British troops and 79,000 Indian troops in Mesopotamia. This was reduced to 10,000 and 44,000 respectively by March, 1920. In December, 1919, there were 18,000 Indian soldiers stationed in Near Eastern areas other than Palestine and Mesopotamia. Cabinet Papers, Cab 24/95, C.P. 342, General Staff memorandum, 12/24/19; *Times* (London), 10/24/19; 3/3/20.

71. Cabinet Papers, Cab. 24/95, C.P. 342, General Staff memorandum, 12/24/19; Cab. 23/20, C.1(20), 1/6/20; Churchill, *Aftermath*, p. 393; "Un Diplomate," *Cambon*, p. 307; Cambon, *Correspondence*, 3:375, 2/18/20. There were two sides to the religious argument. Hohler summarized the other side as follows: "I cannot find that there is, in actual fact, any real basis for the argument which has of late been frequently advanced that Constantinople is in any way whatever a Holy City of Islam. The edifice of Santa Sophia is merely a symbol of the Turkish conquest of the Greek Empire, and it is no more the symbol of this than is the tenure of Constantinople as a whole, and the fane is venerated by the Turks as such, but it is no object of pilgrimage and has no peculiar sanctity for other Turkish Moslems. The only two spots in the city which are held genuinely sacred are the two shrines: the one is the old seraglio in which the relics of the Prophet are preserved, and which the Sultan only is allowed to visit, but which owes its sanctity merely to the presence of the relics; and the other, the alleged tomb—spurious, however, and nothing more than a pious fraud—on the upper waters of the Golden Horn of Eyoub, who was a companion of the Prophet and who fell in the Arab attack on Byzantium in 675. Apart from these, the mosques and other religious buildings, splendid as many of them are, have no sanctity beyond that which attaches to all time-honoured places of worship in all countries; the sentiments of pride and of affection of the Turks would be hurt by seeing these places fall from their control, but not those of piety or religious fervor." *Br. Doc.*, 4:854, Hohler to Curzon, 11/4/19. For more discussion of the views of the War and India Offices, see ibid., p. 909, Kidston to Crowe, 11/28/19; p. 913, Crowe to Kidston, 12/1/19.

72. Cabinet Papers, Cab. 23/20, C.1 (20), App. 4, Curzon memorandum, 1/7/20; also in Ronaldshay, *Curzon*, 3:270–71. See also *Br. Doc.*, 4:1026–28, Forbes-Adam to Kidston, 1/13/20, enclosure; Nicolson, *Curzon*, pp. 99, 113–15; Cambon, *Correspondance*, 3:369, 1/7/20.

73. *Le Temps*, 1/1/20; *R.F.P.: Political Review*, 1:1/16/20, 1/23/20. See also *New York Times*, 12/27/19, 1/2/20.

74. *Br. Doc.*, 4:1013–14, Webb to Curzon, 1/9/20; Cambon, *Correspondance*, 3:369, 1/7/20; p. 370, 1/8/20; pp. 375–76, 1/18/20; *Times* (London), 1/5/20, 1/10/20; Woods, "Sévres," p. 550; *Correspondance d'Orient*, p. 37, 1/15/20; pp. 81–84, 1/30/20.

75. *Br. Doc.*, 4:1016–25, Vansittart to Curzon, 1/12/20, enclosure. Whether this was a diplomatic way of making it easy for the British to shift or whether it constituted an attempt by the French to recede from the London agreements regardless of the British attitude is

hard to say. Poincaré later claimed that "Clemenceau, back in France, convinced himself of the grave complications which might break out in Asia Minor, and the clashes that threatened to develop between the Allies if the Sultan were obliged to cross the sea of Marmora. He therefore returned with rejuvenated vigor to M. Pichon's conclusions [that Constantinople should go to the Turks] and held on to them firmly." Although this may have been the case, it is equally possible that this constituted an effort after the fact to gain favor with the Turks by giving the impression that France was responsible for bringing about the policy change. R. Poincaré, 3/15/20, as quoted by Cumming, *Franco-British Rivalry*, p. 94.

76. *Br. Doc.*, 4:1037-42, Forbes-Adam to Phipps, 1/19/20, App. A; Cabinet Papers, Cab. 23/35, S-6, Conference of Ministers (Paris), 1/11/20; Cab 29/29, A.J. 10, Counter-draft to Montagu memorandum, prepared by Vansittart and Forbes-Adam, 1/15/20; Cab 23/35, S-9, Conference of Ministers (Paris), 1/15/20.

77. Cabinet Papers, Cab 23/35, S-8, Conference of Ministers (Paris), 1/13/20; *Br. Doc.*, 4:1044-47, 1060-61, Forbes-Adam to Phipps, 1/19/20, Apps. C and E.

78. Lloyd George Papers, F12/3/3, Curzon to Lloyd George, 1/21/20.

79. Ibid.; *Br. Doc.*, 4:1047-60, Forbes-Adam to Phipps, 1/19/20, App. D.

80. J. Martet, *Georges Clemenceau*, p. 315. See also editorial in *Le Temps*, 1/19/20.

81. Cambon, *Correspondence*, 3:354, 9/20/19; pp. 366-67, 12/7/19; pp. 370-71, 1/17/20; p. 372, 1/24/20; p. 373, 1/24/20; p. 376, 2/18/20; G. Bruun, *Clemenceau*, p. 199; Lloyd George, *Truth*, pp. 1102-03; J. H. Jackson, *Clemenceau and the Third Republic*, pp. 209, 219-23; Martet, *Clemenceau*, pp. 312-15; G. Adam, *The Tiger, Georges Clemenceau, 1841-1929*, pp. 260-61; G. Wormser, *La République de Clemenceau*, p. 498; R. L. Buell, *Contemporary French Politics*, chap. 6; P. Erlanger, *Clemenceau*, pp. 597-617; G. Monnerville, *Clemenceau*, pp. 682-86. For a general survey of French press reaction see *R.F.P.: Political Review*, 1/30/19.

82. Cambon, *Correspondance*, 3:371, 1/17/20.

83. Over three hundred delegates abstained from voting on the confirmation ballot.

84. In a letter to Curzon on December 10, 1919, Lloyd George complained that having the Conference in Paris meant leaving France with first-rate representatives while the rest had second-rate negotiators who were all too susceptible to the French press and other pressures. "We must break up this dangerous enclave where the Foreign policy of the world is run by the nation which is the least fitted by temper, temperament and tradition to run it at the present moment." Lloyd George Papers, F12/2/11, 12/10/19. See also *Br. Doc.*, 4:881, Curzon-Pichon conversation, 11/2/19; Foreign Office, F.O. 608/117/385-3-3/20932, Curzon to Derby, 11/25/19; Norman to Curzon, 12/3/19; *Br. Doc.*, 2:963-65, Allied Conference, 1/21/20; 4:1068-69, Derby to Hardinge, 1/21/20; pp. 1069-71, 1071-74, Vansittart to Hardinge, 1/22/20, (2); pp. 1081-82, Derby to Curzon, 1/31/20; pp. 1082-83, Curzon to Derby, 2/2/20; p. 1083, Derby to Curzon, 2/4/20; pp. 1083-85, Vansittart to Hardinge, 2/4/20; Cabinet Papers, Cab. 23/20, C.8 (20); 2/4/20; Cab. 23-37, Conference of Ministers, 2/9/20. Cambon commented sarcastically several times about the Conference that "was established at London, but pretended all the time that it existed at Paris." Cambon, *Correspondance*, 3:381, 3/14/20; p. 383, 3/29/20.

85. The Italians had already expressed their alarm at statements in the French press that the Straits issue had been settled. *Br. Doc.*, 4:992, Tilley conversation with Italian ambassador, 12/31/19.

X ❋ THE TURKISH NATIONALISTS AND THE PEACE NEGOTIATIONS

T HE Nationalist movement, which first appeared in May, 1919, was founded by Mustapha Kemal Pasha, later to be known as Ataturk.[1] A general on the Syrian front at the end of the war, Mustapha Kemal had distinguished himself as commander of the successful defense against the British in the Gallipoli campaign. An ardent nationalist, he long had opposed the leadership of Enver Pasha and the Committee of Union and Progress (C.U.P.). The Nationalist movement was independent of the Young Turks in its origins, and subsequent Allied charges that the Nationalists were merely a continuation of the old C.U.P. were without foundation.

Program of the Nationalists

Arriving at Samsun on May 19, 1919, where he had been sent by the Constantinople government as inspector general of the Third Army, Kemal immediately made contact with resistance leaders. Slowly an organization grew that had definite nationalistic aims based upon concepts of Turkish national identity, popular sovereignty, and cultural and social secularization. Kemal realistically confined his territorial ambitions to the preservation of an independent Turkish state in that area where Turks constituted the majority of the population.[2]

A series of conferences with various important leaders and delegates culminated in September with the Congress of Sivas, at which elected delegates from all regions in Anatolia were present. The congress adopted a series of resolutions that outlined the basic foreign policy to be followed by the Nationalists. These indicated a willingness to accept the frontier outlined in the Armistice of Mudros as the boundary of the future Turkish state. At the same time, the congress pledged open and forceful resistance to any attempt to create an independent Armenia out of this territory or an autonomous Greek state at Smyrna. Although completely rejecting any implementation of the old system of foreign preferential judicial and economic rights known as the Capitulations, the resolutions stated that Turkey would accept "with pleasure the scientific, industrial, and economic assistance of every state which will not set forth imperialistic tendencies with respect to our country and which will respect the principles of nationality." [3] The congress, which called itself "The Assembly to Defend the Rights and the Interests of the Provinces of Anatolia and Roumelia," called upon the government in Constantinople to convoke immediately a National Assembly and submit all decisions to it.[4]

Kemal, as chairman of the Representative Committee of the Assembly, headed the Nationalist organization. Heavy pressure was exerted upon the Damad Ferid government in Constantinople in an effort to force its resignation. This was done by means of telegrams to the Ottoman Parliament demanding the formation of a new cabinet favorable to the Nationalists and by the rupture of all communications between Constantinople and Anatolia (which effectively proved Kemal's control of the area). When the Damad Ferid cabinet fell on October 2, the new grand vizier, Ali Riza Pasha, immediately sent his naval minister, Salih Pasha, to confer with Kemal. The two men reached an agreement known as the Amasya Protocol, which theoretically constituted government recognition of the aims and ambitions of the Nationalist movement. Actually, although Salih Pasha signed this document, the government in Constantinople never paid any particular attention to it. This was probably due as much to Allied pressure as to any basic unwillingness on the part of the government to work with the Kemalist organization.[5]

Despite a specific prohibition against it in the Amasya Protocol, the government insisted that Parliament should convene in Constantinople. Elections in October returned a strong Nationalist majority. Kemal immediately held a series of caucases at Ankara with most of the delegates, out of which emerged the National Pact that was officially adopted by the Parliament in Constantinople on January 28, 1920. Based on the principles of the Sivas Declaration, this document in addition demanded a plebiscite in Thrace and the disputed areas of Kars, Batum, and Ardahan. The necessity of maintaining the government, the sultan, and the caliphate at Constantinople was vigorously stated, although a conciliatory clause was included relative to a possible international agreement on the administration of the Straits. The pact reiterated the renunciation of the capitulations evident in the Sivas Declaration and the Amasya Protocol, and added a clearly worded clause prohibiting any outside interference in "political, financial, and other matters." Finally, a willingness to conclude minorities agreements similar to those undertaken by other nations was expressed.[6]

With the acceptance of the Nationalist doctrine by the sultan's government, the two factions appeared to be united in a single foreign policy. In effect, the Allies had been officially notified on the eve of the Conference of London as to the kind of peace that the Turks considered "the maximum of sacrifice" they could undertake.[7]

The Allies and the Nationalists

All this suggests correctly enough a movement of considerable size and significance. But what was the reaction of the Allies to the Kemalist movement as it appeared and rapidly grew stronger during 1919 and early 1920? How well informed were the negotiators in Paris and London concerning the Nationalist movement, and what effect did it have on their own negotiations and plans for peace in the Near East?

It is clear that Kemal's program, his activities, and his plans were all well known. In fact, he did his best to publicize them. During the spring, summer, and early fall of 1919, Kemal managed to establish contact with several Allied groups and agents. To all he expressed the same nationalistic ambitions. In a long meeting with General Harbord, head of the American investigating committee that had been sent to Armenia, he hinted that American commercial and administrative help would be welcomed and left Harbord with the impression that the Nationalists would come out publicly in favor of an American mandate. From time to time Kemal also met with various British and French agents, one of whom even saw Curzon personally in the early fall and warned him of the Nationalist danger.[8]

In September, 1919, Kemal notified the Supreme Council that the Turkish delegation headed by Damad Ferid was not representative of the will of the people and served notice that subsequent Turkish delegations must be recruited from Nationalist forces. He also issued specific protests against the French occupation of Cilicia and the Greek invasion of Smyrna.[9]

The outward attitude of both the Turkish regime in Constantinople and the Allied governments was one of relative unconcern. Dispatches to the *Times* and to the European press in general tended to write off the movement as having at best an harrassment potential.[10] However, British and American agents in Turkey were watching and worrying about the Kemalist movement from the middle of June, and it is evident that the French were equally concerned, for both Calthorpe's and Robeck's reports indicate that they were in close consultation on this matter with the French high commissioner, Albert DeFrance.[11] Although the Turkish government at Constantinople testified to the contrary, the high commissioners persisted in regarding the Kemalist movement as a revival of the C.U.P. in different plumage. They compelled a reluctant Turkish government to order Kemal's recall (Kemal refused and instead resigned from the army) and called for the arrest and outlawing of all the Nationalist leaders.[12]

Actually, Allied policy was far less anti-Nationalist than it seemed. As early as July both Admiral Calthorpe and his second-in-command, Admiral Webb, had become extremely concerned over the obvious weakening of the Constantinople regime. The majority of the reports sent to London were increasingly pessimistic about the future of the Constantinople government, the ability of the Allies to dictate a peace treaty, or the possibility of a collapse of the Nationalist movement. The British and French high commissioners decided that Britain and France would take no part in political matters, but would support legally constituted sources of authority (the sultan), and would oppose any kind of revolution.[13] Calthorpe, however, did not at first regard a Nationalist takeover as hazardous to Allied plans; in fact he commented that there would be "more satisfaction, even if there should be more difficulty, in exacting hard terms from the Unionists rather than those who, one has reason to believe, are fundamentally well intentioned and friendly."[14] He remained confident that the Allies could easily control a Nationalist government if it were retained at Constantinople.[15]

Despite this yearning for "satisfaction," the British in Constantinople became alarmed when plans for parliamentary elections were announced. When they suddenly realized that a Nationalist parliamentary majority was an actual possibility, the idea no longer seemed so satisfying. The result was a combined Franco-British decision to depart from their political neutrality and encourage the sultan to oppose the Nationalist organization more vigorously. This policy of support was only verbal, and was limited by very explicit instructions from Curzon that it "should on no account be extended to cover use of force to prevent accession to power of Committee of Union and Progress, nor against individual supporters of Committee as such."[16] In other words, in a physical sense the "hands off" policy remained in force.[17]

The Sivas Conference in September had a profound effect, not only on the Turkish government, but on the British and French as well. In private conversations, Damad Ferid admitted a total lack of control and asked for an Allied military expedition or at least permission to send Turkish troops to the interior. British agents in the Near East became openly doubtful about controlling the Nationalist movement, and for the first time conceded that the organization might not be just a revival of the C.U.P. By the middle of September, the British and the French high commissioners had decided that the Allies "were powerless to apply or give any effective support to [the] present Government."[18] The fact that Turkey had two governments of at least equal strength was tacitly admitted, and it is evident that the high commissioners held little real hope for rees-tablishment of authority by the Constantinople government. Both commissioners pleaded for a speedy peace treaty and the complete withdrawal of Italian and Greek troops from Anatolia, for they were agreed that this was the one possible way to prevent a Nationalist takeover.[19]

By the end of September, Nationalist forces were virtually in control of all of Anatolia except for territory occupied by Allied troops. All telegraphic communication with Constantinople had been stopped, and rail lines were being continually harassed. The grand vizier desperately pleaded for permission to send Turkish troops to the interior. The British, French, and Italian high commissioners sought the opinion of the commander of the Allied forces in Anatolia, General Milne, and after much consultation, his advice was unanimously accepted.

We therefore decided to tell the Grand Vizier (1) that despatch of 2,000 men would be altogether insufficient to re-establish order; . . . (2) that despatch of a larger force would throw country into civil war; (3) that to anticipate such an event Allied Military Authorities think that they would have to withdraw their troops on Anatolian line at least to Gulf of Ismid; (4) that result of this would be to deliver immediately to insurgents the railway thus cutting off capital from all connection with Interior and rendering revictualing of population impossible; (5) that therefore under Article V of Armistice High Commissioners felt unable to authorize proposed despatch and disposition of troops.[20]

This report, when read in London, was minuted by Lord Hardinge, "I must say that we do not really give Damad Ferid a chance, but we ought to encourage him if possible," [21] to which Curzon added his initials.

Unable to act, and faced with increasing pressure from the Nationalists, Damad Ferid resigned on October 2. Allied responsibility for this was extensive. Thomas Hohler summed up the situation well:

Ferid . . . was always anxious up to the last minute to go in person with a force or at least to send a force and we prevented him from doing this. The result was that we really helped Mustafa, whose freedom of action we could not check, whilst we could, and did check that of Ferid, i.e., the "constituted Government," but on the whole we were undoubtedly right for if a force had gone against Mustafa, one of two things would have happened. The most probable that the force would have gone over to Mustafa's side; the second that a civil war would have been let loose on the country, the burden of which in all probability would have fallen on the Christians. . . . I never contemplated that the Allies would reduce their military forces so thoroughly before they had made peace and imposed their conditions. We have acted on the reverse principle of the Japanese, whose old proverb is, that the end of the fight is the right time to tie on your helmet.[22]

So pessimistic had the British command at Constantinople become that a memorandum by Webb, which was sent with de Robeck's approval on October 10, stated:

I cannot too strongly repeat and emphasize that the time has gone by when it was possible to assume that any Turkish Government must accept any peace which the Allies might choose to offer, and when it was legitimate to prefer, if anything, that the reins of power here should be in the hands of the Committee of Union and Progress for the sake of the moral effect of poetic justice of making those who ruined Turkey subscribe to her death warrant. Every day the Armistice is prolonged sees the Turk recovering more and more from the overwhelming sense of disaster which General Allenby's victorious advances, followed by crushing Armistice terms, instilled into him. . . . The possibility (which every week's delay tends more and more to transform into probability) that Turkey will reject the proposals of the Allies, must therefore be taken into serious consideration, necessitating a review of what means the Allies will, in the event, be prepared to employ, in order to secure the execution of the Peace terms they mean to impose.[23]

This communication definitely impressed Curzon, for he had it sent for examination to British ambassadors at all major capitals.[24] It may have been this that led him to remark to Pichon on November 12, that unless the peace was made quickly it might not be made at all, for there might shortly be no Turkish government with which to negotiate. It would have been more accurate had he said that a future Turkish government might well be one with which it would be impossible to deal.[25]

Not only the Foreign Office was impressed by Kemalist strength in the fall of 1919. The British War Office was concerned over the possible inability of British troops stationed along the Anatolian railway to protect the railway and the British civilians operating it. In fact the War Office proposed to evacuate all civilians and perhaps even the military detachments should Nationalist pressure become too strong.[26]

Although Curzon concurred and authorization was granted, the decision was greeted with bitter protests from all sides. Robeck complained that this retreat would destroy what little British prestige remained after previous withdrawals from the Caucasus and Samsun. Moreover, a British withdrawal would mean in all probability that the French would move in and all Anatolia would come under French influence. Robeck strongly opposed giving up the railroad "unless it is policy of His Majesty's Government to disinterest themselves totally in the future of Turkey." [27] However, the British high command in Constantinople urged an end to any form of Turkish authority over Constantinople and the Straits. Similar protests came from Sir Eyre Crowe and General Milne. The result was that although the authority to withdraw from Anatolia was not rescinded, the plan was not immediately put into effect.[28]

Effect of the Nationalist Movement on the Anglo-French December Conversations

There is conclusive evidence that the seriousness of the situation was recognized and reported by British agents in the Near East. That the French representatives were equally aware of the danger is also clear, and it may be assumed that reports similar to those sent to the British Foreign Office also reached the Quai d'Orsay.[29] By the end of the year the press of both nations were expressing fear and apprehension regarding the Nationalist movement.[30] Yet, from a first examination of the Anglo-French negotiations that took place during December and January, one would hardly guess that anyone had ever heard of Mustapha Kemal or the Nationalist movement. The only reference made to Kemal was a brief comment by Curzon that "it would be disastrous to dictate a peace which the Allies had not the military strength to enforce," to which Berthelot replied that he "thought the Nationalist movement . . . was largely bluff, and that a show of force from the points where the Allies had troops would be sufficient to show this." [31] Curzon, although stating that he was less optimistic, agreed that a way certainly could be found to impose peace conditions if the Allies acted in concert.

Other than this brief discussion, the Nationalist movement was not mentioned. Nevertheless, the results of the Anglo-French December conversations seem to indicate a far greater concern with the Nationalist movement than appears on the surface. The decision to separate Constantinople and the Straits from Turkey may well have reflected a realization of the strength of the Nationalists. Certainly, in the British cabinet meetings the Nationalist threat was discussed.[32] It will be remembered that one of Curzon's main reasons for wanting the Turks out of Constantinople and the Straits was his desire to separate the area completely from the authority and control of the weak and unstable regime of the sultan, a regime that he realized might well be overthrown by the Nationalists. A similar concern over the possibility of a Nationalist takeover in Anatolia may help to explain both the Picot-Kemal conversations and the French willingness to accept Curzon's arguments relative to the Straits area.

The peace treaty, as outlined in the December Anglo-French discussions, was a two-part affair. If all the plans for the control of Turkey could be achieved, fine; if not, Anatolia could be released and discarded easily, with no loose ties or connections with the important areas of the Arab world or with Constantinople and the Straits. Only Smyrna remained to hinder the separation. Here Curzon had long opposed the Greek military action, and he agreed with Berthelot that Turkish sovereignty should be restored. Thus it would seem that the scheme as envisaged by the negotiators in December was a combination of "what we would like" and "what we must have," with great care taken to keep the two from becoming inextricably entangled. The refusal of the British cabinet to accept this program on January 6, 1920, immediately mixed the necessary and the merely desired completely together. What the cabinet, and particularly the War Office, apparently failed to realize was that even if Allied forces were withdrawn from Anatolia, as long as Constantinople remained the capital of Turkey and under foreign occupation,

Allied responsibility for events in Asia Minor was unavoidable. As a result, from that time on the negotiation of the Treaty of Sèvres proceeded on the premise of Allied involvement in all of Turkey, and Curzon's efforts to maintain carefully drawn and clearly defined distinctions between the essential and the nonessential went for naught.

Therefore, it would seem that the December conversations showed evidence of an unmentioned, but great, underlying concern about the Nationalist threat and the limitations on the peace treaty that it might well impose. Had the final peace treaty been formulated along the lines drawn up at that time, it might have had a chance at long-range success. This is not to say that Curzon's wish to deprive the Turks of their capital was "right" in any moral or ethical sense, but it was practical, and had both the advantage of being reasonably attainable and of giving the Allies control of the Straits without involving them in Anatolian-Turkish affairs. But by the time the Conference of London opened in February, all this had gone by the boards. The decision to ignore reality had been made. It would be all or nothing in the best traditions of nineteenth-century control and the establishment of spheres of influence.

1. There is no intention to undertake here a detailed examination of the growth and development of the Kemalist regime. The concern of this study is only the effect which the Nationalist movement had upon the course of the peace negotiations. For the rise of Kemalism, see D. Webster, *The Turkey of Ataturk;* E. Smith, *Turkey: Origins of the Kemalist Movement and the Government of the Grand National Assembly, (1919-1923);* Kinross, *Ataturk,* section 2; I. and M. Orga, *Ataturk;* N. Berkes, *The Development of Secularism in Turkey,* chaps. 15-17. For Kemalist foreign policy, see Davison, "Turkish Diplomacy."

2. Berkes, *Secularism in Turkey,* chap. 15; S. N. Fisher, *The Military in the Middle East,* pp. 25-29. It is generally accepted that the event which triggered the formation of the Nationalist movement was the Greek landing at Smyrna. Davison, "Turkish Diplomacy," pp. 173-74; Kinross, *Ataturk,* pp. 179-85. Kemal apparently had been in touch with leaders of the various nationalist "defense" organizations before leaving Constantinople. See K. Karpat, *Turkey's Politics,* pp. 33-34; Kinross, *Ataturk,* pp. 163-79. Adkisson suggests that Damad Ferid was aware of Kemal's plans to oppose the Greeks and Armenians, but did not realize that this would include rebellion against the government at Constantinople. *Britain and the Kemalist Movement,* p. 168.

3. *U.S. Doc., 1919,* 2:887, Exhibit E of the Harbord Report.

4. Ibid., pp. 886-88. For the previous Erzerum Resolutions, see M. Larcher, *La Guerre Turque dans la Guerre Mondiale,* pp. 554-55, 7/10/19; Webster, *Turkey of Ataturk,* p. 79; Frangulis, *Crise Mondiale,* 2:146-53.

5. Webster, *Turkey of Ataturk*, pp. 80-81; *Br. Doc.*, 4:787, Robeck to Curzon, 10/2/19; pp. 787-88, 10/3/19 (2); pp. 802-10, 10/10/19; pp. 887-91, 11/16/19, plus enclosures 1 and 2; Pech, *Alliés et Turquie*, p. 82, 9/23/19; Smith, *Turkey*, pp. 21-23; Adkisson, *Britain and the Kemalist Movement*, pp. 211-13; *Times* (London), 9/15/19, 10/7/19, 10/11/19.

6. For the text of the National Pact, see Webster, *Turkey of Ataturk*, pp. 81-82; Temperley, *Peace Conference*, 6:605-6; Toynbee and Kirkwood, *Turkey*, pp. 85-86; Larcher, *Guerre Turque*, pp. 555-56. See also N. Sousa, *The Capitulatory Regime of Turkey, its History, Origin and Nature*, p. 206.

7. Davison, "Turkish Diplomacy," p. 180; Smith, *Turkey*, pp. 25-26.

8. This was Col. Alfred Rawlinson. Curzon was interested enough to send Rawlinson back to Anatolia, ostensibly to oversee the confiscation of weapons, but actually with verbal instructions to meet again with Kemal "and endeavor to ascertain as definitely as might be possible from him what Peace terms his party were expecting to obtain, and what conditions . . . they would be prepared to accept." Rawlinson returned to Anatolia and was subsequently imprisoned because of Nationalist reaction to the Allied occupation of Constantinople in March, 1920. See A. Rawlinson, *Adventures in the Near East, 1918-1922*, pp. 188-90, 231, 234, 249-52; Kinross, *Ataturk*, pp. 203-4, 210; Foreign Office, F.O. 608/112/385-1-15/18202, Rawlinson Report, 8/18/19; 18356, Webb to Curzon (Rawlinson Report), 8/30/19; F.O. 608/278/394/461, Osborne to Vansittart, 7/29/20. Also *Br. Doc.*, 4:737, Webb to Curzon, 8/22/19; Foreign Office, F.O. 406/41/128, Robeck to Curzon, 10/10/19; *U.S. Doc., 1919*, 2:888-89, Congress of Sivas to U.S. Government, 9/9/19; Harbord Report, 10/16/19; pp. 858-59; pp. 875-85; Exhibit C; Bristol Papers, Box 27, Bristol to Polk, (from Harbord), 10/6/19; Box 16, Diary, 10/7/19, 11/5/19; J. Harbord, "Mustapha Kemal Pasha and his Party," pp. 176-93; Davison, "Turkish Diplomacy," p. 178; M. Kemal, *A Speech delivered by Ghazi Mustapha Kemal, President of the Turkish Republic, October 1927*, pp. 67-70, 136-37, 147-48, 151, 154, 156; "Turkey at the Coming Peace Conference," p. 212.

9. State Department, A.C.N.P., 185.5/46, Bristol to Paris, 10/2/19; Turkey, 867.00/913, Ravndal to Sec. State, 8/22/19; Davison, "Turkish Diplomacy," p. 179; *Br. Doc.*, 4:538, Robeck to Curzon, 11/19/19, enclosure 2; pp. 932-33, 12/12/19, enclosure; Kemal, *Speech*, p. 168; Mustafa Kemal, *Die Dokumente zur Rede vom 15 bis 20 Oktober, 1927*, pp. 114-15, no. 127.

10. Gontaut-Biron, *Comment*, pp. 335-37; *Times* (London), 5/22/19, 7/16/19, 8/7/19; *Correspondance d'Orient* until the middle of December discounted the Nationalists. *Le Temps*, on the contrary, took the Kemalist movement very seriously. See 9/10/19.

11. The sending of Kemal to the interior and the early revolt apparently went almost unnoticed by Allies. Ryan, *Dragomans*, p. 130. Foreign Office, F.O. 608/112/385-1-15, F.O. 608/112/385-1-16, F.O. 608/114/385-1-25 all contain numerous reports from British agents in the Near East during 1919 attesting to the growth and danger of the Nationalist movement. See also Bristol Papers, Box 27, Bristol to Paris, 6/11/19; 9/5/19; Box 16, Reports for weeks ending 7/13/19, 7/20/19; State Department, Turkey, 867.00/892, Ravndal to Sec. State, 7/1/19; 907, 8/5/19; 908, 8/14/19.

12. The very reluctance of the Constantinople regime to take any action against Kemal stemmed from the fact that it sympathized fully with the Kemalist opposition to the Greek landings at Smyrna. Kemal, *Speech*, pp. 26-27; Foreign Office, F.O., 608/112/385-1-15/13529, Calthorpe to Curzon, 6/23/20; *Br. Doc.*, 4:654-57, Webb to Curzon, 6/28/19; pp. 667-68, Calthorpe to Curzon, 7/8/19; pp. 668-69, 7/9/19; pp. 688-90, 7/17/19, enclosures 1, 2 and n. 3; p. 714, 8/1/19; pp. 720-21, Webb to Curzon, 8/8/19, enclosure 1; *Times* (London), 7/21/19; Bristol Papers, Box 27, Bristol to Paris, 8/2/19.

13. *Br. Doc.*, 4:696-98, Calthorpe to Curzon, 7/23/19.

14. Ibid., p. 709, 7/31/19.

15. Ibid., p. 697, 7/23/19.

16. Ibid., p. 734, Curzon to Webb, 8/18/19.

17. It was also hoped that the announcement of the boundary delimitation around Smyrna, which had just been agreed on in Paris, would have a beneficial effect on the authority of the Constantinople regime. Ibid., p. 714, Calthorpe to Curzon, 8/1/19; p. 717, Hohler to Kidston, 8/4/19; pp. 717-19, Calthorpe to Curzon, 8/5/19. See above, Chapter 7.

18. Ibid., pp. 761-62, Robeck to Curzon, 9/17/19.

19. Ibid., p. 719, Calthorpe to Curzon, 8/5/19; pp. 722-23, Webb to Curzon, 8/9/19; pp. 730-32, 8/17/19; p. 733, 8/17/19; pp. 760-61, Robeck to Curzon, 9/13/19; pp. 761-62, 9/17/19; pp. 763-66, 9/17/19; pp. 802-10, 10/10/19; pp. 869-73, 11/10/19; pp. 970-72, 12/23/19; pp. 998-99, Curzon memorandum, 1/4/20, n. 12; Foreign Office, F.O. 608/113/385-1-16/19040, Report by Calthorpe's staff, 10/28/19; State Department, A.C.N.P. 185.5/43, De France to Peace Conference, 8/28/19; Davison, "Turkish Diplomacy," p. 179; Pech, *Alliés et Turquie,* p. 89, 10/15/19.

20. *Br. Doc.,* 4:785-86, Robeck to Curzon, 9/30/19. One of the most interesting aspects of this whole sequence of events is that while De France and Robeck worked together closely and on occasion consulted the Italian high commissioner, no attempt was made to include Bristol in the decisions. This was probably because of Bristol's awkward position as high commissioner of a country that had never been at war with the Ottoman Empire. Bristol's own estimation of the situation was approximately the same as that of the other commissioners, though he did not view the Nationalists with as much suspicion and distrust. Bristol Papers, Box 16, Reports for weeks ending 8/17/19, 9/14/19, 9/21/19; Box 27, "Turkey," passim; State Department, Turkey, 867.00/916, Bristol to Sec. State, 8/28/19.

21. *Br. Doc.,* 4:786, Robeck to Curzon, 9/30/19, n.7.

22. Ibid., pp. 788-89, 791, Hohler to Kidston, 10/4/19.

23. Ibid., p. 809, Robeck to Curzon, 10/10/19. See also rest of dispatch, ibid., pp. 802-10; pp. 819-23, 10/18/19, and enclosure 1; p. 847, 10/29/19; pp. 869-73, 11/10/19, pp. 998-99, Milne to War Office, 10/20/19, in Curzon memorandum, 1/4/20, n. 12.

24. Ibid., p. 847, Curzon to Robeck, 10/29/19.

25. See above, Chapter 8.

26. Cabinet Papers, Cab. 24/89, G. T. 8292, General Staff memorandum, 10/9/19; *Br. Doc.,* 4:764, Robeck to Curzon, 9/17/19, n. 7; pp. 881-82, 11/13/19, and n. 1; p. 906, Curzon to Robeck, 11/26/19.

27. *Br. Doc.,* 4:932, Robeck to Curzon, 12/11/19.

28. Ibid., p. 845, Curzon to Robeck, 10/26/19; p. 852, Curzon to Buchanan, 11/4/19; p. 881, Robeck to Curzon, 11/13/19; pp. 911-12, Crowe to Curzon, 11/29/19. For views of the British High Command regarding Constantinople, see above, p. 191.

29. See above, pp. 232-35 and *Br. Doc.,* 2:236, S.C., 11/8/19.

30. "Turkey at the Coming Peace Conference," pp. 21-22; *Correspondance d'Orient,* pp. 453, 460-61, 12/30/19; "The New National Movement in Turkey," pp. 266-67; "Europe's Perplexity over the Upheaval in Turkey," pp. 284-85; *R.F.P.: Political Review,* p. 17, 11/14/19.

31. *Br. Doc.,* 4:965, Curzon-Berthelot second meeting, 12/22/19.

32. Cabinet Papers, Cab. 23/37, Conference of Ministers, 1/5/20; Cab. 23/20, C. 1(20), 1/6/20.

XI ✿ THE CONFERENCE OF LONDON:
THE TURKISH STATE

T HE Conference of London convened on February 12, 1920, and continued to meet until April 10. Progress was slow because Premier Millerand was only able to take part in discussions for the first three days of the conference and again from February 23 to February 25.[1] His absence proved quite irritating to Lloyd George, who had spent so much time in Paris during the previous year.

During the first two weeks of the conference, the Supreme Council considered the whole range of topics relating to the Turkish peace treaty. In most cases, the questions were then referred to special commissions for further study. The commissions were requested to submit their recommendations in the form of draft articles, and their reports were eventually considered by the Committee of Foreign Ministers and Ambassadors.

This committee, which was created on February 27 at Lloyd George's suggestion, deserves a word of explanation and comment. It was established for a number of reasons. By delegating the drafting of the treaty to this subordinate group, the Supreme Council was able to discuss other business such as the problem of high prices and the exchange of currency in Europe, which was a major concern during March and early April. In addition, with Millerand gone most of the time and Nitti absent after March 4, Lloyd George was freed from attending many meetings from which his Italian and French counterparts were absent. By absenting himself, he, like

Millerand and Nitti, was able to maintain the position of reserving final assent on issues decided by the committee. With this one major restriction, the Committee of Foreign Ministers and Ambassadors was empowered to draft and approve clauses of the final treaty, and between February 27 and April 10 it was able to reach a final settlement on many difficult problems.[2]

Constantinople

Constantinople provided very little difference of opinion among the powers. At no time in the discussions was the slightest reference made to the events and decisions of the past two months. Aware that Lloyd George's hands were tied by the cabinet decision of January 6, Millerand strongly supported keeping the Turks in Constantinople. He argued that conditions had altered considerably since 1918 and that the expense of forcing the Turks out was more than France could undertake. Nitti was even more blunt: "We must not antagonize the populations of Turkey; we must be liberal, and we must pursue economical advantage . . . rather than political changes."[3]

How this must have infuriated Lloyd George and Curzon! Lloyd George could not refrain from listing reasons for Turkish expulsion. He emphasized that in his own personal view "we might now really be missing a great opportunity of ridding Europe once and for all of this pest and potential source of trouble."[4] But ultimately, bound as he was by the cabinet decision, there was nothing for him to do but give in.

This decision appeared almost immediately in the French press. In Britain the general reaction was hostile. The government was bitterly attacked in most of the newspapers and periodicals, and the announcement touched off a lengthy debate and questioning of Lloyd George in the House of Commons. In contrast, the French and Italians greeted the news enthusiastically, the Italian press mistakenly ascribing the decision to a firm Italian-French stand that had forced the British to give in. In Constantinople, a delighted Turkish government tended to credit a combination of Mustapha

Kemal and the French for reversing the British position, while in the United States demonstrations opposing the decision occurred.[5]

The Straits

The question of the administration, control, and extent of the Straits zone was far more difficult to resolve. It was necessary to determine whether any of the land in the Straits area should be placed under international control, and how much, if any, should be left to Turkey. Moreover, since Constantinople would be a part of Turkey, the issue of control of the Straits was inextricably entwined with the problem of the degree and kind of authority that the Allies would wield over the Turkish nation. This involvement was exactly what Curzon had desperately sought to avoid, and it must have been a bitter man who found himself the chief architect of a treaty much of which he personally opposed.[6]

All of these questions were referred to various commissions, whose reports were eventually considered either by the Supreme Council or the Committee of Foreign Ministers and Ambassadors. After much discussion and redrafting, an agreement was eventually reached. The draft called for the creation of a Straits Commission made up of representatives of France, Britain, Italy, Japan, Greece, and Rumania. The four great powers were each to have two votes, the others only one. Provision was made for the eventual participation of the United States, Russia, and Bulgaria. The commission would be completely separate from all organizations having anything to do with the government of Turkey and would have its loans secured "as far as possible"[7] by the tolls levied on ships passing through the Straits.

Although the commission was to have no sovereignty over any territory it would have the right to occupy militarily a demilitarized zone on both sides of the Straits and the Sea of Marmara. The Straits themselves were to be open in times of war and peace to ships of all nations that belonged to the League, had received the approval of the League of Nations, or were members of the Allied and Associated powers. Should Turkey become a belligerent, but not an aggressor nation, materials or ships of war belonging to its enemies would not be allowed to pass through the Straits. The commission would regulate everything relating to the passage of ships through the Straits or to shipping in the port of Constantinople. Therefore, matters such as sanitation, control of quarantine, and loading and unloading of goods would come within its purview. Moreover, the commission would have control over any judicial questions that arose in connection with the administration of the Straits and the passage of ships through the area, or with men attached to such ships.[8]

In the negotiations that led to the final framing of these articles, only the admission of Japan as a two-vote member of the commission presented a problem worthy of note. Rarely voicing an opinion or taking part in the discussion, the Japanese delegates were often overlooked by the other powers, who forgot that Japan was there as a full-fledged equal of the other nations. Thus, the Western delegates were completely taken aback when Japan insisted on its right to membership on the Straits Commission. The Japanese argued that since the Straits were to be opened to the world as an international waterway, Japan, as one of the major Allies, should have a place on the governing commission. It was intolerable and unjust that Japan should be left out when provision was made for the eventual membership of Russia and the United States.[9]

The other powers were so thoroughly surprised that they agreed at first, but soon Britain and France began to object.[10] Their position centered on Japan's lack of commercial interest in the Mediterranean and the fact that it was not a Mediterranean power, but their arguments were weak and lacking in conviction.[11] What really bothered Britain and France was that Japan would have to be admitted as a two-vote member and would, therefore, expect to take a regular turn as chairman. Whereas Russian and American membership was unlikely in the near future, Japanese membership would be immediate and would provide a threat to the closed group administration of the Straits that Britain and France had in mind. Instead of controlling half of the votes on the commission, France and Britain would be in a minority. From the beginning the Italians, who technically supported their Western allies, made it clear that should Japan insist Italy would not oppose Japanese membership on the Straits Commission.[12]

Eventually the powers agreed, with a total lack of grace, to Japan's admission. Lord Curzon could not resist asking whether Japan was willing to undertake military responsibility in the Straits, to which Viscount Chinda smoothly replied that this would depend on the share that Japan was granted in the actual administration of the area.[13]

Financial Control of the Turkish State

Closely tied in with the questions involving the Straits Commission were those of financial control of the whole Turkish state. The task of formulating specific provisions was delegated to a special subcommission, which was instructed that no large-scale indemnity was to be demanded from Turkey. At the same time, all occupation costs, damages to foreign or Turkish Christian refugees, and the Turkish share of the prewar Ottoman Debt were to be safeguarded.[14]

Eventually, financial clauses were drawn up, examined by the Supreme Council and the Committee of Foreign Ministers and Ambassadors, and revised several times. Agreements were reached, broken, re-argued, and reached again. In time all disputes but two were resolved, and by the time the London conference adjourned a series of draft articles had been approved.[15]

Financial Clauses

The provisions for financial control called for the formation of a three-power Financial Commission that would oversee the workings and personnel of the Turkish financial system through a network of Turkish supervisors. The Financial Commission would have to approve the government's budget before it was submitted to the Turkish Parliament, and no amendment would be allowed that did not meet with the approval of the commission. The commission would have a hand in the regulation of the currency and would retain a veto over the contracting of internal or external government loans.[16]

Formal reparations were specifically renounced, although it was decided that in lieu of reparations the territories that were being separated from the Turkish state would not have to pay for property formerly owned by the Ottoman government. The Turks were to be held responsible for obligations pertaining to occupation costs and damages to foreign nationals, though no provision was made for the claims of displaced Turkish Christians. To meet these obligations, "all resources of the Turkish government," with the exception of those pledged to the Ottoman Debt, were to be "placed at the disposal of the Financial Commission." [17]

The priority scale for the dispersal of these revenues became the source of much animated Anglo-French discussion. Although all the Allies agreed that revenues that had previously been pledged to cover the service of the Ottoman Debt should continue to be at the disposal of the Debt Council, the French were fearful that these revenues would not be enough to meet the Debt service allotted to the new Turkish state. Therefore, they demanded that the Financial Commission use its funds first and foremost to cover any such deficiency should it arise. The British were far less concerned about the Debt, for only 11 percent of the bonds were held by British shareholders compared to 60 percent by French. Instead, they insisted that the primary charge on the commission, after its own expenses and current occupation costs were taken care of, should be for Allied occupation costs incurred since the armistice in areas that remained part of the Turkish state.[18]

The dispute was eventually bypassed, if not solved, by giving priority to occupation expenses, both past and present, and then inserting a provision that the Financial Commission should arrange to meet these expenses in such a manner as to enable it to cover any deficiency in the Debt service that might appear. Although all were agreed that no charge should be made for occupation costs in areas detached from Turkey and retained as mandates by the Allies, the British maintained that someone should pay the cost of the British occupation of Syria. The logical power was France. The matter was referred to Paris and apparently met with a refusal, for the financial clauses as finally formulated called for Turkish payment of the expenses of occupation forces in territory "ceded . . . to a Power other than the Power which had borne the expenses of occupation." [19]

One other issue caused some difficulty. The British, French, and Italians sought to insert a clause granting the Financial Commission sole power to raise or lower customs rates from the flat 11 percent that had been in effect on all items before the war. The Japanese, who were not to be represented on the Financial Commission, opposed this clause because they felt that higher tariffs on a specific type of goods might hurt one country more than another. To meet this criticism, the others reluctantly agreed to let the initiative for tariff changes come from the Turkish government, with the commission only retaining the right of approval. Although the ultimate decision still remained with the Financial Commission, this meant that all customs changes would have to be requested by the Turkish regime instead of being imposed directly by the commission, and therefore the commission's ability to impose swift and arbitrary tariff alterations was greatly reduced.[20]

Ottoman Debt

The question of the Ottoman Debt was also the source of differences between the Allies. The British sought the abolishment of the old Ottoman Debt Council and the merging of its functions with that of the new Financial Commission. From an administrative point of view such a solution made great sense, yet it was vigorously opposed by the French. Ottoman Debt bondholders in France constituted a vociferous and powerful lobby, so much so that the French government would agree to nothing that might displease them. Therefore, Berthelot and Cambon steadfastly maintained that since the Debt Council was the organization that had been agreed upon at the time the loans were negotiated, no alteration in its structure could be made without the bondholders' consent.[21]

A tentative settlement was finally reached when the British gave up their insistence on a firm commitment regarding the ending of the Debt Council and accepted a milder statement that the consent of the bondholders would be necessary for the unification of the two bodies. This consent would be sought "as soon as possible, with a view to the fusion of the two bodies taking place not later than the expiry of the present term of the Council" (1923).[22] Even this solution was not approved by the French, and the clause was left in the draft articles subject to the receipt of new French instructions from Paris and a final decision by the Supreme Council.[23]

A second question concerning the Debt Council involved the dispersal of funds. Some £5,000,000 in gold had been deposited in German banks, either by the Ottoman Debt Council or the German government as security against wartime issues of Turkish currency. The French and Italians wanted this money pledged to the Financial Commission for the restoration and stabilization of Turkish currency. The British, concerned with recouping the cost of their heavy military expenditure in the Near East, wanted no such restriction. Eventually, a compromise was reached. The funds that had been deposited by the German government were to be given to the Financial Commission with no strings attached. The smaller amount that had been loaned by the Ottoman Debt Council to the Ottoman government was to be returned to the council.[24]

A decision was also reached on an apportionment formula by which the various shares of the Ottoman Debt would be divided among the territories of the old empire:

> The amount shall bear the same ratio to the total required for the service of the debt as the average revenue of the ceded territory bore to the average revenue of the whole Empire (including in each case the yield of the customs surtax imposed in the year 1907) over the three financial years 1909–10, 1910–11, 1911–12.[25]

Economic Clauses

The economic clauses, which dealt with property and commercial affairs, never provoked much high-level disagreement or, for that matter, even discussion. They provided for the restoration of all concessions, agreements, and property rights involving Allied nationals on the basis of their status before August 1, 1914. In areas in which a power had a mandate it would have to buy out concessions belonging to other nations or their nationals. All German, Hungarian, or Bulgarian interests would have to be liquidated. If necessary, the price would be arbitrated by a three-man committee, one from each side and a third either agreed on by the nations concerned or appointed by the League of Nations.

All concessions granted after the signing of the armistice were declared null and void; the same held true for concessions granted to enemy nations since the outbreak of the war. Disposition of concessions granted to Allied nationals during the war years was to be left to the discretion of the Allies. The right to transfer concessionary rights from one Allied company to another was recognized.[26]

Capitulations

The question of the capitulations, covering as it did a wide variety of problems, could not be settled in London. For some time the European powers had advocated abandoning most of the intricate system of economic and judicial rights and privileges that had accrued over the years to the various foreign nations and their nationals residing in Turkey. Yet there was great disagreement as to the speed and means required to obtain this end. The French pressed for a quick settlement by a commission that would sit in either London or Paris. The British were in far less of a hurry and argued that the committee should sit in Constantinople where it could consult those affected by the capitulations, that is, the British, French, and Italian residents of Turkey. The outcome was generalization and postponement. The draft provision called for the establishment of a four-power commission after the ratification of the treaty, but no mention was made of either its location or its method of procedure. Turkey was to agree in advance to accept whatever reform system was eventually worked out. Until such time, the old capitulatory system would be continued.[27]

An examination of the financial and economic provisions drawn up in London and eventually incorporated into the Treaty of Sèvres leads to the conclusion that the powers had no intention of leaving any real authority or control in these matters to the Turks. Although all the provisions were supposedly undertaken solely for Turkey's benefit, the conclusion reached by Donald Blaisdell best sums up the actual situation:

Not a single item of the economic order in Turkey as forecast by the Sèvres Treaty would have remained within the sole jurisdiction of the Turkish Government. . . . By this ring of economic servitudes, Turkey would have become effectively shackled to the Allied powers. Such, it seems, is the only rational interpretation to be placed upon their phrase "to afford some measure of relief and assistance to Turkey."[28]

Spheres of Influence in Turkey

Perhaps the thorniest issue that confronted the powers during the initial stage of the London conference was that of zones or spheres of influence within the proposed Turkish state. This was necessitated by French interests in Cilicia and Italian claims for compensation for British and French mandates in Mesopotamia, Palestine, and Syria. Even though the validity of the Saint Jean de Maurienne Agreement was denied by Britain and France, they realized that some sort of adjustment for Italy would have to be made. Indeed, Article 9 of the Treaty of London specifically stated that compensation would be arranged. Therefore, in the December discussions Berthelot and Curzon had agreed that an Italian economic sphere of some sort in Turkey might serve the purpose.[29]

Extent of Allied Control

This problem, however, was only part of the larger question of the extent and type of control the Allies would wield over Turkey. All were agreed that whatever forms such control took, it must be indirect. All were of the opinion that a close control of financial affairs was essential. The real issue was whether this control should extend into other areas. Both Italy and France advocated a great deal of Allied administrative as well as financial authority in Anatolia. As Cambon put it: "The power [of] controlling the purse would really mean control of the whole Government."[30] Cambon readily admitted that in his view the plans for financial supervision called for governing the country, albeit indirectly. The Turks liked having someone tell them what to do. Besides, "if the Powers did not govern the country, who would? . . . If the Powers did not seize this opportunity to intervene and to control the administration of Turkey, the Turks would merely relax into their old corrupt ways."[31]

This went far beyond anything the British wanted, and Lloyd George immediately placed himself in opposition. "If Turkey desired to govern herself in her own way, he did not see how we could resist her [in] this demand. After all, Turkey was no more incompetent than Persia." [32] Moreover, he was afraid that any joint Allied administration of the country would result in endless antagonisms and quarrels among the powers. Finally, he broached the important question of enforcement. The more administrative control that was undertaken, the more committed the Allied powers would be to insist upon enactment of governmental provisions even if it necessitated military action.

This was exactly what Lloyd George and Curzon had most wanted to avoid with their scheme for separating Constantinople from Turkey. As long as Constantinople was to be kept apart, Britain had been willing to accede to France's views regarding control of the Turkish state since their success or failure would not affect the administration of the Straits zone. However, now that Constantinople and the Straits were to be part of that state, the powers would be obliged to exercise fully any administrative authority they undertook within the Turkish state. Therefore, from the British viewpoint, it seemed imperative that control should be held to an enforceable minimum, aimed only at "measures to ensure the liquidation of the Turkish debt." [33]

The Italian-French position was motivated by hopes of achieving spheres of influence within the Turkish state. In this the French took the lead due to their heavy involvement in Cilicia, but they received strong support from the Italians, for Italy recognized that the status of France in Cilicia would basically determine Italy's position in whatever zone of influence it eventually received.

In Cilicia, the French found themselves in an increasingly uncomfortable position. Opposition in Cilicia had pointed up the difficulty of maintaining authority against the wishes of the population. By the beginning of February, this opposition had turned into a full-scale revolt in which the local inhabitants were assisted by Nationalist troops. The French had recruited many Armenians into their army, in fact the vast majority of the occupying troops were Armenians or black-African colonials. The Turks especially resented this, and the revolt brought forth a general massacre of the Armenians in Cilicia, particularly in the area around Marash. It was apparent that military measures on a considerable scale would be necessary to maintain order.[34]

All of this led Berthelot to announce on February 16 that "the French Government did not intend permanently to occupy Cilicia, they intended eventually to withdraw, merely maintaining a certain control, probably similar to the financial control which had been proposed by the French to be applied to Turkey." [35] The withdrawal would, of course, "depend on the intentions of Italy in Asia Minor." [36]

This brought the issue out in the open. The French advocacy of supervisory authority over Turkey was based on the desire to withdraw troops, yet maintain administrative and financial control over Cilicia, which would be part of the Turkish state. Not only did the French envisage having economic priority in Cilicia, but they wanted "French officers . . . appointed to supervise the gendarmerie and French advisors or councillors to control the finances and other branches of administration." [37] This, they asserted, would be no different from what was done for all of Turkey except that the instructors and advisors in Cilicia would all be French.[38]

Lloyd George vehemently opposed any such solution. He objected to the extension of control from the financial into the police and judicial fields. Moreover, Lloyd George claimed that the French plan meant a virtual mandate, plus the right of economic priority in industrial development, which was not part of a normal mandate. The appointment of only French, British, or Italian advisors in any one area would constitute in effect the partitioning of Turkey. This would be in direct opposition to the Covenant of the League of Nations and would arouse the wrath of other nations, particularly the United States.[39]

Berthelot in turn argued that the United States had forfeited its right to impose its views on the conference or to be the "arbiter of the affairs of all the world." [40] However, instead of requiring the Turks to accept military and political advisors, the Allies might offer to supply them if the Turks so wished. This would meet Lloyd George's objection that neither British nor world opinion would allow them to force advisors on the Turks. "If the Turks asked for them,

we could hardly refuse to supply them." [41] As to Cilicia, he was willing to waive the right of France to choose all advisors, as long as
in practice the vast majority would be French.

At this point Curzon came up with a suggestion that proved to
be the foundation of the ultimate solution to the problem:

[This] led to the following general conclusion, to which he believed they
all subscribed. Whatever arrangements we might make regarding the em-
ployment of instructors or the granting of economic concessions could not
be put down in black and white in the treaty, but must be a matter of
mutual arrangement between the Powers. If in the treaty we made it appear
that Turkey was to be partitioned into spheres, Turkey would never accept
these conditions, the United States would reject them, and the sentiments
of the civilized world would be offended. He urged, therefore, that nothing
about partitioning should appear in the treaty. If, however, Turkey should
ask for the assistance of instructors, the Powers could arrange among
themselves for their provision. As regards spheres of influence, he suggested
that the Allies should work on the lines of what was known in England
as a 'self-denying ordinance'; that is to say, that they should mutually
arrange that Great Britain would not interfere in the areas allotted to France
and to Italy, and would, moreover, actually support those countries in their
administration of such areas, and *vice versa*. Lastly, he would urge that,
whatever arrangement of this character might be made by the Powers,
it should be widely published, and not kept secret, as nothing else would
satisfy the feelings of the civilized world. [42]

To this suggestion both Lloyd George and Berthelot readily agreed.
All that would be necessary would be to insert a clause in the treaty
indicating the willingness of the Allies to supply advisors and instructors if asked. To prevent the Turks from turning to an outside power
for aid, they would be required to obtain the consent of the Allies
regarding all advisors. It did not seem to occur to any of the negotiators that the Turks might not ask for help. As Berthelot put it:

The Turks were all in favour of having a sound administration. They
favoured financial and administrative organizations which were controlled
by Europeans and which gave themselves good openings, as they liked
handsome salaries, regularly paid, which they did not get under their own
Government. [43]

Moreover, the British high commissioner had reported from Constantinople on January 8, 1920, that the Ottoman government had formally signified its willingness to undertake a program of judicial, financial, and police reform with the assistance of one power. A foreign inspection corps, a council of justice with some foreigners, and a foreign administration at the top of the police system had been suggested. The negotiators in London were agreed that there should be little trouble in substituting a group of two or three powers for a single one.[44]

The Tripartite Pact

The idea of a self-denying agreement solved the problem of conflict with the League Convenant. It enabled the three powers to make a tripartite arrangement that defined areas of priority and the rights each power would have in its sphere. But because it would be a self-denying agreement, it would have no effect on other nations. It did not, as Nitti put it, "protect the Allies against outside Powers." [45] This was recognized as a serious defect, but Lloyd George argued cogently that there was little alternative:

If they insisted upon inserting in the treaty their demand for preferential rights, the first thing that would happen would be that they would receive a note from the United States saying that this action was contrary to the terms of the covenant. The Turks would be well aware that the United States was taking this line, and they would consequently refuse to sign the treaty. In his opinion, it would be much better for the Allies to generalize in the treaty and to come to certain mutually amicable arrangements in regard to concessions and priorities. The other course was, in his view, much too dangerous for them to adopt. He thought the council would be much wiser to accept Lord Curzon's suggestion, although it did not give them all they wanted.[46]

The self-denying ordinance had a further advantage. The League Covenant allowed no rights of economic priority in mandated areas. The British in particular were concerned about this, for the whole of their sphere of influence would consist of mandated territory, rather than zones of priority in Anatolia. Thus the British sternly insisted that any rights recognized in the French and Italian areas must be reciprocated in the areas under a British mandate. The technique of a self-denying ordinance allowed for this, because it did not specifically prohibit any nation from economic investment anywhere. Rather, such an agreement would be a voluntary commit-ment on the part of the three Allies not to compete with each other and to recognize and support the economic priority of the designated nation in each area. This pleased the French as well as the British, for France was anxious to have all rights given in Cilicia extended to Syria.[47]

Much time was spent between February 17 and March 3 on discussion of the form the Tripartite Pact should take. In the process several other issues relating to boundaries, railroads, and minorities were provisionally settled so that the pact grew considerably. What had originally been envisaged as a simple two- or three-part statement became a rather lengthy document of more than a dozen articles.[48] It called for a self-denying ordinance by which each nation would not only refuse to compete for rights of economic investment and development in an area allotted to another nation but would also support the aspirations of the favored nation in negotiations with the Turkish government. At British insistence, trade and commerce were excluded from this provision and were to remain totally unhin-dered. Each nation assumed responsibility for the protection of mi-norities in its sphere of economic interest. The right of the interested nation to appoint political, judicial, and military advisors should the Turks request them was also accorded. French and Italian troops would be withdrawn from areas within the Turkish state as soon as the treaty was successfully executed. Instead of requiring the Turks to sign the pact, a clause signifying Allied willingness to provide advisors would be included in the draft articles of the peace treaty. The terms of the Tripartite Pact, it was agreed, would be made public at the time of the formal signing of the peace treaty, so that its consistency with the letter of the League Covenant would be evident.

The zones of influence were tentatively set as those of the 1916 Sykes-Picot and the 1917 Saint Jean de Maurienne Agreements. The Italian zone was modified by loss of the Smyrna area, while the British zone was not fully determined because of the somewhat unsettled status of Mosul and Kurdistan. Both the French and Italians advanced claims for the territorial extension of their spheres of influence, and reserved the right to reopen this matter later.

On one question no agreement could be reached. This was the disposition of German property in Turkey. Although all agreed that it should be confiscated, the French and Italians supported a proposal that the property found in each zone should be allotted to the favored power. This the British bitterly opposed, undoubtedly because there were few German holdings in Mesopotamia, whereas France and Italy stood to gain considerably in their zones from such an arrangement. The British were particularly opposed to a splintering of control over the railway lines that constituted most of the German holdings. Instead, Britain sought common control of the railroads with a proportional split of the total revenues. The French and Italians admitted that the British were probably correct, and the matter was referred to a commission for further study.[49]

Thus, although final discussion and ratification of the Tripartite Pact awaited the signing of the Turkish treaty, the basic terms had been formulated by early March. The settling of this difficult question of economic and administrative priorities in turn contributed much to easing the process of drafting the rest of the Turkish treaty.

Military Provisions

A treaty of the type envisaged by the Allied Powers necessitated complete subjugation and control of the Turkish military establishment, yet the military clauses provided little difficulty.[50] The provisions for demilitarization in terms of equipment followed much the same pattern as in the peace treaties with other nations. The draft terms stipulated that Turkey should have no long-range artillery (with the exception of mountain guns), no tanks or other motorized equipment, no air force, and a navy only large enough to permit patrolling of the coastline. The number of rifles, machine guns, and revolvers, as well as rounds of ammunition, was to be closely regulated.[51]

The ultimate size of the Turkish military force provoked a good deal of discussion. The initial recommendation of the military experts called for an army of 50,000–60,000 men. In the discussions at London the delegates, with the notable exception of Churchill, all thought that this was far too large, especially when considered against the 100,000 allotted to Germany. Churchill alone believed that transportation problems necessitated a larger force because it would have quite limited mobility. He was overruled, and eventually it was decided that a force of 50,000 should include the gendarmerie, with the regular army limited to 15,000 men. Between 10 and 15 percent of the officers in both units were to be from either Allied or neutral nations. In addition, the sultan would be allowed a small personal bodyguard, which would be the only regular army force allowed within the Straits zone.[52]

One other question assumed major proportions in relation to the military clauses. All the peace treaties contained a clause stating that the Allies would not enlist or employ any citizen of the defeated nation in any of its military forces. In every treaty a proviso had been added exempting the French Foreign Legion from these conditions. This reservation had always been accepted without argument by the other powers. At London, however, Curzon suddenly raised a strong protest against the inclusion of a similar provision in the Turkish treaty. He saw this as an opportunity for the Turks to train hundreds of extra men and for the French to enroll Turks in their forces in Syria, while Britain would not be able to do the same in Mesopotamia. He protested:

The recruitment of large Asiatic and African armies by the European Powers was highly objectionable. The present troubles which the French Government were experiencing in Cilicia were due to a large extent to the presence of Senagalese and Armenian troops in French uniforms. The peace of the world would be seriously threatened unless the European powers agreed to limit their recruitment of Asiatic and African troops.[53]

This from the foreign secretary of a nation that had employed and was still employing thousands of Indian troops in Mesopotamia!

The French were totally taken aback by this sudden attack. While stating a willingness to refrain from recruiting amongst the Turks, the French refused to concede the time-honored Legion tradition of accepting all physically qualified enlistees without asking questions concerning nationality or past. The question was reserved, at Curzon's insistence, for consideration by the Supreme Council.[54]

Why did the British suddenly object to this rather routine provision? Part of the reason probably lay in a genuine concern that Turkish battalions might well be employed in France's Syrian mandate, a prospect that would not at all be to the liking of Britain's Arab allies. But behind this one suspects a general British distrust of Franco-Turkish relations. During most of 1919, the French had shown a rather conciliatory attitude toward the Constantinople government, only to shift late in 1919 to negotiations with Kemal. This they had coupled with a sudden decision to withdraw eventually from Cilicia. It is quite conceivable that Curzon feared that France would use the special privileges accorded to the Foreign Legion as a means for obtaining Turkish favor by secretly agreeing to train a good-sized Turkish contingent. Such an eventuality would never have occurred to the British in considering the possible course of future French relations with any of the other defeated nations.[55]

Minorities

The problem of protecting the various minorities in Anatolia was one of great concern to the Allied powers. The special provisions for a percentage of foreign officers in the gendarmerie and local police forces, as well as a requirement that these units reflect in their ranks and officer corps the ethnic proportion of the given area, resulted from specific requests by a special minorities commission that had been entrusted with the task of drafting the minorities clauses of the Turkish peace treaty. The Minorities Commission also suggested that Turkey be told that a continuation of Turkish sovereignty over Constantinople would be made contingent upon fulfillment of the minority regulations. All of these suggestions were approved for incorporation in the final treaty. In the same way, the Tripartite Pact specifically stated that each power would be responsible for enforcing the minority provisions of the treaty in its sphere of influence.[56]

The minorities provisions themselves were similar to those which had been included in other treaties. Complete religious, civil, political, and economic freedom was guaranteed. Restoration of property and land belonging to minority elements that had been confiscated during the war was called for. Minority languages were to be recognized in the courts, and private ethnic or religious educational systems were to be allowed.[57]

One clause in particular differed from those found in the other treaties. During the war, many non-Moslems had been forced upon pain of death to convert to Islam. Many of these had been women and children who had been forced against their will to become part of a Turkish family. The women had often been required to take the veil and follow the custom of female seclusion. Therefore, all conversions to Islam after August 1, 1914, were declared null and void unless the ceremonies were now performed again. Provision was made for the searching of private institutions or homes, should this be necessary, to find individuals who were sought by their families, or, if they had none, by their former religious or ethnic community.[58]

This provision provoked considerable discussion in the Committee of Foreign Ministers and Ambassadors. Both the Italians and the French warned of the tremendous tensions and antagonisms that would be created by any male invasion of the women's quarters in a Turkish home. Nevertheless, it was decided that the clause must be maintained, with the provision that any search should be carried on jointly by a representative of the Turkish government, a member of the minority community involved, and a representative of the Allied powers.[59]

The question of the role of the League of Nations in the protection of minorities in Turkey was not settled in London. All previous minority conventions had included a clause placing the provisions under the guarantee of the League and granting the League Council sole power to modify them. The League generally was given the right to hear, investigate, and adjudicate individual complaints of violations of the convention. In the case of Turkey, the Minorities Commission had also recommended the appointment of a resident representative of the League of Nations at Constantinople who would investigate immediately all infringement of the minorities clauses.[60]

This plan ran into heavy opposition from the Italian and French delegates in London. They questioned having two sources of authority at Constantinople, the League representative and the Allied commissions. They argued that either the League delegate would serve no purpose or he would become very powerful, interfering in the Allied administration and serving as an avenue for endless Turkish appeals against the decisions of the Allied commissions. However, when the Committee of Foreign Ministers and Ambassadors turned to the League for advice, it found that not only did the League Council have grave reservations about the advisability of stationing a League representative at Constantinople but that it was dubious about giving any guarantee at all to the minorities convention in a state as unorganized as Turkey. The League Council asked for more information and promised a definite answer after its next session on April 25.[61]

This created a problem, for the powers had planned to present the draft articles to the Turks before then. They therefore decided to omit all reference to the League in the minorities provision, including the traditional League guarantee. Instead they substituted a suspensory clause that bound the Turks to accept all decisions subsequently taken concerning "what measures were necessary to guarantee the execution of the clauses."[62]

The settlement of the minorities question brought to a close the discussion of treaty terms relating directly to the Turkish state. What emerged was a treaty drafted by powers that seemed supremely confident of their ability to partition and control Turkey as they saw fit. Coupled with the separate Tripartite Pact, the provisions ensured sweeping Allied control, directly or indirectly, of every aspect of Turkish fiscal, economic, political, and military administration. Under the treaty's terms, Turkey as a truly independent nation would cease to exist.

---

1. Internal affairs in France were in a serious state, for a railway strike threatened to trigger a series of strikes throughout the nation.

2. *Br. Doc.,* 7:268–69, S.C., 2/27/20.

3. Ibid., pp. 44–45, 2/14/20. See also *R.F.P.:Political Review,* 2/13/20, 3/5/20; *Bulletin périodique de la presse Italienne,* no. 132.

4. *Br. Doc.,* 7:46, S.C. 2/14/20.

5. *Le Temps,* 2/16/20; *Br. Doc.,* 7:240–42, 2/25/20; 13:1, Robeck to Curzon, 2/12/20;

p. 2, Curzon to Robeck, 2/16/20; pp. 4–7, Robeck to Curzon, 2/23/20; Foreign Office, F.O. 406/43/80, Robeck to Curzon, 2/21/20; Waley, "Life of the Hon. Edwin Samuel Montagu," p. 286; Bonar Law Papers, 98/7/8, Montagu to Bonar Law, 2/16/20; *Times* (London), 2/16/20, 2/18/20, 2/20/20, 2/21/20, 2/23/20–2/28/20, 3/3/20; *Parliamentary Debates* (Commons), 5th ser., 125:1949–2060, 2/26/20; *R.F.P.:Political Review,* 3/12/20, 3/19/20, 3/26/20; *Bulletin périodique de la presse Italienne,* no. 133; Pech, *Alliés et Turquie,* p. 113, 2/15/20; 2/20/20; Bardoux, *De Paris à Spa,* pp. 316–17; *Correspondance d'Orient,* pp. 229–30, 3/15/20; p. 370, 4/30/20; Dumont-Wilden, "La Question de Constantinople," pp. 151–54; A. Toynbee, "Meaning of the Constantinople Decisions," pp. 129–31; J. Gerard, "Civilization's Surrender to Barbarism: Proposed Retention of the Turks in Europe," p. 345; "The Turks to Stay in Europe," pp. 103–8; Adkisson, *Britain and the Kemalist Movement,* pp. 270–71; Evans, *U.S. and Partition,* p. 281; *New York Times,* 2/19/20, 2/24/20.

6. On February 18 Curzon wrote Montagu: "As you know I deplore the decision, which is fraught with certain disaster in the future. I have seldom prophesied with greater confidence and you will live to see that you have won a Pyrrhic victory. Even the Viceroy had to admit in one of his telegrams that the Indian Moslem agitation was artificial and would collapse without explosion." Waley, "Life of the Hon. Edwin Samuel Montagu," p. 287. Subsequently, Curzon commented in a letter to his wife on March 11: "The treaty with Turkey is going badly and we are in for great trouble at Constantinople." Ronaldshay, *Curzon,* 3:271.

7. *Br. Doc.,* 7:323, 3/1/20, App. 1.

8. Ibid., pp. 46–50, 54, S.C., 2/14/20; pp. 122, 2/18/20; pp. 124–25, App. 1; pp. 313–21, For. Min., 3/1/20; pp. 321–25, App. 1; pp. 352–57, 3/2/20; pp. 372–73, 3/3/20, App. 1; pp. 716–17, 4/7/20; pp. 725–26, App. 1; Cabinet Papers, Cab. 24/99, Lloyd George to Foch, 3/2/19; Cab. 29/20, A.J. 51, 51A, Report of the Committee on the Administration of the Waterways of the Straits and the Sea of Marmara, 2/27/20.

9. *Br. Doc.,* 7:180, S.C., 2/21/20; pp. 393–94, For. Min., 3/4/20.

10. Ibid., p. 180, S.C., 2/21/20.

11. Ibid., pp. 394–99, For. Min., 3/4/20.

12. Ibid., pp. 396–97. For Franco-British plans regarding a closed-group administration of the Straits, see ibid., 4:940, Curzon-Berthelot first meeting, 12/22/19.

13. Ibid., 7:719–21, For. Min., 4/7/20.

14. Ibid., pp. 59–60, S.C., 2/14/20; p. 86, 97–98, 2/17/20; pp. 191–92, 2/21/20; p. 405, For. Min., 3/4/20; p. 707, 3/31/20. For the minutes of the meetings of the Turkish Financial Commission, 2/17/20–3/27/20, see Cabinet Papers, Cab. 29/29, A.J. 20, 29, 32, 33; Cab. 29/30, A.J. 62, 67, 86, 99; Cab. 29/31, A.J. 121, 122, 126, 132. The report of the commission to the Supreme Council was submitted on February 26, 1920.

15. The French did all in their power to circumvent the Foreign Ministers and Ambassadors Committee, maintaining that only the experts or the top politicians could decide. This was a rather obvious attempt to cold-shoulder Lord Curzon, whom the French had always distrusted because of what they felt was his anti-French bias. Curzon did not take this slight lightly, and at times became quite bitter and indignant in the Foreign Ministers and Ambassadors meetings. *Br. Doc.,* 7:463–66, For. Min., 3/11/20; pp. 610–12, 614, 3/24/20; pp. 617–22, App. 2.

16. Lloyd George Papers, F206/3/21, Berthelot to Lloyd George, 2/16/20; *Br. Doc.,* 7:400–401, For. Min., 3/4/20; pp. 707–8, 3/31/20, Articles 1–4.

17. *Br. Doc.,* 7:401, 403–8, For. Min., 3/4/20; pp. 707–9, Articles 1, 5, 6, 10, 3/31/20, App.

18. Ibid., pp. 156–57, S.C., 2/20/20; 344, 3/2/20; p. 612, For. Min., 3/24/20; pp. 618–19, App. 2. n.8 (For an English translation see Cabinet Papers, Cab. 29/31, A.J. 113.).

19. *Br. Doc.,* 7:708, For. Min., 3/31/20, App., Article 6. See also ibid., pp. 344–45, S.C., 3/2/20; pp. 410–13, For. Min., 3/4/20; pp. 582–83, 3/22/20; pp. 701–2, 708–9, 3/31/20.

20. Ibid., pp. 341–44, S.C., 3/2/20; pp. 408–10, For. Min., 3/4/20; p. 711, 3/31/20, App., Article 16.

21. Ibid., pp. 410–11, For. Min., 3/4/20; pp. 612–13, 3/24/20; p. 620, App. 2, n. 8. For the best discussion of the history of the Ottoman Debt, see D. C. Blaisdell, *European Financial Control in the Ottoman Empire.*

22. *Br. Doc.,* 7:711, For. Min., 3/31/20, App., Article 16.

23. Ibid., pp. 703–6; pp. 710–11, App., Article 16.

24. Ibid., pp. 346–48, S.C., 3/20/20; pp. 612, 614, For. Min., 3/24/20; p. 621, App. 2, n. 8; p. 712, 3/31/20, App., Articles 23–24. See also *U.S. Doc., P.P.C.,* 12:539–40, Treaty of Versailles, Article 259; Miller, *Diary,* 17:473; 19:398–401.

25. *Br. Doc.,* 7:710, For. Min., 3/31/20, App., Article 13. See also, Foreign Office, F.O. 608/226/1072-2-1/1374, General Debt of the Ottoman Empire, n.d.

26. Foreign Office, F.O. 608/276/185/185, British delegation report regarding economic clauses, 1/30/20; *Br. Doc.,* 7:525, For. Min., 3/18/20; pp. 538–39, App. 5, and n. 14; pp. 669–74, 3/29/20, and n. 6; pp. 675–76, App. 1; Cabinet Papers, Cab. 24/101, C.P. 914, Report of the Economic Commission, 3/26[?]/20.

27. Foreign Office, F.O. 608/117/385-303/15018, Economic Commission report, 7/9/19; *Br. Doc.,* 7:87–89, S.C., 2/17/20; pp. 157–58, 2/20/20; pp. 660–61, 3/27/20; p. 663, App. 3. The United States, which had no capitulatory rights of its own, could only demand equal rights with other nations. Therefore, while Britain, France and Italy were chiefly concerned with the judicial aspects of the Capitulations, the United States maintained continuous pressure for fulfillment of the economic, customs, and tax provisions. Since the Allies had already agreed to invest all financial control in the Ottoman Debt Council and the new Financial Commission, they were not at all concerned about enforcing these particular provisions. See *U.S. Doc., 1919,* 2:814–17; *U.S. Doc., P.P.C.,* 3:1008; 11:68–69, 74, 310–11; United States, *Papers Relating to the Foreign Relations of the United States, 1920,* 3:757–66; Evans, *U.S. and Partition,* pp. 308–9. See also the large number of documents in Foreign Office, F.O. 608/109/385-1-3; *Br. Doc.,* 4:948, 960.

28. Blaisdell, *Financial Control,* p. 196.

29. See above, Chapters 4 and 8.

30. *Br. Doc.,* 7:47, S.C., 2/14/20.

31. Ibid., p. 58. See also ibid., p. 56; pp. 69–71, 2/16/20, App. 8; p. 90, 2/17/20; Lloyd George Papers, F206/3/21, Berthelot to Lloyd George, 2/16/20.

32. *Br. Doc.,* 7:57, S.C., 2/14/20.

33. Ibid.; Cabinet Papers, Cab. 23/35, S-9, Conference of Ministers (Paris), 1/15/20.

34. Bristol Papers, Box 28. File on Syria and Cilicia, 1920, contains a series of reports concerning events in Cilicia. For a further discussion of this problem, see below, Chapter 12.

35. *Br. Doc.,* 7:85, S.C., 2/16/20.

36. Ibid.

37. Ibid., p. 94, 2/17/20.

38. Ibid., pp. 59, 68, 2/14/20; pp. 94–95, 2/17/20; p. 130, 2/18/20; pp. 153–57, 163–73, 2/20/20.

39. Ibid., p. 94, 2/17/20.

40. Ibid., p. 96.

41. Ibid., p. 101.

42. Ibid., pp. 100–101. See also ibid., pp. 130–31, 2/18/20.

43. Ibid., p. 101, 2/17/20.

44. Ibid., p. 132, 2/18/20; pp. 154–56, 2/20/20; 4:1012–13, Webb to Curzon, 1/8/20.

45. Ibid., 7:131, S.C., 2/18/20; see also ibid., p. 169, 2/20/20.

46. Ibid., p. 132, 2/18/20.

47. Ibid., pp. 128–30; p. 169, 2/20/20; pp. 382–83, 3/3/20.

48. For text see ibid., pp. 164–73, 2/20/20; or State Department, A.C.N.P. 185.5/42. See also *Br. Doc.*, 7:156–57, 160–62, S.C., 2/20/20; pp. 256–62, 2/26/20; pp. 381–84, 3/3/20; p. 391, App. 2.

49. *Br. Doc.*, 7:164–72, S.C., 2/20/20; p. 262, 2/26/20; p. 382, 3/3/20; Foreign Office, F.O. 608/102/378-1-1, through 5. These files deal with the problem of railroads in various parts of the Ottoman Empire. See especially, 378-1-5/17719, Tentative Anglo-French agreement regarding railroad interests in Asiatic Turkey, 8/11/19.

50. For the various drafts of the military clauses, see *Br. Doc.*, 7:368–77, S.C., 3/3/20, App. 1; pp. 563–68, For. Min., 3/19/20, App. 1; pp. 723–25, 4/7/20, App. 1.

51. Ibid., pp. 339–41, S.C., 3/2/20; pp. 372–75, 3/3/20, App. 1.

52. Ibid., pp. 124–25, S.C., 2/18/20, App. 1; p. 126, App. 2; p. 181, 2/21/20; pp. 358–61, 3/3/20; pp. 367–69, App. 1; pp. 555–59, For. Min., 3/19/20; pp. 562–63, App. 1; pp. 715–16, 4/7/20; pp. 723–24, App. 1; Foreign Office, F.O. 608/271/10/10, Gribbon memorandum, 1/10/20. The gendarmerie constituted a force somewhat similar to the United States National Guard.

53. *Br. Doc.*, 7:576, For. Min., 3/20/20.

54. Ibid., p. 361, S.C., 3/20/20; p. 377, App.; pp. 575–78, For. Min., 3/20/20; pp. 651–52, 3/26/20.

55. *Br. Doc.*, 13:11–14, Curzon to Cambon, 3/5/20, and enclosure; Foreign Office, F.O. 608/274/211/212, Webb to F.O., 1/28/20; *Le Temps,* editorials 2/16/20, 2/20/20, 2/25/20.

56. *Br. Doc.*, 7:178, S.C., 2/21/20; p. 381, 3/3/20; p. 467, For. Min., 3/11/20, n.4; p. 485, 3/12/20; pp. 715–16, 4/7/20; pp. 722–24, App. 1.

57. Ibid., pp. 467–71, For. Min., 3/11/20, n.4; p. 523, 3/18/20; pp. 530–36, App. 1; pp. 580–81, 3/22/20, and n.6; pp. 733–34, 4/10/20; p. 739, App. 2.

58. Ibid., p. 468, 3/11/20, n.4, Article 3.

59. Ibid., pp. 471–72, 475–76.

60. Ibid., pp. 470–71, n.4, Articles 11–14.

61. League of Nations, *Official Journal, 1920,* pp. 15–17, 31, Third Council Session, 3/13/20; *Br. Doc.*, 7:472–75, For. Min., 3/11/20; pp. 479–82, 3/12/20; pp. 507–8, 3/16/20; Cabinet Papers, Cab. 29/32, A.J. 156, Memorandum agreed to by the Council of the League of Nations, "Protection of Minorities in Turkey," 4/11/20.

62. *Br. Doc.*, 7:509, For. Min., 3/16/20.

XII ❀ THE CONFERENCE OF LONDON: NON-TURKISH TERRITORIES AND TREATY ENFORCEMENT

DURING its sessions, the Conference of London dealt with a wide variety of non-Turkish problems ranging from Greek claims in Thrace to the elimination of the last ties between the old Ottoman Empire and its North African territories. Of these, the Greek and Armenian questions also particularly affected the formation of the new Turkish state.

Greek Claims

The disposition of Greek claims in Thrace involved the determination of the boundaries of Turkey in Europe, and the question of Smyrna necessitated a decision as to whether or not Anatolia should belong completely to Turkey. In both cases it was necessary to deal with not only a difference in views among the powers at the conference, but also the powerful influence and strong Greek nationalism of the Greek prime minister, Eleutherios Venizelos.

Thrace

After the powers had delineated the southern frontier of Bulgaria in the summer of 1919, Allied troops were sent into that part of Thrace which had been taken from Bulgaria. Greek troops were allowed to occupy only the small area in western Thrace that all the Allies, including the United States, agreed should go to Greece. Failure to reach a final settlement had been due entirely to American opposition to Greek annexation of all Thrace. However, at the London conference, objections of the United States no longer carried any great weight. Now that it was evident that the United States could not be expected to take part in the enforcement and administration of the Eastern settlement, the British and French made no effort to conceal their annoyance at American interference in both the Eastern and Adriatic questions.[1]

With the need to consider American desires removed, the Thracian problem was greatly simplified. All were agreed that eastern and western Thrace should go to Greece. Only the question of whether Greece should receive territory to the Enos-Midia or the Chataljah line remained. Neither Britain nor France was anxious to see the Turkish state extended far beyond Constantinople. Venizelos, as would be expected, strongly supported the Chataljah boundary, and he readily assented to the suggestion that Adrianople, with its Turkish majority and many Moslem mosques and shrines, should be granted a local form of administration that would be Turkish in nature. This settlement was provisionally accepted by the conference on February 18, 1920. As to the question of Bulgarian access to the Aegean through the port of Dedeagatch, it was decided that because Turkey would possess no rights in the area, no mention of this need be made in the treaty.[2]

Smyrna

In December, the British and French had decided that Smyrna should remain in Turkish hands, with guarantees regarding Greek local administration similar to those granted the Turks in Adrianople. At London this basic decision was outwardly adhered to, although Lloyd George and Millerand put up a violent anti-Turkish smoke-screen for the benefit of the Italians and the Japanese. Yet Millerand, after inveighing against the Turks, stated that "it was a bitter conclusion to arrive at, but . . . he thought the Greeks must leave

Smyrna." [3] Lloyd George, who personally supported the Greek position, spent much time presenting the case for Greek retention; then, almost as an afterthought, he commented that "he would like to add that if any arrangement could be come to of giving nominal sovereignty to the Turks in order to save their face, by allowing them to show the Turkish flag at Smyrna, it might be a solution of the difficulty." [4]

The Italians, always antagonistic to Greek claims, readily accepted this decision. Only Venizelos was opposed, asserting that Greece had every right to the area and that it could easily handle without outside assistance the challenge of the Nationalist movement. Nevertheless, the decision stood. [5]

There remained questions involving the degree of Turkish sovereignty (or "suzerainty," as Lloyd George insisted on calling it), the amount of local autonomy and connection with Athens that the area would be allowed, and the ultimate delineation of the boundaries of this privileged zone. Of these, the territorial question proved the easiest to settle. Although not as large as that recommended by the British and French delegations on the Greek Committee in March, 1919, the final territory was somewhat greater than that recommended by General Milne in September, 1919. However, it did provide for Greek withdrawal from the region around Aidin back to the southern boundary of the sanjak of Smyrna. [6]

The form of government and the degree of Turkish suzerainty were not taken care of so easily. Lloyd George was determined to allow the Anatolian Greeks not only local autonomy but also many ties with Greece itself. Already bitter over the Constantinople decision and the recognition of any Turkish authority in Smyrna, he was adamant in insisting that Turkish sovereignty should be of the most nominal variety. He argued that the Greek government should be accorded the right to choose the administration of Smyrna, that the district should be represented in the Greek parliament, and that Greece should be allowed to enlist recruits for its army from Smyrna. [7]

Acceptance of this plan would have meant that for all intents and purposes Smyrna would be administered as an integral part of Greece. This was a far cry from the agreement reached in December by Berthelot and Curzon which, although calling for a permanent Greek governor, had made no mention of the nomination coming from Athens or of sending deputies and drafting soldiers. Both Nitti and Millerand refused to consider the idea of representatives from Smyrna sitting in the Greek parliament. Even Venizelos felt sure that "such a proposal would naturally be refused by the Turks as infringing on their sovereign rights." [8]

Faced with this opposition, Lloyd George reverted to his preferred policy of outright Greek annexation. This was completely rejected by the others. In the course of lengthy discussion it became evident that the chief concern of both France and Italy was to find a solution that would prevent too great a loss of Turkish "face." Some formula that would allow a slow adjustment to the situation seemed to be in order. [9]

It was Curzon who came forward with a five-point proposal that outlined just such a scheme. It called for the retention of the Turkish flag as "sole evidence of Turkish suzerainty." [10] The area would have a Greek garrison and a Greek administration. There would be a local parliament representing both the Greek and Turkish population, which, after two years, would have the right to apply to the League of Nations for incorporation of the territory into Greece. If such a request were made, the League would have the right to insist on a plebiscite if it thought one necessary.

Venizelos, who had sought outright annexation, reluctantly accepted this solution. He requested that the Turkish flag be flown on a fort outside, rather than within, the city; this was quickly granted. It was decided that Smyrna should be constituted as a free port, with the commercial rights of all nations carefully protected. The draft articles were eventually approved by the Committee of Foreign Ministers and Ambassadors on March 16. [11]

News of the Supreme Council's decision was greeted with dismay by the British, French, and Italian high commissioners in Constantinople, who immediately drafted an identic telegram to their governments protesting the decision and warning of the problems of enforcement that would ensue. [12] De Robeck was even more specific in a personal letter to Curzon. Pointing out that both the Thrace and Smyrna decisions violated every principle of self-determination, he warned:

It is unthinkable, as the Foreign Office has consistently been informed by us here, that the Mussulmans in those areas will peacefully accept Greek annexation, especially after the sample of Greek methods which they have had since the Greek occupation of Smyrna. . . .

The terms are such that no Turk, Committee of Union and Progress or pro-*Entente* can very well accept. The Supreme Council, thus, are prepared for a resumption of general warfare; they are prepared to do violence to their own declared and cherished principles; they are prepared to perpetuate bloodshed indefinitely in the Near East; and for what? To maintain M. Venizelos in power in Greece for what cannot in the nature of things be more than a few years at the outside. I cannot help wondering if the game is worth the candle. . . . M. Venizelos's deserts *vis-a-vis* the *Entente* are great; but is it wise to run the almost certain risk of plunging Asia in blood in order to reward Greece according to the deserts of M. Venizelos, which are very different from the deserts of Greece? [13]

Curzon, who fully agreed with these views, circulated the letter to the members of the British cabinet but to no avail.[14] The Smyrna issue was finally settled. All in all, the decision constituted a distinct victory for Lloyd George and Venizelos. To all intents and purposes, Smyrna had been turned over to Greece, for Article 4 of the draft articles called specifically for Turkey to recognize Greece's right to "all acts of sovereignty" in the area.[15] The one restriction was the right of Turkey to fly a flag over a single fort in technical recognition of its suzerainty, and even this right could be rescinded after two years.

Armenia

At London, the attitude of the negotiators was one of reluctant resignation to the concept of an independent Armenia.[16] There was little, if any, enthusiasm for Armenia or the Armenians. Since it was obvious that the United States was unlikely to assume the Armenian mandate, the conference faced the problem of finding some other protector. Whereas in the summer of 1919 the forces of General Denikin had seemingly posed a threat to an independent Armenia, in March, 1920, the apparent imminent victory of the Bolshevik forces in the Caucasus constituted an even more serious one. None of the powers at the conference was willing to undertake the mandate or to commit itself to any long-range support. It was decided, therefore, that Armenia should be independent and placed under the guarantee of the League of Nations, which would finance and recruit a voluntary military force to maintain Armenian security. However, when this solution was referred to the League Council, it met with a cool reception. Pointing out that it had no forces at its command, the League Council asked for more information concerning what might be involved in terms of men and expenses and agreed to reconsider the question when this information was received. Since this precluded any final decision by the London conference, the question was held over for consideration by the Supreme Council when it met at San Remo in April.[17]

Regarding the definition of boundaries, the powers quickly decided in favor of a small and, they hoped, more viable state than the one envisaged in the grandiose claims originally put forward by the Armenians and supported by Woodrow Wilson. It was decided to exclude Trebizond and Erzinjan; Mush, Bitlis, Van, and Erzerum would be included, although the latter was put in reluctantly and only because it seemed geographically and strategically necessary. Despite the growing strength of the Kemalist movement, the negotiators evidenced no apparent concern regarding the physical implementation of a boundary that would detach a considerable portion of Anatolia from the Turkish state. The Armenian boundary with Azerbaijan was to be negotiated directly by the two states, with the Allies committed to intervene if no agreement were reached within six months after the signing of the treaty.[18]

Batum

Other than Trebizond, Batum constituted the only decent port along the southeastern Black Sea littoral. It was therefore of prime importance not only to Armenia, but to Georgia, Azerbaijan, the northern part of Persia, and the Caspian area of Russia as well. It provided a major commercial terminus, not only for trade in cotton, timber, and wool in the Caucasus and northern Persia, but also for rail and pipeline connections with the rich oil fields around Baku.

Although there was little doubt that the city belonged ethnically and geographically to Georgia, the Allies placed no trust in Georgian promises of equal trading rights and privileges in Batum for all nations. Moreover, it was becoming all too evident that Georgia might well fall to the advancing Russian Bolshevik forces.[19]

Batum had been occupied by British forces since the end of the war. Originally it was scheduled to be evacuated at the time of the general British withdrawal from the Causasus in the late summer and early fall of 1919. However, because of the considerations mentioned above, the cabinet at the last moment had decided to retain a small garrison in Batum. Again, in early February, 1920, the cabinet decided to proceed with the evacuation, only to reverse itself a few days later as a result of stringent protests from Curzon and British diplomatic, commercial, and military representatives in the area. Instead it was decided to postpone the evacuation until the Supreme Council completed its deliberations on the future status of the city.[20]

To the Supreme Council, the League of Nations again seemed to provide the ideal solution. It was decided to ask the League Council for its opinion regarding the creation of a free port with an autonomous hinterland. Batum would become a free and independent state under the protection of the League of Nations with an administrative high commissioner appointed by the League. An inter-Allied military garrison would be provided until such time as the League assumed control. The tentative boundaries for this city-state were drawn up in detail and included in the draft articles concerning Armenia.[21]

However, the League Council's response regarding the protection of Armenia made this solution impossible. If the League had no forces to protect and administer the new Armenian state, it would be even less likely to have them for Batum. It seemed there was no choice but to grant to Georgia territorial sovereignty over the city, and the powers reluctantly acceded to that fact. It was decided, however, to approach the League again to see if it would undertake to garrison the city with inter-Allied voluntary forces in order to enforce its status as a free port. Should the League refuse, as was thought likely, the Allies themselves would then consider whether they would undertake to finance and supply such a garrison. In the meantime a contingent of three battalions, British, French, and Italian, would be kept in the city in order to prevent a complete Georgian takeover before these issues were resolved.[22]

Lazistan

The territory known as Lazistan fronted on the Black Sea and constituted the eastern half of the vilayet of Trebizond. Georgian in character and Moslem in religion, the inhabitants were a mountain people who, as Lord Curzon put it, "would brook no interference." [23] If they inclined toward any outside authority, it was toward Turkey. The Allies, however, did not want Turkey to control the area, for this might endanger Armenian independence and encourage Turkish pretensions toward recovering Batum. Therefore it was provisionally decided to grant Lazistan virtual autonomy, while technically placing it under nominal Armenian sovereignty. This decision was subsequently repudiated when it became necessary to find something with which to compensate Armenia for the commitment of Batum to Georgia. It was decided that Lazistan should be included in the Armenian state without restrictions. The traditional minorities convention that Armenia would be required to sign would adequately protect the rights of this ethnic minority in Armenia.[24]

By the time the London conference closed, the problems involving Armenia that still remained unsettled concerned long-range protection, financial aid, and the status of Batum. The boundaries of the proposed state had been clearly defined, at least as well as they could be until a team of engineers and experts could delineate them on the spot. The territorial question, at least, seemed solved.

Syria and Palestine

During the first two weeks of the Conference of London, the British and French finally reached an agreement on the long-standing question of the Syrian-Palestine border. In December, the British had

indicated that they would no longer insist that the planned Mesopo-
tamia-Mediterranean railway run through Palestine. However, a new
issue involving water rights, so precious in that semidesert area, had
emerged. Now, in a compromise settlement, the French agreed to
the inclusion within Palestine of the headwaters of the Jordan, while
the British in turn dropped all pretensions to water supplies located
further north, including a claim to the Litani River area. The French
promised to work out an arrangement with the Zionists guaranteeing
an adequate supply of water to those areas that would be dependent
on streams originating in Syria. At the same time, the British acceded
to a French request that defined the northern Syrian boundary in
such a way as to include the Bagdad Railroad line within Syria.
Both of these agreements were reached with a minimum of debate
and quibbling and remained the same in the final Treaty of Sèvres.[25]

Although settlement of these issues removed the last major area
of Syrian-Palestine disagreement between the British and French,
the relationship of the two states with Feisal and the other Arab
leaders was rapidly deteriorating. During the spring of 1920, native
unrest in Syria, and to a lesser extent in Mesopotamia, increased
considerably. In Syria, Feisal found no support for his proposed
agreement with the French and instead threw in his lot with the
extreme nationalists. A congress of Syrian notables in Damascus in
early March proclaimed the formation of an independent Syrian
state with Feisal as its ruler. Subsequently, Feisal's brother, Abdullah,
was declared ruler of an independent Mesopotamia.[26]

Both Britain and France refused to recognize the existence of the
Syrian Congress or its right to deal in any way with matters relating
to the future of territories that had been taken from Turkey by the
Allied armies. Such decisions, they stated in warnings to Feisal, could
only be made at the Peace Conference by all the Allied powers.
At the same time they invited Feisal to come to San Remo in April
for the final sessions of the Peace Conference in order to discuss
these matters. Feisal, however, refused unless he received private
assurances from the British that they recognized the independence
of these states. This the British could not provide, and as a result
Feisal remained in the Near East.[27]

Oil Rights

The question of oil was discussed in only the briefest way during the London conference. The French, eager for a definite settlement, referred to the terms of the Greenwood-Berenger Agreement that had been formulated during the previous December. Lloyd George would have none of it:

He hesitated to accept the agreement because of the rights thereby conferred on certain companies. The administration of Mesopotamia would cost an enormous sum of money, and whatever benefits could be obtained would have to go towards the cost of that administration. The cost of administration was going to be far heavier than the revenue; it was now costing eight times as much as Turkey ever screwed out of the country. It was not at all certain whether it would be worth Great Britain's while to administer the country at all, but whatever happened, the profits derived from the working of the oil-fields should not go to private companies. He personally recognized no rights in any Turkish petroleum concession, since all these agreements were worthless and could not be enforced in any court of law. He would only be prepared to recognize an agreement whereby France would obtain her share of the oil; but he must refuse to have any dealings with private companies.[28]

This apparent reversal of Lloyd George's December willingness to formalize a petroleum agreement was the result of a policy decision taken by a British conference of ministers on January 23. At that time they agreed as a matter of principle that oil revenues should benefit the state rather than joint stock companies.[29] The reasons behind this decision were twofold. There remained the aversion Lloyd George had expressed the previous July when he wrote: "I feel strongly that the discussion between France and ourselves on important questions of policy ought not to be mixed up with arrangements about oil in which private companies are involved."[30] But there was also the realization, which had not been the case in the previous summer, that the Mesopotamian fields were "so extensive that sufficient revenue should be forthcoming from them to pay for the whole administration of the country, and that for that reason private exploitation should be prevented."[31] The British ministers had agreed that the War Office could continue with its program of prospecting, but only for the ultimate benefit of the state.

Since the Greenwood-Berenger Agreement called for the awarding of concessions to various private companies, it was therefore unacceptable. Because of the British position, the Supreme Council instructed Berthelot and Greenwood to meet again in an effort to draft a new arrangement for consideration by the two governments.[32] The oil question was effectively tabled, and Lloyd George had again succeeded in keeping political issues and private business interests separate. However, Britain's reasons for doing so were somewhat different from what they had been nine months earlier. Originally, oil had been regarded as a subject of minor import in comparison to territorial, administrative, and other economic questions that faced the Peace Conference.[33] Now it loomed as an important element of national concern, with the result that the exclusion of private companies to the benefit of the national governments had become a major element in British policy formulation.

North Africa

It was during the Conference of London that the Allies finally got around to discussing the African territories that, although long since dominated by European powers, technically remained under Turkish sovereignty. Clauses stipulating Turkish renunciation of all rights to Libya, Tunis, Morocco, and the Sudan were quickly agreed upon by the Committee of Foreign Ministers and Ambassadors.[34] However, a British memorandum proposing a series of clauses relative to Egypt hit a snag of major proportions in the form of French objections.

The French did not object to provisions requiring Turkey's renunciation of its Egyptian claims and recognition of the British protectorate there. Rather they protested a clause transferring to the British all rights concerned with the navigation of the Suez Canal. This involved certain rights of intervention in cases of outside agression. The French government, much to Berthelot's obvious discomfort, maintained that granting these rights to Britain alone would involve a concession on the part of France, inasmuch as France had signed the original canal convention and many of the Suez Canal bonds were held by French investors. The British were able to demolish this argument by pointing out that Turkey could not cede anything beyond its own rights, and, since Britain held the Egyptian protectorate, it was only reasonable that authority concerning the canal should be accorded it as well.[35]

The real reason for French concern came out in a much more serious and determined French resistance to a British-sponsored clause calling for the dissolution of the international Commission of the Egyptian Public Debt. The British government indicated its willingness to "relieve Turkey of all liability in respect of the Turkish loans secured on Egyptian tribute." [36] Since Britain would, in effect, guarantee the Egyptian Public Debt, the Debt commission was no longer needed to protect the stockholders. The French government protested bitterly, arguing that since the commission was European in composition, its dissolution did not involve Turkey and therefore need not be mentioned in the treaty. Moreover, France could only accept such a provision "in exchange for correlating advantages in Morocco." [37]

Here was the crux of the matter. The 1904 Anglo-French Convention had called for recognition of reciprocal advantages in Egypt and Morocco. In the period since the end of the war the two powers had negotiated a convention in which France agreed to a renunciation of its Suez Canal rights and the abrogation of the Egyptian Debt commission. In return, Britain was to renounce all its rights and interests in the State Bank of Morocco. The convention had never been signed, however, for France sought and Britain refused to give prior consent to any arrangements France might be able to work out subsequently with Spain for French acquisition of Spanish Tangier.[38]

The French regarded the inclusion of the canal and Egyptian Debt provisions in the Turkish treaty as an unbalancing of the carefully worked out details of the Anglo-French Convention, for the peace treaty would probably be signed and ratified by the powers without reference to the Moroccan bank issue. In relation to the canal clause this argument had little validity, because Turkey was to renounce only its own rights, not those of France. But in case of the Debt commission, the French were on much more solid ground. At the close of the London conference the question remained undecided.

Berthelot did agree to consult Paris again; Curzon, in turn, threatened the withdrawal of all British guarantees of the Egyptian Debt should France fail to agree to the ending of the Debt commission.[39]

The Occupation of Constantinople

During the course of the London conference, the threat of the Turkish Nationalist movement became increasingly severe. Although this did not affect the negotiators in their formulation of the treaty terms, the conference did discuss possible means of enforcing the will of the Allies on a dissident Turkish population. This question became particularly acute because massacres of Armenians had taken place in Cilicia as a result of Turkish uprisings there. The actual extent of the massacres was unknown, but it was estimated that the number of Armenians who had lost their lives might well be in the thousands. These atrocities constituted a great embarrassment to the French, whose troops had so recently replaced the British in the area, and who had now been compelled by the Nationalists to withdraw from the town of Marash. The British did not hesitate to point out that complete peace and quiet had prevailed while they were in occupation. Although correct, the inference was hardly fair, for the strength of the Nationalist movement had increased many times over since September.[40] More justified was British criticism of the French practice of local recruiting. Close to one-third of the French forces in occupation were Armenians native to the area. The sight of the hated Armenian in the uniform of the conqueror understandably irritated the Turkish population, and they turned against the Armenians as soon as the uprisings began.[41]

There was little question that the uprisings, though primarily local in nature, were Nationalist sponsored. Nationalist units had even taken part in some places. Moreover, since January, 1920, the Nationalists had been in control of the government in Constantinople. The National Assembly had approved the National Pact and the sultan and his regime showed every sign of being dependent on the Nationalist movement. In fact, Kemal had officially made peace with the Constantinople regime and had recently been appointed governor of Erzerum (which was slated by the Allies to become part of the new Armenian state).[42]

The Allied statesmen were therefore convinced that the Turkish government at Constantinople must be held responsible for the Cilician massacres. It seemed imperative that some punitive action should be taken. Lloyd George made the point clearly:

> Were the Allies to do nothing? It was not enough to warn the Turks. We had done that again and again. . . . It was no use the Allies proceeding with the terms of a Peace Treaty until they could once more restore order. . . . It was all very well to insert in the treaty provisions about "powers of patrolling," "spheres of influence," and so on, but not the slightest attention would be paid to these by the Turks, and the stipulations that would be made mutually in regard to the protection of minorities—well, he doubted whether these had the slightest value. The fact was that, on the eve of making peace with Turkey, the Powers found themselves practically impotent to deal with a situation of extreme gravity. . . . The time had now arrived to take strong action and to do something dramatic.[43]

What this action might be Lloyd George went on to reveal. If the information concerning the massacres were true, "they should take charge of the Turkish government; . . . they should arrest the Grand Vizier and his War Ministers [Minister], along with other Ministers, if necessary, and either imprison them on the other side of the Straits or place them in custody on one of the Allied ships till steps had been taken by the Government to remedy the situation." [44] Curzon put the finishing touches on the argument:

> Why had the Supreme Council decided to retain the Sultan in Constantinople? It was in order that he should be at their mercy in the event of any trouble arising in Turkey in the future. The case had now arisen . . . now was the moment to show to the world, and to the Turk in particular what our policy was worth. By what the Powers decided to do now their Turkish policy would be judged.[45]

To this the French agreed, and the Italians, with some foot-dragging, also concurred. Since the French were so involved in the Cilician problem, there was little they could say in opposition to the proposals of Lloyd George and Curzon. However, both Berthelot and Cambon expressed reservations as to the ability of the Constantinople government to influence and control Kemal. Nitti also expressed similar reservations and questioned whether the general effect would not be to lessen rather than increase the authority of the Constantinople government over the Anatolian interior. He suggested that if the Allies sought to maintain the authority of the sultan, perhaps some attention should be paid to encouraging him to resist the Nationalists.[46]

Within the British delegation, the chief opposition to an Allied occupation of Constantinople and a crackdown on the Constantinople government came from the secretary of state for war, Winston Churchill. Britain was scheduled to end conscription on March 31, the first of the Allies to do so, and all conscripts had the right to be released from military service by the end of April. Having only the previous week defended the proposed military budget before a critical House of Commons, Churchill strenuously opposed any further extension of British military obligations and argued that an occupation of Constantinople would serve no purpose, be extremely costly, and needlessly irritate the Turks.

He agreed that the power of the Allies, as represented by their fleet and armies, over Constantinople and the Turkish administration was unlimited. Any action could be taken under the menace of the guns of the ships, and Great Britain alone could do all that was necessary in Constantinople. But the fact must not be overlooked that the real difficulties would have to be faced in districts remote from Constantinople and from the sea. It would be in these far off districts that sullen resistance to the terms of the Peace Treaty would arise, and in those districts the Allies at present possessed no power or forces sufficient to exercise any satisfactory control. He agreed that the Turkish armies in Asia could not be compared in efficiency to the trained forces employed by Turkey during the war, but they would be quite good enough to inflict heavy losses on any small force[s] sent against them. Consequently, military operations must be comtemplated if the conference desired to enforce its decisions. It must be fully realized that the Turkish armies in Asia would not be controlled by any decision of violence extorted from the Turkish Government in Constantinople, the same would never result in compliance by Turkey as a whole and, furthermore, the Allies did not possess sufficient forces to take the necessary action outside Constantinople.[47]

In answer to Churchill's criticism, Lloyd George argued that there were 160,000 Allied troops (of which 90,000 were Greek) in European and Anatolian Turkey. The Turkish forces of Kemal were estimated at 80,000. "He could not help thinking that if two soldiers—French, British, Italian or Greek—could not defeat one Turk, the Allies ought to start their conference anew and ask the Turk upon what terms he would condescend to make peace." [48]

When the views of the Allied high commissioners in Constantinople were sought, they proved to be quite similar to those of Churchill. The general opinion was that no action taken in Constantinople could in any way alter or retrieve the situation in Cilicia. As Admiral de Robeck put it, "What we have to face and what we have to adjust our action to is the wider issue raised by [the] Nationalists to resist drastic peace and [the] apparent intention of [the] Peace Conference to impose one." [49] As an alternative to the hard-line approach, the high commissioners offered what Curzon described as the *bloc* method of handling Turkey. This consisted of a policy of support for the sultan, the treatment of him as an ally, and the taking of steps that would strengthen his position and better enable him to ward off the challenge of the Nationalists. These steps would consist of very lenient peace terms, including the "maintenance of Turkish sovereignty over Smyrna and Eastern Thrace including Adrianople," as well as suzerainty over the territory planned for the Armenian state.[50]

In reply, the Supreme Council telegraphed an outline of the proposed peace terms with a request for an estimate of what the Turkish reaction would be.[51] The answer was hardly encouraging:

[The High Commissioners] regard it as incumbent upon them once more to express their unanimous opinion on the consequences of presenting a treaty as severe as that now proposed. In their view the said consequences may be: First, a refusal by Turkey to sign the treaty or to ratify it if it is signed or to execute it if it is ratified. Second, creation of a new Government in Asia, the flight of Parliament to Anatolia, the rising of the whole of the Turkish elements and widespread massacre of Christians in Asia Minor and Thrace. As soon as the stipulations become known there is danger that these consequences and in particular the massacres, will at once ensue. Third, attempts in Europe which may be continued indefinitely to secure any action against the Greeks between the Bulgarians and the

Turks. Fourth, the possibility of combined action in the future in Asia between the Bolsheviks, the Arabs, and the Turks.[52]

Despite such clearcut warnings, the Supreme Council never considered the possibility of formulating a more lenient set of peace terms. As Curzon put it, this "would involve an absolute reversal of the policy the Allies had decided to adopt." [53] The terms to be imposed "were so drastic as to exclude the *bloc* policy, and . . . it was evident that they must be imposed by force of arms." [54] Whether this could effectively be done was not discussed; only the questions of when and with what strength were considered. Both Lloyd George and Curzon argued that sooner was better than later and that only action, not threats, would have any chance of showing any real effect. It was necessary to seize and hold territory that could be used as a hostage for better Turkish behavior in the future. If necessary, Britain would occupy Constantinople alone. Parliament had been promised that Constantinople would be held as a hostage to protect the Armenians, and this must at all costs be carried out.[55]

Faced with such an adamant stand, the other powers could do little but agree, especially because they all recognized the need for some action and could offer no alternative plan. It was decided that Allied sentries should be stationed at various municipal buildings, that the War Office should be seized, and that Allied censorship should be imposed on all orders issued by the Turkish War Department. The post and telegraph systems would also be brought under Allied control as well as the administration of the police. The policy of arrest and deportation of leading Nationalists was specifically sanctioned.

Other punitive measures involving the dissolution of the Turkish parliament, the taking over of civil government, or the arrest of the grand vizier and other political figures in Constantinople were considered and discarded. With the center of power in Anatolia, such action could do little good, especially since the Supreme Council seemed to be agreed on the impossibility of any extensive military operations in Anatolia. The problem of what further military action could be taken to enforce the treaty was referred to the Allied military experts at Versailles and became one of the main topics of discussion at the San Remo conference in April.[56]

Despite this growing concern with treaty enforcement, the general attitude of the London conference was still one of easy optimism, best summed up in Lloyd George's remark about two Allied soldiers being easily able to handle one Turk. Although the powers no longer had any doubts that the Kemalists were the dominant political force in Turkey, they still did not see in the Nationalist movement a serious threat to eventual enactment of any peace treaty they might wish to impose upon the Turkish state.[57]

The occupation of Constantinople was carried out on March 16 by a contingent of British, French, and Italian forces. Proclaiming that the occupation was provisional, the Allies officially declared that they had no intention of destroying the authority of the sultan but instead sought to strengthen it. Although asserting that the Allies still intended to leave Constantinople with Turkey, a warning was issued that "if, God forbid, widespread disturbances or massacres should occur, this decision would probably be altered." [58]

This was what Lloyd George and Curzon had meant when they stated that territory should be held as a hostage for Turkish good behavior. Yet it is hard to believe that Curzon and Lloyd George really believed that the occupation of Constantinople would restrain the Nationalists, when from all sides they had been warned that this would not be the case. Their original intention of driving the Turks out of Constantinople may have helped to blind their eyes to the true situation. It is quite possible that, apart from any beneficial effect the occupation of Constantinople might have on the Anatolian situation, Curzon and Lloyd George welcomed the excuse to separate Constantinople even temporarily from Turkey and would not have been upset if the separation ultimately had become permanent.

One old issue reappeared as a result of the decision to intervene in Constantinople. This was the question of the command in Constantinople and the status of British General Milne and French General Franchet d'Esperey. The French were quite willing to accede to British requests that Franchet d'Esperey be removed, for they conceded that the general had shown "an almost complete lack of tact and judgment." [59] However, they would not accept the British contention that General Milne, who was in charge of the Constantinople garrison, should be freed from the supervisory command of a French commander-in-chief of European Turkey. To further complicate the situation the Supreme Council compromised by deciding that in the city of Constantinople there should be "complete equality between the Allied generals . . . ,who should meet together and decide on the steps to be taken by the commanders of each of the Allied forces." [60] As a result of this stalemate, Franchet d'Esperey remained, and Milne, who had direct command of the occupying forces, in turn refused to work with him. The situation was clearly untenable, and the French, unwilling to concede the principle, solved the problem by placing Franchet d'Esperey on extended leave. The result was that the British assumed sole military command in fact, if not in theory, of not only Constantinople but the Straits zone as well. [61]

The Conference of London and the United States

Before bringing discussion of the London conference to a close, a comment on the role of the United States is in order. The attitude of the European Allies toward America during the conference is best exemplified in Lloyd George's proposal that America should be asked to take part in the occupation of Constantinople.

We had received endless telegrams from the United States asking why nothing was done to help Armenia, and the American press had strongly criticized our alleged impotence to stop the massacres. An American school had been attacked in Cilicia, and several American citizens had been murdered. Moreover, the Armenians were the special protégés of the Americans. He thought we might tell the United States Government that the Allies intended now to take strong action, and to ask if the Americans were prepared to join. The Americans had always taken a very exalted position and had lectured us severely on our inaction. They appeared to assume responsibility for the sole guardianship of the Ten Commandments and for the Sermon on the Mount; yet when it came to a practical question of assistance and responsibility, they absolutely refused to accept these. He suggested, therefore, that a telegram should be sent to Washington pointing out that massacres of Armenians had taken place; that the Armenians were the special protégés of the Americans; and that American citizens had also been murdered, and asking whether the United States were prepared to join the Allies in the strong action they proposed to take. . . . He was quite certain the Americans would do nothing, but their refusal to assist would make it easier for us in the future to deal with them.[62]

The Supreme Council readily agreed with Lloyd George's proposal. The next day Curzon met with Ambassador Davis and informed him of the council's decision and the proposed action. Although he made no specific request for American participation, he made it clear that it would be welcomed. As it turned out, no reply was ever forthcoming from Washington.[63]

Throughout the Conference of London, the American government, though refusing to participate in the proceedings, requested that it be kept apprised of the work being done.[64] On March 12, the French ambassador to America, Jules Jusserand, informed Acting Secretary of State Frank Polk of the tentative outline of the Turkish settlement. This elicited a long reply in which Wilson personally protested the granting of Constantinople to the Turks, expressed reservations concerning spheres of economic priority, insisted on a greater Armenia that would include Trebizond, and bitterly opposed the cession of the northern part of eastern Thrace to Greece.[65]

The reaction of the conference was basically one of impatience. President Wilson's physical collapse in September 1919 had rendered him a shadow president. Isolated by the understandably protective screening provided by his wife, he remained invisible and inaccessible to all but a few chosen aides. It was obvious to the powers in London that the president's influence on American politics had declined greatly. Popular attitude in America concerning mandates was generally one of indifference, while the Senate, fresh from its bitter battle over the Versailles treaty, evidenced open hostility to the idea of American participation in any such scheme. The powers therefore saw little reason to consider protests from a country that had refused both a seat at the London conference and an active part in cooperative action in the Near East. Generally, the Supreme Council's position remained the same as it had been throughout the conference: that even though the United States had not declared war on the Ottoman Empire and had refused to participate in the Conference of London, it should be given the opportunity to comment on, and even sign, the final treaty if it wished. However, the Allies would in no respect be bound to consider or adopt any American-sponsored revisions. In other words, America was welcome to participate, but only on a take-it-or-leave-it basis.[66]

It is difficult to overestimate the importance of the Conference of London. At the beginning of the conference, the Turkish settlement had consisted of a series of general principles and broad policy decisions. During February and March, the conference implemented most of the basic decisions made by the French and English during December and January, and initiated new decisions relating to Smyrna, financial control, and economic spheres of priority. By the time the conference closed, a draft treaty had been pretty thoroughly hammered out, and only a series of specific decisions on particular clauses, plus final overall approval, awaited the Supreme Council at San Remo.

Not everyone was happy with the results. The Italians complained that they were receiving very little and believed that Italy was not being accorded its fair share.[67] Nor were the French particularly happy. Paul Cambon, one of the chief negotiators on the Committee of Foreign Ministers and Ambassadors, commented that France had given away much, obtained little, and had played directly into British hands. By allowing the occupation of Constantinople and the virtual domination of Smyrna by Greece, France had alienated the Turks while gaining no support elsewhere. Believing that the Turks were only waiting "to throw themselves into our arms," Cambon complained that as a result of these actions, "Turkey will detest us the more, since she had had more hope of our support." [68]

For the British, the treaty was a tribute to their negotiating ability if not their foresight. They had succeeded in minimizing both French and Italian influence in the Near East. At the same time, Greek interests had been protected and the Greeks had virtually obtained Smyrna as well as Thrace. The occupation of Constantinople by a predominantly British military force commanded by General Milne gave Britain general control of Constantinople and the Straits. All in all, in terms of British aims, the London conference must be regarded as a triumph for British diplomacy.

Yet it was a triumph that could lead only to disaster, and none realized it better than Paul Cambon:

The Turks will accept all the rest but Smyrna. . . . .It is probable that this council [military experts] will recognize that to quell the Turks, almost certainly several hundred thousand men will be needed. The Italians have declared that they cannot send anyone, we are in the same position. Thus the English must assume all the load. Lloyd George will recoil before this prospect and Venizelos with 80,000 men will find himself alone, facing an aroused country and an organized guerilla force. Then we will be forced to revise the Treaty. That is how I see things.[69]

Few statements have been more prophetic.

1. See above, Chapter 7; also *Br. Doc.*, 7:1, S.C., 2/12/20; pp. 43, 48, 53, 2/14/20.

2. Cabinet Papers, Cab. 23/35, S-9, Conference of Ministers (Paris), 1/15/20; *Br. Doc.*, 7:50, S.C., 2/14/20; p. 64, 2/16/20; pp. 121–22, 2/18/20; p. 179, 2/21/20; Frangulis, *Crise Mondiale* 2:128, Venizelos to Greek foreign minister, 3/16/20.

3. *Br. Doc.*, 7:54, S.C., 2/14/20. See also editorial in *Le Temps*, 2/17/20.

4. *Br. Doc.* 7:55–56, S.C., 2/14/20. In private, the French did not hesitate to tell Venizelos that they felt the decision to send Greek troops to Smyrna had been a mistake. See Frangulis, *Crise Mondiale*, 2:139–40.

5. *Br. Doc.*, 7:63, 65–68, S.C., 2/16/20; pp. 121–22, 2/18/20.

6. Ibid., p. 98, 2/17/20, App. 2; pp. 244–47, 2/25/20, and n.5

7. Ibid., p. 127, 2/18/20, App. 2; p. 187, 2/21/20.

8. Ibid., p. 65, 2/16/20. See also ibid., pp. 186–88, 2/21/20.

9. Ibid., p. 88, 2/17/20; pp. 189–90, 2/21/20; pp. 219–20, 229–33, 2/24/20.

10. Ibid., p. 233, 2/24/20.

11. Ibid., pp. 238–39, 247, 2/25/20; pp. 511–12, For. Min., 3/16/20; pp. 517–20, App. 2; Lloyd George Papers, F55/1/27, Venizelos to Lloyd George, 2/26/20.

12. *Br. Doc.*, 7:500, S.C., 3/15/20, App. 3; 13:14–16, Robeck to Curzon, 3/7/20. Though he was not consulted by the others, American High Commissioner Admiral Mark Bristol took a similar view. He continually urged American action to thwart Greek ambitions, but was told by Washington that Congress would neither take a mandate nor authorize money for work in the Near East. State Department, Turkey, 867.00/1190, Bristol to Sec. State, 3/30/20; Colby to Bristol, 4/6/20; ibid., 867.00/1195, Bristol to Sec. State, 4/1/20.

13. *Br. Doc.*, 13:18, Robeck to Curzon, 3/19/20.

14. Cabinet Papers, Cab. 24/101, C.P. 967, Curzon to Cabinet, 3/26/20; Lloyd George Papers, F12/3/26, Curzon to Lord George, 4/9/20; Ronaldshay, *Curzon*, 3:272.

15. *Br. Doc.*, 7:518, For. Min., 3/16/20, App. 2.

16. Armenian independence was formally recognized by Great Britain, France and Italy on January 19, 1920, and by the United States on April 23, 1920 (Senate confirmation was received on May 13, 1920). President Wilson proposed an American mandate for Armenia on May 24, 1920. It was rejected by the Senate on June 1, 1920. *Br. Doc.*, 2:922–25, Allied

Conference, 1/19/20; Foreign Office, F.O. 608/272/16/102, 109, 187; *U.S. Doc., 1920*, 3:775–78; De Novo, *American Interests*, pp. 126–27; Evans, *U.S. and Partition*, pp. 261–62; Gidney, *Mandate*, chap. 10.

17. It should be noted that in all the discussions concerning League administration of Armenia it was assumed that a great deal of the money could be obtained from American sources that were sympathetic to the Armenian cause. It was felt that the League could better appeal to and tap this source than could the Allied nations themselves. *Br. Doc.*, 7:81, S.C., 2/16/20; p. 126, 2/18/21, App. 2, Part 4, Article 1; pp. 283–85, 2/27/20; pp. 477–79, For. Min., 3/12/20; pp. 507–9, 3/16/20; 4:1024–25, Vansittart to Curzon, 1/12/20, enclosure; Cabinet Papers, Cab. 24/104, C.P. 1186, Correspondence between the Supreme Council and the Council of the League of Nations concerning Armenia, March–April, 1920; League of Nations, *Journal, 1920*, p. 19, Third Council Session, 3/13/20; p. 33, Annex 29, Curzon to Derby, 3/12/20; Aharonian, "From Sardarapat to Sèvres to Lausanne," *Armenian Review* 16 (Fall, 1963), 3/22/20; Gidney. *Mandate*, pp. 216–17.

18. *Br. Doc.*, 7:98, 2/17/20, App. 3; pp. 280–82, 2/27/20; p. 641, For. Min., 3/25/20; pp. 644–46, App. 1: Cabinet Papers, Cab. 24/103, C.P. 1061, Report of the Armenian Commission, 4/9/20. The Trebizond-Erzinjan area was to be demilitarized.

19. Foreign Office, F.O. 406/42/73, McDonell memorandum, 11/15/19; *Br. Doc.*, 12:558, Wardrop to Curzon, 2/5/20; p. 562, Hardinge to Goode, 2/13/20; p. 572, Wardrop to Curzon, 3/7/20; p. 573, 3/9/20; p. 574, Curzon to Wardrop, 3/15/20 and n. 2; pp. 574–75, Wardrop to Curzon, 3/15/20; p. 576, Robeck to Curzon, 3/18/20; p. 582, Wardrop to Curzon, 3/26/20; pp. 586–89, Robeck to Curzon, 4/6/20; Ullman, *Anglo-Soviet Relations*, 2:321 ff.

20. Cabinet Papers, Cab. 23/12, W.C. 622, 9/18/19; Cab. 24/92, C.P. 93, Future of Batum, 11/11/19; Cab. 23/20, C.4(20), 1/14/19; C.7(20), 1/29/20; C.10 (20), 2/11/20, App. 2, Conference of Ministers, 2/3/20; C. 11(20), 2/18/20; Cab. 23/35, S-11, Conference of Ministers, 1/18/20; Foreign Office, F.O. 406/43/55, War Office to F.O., 2/5/20, enclosure, War Office to Milne, 2/3/20; *Br. Doc.*, 12:558–59, Wardrop to Curzon, 2/6/20; pp. 559–60, Curzon memorandum, 2/9/20; p. 562, Wardrop to Curzon, 2/12/20; p. 565, Stevens (Batum) to Curzon, 2/16/20; p. 566, Wardrop to Curzon, 2/16/20; p. 567, Curzon to Wardrop, 2/17/20; p. 568, Curzon to Wardrop, 2/20/19.

21. *Br. Doc.*, 4:1024–25, Vansittart to Curzon, 1/12/20, enclosure, Berthelot note, 1/11/20; 7:253–55, S.C. 2/25/20; p. 281, 2/27/20; pp. 514–15, For. Min., 3/16/20; pp. 520–22, Apps. 4 and 5; pp. 647–50, 3/25/20, Apps. 1 and 2; pp. 728–30, 4/7/20, App. 5; 12:564, Curzon to Wardrop, 2/14/20; pp. 565–66, Wardrop to Curzon, 2/16/20; p. 568, Curzon to Wardrop, 2/27/20; pp. 571–72, 3/3/20.

22. Ibid., 7:639–41, For. Min., 3/25/20; p. 643, App. 1; pp. 654–56, 3/26/20; 12:577, Curzon to Wardrop, 3/21/20; 8:51, S.C., 4/20/20; Callwell, *Henry Wilson*, 2:228, 2/7/20.

23. *Br. Doc.*, 7:281, S.C. 2/27/20.

24. Ibid., p. 82, 2/16/20; pp. 281–82, 2/27/20; pp. 640–41, For. Min., 3/25/20; pp. 643 and 647, App. 1; 12:583, Wardrop to Curzon, 4/1/20; p. 590, Curzon to Robeck, 4/12/20.

25. Ibid., 7:104–11, S.C. 2/17/20; pp. 113–16, 3/18/20; p. 160, 2/20/20; pp. 182–84, 2/21/20; Foreign Office, F.O. 608/274/76, File on Syrian-Palestine border disputes, 1920.

26. *Br. Doc.*, 13:215–16, Wilson to Montagu, 2/12/20; p. 221, Allenby to Curzon, 3/7/20; p. 222, Curzon to Allenby, 3/8/20; p. 223, Allenby to Curzon, 3/8/20 (2); pp. 224–25, 3/13/20; pp. 236–37, Meinertzhagen to Curzon, 3/26/20; Foreign Office, F.O. 608/274/77/78, Forbes-Adam memorandum, 1/17/20; Antonius, *Arab Awakening*, p. 304; Callwell, *Henry Wilson*, 2:230, 3/19/20; Cumming, *Franco-British Rivalry*, pp. 103–4; *Correspondance d'Orient*, pp. 15–22, 1/15/20; p. 67, 1/20/20; p. 116, 2/15/20; G. Samné, "Les variations de L'Emir Faycal et le nationalisme turc," pp. 149–52; A. Hourani, *Syria and Lebanon: A Political Essay*, pp. 53–54; Kedourie, *England and the Middle East*, chaps. 6 and 7; J. Loder, *The Truth about Mesopotamia, Palestine and Syria*, pp. 89–98; Longrigg, *Syria and Lebanon*, pp. 97–99; Wilson,

Loyalties, 2:237, 314–16; H. Young, *The Independent Arab,* p. 305; Zeine, *Arab Independence,* chap. 7.

27. *Br. Doc.,* 13:224, Cambon to Curzon, 3/11/20; p. 225, Curzon to Allenby, 3/13/20; pp. 226–29, Curzon to Derby, 3/13/20; pp. 229–30, Allenby to Curzon, 3/14/20; p. 231, 3/18/20; pp. 231–32, Curzon to Allenby, 3/19/20; p. 233, Meinertzhagen to Curzon, 3/19/20; pp. 233–34, Allenby to Curzon, 3/20/20; p. 235, Curzon to Allenby, 3/22/20; pp. 235–36, Allenby to Curzon, 3/23/20; pp. 237–39, Curzon memorandum of meeting with Cambon, 3/20/20; p. 239, Curzon to Allenby, 4/1/20; pp. 239–40, Cambon Memorandum, 4/1/20; p. 246, Meinertzhagen to Curzon, 4/4/20; pp. 251–52, Curzon to Hardinge, 4/26/20; *Le Temps,* 3/29/20.

28. *Br. Doc.,* 7:108, S.C., 2/17/20.

29. Cabinet Papers, Cab. 23/20. C.8(20), 2/4/20, App. 2, Conference of Ministers, 1/23/20. See also *Br. Doc.,* 13:257, Curzon to Geddes, 5/7/20, n. 4, Curzon memorandum, 12/12/20.

30. Lloyd George Papers, F.12/1/55, Lloyd George memorandum, 7/10/19. See above, Chapter 9.

31. Cabinet Papers, Cab. 23/20, C.8(20), 2/4/20, App. 2, Conference of Ministers, 1/23/20.

32. *Br. Doc.,* 7:185, S.C., 2/21/20.

33. For a further expression of this viewpoint, see the editorial in the *Times* (London), 3/27/20. See also above, Chapter 9.

34. *Br. Doc.,* 7:596–99, For. Min., 3/23/20; p. 605, App. 6; pp. 736–37, 4/10/20; pp. 743–44, App. 6.

35. Ibid., p. 603–5, 3/23/20, App. 5; p. 651, 3/26/20; pp. 686–88, 3/31/20; pp. 693–96, App. 1.

36. Ibid., p. 695, 3/31/20, App. 1.

37. Ibid., p. 697, App. 2. See also ibid., pp. 688–90.

38. Ibid., pp. 696–700, App. 2, n. 11; 4:492–95, Peterson to Forbes-Adam, 10/20/10, enclosure and n. 5; *U.S. Doc., P.P.C.,* 4:127–37, C. of Ten, 2/25/19.

39. *Br. Doc.,* 7:690–91, For. Min. 3/31/20; pp. 736–37, 4/10/20; pp. 743–44, App. 6.

40. State Department, Turkey, 867.00/1106, Bristol to Sec. State, 2/7/20; 1102, 2/14/20; 1113, 2/17/20; 1114, 2/17/20; 1124, 2/26/20; 1128 n.d.; 1130, 3/4/20; 1131, n.d., 1136, 3/5/20; 1234, Jackson to Sec. State, 3/4/20; Foreign Office, F.O. 406/43/54, Robeck to Curzon, 2/4/20; 67, Williams to Phipps, 2/13/20; 86, Robeck to Curzon, 3/2/20; 109, 2/11/20; *Br. Doc.,* 7:285, For. Min., 2/27/20; pp. 291–94, 2/28/20; pp. 298–99, S.C., 2/28/20; pp. 301, 303–4; *Times* (London), 2/7/20, 2/14/20, 2/17/20, 2/28/20; *Le Temps,* 2/20/20; France, *Journal Officiel, Débats parlementaires: Chambre des Députés, 1918–1925,* pp. 739–62, 3/26/20–3/27/20; "Dangerous Complications in Syria, The Massacres at Marash," pp. 108–12.

41. The Turks also disliked the contingents of black African colonial troops stationed by the French in Armenia. State Department, Turkey, 867.00/1118, Bristol to Sec. State, 2/21/20; 1129, 3/6/20; 1149, 3/9/20. See also, generally, file entitled "Syria and Cilicia, 1920," Bristol Papers, Box 28; Foreign Office, F.O. 406/43/112, Robeck to Curzon, 2/17/20; *Br. Doc.,* 7:185, S.C., 2/21/20; Cambon, *Correspondance,* 3:377, 2/29/20.

42. *Br. Doc.,* 4:1088, Robeck to Curzon, 2/10/20; 13:1, Robeck to Curzon, 2/13/20, pp. 2–3, 2/17/20; pp. 4–7, 2/23/20; 7:299–300, 302, S.C., 2/28/20; Foreign Office F.O. 406/43/128, Robeck to Curzon, 3/1/20; Adkisson, *Britain and the Kemalist Movement,* pp. 227–31; Rémusat, "Cilicie, 1918–1922," pp. 350–61.

43. *Br. Doc.,* 7:301–2, S.C., 2/28/20. See also ibid., p. 293, For. Min., 2/28/20.

44. Ibid., p. 302, S.C., 2/28/20.

45. Ibid., pp. 298–99. The *New York Times* expressed a similar view in an editorial on March 6.

46. *Br. Doc.*, 7:294–96, For. Min., 2/28/20; pp. 304–5, S.C., 2/28/20; p. 362, 3/3/20; 13:10–11, Derby to Curzon, 3/5/20; *Le Temps*, 3/1/20; *R.F.P.: Political Review*, 4/2/20.

47. *Br. Doc.*, 7:364, S.C., 3/3/20; also p. 305, 2/28/20; pp. 453–4, 3/10/20. Churchill, *Aftermath*, p. 401, Churchill to Lloyd George, 3/29/20. Churchill was supported in his criticism by Sir Henry Wilson. Callwell, *Henry Wilson*, 2:229, 3/3/20. See also *Times* (London), 2/24/20.

48. *Br. Doc.*, 7:416–18, S.C., 3/5/20.

49. Ibid., p. 423, S.C., 3/5/20, n. 7. Bristol subsequently reported to Washington that neither the high commissioners nor General Milne, who commanded the forces that occupied Constantinople, regarded it as a wise policy decision. Bristol Papers, Box 28, Bristol to Washington, 3/16/20; Box 17, Diary, 4/18/20.

50. *Br. Doc.*, 7:379, S.C., 3/3/20, App. 2. See also ibid., p. 306, 2/28/20, App.; pp. 377–79, 3/3/20, App. 2 and n. 24; 13:9–10, Robeck to Curzon, 3/5/20; pp. 14–16, 3/7/20; Foreign Office, F.O. 406/43/84, Robeck to Curzon, 2/29/20.

51. Foreign Office, F.O. 406/43/95, Curzon to Robeck, 3/6/20; *Br. Doc.*, 7:411–21, S.C., 3/5/20; pp. 421–23, App. 1.

52. *Br. Doc.*, 7:500, S.C., 3/15/20, App. 3. See also ibid., 13:16, Robeck to Curzon, 3/8/20; pp. 21–22, 3/10/20.

53. Ibid., 7:413, S.C., 3/5/20.

54. Ibid., p. 414.

55. The Allies had had troops stationed in barracks within the city limits ever since 1918. Ibid., pp. 413, 417, S.C., 3/5/20.

56. Ibid., pp. 415–20, S.C., 3/5/20; pp. 450–57, 3/10/20; Foreign Office, F.O. 406/43/105, Curzon to Robeck, 3/10/20.

57. *Br. Doc.*, 7:413–15, S.C., 3/5/20; p. 456, 3/10/20.

58. Ibid., 13:45, Robeck to Curzon, 3/21/20. See also p. 24, Curzon to Robeck 3/13/20; pp. 25–26, Curzon to Cambon, 3/13/20; pp. 38–40, Robeck to Curzon, 3/16/20; p. 43, 3/18/20; pp. 43–44, 3/21/20; 7:438–39, S.C., 3/8/20; p. 507, 3/16/20; Foreign Office, F.O. 406/43/105, Curzon to Robeck, 3/10/20; Pech, *Alliés et Turquiè*, pp. 117–18, 3/16/20; *Times* (London), 3/17/20, 3/18/20; Howard, *Partition*, pp. 256–57; Adivar (Edib), *Ordeal*, pp. 67–69; Luke, *Cities and Men*, 2:71–72.

59. *Br. Doc.*, 13:41, Curzon to Derby (conversation with Cambon), 3/17/20.

60. Ibid., 7:462, Franco-British conversation, 3/10/20.

61. Ibid., pp. 239–41, 2/25/20; pp. 458–62, 3/10/20; 13:13–14, Curzon to Cambon, 3/5/20; pp. 21–22, Robeck to Curzon, 3/10/20; p. 24, Curzon to Robeck, 3/13/20; pp. 41–42; Curzon to Derby (conversation with Cambon), 3/17/20; pp. 46–47, Robeck to Curzon, 3/24/20; p. 58, Curzon to Cambon, and nn. 1, 2; p. 60, Grahame to Curzon, 4/5/20; 9:343–44, Curzon to Derby (conversation with Cambon), 4/8/20; 13:93–94, Curzon to Derby, 6/25/20; pp. 96–97, Derby to Curzon, 6/27/20; Cabinet Papers, Cab. 24/100, C.P. 892, Churchill memorandum, 3/18/20; Foreign Office, F.O. 406/43/237, Duncan to Buchanan, 5/17/20; Callwell, *Henry Wilson*, 2:226–27, 2/14/20; Toynbee and Kirkwood, *Turkey*, p. 87: Azan, *Franchet d'Esperey*, p. 257; *Le Temps*, 4/17/20.

62. *Br. Doc.*, 7:428–29, S.C., 3/5/20. For examples of the kind of American statements that so irritated Lloyd George, see Gidney, *Mandate*, pp. 208–9.

63. *Br. Doc.*, 7:428–30; p. 496, 3/15/20; Lloyd George Papers, F206/4/16, Curzon memorandum, "The Turkish Situation and the American Government," 3/6/20; *Br. Doc.*, 12:22–24, Curzon to Lindsay, 3/12/20.

64. The Allied invitation to the United States to participate in the Conference is in *Br. Doc.*, 2:965–67, Allied Conference, 1/21/20; pp. 968–70, App. A. In November, 1919, Polk, who shortly after became acting secretary of state, recommended from Paris that America

should "have nothing to do with the [Turkish] Treaty." When Wilson nominated Bainbridge Colby as secretary of state, Wilson suggested that Polk go to London to take part in the London conference as the American commissioner. Polk refused, and pressed his view that the United States should stay clear of the Turkish negotiations. Polk Papers, Dr. 78, fol. 13, letter, Polk to Lansing, 8/12/19; fol. 12, 8/31/19; Dr. 73, fol. 121, Polk to Davis, 11/15/19; Dr. 89, fol. 128, Wilson to Polk, 2/24/20; Polk to Wilson, 2/25/20; De Novo, *American Interests*, pp. 123-24.

65. *U.S. Doc., 1920*, 3:748-50, Jusserand to Polk, 3/12/20; pp. 750-53, Colby to Jusserand, 3/24/20; *Br. Doc.*, 7:495-96, S.C., 3/15/20; p. 501, App. 4. See also Polk Papers, Dr. 89, fols. 129, 130, 132, Polk-Wilson correspondence regarding Turkish treaty, March, 1920; *Times* (London), 3/25/20; *New York Times*, 4/1/20.

66. *Br. Doc.*, 7:95-96, S.C., 2/17/20; p. 278, For. Min. 2/27/20; pp. 666-67, 3/29/20; pp. 679-81, 3/30/20; "Effects of America's Exit from the Near East," pp. 162-65; Gidney, *Mandate*, chap. 10.

67. *Br. Doc.*, 7:160-62, S.C., 2/20/20; pp. 258-60, 2/26/20.

68. Cambon, *Correspondance*, 3:381, 3/9/20. See also ibid., pp. 376-77, 2/27/20; pp. 377-78, 2/29/20; pp. 378-79, 3/4/20; pp. 381-82, 3/14/20.

69. Ibid., p. 382, 3/14/20; pp. 382-83, 3/17/20. See also ibid., p. 381, 3/9/20.

XIII ✸ THE CONFERENCE AT SAN REMO

B Y THE TIME the Supreme Council reconvened at San Remo on April 18, 1920, most of the basic decisions regarding the Turkish peace treaty had long since been made, and a nearly complete draft of the treaty was in existence. What remained for the Allied representatives to settle was, on the whole, a series of relatively minor and specific issues that the various expert commissions and the Committee of Foreign Ministers and Ambassadors had failed to resolve during the Conference of London. In general, this was accomplished rapidly and amicably; what tension existed at the conference was engendered by European questions, particularly the enforcement and fulfillment of the reparations provisions of the German peace treaty.

The Turkish State

When the statesmen at San Remo reviewed systematically all the agreements reached during the London conference, they found little to alter. The provisions relating to Turkey's European frontier, the Straits Commission, and financial control of Turkish Anatolia were approved with only a few minor changes. In the same way, the French reluctantly accepted what had basically been the British position regarding the probable dissolution of the Ottoman Debt Council when its term expired in 1923.[1]

Smyrna

The draft provisions regarding the boundaries of the Smyrna area were approved without discussion, and only one significant change was made in the political clauses governing the administration of the territory. At the insistence of Curzon and the French, the waiting period prior to application for a League plebiscite, which might lead to Greek annexation of the territory, was extended from two to five years. This decision was the only real rebuff suffered by Venizelos during the entire Peace Conference, for he had sought to have the waiting clause removed entirely. However, Venizelos accepted the decision calmly, and three days later wrote Lloyd George thanking him effusively for all he had done to further Greek aims, the achievement of which Venizelos recognized was due primarily to Lloyd George's "powerful and effective support." [2] Rarely had such praise been more richly deserved.

Heraclea Coal Fields

Only one question regarding the spoils envisaged by the powers in the separate, "self-denying" Tripartite Pact provoked any discord at San Remo. In addition to a sphere of economic priority in Anatolia, the draft of the Tripartite Pact gave Italy the right to exploit the coal resources in the vicinity of Heraclea. For the previous twenty-five years, a French company had been developing a concession there of some sixty-five square kilometers, which it had received from the Turkish government. By the draft terms of the Tripartite Pact, the company was to keep its original concession, but was denied any rights of further expansion.[3]

At San Remo, Millerand vehemently protested this provision. Instead he asked that France be accorded all concessions granted or asked for by the French up to the time of the signing of the treaty and that the remaining area should be developed equally by France and Italy. This, of course, was unacceptable to Nitti, and after some intense bargaining a compromise was reached. Concessions held or asked for by France were to be allowed, but the terminal date was to be that of the signing of the Armistice of Mudros. Italy would be allowed unrestricted development of the remaining area until its rate of production equalled that of the other foreign concessions on January 1, 1920. When this occurred, the French would be allotted a one-fourth share of the remaining concessions and interests. This agreement was embodied in the Tripartite Pact.[4]

The Tripartite Pact was signed by France and Italy on May 11, 1920. Though the British had indicated they would sign as well, Curzon changed his mind at the last moment on the ground that there was no point in signing in advance a pact that could neither take effect nor be published until the Turkish peace treaty was signed. It was always possible, Curzon maintained, that significant modification of the treaty might be considered in the final negotiations with the Turks, particularly given the unstable political situation in Turkey. If this did happen, the Tripartite Pact would have to be altered as well. Although the Italians were not happy with Curzon's decision, there was little they could do about it; in contrast, Millerand, Derby reported, "was, I think, much relieved at our not signing." [5]

Non-Turkish Territories

In contrast to questions relating directly to the Turkish state, issues involving territories that were to be separated from Turkey provoked some controversy at San Remo. Yet even here, there was little that approached crisis proportions, and, in general, all problems were resolved swiftly and amicably.

Armenia

At London, the powers had decided to place Armenia under the protection of the League of Nations and had hopefully asked the League what measures it was prepared to take to assist the new state militarily and financially. The reply of the League Council, which was received just before the opening of the San Remo conference, pointed out that League protection meant little, that a mandate was necessary, and that the League possessed no military means of assisting the Armenians. Although the League might appeal to its members to subscribe to and guarantee a loan for Armenia, this would take time. The council inquired whether the Allies could provide the necessary credits during the interim period.[6]

This reply did not please the heads of state at San Remo, for it effectively tossed the Armenian question back to the Supreme Council. Neither the French nor the Italians were prepared to supply military or financial assistance; in fact the Italians stated emphatically that aside from fulfilling obligations in the Straits zone, Italy would not undertake military action to uphold the treaty provisions in any part of Asia Minor.[7] The British likewise were unwilling to send troops to Armenia, but thought that the Allies could undertake to supply equipment and officers.[8] As to a loan, Lloyd George became rather vehement:

He was told that Armenia would require about £10,000,000. Who was prepared to advance such a sum? America, he was told, could easily find it. Why did the League of Nations not appeal to America? Why did they refer their difficulties to the Supreme Council, which was already overburdened by its own tasks? The League of Nations did not discharge its whole duty by making pious speeches. He believed an appeal from the League of Nations to America would be successful. At least it might have the effect of stopping President Wilson from addressing any further notes to the Supreme Council. He thought the League of Nations was quite able to negotiate a loan and to find a mandatory.[9]

To this Lord Curzon rather testily replied that he "deprecated ridicule of the League of Nations, seeing that the Council, whenever it found itself in a perplexity, referred its difficulties to the League of Nations."[10]

The conference thus found itself squarely faced with the problem of Armenian protection and finance. Though the French agreed to the proposal to send officers and equipment, this assent still did not solve the problem of providing funds to keep the new state going. In desperation, the statesmen again turned their thoughts toward the United States. Lloyd George in particular sought to create a situation that would force America to take a stand on the Armenian situation. It was decided to ask the United States to provide the necessary financial aid for Armenia.[11]

Ensuring the enforcement of the Armenian settlement was the most difficult problem of all. An Armenian army as such still remained to be equipped and organized, and it was estimated by the British that the Turks "might well be able to concentrate a force of close on 40,000 men in this area." [12] Much of the territory allotted to Armenia at the London conference was in Turkish hands and had a predominantly Moslem population. Both Curzon and Marshal Foch, the head of the inter-Allied Committee of Military and Naval Experts, were doubtful as to whether acceptance of the proposed boundaries could be enforced. Moreover, it was evident that available Allied forces were so limited that any attempts to enforce the Turkish treaty provisions in the rest of Anatolia would preclude the sending of Allied contingents to Armenia, and vice versa. [13]

In a special report to the conference, the committee of military experts stated that in order to enforce the treaty provisions a total of nineteen divisions would be needed for the occupation of Thrace, Smyrna, Armenia, the Straits, northern Syria, and Mesopotamia, while an additional eight would be necessary to enforce the general disarmament and minority provisions. [14] If, however, protection and guarantees to Armenia were excluded, the total number of divisions could be reduced from twenty-seven to twenty-three. The Allies had nineteen divisions available for duty in the Near East, and Venizelos promised that he could provide three more. The powers therefore decided that they could readily enforce the treaty provisions in the occupied territories and withstand any attack by Kemalist forces so long as no attempt was made to advance into the interior. Turkey could be "strangled" by seizing her "vital parts, . . . her capital and . . . her ports on the seacoast. . . . If they could cut off . . . the source of revenue which Turkey had received from Smyrna and elsewhere, Turkey could not hold out very long. Her main arteries would be cut and she would be compelled to give in." [15]

In this way the Conference of San Remo blithely disposed of the enforcement and Turkish Nationalist problems in one easy decision, but did so at Armenia's expense. None of the European states had ever intended to become heavily involved in Armenia, despite all their pious pronouncements. Now, finally faced with the necessity of making a decision, they coldly and ruthlessly pushed aside the

Armenians and their newborn state. At the same time they attempted to salve their consciences by agreeing to officer and equip an Armenian military force, which supposedly would be able to defend Armenia by itself.[16]

The decision was realistic. The powers had long since recognized, as Nitti put it, that "it would not be necessary . . . to declare war on Turkey to have the treaty executed [in Armenia], but in effect it would be necessary to wage it." [17] By forgetting Armenia, the enforcement problem was greatly simplified. All the other territories to be taken from Turkey were already in Allied hands and could easily be reached. Aside from the Armenians, the large minority elements in Turkey all lived near the seacoast, where their rights could be protected relatively easily. Therefore, once Armenia was excluded from plans for the disposition of Allied forces, problems of disarmament of the interior and guarantees for minorities became less important.

In the light of the decision not to send Allied troops to Armenia, Nitti suggested that it might be wise to reconsider the proposed Armenian-Turkish boundary. He pointed out that "Erzerum was at present the centre of the Turkish nationalists. Someone would have to drive the Turks out. If this were done there would be a massacre of Armenians." [18] Lloyd George immediately came to Nitti's support:

Before the war, and before any massacres took place, the population was emphatically Mussulman. Consequently, by no principle which had been laid down by the Allied Powers could they defend surrendering the place, which had a preponderant majority of Mussulmans, to the Armenians. . . . He strongly deprecated encouraging illusive hopes in the breasts of poor creatures who had been persecuted for centuries, when the Allied Powers were perfectly well aware that they could not justify those hopes. It was quite possible that the cession of Erzerum might not be the one thing which would prevent the Turks from signing the treaty, but the Turks might think and say that "the other parts of our Empire which you have taken away are regions of which you are already in possession, but we know that Erzerum is a place where you cannot touch us." He would not, however, put his case on that ground but would put it to the Supreme Council that it was not honorable to the Armenians to cede Erzerum on false pretensions, as the Allied Powers had no intention to do anything except to write letters to President Wilson, or to assemble conferences, or to address appeals to the League of Nations. He could say this: that no one in Great Britain would take the responsibility of asking for even £1,000,000 in order to send troops to conquer Erzerum. The Armenians could not conquer it themselves, and its cession to Armenia would be a purely provocative measure. . . . It was not fair to the Armenians to give them on paper a territory which we had no intention of assisting them to secure.[19]

In opposition to this point of view, Curzon, Millerand, and Berthelot argued that Erzerum was so located geographically as to make its inclusion within the Armenian state a necessity, not only for military reasons but as the terminus of the railway from Erivan and the center of Armenia's road system. Moreover, the Armenians had been told that they could have Erzerum, and the Allies could not honourably go back on their word. It was very important "to constitute a frontier up to which Armenia could work in the future."[20] Retaining Erzerum would not make the Turks any more willing to sign the treaty, since it would hardly make up for the loss of Smyrna.[21]

In an effort to resolve this deadlock, the Armenian delegates to the Peace Conference[22] were questioned regarding Armenia's ability to fend for itself. They appeared extremely confident that Armenia could raise an army that not only could defend the territory it held, but that would be able to establish itself in Erzerum as well. All that would be needed was equipment and Allied officers.[23]

The Armenian attitude only served to increase the boundary dispute within the conference. The French maintained that the question must be decided in the treaty and that the best way out of a bad situation was to adhere to the decision of the Conference of London.[24] Moreover, it was all important that Armenia be given legal title to Erzerum, for "the law had some force of realization in its very nature."[25] This argument Lloyd George refused to accept:

The real danger in conferences was that they lived in a world of illusions and did not face facts. Conferences were inclined to think when they had framed resolutions and adopted clauses they had solved difficulties. M. Berthelot seemed to think that the ownership of Erzerum could be decided in the conference. It could not. If six representatives round the table ordered the Drafting Committee to declare Erzerum Armenian, would this be giving Erzerum to Armenia in M. Berthelot's sense? Erzerum would have to be taken by force, and blood spilt in the taking. . . . The Allied Powers had decided that they could not send troops to take the place. . . . Could the Armenian republic take Erzerum unaided? Marshal Foch's report and that of all the military experts gave an unhesitating answer in the negative.[26]

As an alternative, Lloyd George proposed that the United States should be asked to assume the responsibility for expelling the Turkish Nationalists from the larger Armenian state defined in the draft terms of the treaty. If it refused, a smaller Armenia should be constituted. This proposal was accepted by Millerand who suggested that it be extended to include a definite request for an American mandate. If America declined, Wilson should be asked to arbitrate the question of Erzerum. To this Lloyd George readily assented.[27]

Ultimately, despite the protests of Curzon that the frontiers of Armenia should be at least hypothetically defined in the treaty, it was decided that the treaty should provide for Turkish, Armenian, and Allied acceptance of whatever boundary President Wilson might draw in the vilayets of Trebizond, Erzerum, Van, and Bitlis.[28] This was going far beyond the original proposition, which had concerned only Erzerum and its immediate vicinity. To give Wilson the authority to decide the whole Turkish-Armenian frontier meant reopening questions involving the Lake Van area and the towns of Erzinjan and Trebizond.

It may be asked why Lloyd George so readily supported Millerand's arbitration proposal, especially when it must have been obvious to all that Wilson was almost certain to grant Armenia more, rather than less, territory than had been provided for in the draft treaty framed in London. It may be that Lloyd George, opposed by his own foreign minister and the entire French delegation, saw a way of backing down without a great loss of face. But it is also true that the proposal provided several benefits that were pleasing to Lloyd George. First, even if the United States refused to take the mandate, it would become involved in Armenia, and this had been a long-time goal for Lloyd George. Second, American arbitration would remove from the Allies the unpleasant task of creating a boundary that inevitably would please neither side. Third, British and French responsibility for enforcing a territorial division that they had not created would be far less than if they had drawn it themselves. As a result, blame for the probable future failure of Armenia to obtain any Turkish territory would be diverted at least partly from Great Britain and, more directly, from Lloyd George himself.[29]

A special message was dispatched to Wilson asking the United States to accept the mandate as defined by the London conference. Whether or not America took the mandate, Wilson was invited to redefine the Armenian-Turkish boundary as he saw fit. As expected, the United States Senate refused the mandate, but Wilson undertook to draw the boundary, which he eventually did in late November, 1920. Although the southern line corresponded roughly with that drawn by the Allies at London, in the center and north Wilson's boundary gave both Erzinjan and Trebizond, as well as Erzerum, to Armenia. But by that time events in Turkey and the Caucasus had made the problem an academic one.[30]

Batum

Directly connected with the Armenian question and the problem of enforcing the treaty was the future of the city of Batum. At the Conference of London it had been decided that Batum should go to Georgia, with the proviso that it would be a free port under either League or Allied guarantee, and that a garrison of three battalions—British, French, and Italian—would be kept in the city at least temporarily to enforce these provisions.[31]

By the time the San Remo conference convened, matters had taken a turn for the worse. Russian Bolshevik forces had decisively defeated the White Russian troops under General Denikin and were advancing rapidly along the Black Sea littoral toward Batum. Instead of enforcing free port requirements on the Georgians, it appeared more probable that an Allied garrison at Batum would find itself defending the city against the Russian Bolshevik army. The Allies so far had avoided any direct military contact with the Bolsheviks; Batum was hardly the ideal spot for such a conflict to begin. Not only could the Georgian national army not be relied on, but Bolshevik sympathy ran high in the city itself. Any defense would have to be undertaken by the Allies alone.[32] Yet the abandonment of Batum would probably mean the end of Allied influence and control in the Caucasus. This not only would hurt Armenia but it would affect oil-pipeline and railroad connections with Baku, the capital of the newly constituted state of Azerbaijan.

No final decision was reached at San Remo. Instead, the Allies asked the British high commissioner, Admiral de Robeck, who was in Batum, to report on the situation. De Robeck's reply was highly pessimistic. Stating that Georgia itself could not be held, he asserted that it would require at least two divisions to prevent Batum from falling into Bolshevik hands. Since the British were loath to maintain their single battalion that was already there, and the French and Italian contingents had not yet arrived, defending the city seemed out of the question.[33]

On April 27, the Bolshevik party in Azerbaijan executed a coup d'état, well coordinated with an almost simultaneous invasion of Azerbaijan by Russian Bolshevik forces. In two days the affair was over. Although the state remained officially independent, it was completely subservient to the wishes of the Russian Bolsheviks. The fall of Baku completely changed the situation regarding the Baku-Batum rail and pipeline communications. The basis of self-interest that had done much to hold the Allies in Batum was gone. As a result, the Italian battalion never was sent, and on July 7 the British and French officially turned the city over to the Georgian government and evacuated their troops. Although the Georgians accepted the provision of maintaining Batum as a free port for Armenia, Azerbaijan, and Persia, the lack of any outside supervision and the subsequent Russian takeover of Georgia and Russian Armenia soon made this provision meaningless.[34]

Kurdistan

In December, Berthelot had agreed to a British suggestion for the creation of an independent state or federation of tribes in Kurdistan that would not officially be under the supervision of any power. However, since the British had taken charge of what had been done since the war in that area, there was little question of whose influence would predominate. In fact, during the negotiations of the Tripartite

Pact in London, the British proposed that the French and Italians should agree not to compete with the British for special concessions in the area of Kurdistan outside of the territory originally granted outright to France in the Sykes-Picot Agreement. Moreover, as Curzon admitted, the Indian government was interested in Kurdistan, for Indian troops had been in service there. Realizing that under these circumstances an independent Kurdistan meant British control, at London the French had reverted to their former advocacy of Turkish sovereignty over Kurdistan. Having already given up much in Mosul, they were not anxious to see British control expanded further. The issue had remained unresolved throughout the course of the Conference of London.[35]

The solution ultimately reached at San Remo constituted a French diplomatic victory. Britain forsook its long-standing advocacy of an independent state with no mandate, and accepted the French plan calling for Turkish retention of the area subject to provisions guaranteeing a degree of local autonomy. The exact terms that would implement this decision were to be formulated by a joint French-British-Italian commission within six months of the signing of the treaty. The Kurds would have the right to appeal within a year to the League of Nations for full independent status. The responsibility for deciding whether or not to grant this, and the problem of aiding and protecting the new state would thus devolve upon the League and not directly on the Allies. The British renounced all claim to areas outside the Mosul vilayet and specifically excluded such territory from their sphere of economic priority in the tripartite agreement.[36]

This settlement reflected a basic change in British policy, which now took the position that Britain should in no way become involved in Kurdish affairs. The rebellious attitude of the various tribes and their opposition to any outside authority undoubtedly had much to do with this.[37] Lloyd George summed up the situation when he said:

He himself had tried to find out what the feelings of the Kurds were. After inquiries in Constantinople, Bagdad and elsewhere, he had found it impossible to discover any representative Kurd. No Kurd appeared to represent anything more than his own particular clan. . . . On the other hand, it would seem that the Kurds felt that they could not maintain their existence without the backing of a great Power. . . . But if neither France nor Great Britain undertook the task—and he hoped neither would—they appeared to think it might be better to leave them under the protection of the Turks. The country had grown accustomed to Turkish rule, and it was difficult to separate it from Turkey unless some alternative protector could be discovered.[38]

Lloyd George thus abandoned a position he had held since the beginning of the Peace Conference.

Syria and Mesopotamia

The negotiators at San Remo formally approved the allocation of mandates in Syria and Lebanon to France and in Mesopotamia and Palestine to Britain. No pretense was made of consulting with, or working through, the League. The boundary between the French and British areas as it had previously been agreed upon was routinely confirmed. It was evident that each nation was free to carry out, without restriction, any policy it wished in the mandated territories.[39]

That this would be the case had been evident for some time, and as a consequence Arab unrest in Syria, and to a lesser extent in Mesopotamia, increased considerably. In Syria, reaction to the announcement of the French mandate was bitter. Arab-French clashes in the no-man's-land between territory held by the Arabs and that occupied by the French continued with unabated intensity. It was obvious that a military showdown between the Arabs and the French was only a matter of time. Nevertheless, these problems could have been nonexistent for all the consideration they received at San Remo.[40]

Palestine

In the discussion of the clauses concerning the administration of Palestine, one major difficulty arose. The French government had long been recognized as the protector of Roman Catholicism in the Near East, and as such was under considerable pressure from the Roman Church and from many French legislators not only to assert this right but to undertake a mandate in Palestine. The French government had no intention of doing the latter. It was obvious, moreover, that to preserve French control over Roman Catholic affairs in a British mandate would be an insult to the British and would constitute an obstacle to the successful administration of the mandate.[41]

Palestine was an area in which Protestants, Catholics, Jews, Moslems, and Orthodox Christians all had an interest. To meet this situation, Nitti suggested that establishment of regulations for the Holy Places and methods of adjudicating disputes between the various sects should be handled by a special commission of all faiths, headed by a president chosen by the League of Nations. He recommended that all previous privileges and prerogatives held by the various religious communities, or by other nations in relation to them, should be rescinded.[42]

Lloyd George immediately agreed to this proposal. "Great Britain would prefer not to have to decide this question herself. . . . Great Britain would infinitely sooner have these questions referred to an authoritative and impartial body whose decisions Great Britain would scrupulously carry out." [43] For Millerand, however, the solution was not so simple. Although he was perfectly willing to agree to Nitti's scheme in practice, and secretly to commit himself to the renunciation of the French religious protectorate, a public renunciation would be political dynamite, and he firmly refused to incorporate such a declaration in the formal treaty. A solution was reached through agreement to excise any reference to the religious protectorate from the treaty. Instead, a formal resolution was incorporated in the secret minutes of the conference as a corollary to Allied acceptance of the rest of the treaty clauses. The resolution read as follows:

To accept the terms of the mandates article . . . with reference to Palestine, on the understanding that there was inserted in the *procès-verbal* an undertaking by the mandatory Power that this would not involve the surrender of the rights hitherto enjoyed by the non-Jewish communities in Palestine; this undertaking not to refer to the question of the religious protectorate of France, which had been settled earlier in the previous afternoon by the undertaking given by the French government that they recognized this protectorate as being at an end.[44]

North Africa

The only other outstanding issue dealt with at San Remo was the Franco-British conflict over the Egyptian clauses. The French objection was not to the clauses as such, but rather to their inclusion in the treaty, for they feared that such action would upset the balance of the unsigned Franco-British convention relative to Morocco and Egypt, which had been pending for some time.[45] The British, in turn, refused to sign the convention because of French insistence that it be revised to include prior British consent to any future Franco-Spanish agreement on French claims to Spanish Tangier.

At San Remo, the issue was quickly settled when Millerand indicated willingness to resume negotiations on the Egypt-Morocco convention, which had almost been signed in Paris, and to do so without extending them beyond issues involving Egypt and Morocco. Having received this assurance, the British in turn agreed to withdraw the offending Egyptian articles from the Turkish treaty, with the proviso that if the convention were signed before the treaty was given to the Turks, they should again be included. However, this did not occur, and the final treaty did not include the controversial clauses.[46]

Oil Rights

The question of the distribution of oil resources did not provoke any time-consuming negotiations or serious misunderstandings at San Remo. Millerand did make a feeble effort to claim the 50 percent participation that Clemenceau had sought in December, 1919. Meeting a solid wall of opposition, he quickly dropped the demand, and the revised agreement brought forward by by the experts was quickly approved.[47]

In its final form, the San Remo Oil Agreement was basically the same as the earlier Long-Berenger and Greenwood-Berenger Agreements.[48] A comparison indicates only a minor amount of editorial revision, mainly in an effort to meet British objections to the mention of private individuals or companies. Though the provision that France should receive 25 percent of the stock in any private oil company in Mesopotamia was retained, the April agreement also provided an alternative that called for the sale to France of 25 percent of all crude oil produced in the Mesopotamian oil fields "in the event of their being developed by Government action." [49] Thus the contingency of either private or public development was covered. The only completely new provision in the San Remo agreement was an additional clause giving the French government the right to purchase up to 25 percent of any oil produced by the Anglo-Persian Company and piped from Persia to the Mediterranean through pipelines that went across French mandated territory.

This settlement was officially approved on April 24, 1920, by the prime ministers of France and England. Its acceptance by the British, where similar proposals had previously been rejected, stemmed from two major considerations. The first was that, as Greenwood put it, "The leading feature of our petroleum policy for a number of years has been the endeavor to secure British control of the Royal Dutch Shell group." [50] The bait for the Shell group was the granting of the Mesopotamia concession to the Turkish Petroleum Company in which Shell held a 25 percent interest. This in turn necessitated the signing of the Anglo-French accord, since its major provision called for France's receiving a 25 percent share in the Turkish Petroleum Company. Without the Anglo-French agreement, it was evident that British control of Shell would not be achieved, and France would most likely ally itself with the American firm of Standard Oil. [51] Even more important, was the fact that agreement had now been reached on other political and territorial issues such as France's role in Syria, the boundary between Syria and Palestine, the fate of Constantinople, and the disposition of Anatolia, Armenia, and Kurdistan. Therefore, the British at last were willing formally to approve the pact.

With the San Remo accord, which was essentially a confirmation of previous Anglo-French agreements, negotiations concerning oil rights were at an end. Instead of dominating the Near East settlement, the question of oil and oil resources had played a surprisingly minor role in the negotiation of a Turkish peace treaty, taking a very definite back seat to other political and territorial issues. [52] Never had its terms provoked any lengthy or serious disagreement. Although formal ratification of the settlement, originally drawn up in February and March, 1919, was postponed for over a year, the pact was among the earliest and most easily attained of all the agreements centering on the Near East, and from the beginning was solely a Franco-British affair in which neither the Italians nor the Americans played a role of any import.[53]

The San Remo Conference and the United States

At San Remo, as in London, the United States played no official role, although the American ambassador in Rome was authorized to attend the Supreme Council sessions during the latter half of the conference.[54] The attitude of the negotiators toward the United States, however, was anything but amicable. On April 26, the Allied Powers approved a reply to President Wilson's critical note to the Conference of London.[55] In it they pointed out that they had sought United States participation, had waited for it, and had been inconvenienced by the waiting. Politely but firmly, the United States was told that the treaty was none of its business, and that as a nonsignatory America could not ask that guarantees regarding American interests should be inserted in the treaty.[56]

This attitude of irritation was even more apparent in the debates preceding the dispatch of the note. Berthelot remarked that "it was impossible that the Allies should waste time explaining to the United States why they took this action or proceeded on such-and-such lines. . . . The treaty could not be subordinated to the whims of the American President." [57] In this Lloyd George concurred. "He thought it was intolerable that the Allies should continue to conduct correspondence with the United States on the subject." [58]

The powers were obviously disgusted with what they considered to be unjustified and unwarranted interference by a nation that refused to take part in the negotiations and to assume responsibilities in the Near East.[59] Even the appeal by the Allies to America for help in Armenia brought forth a caustic comment from Lloyd George:

He could not see that there was any harm in making an appeal of this nature. If America refused to assist, the Allies would be no worse off, and, in one respect, they would be better off. President Wilson could continue to lecture the Allies about the way they were handling the Turkish question, but if the Allies could retort that they had asked America to come in and assist, and that America had refused, the United States could not continue to complain of the inability of the Allies to protect Armenia.[60]

Thus by the time the negotiations of the Turkish peace treaty were concluded, the influence of the United States on the powers was nonexistent, and in the final analysis it must be said that the treaty as drafted manifested little or no evidence of American attitudes or aims regarding a Near East Settlement.

The San Remo Conference and the Turkish Nationalists

The role played by the Nationalist threat in the final formulation of the treaty is harder to ascertain. Certainly the Allies were concerned about the Kemalists in a military sense. They were obviously skeptical about Allied ability to enforce the treaty terms in the interior of Anatolia. Without question, the decisions taken at San Remo regarding Armenia were due to anxieties about the strength of the Nationalist movement.

However, regarding the coastal regions there was little concern. The Allied military experts were agreed that all territories except Armenia which were to be separated from Turkey or occupied by the Allies could easily be held. The Allied occupation of Constantinople on March 16, 1920, had brought the Straits area totally under Allied control. This had been followed by the arrest and deportation of some forty members of the Turkish parliament, which was dissolved by the sultan at the insistence of the Allies on April 11. On the same day, Damad Ferid, who was once again grand vizier, proclaimed the Nationalists as rebels, and a *fetva* was issued in the name of the sultan as caliph, stating that it was religiously permissible to kill all those supporting the Nationalist cause.[61]

For Mustapha Kemal, the occupation of Constantinople served as a signal for a total break with the Constantinople regime. On the day of the occupation, he sent a message to all civil and military authorities urging them to remain calm and promising that action would be forthcoming shortly. At the same time, he addressed a sharply worded protest to the diplomatic representatives of the Allied powers and the United States in Constantinople, the foreign ministers of neutral nations, and the legislatures of Britain, France, and Italy. Three days later he issued a manifesto calling for the election of delegates to a new "Extra-Ordinary" Assembly and inviting members of the old parliament to attend.[62]

The Grand National Assembly, as it called itself, convened on April 22 in Ankara with the express purpose of "securing the independence of the country and the deliverance of the seat of the Caliphate and Sultanate from the hands of our enemies." [63] Within a matter of hours it adopted the following resolution:

1. The founding of a government is absolutely necessary.
2. It is not permissible to recognize a provisional chief of state nor to establish a regency.
3. It is fundamental to recognize that the real authority in the country is the national will as represented by the Assembly. There is no power superior to the Grand National Assembly.
4. The Grand National Assembly of Turkey embraces both the Executive and the Legislative functions. A council of state, chosen from the membership of the Assembly and responsible to it, conducts the affairs of the state. The president of the Assembly is *ex officio* president of the Council. Note: The Sultan-Kalif as soon as he is free from the coercion to which he submits shall take place within the constitutional system in the manner to be determined by the Assembly.[64]

This was nothing less than a declaration of political revolution and independence. The next day the Assembly elected Mustapha Kemal as its president and created an executive commission and a parliamentary commission. On April 30, the Allied Powers were officially notified of the creation of the new government and its claim to represent the will of the people.[65]

By that time the Conference of San Remo had closed. Yet during the conference the powers must have been aware that the Grand National Assembly was meeting in Ankara, and they undoubtedly recognized the purpose and intent of Kemal in convening the assembly.[66] Kemal later maintained that even by the time of the occupation of Constantinople, he was receiving "private assurances from French and Italian officials that British policy was not theirs—that Millerand and Nitti did not agree with Lloyd George." [67] If this were the case, it was hardly evident in the talk and actions of Millerand and Berthelot at San Remo. Nitti, it is true, was more cautious than the others, and several times spoke of the necessity of drafting a treaty that the Turks would accept and that could then be enforced.[68] But at no time during the whole course of the conference was any mention made of the political action then taking place at Ankara. Aside from recognizing the Nationalist forces as a military annoyance, the negotiators at San Remo seemed unconcerned about the Kemalist movement and totally indifferent to Kemalism as a political force.[69] Instead, a delegation from the Constantinople government was instructed to come to Paris. On May 11, 1920, the treaty was presented to the members of this delegation, and they were given a month in which to formulate a reply.[70]

Until quite recently, historians regarded the San Remo conference as the time when the major negotiations and drafting of the Turkish peace treaty took place. In retrospect, it is now evident that such was not the case. Aside from the decision taken in January, 1919, to create mandates in the Arab portion of the old Ottoman Empire, the general principles on which the treaty was based (with the exception of the Armenian issue) were agreed upon during and shortly after the bilateral Anglo-French discussions in December, 1919. On the basis of these principles a draft treaty was hammered out in conjunction with the Italians at the meetings in London during February and March, 1920. In addition, many policy decisions relating to specific problems were arrived at in London. As far as the Turkish peace is concerned, the Conference of San Remo, apart from the decision regarding Allied noninvolvement in Armenia, dealt almost, if not entirely, with routine matters involving final approval and minor revisions of clauses already drafted during the Conference of London.

1. See *Br. Doc.*, 8:45–143, 172–95, passim, 4/20/20–4/23/20, 4/25/20.

2. Lloyd George Papers, F55/1/28, Venizelos to Lloyd George, 4/26/20. See also *Br. Doc.*, 8:123–26, S.C., 4/23/20; p. 130, App. 1.

3. *Br. Doc.*, 7:165–66, S.C., 2/20/20; p. 384, 3/3/20; p. 391, App. 2; 8:134–36, 4/23/20; pp. 141–43, App. A. See also Sonnino Papers, Reel 51, Memorandum on Heraclea Coal Fields, 1/30/19.

4. *Br. Doc.*, 8:134–36, S.C., 4/23/20; p. 143, App. B; pp. 211–14, 4/26/20, and n.2. The final text of the Tripartite Pact may be found in Great Britain, *Parliamentary Papers, 1920*, Cmd. 963, "Tripartite agreement between the British empire, France and Italy respecting Anatolia. Signed at Sèvres, August 10, 1920"; "The Secret Treaty Dividing Turkey," *Nation* 3 (December, 1920):697–99; *R.F.P.: Political Review*, 5/14/20; *Bulletin périodique de la presse Italienne*, no. 136.

5. Foreign Office, F.O. 608/278/301/310, Derby to Curzon, 5/11/20; See also ibid., 301, Vansittart to Curzon, 5/10/20; 308, Tripartite Pact text as signed by French and Italians; 310, Curzon to Derby, 5/11/20; 315, Curzon to Derby, 5/10/20; *Br. Doc.*, 13:74–76, Curzon to Buchanan (Rome), 5/17/20.

6. Cabinet Papers, Cab. 29/32, A.J. 156, Memorandum agreed to by the Council of the League of Nations, "Future Status of Armenia," 4/11/20; A.J. 185, Draft reply of Supreme Council of League of Nations, 4/26/20; League of Nations, *Official Journal, 1920*, Fourth Council Session, pp. 3–7, 4/19/20; pp. 11–13, 15, 4/10/20; pp. 19–21, Annex 30A; pp. 27–29, Annex 30B; Fifth Council Session, p. 15, 5/14/20; p. 19, 5/15/20; pp. 149–59, Annex 43, 43A; *Br. Doc.*, 8:46–51, S.C., 4/20/20. It is interesting to note that Venizelos led those supporting League responsibility for Armenia in the League Council, conversely it was the British and French delegates, Balfour and Bourgeois, who successfully opposed any League action. J. Bassett, *The League of Nations, A Chapter in World Politics*, pp. 40–42; *Times* (London), 4/28/20; Mandelstam, *Problème arménien*, pp. 64–69; "The Tangled Turkish Question," pp. 323–30.

7. *Br. Doc.*, 8:90–91, S.C., 4/21/20.

8. The British General Staff was emphatic in its assertion that it "could not point to any sources from which the necessary expeditionary force for Armenia can be found," especially given the industrial unrest in England and the condition of affairs in Ireland. *Br. Doc.*, 13:37, General Staff memorandum on the situation in Turkey, 3/15/20; p. 55, General Staff memorandum on the Turkish Peace Treaty, 4/1/20; 8:46–50, S.C., 4/20/20.

9. Ibid., 8:50, S.C., 4/20/20. At San Remo, rumors were circulating that Norway might be willing to accept an Armenian mandate, and the conferees indicated they would be more than willing to agree to such an idea. Ibid., pp. 47–48.

10. Ibid., p. 50. The *Times* (London), expressed an opinion similar to Curzon's on April 5.

11. *Br. Doc.*, 8:57–58, S.C., 4/20/20; pp. 61–64.

12. Ibid., 13:35, General Staff memorandum on the situation in Turkey, 3/15/20.

13. Ibid., 8:58–60, S.C., 4/20/20; p. 92, 4/21/20.

14. Cabinet Papers, Cab. 24/103, Foch to Lloyd George, report of the military representatives, 3/30/20.

15. *Br. Doc.*, 8:56, S.C., 4/20/20. See also ibid., pp. 54–58, and pp. 66–67, App. 4; Baron Riddell, *Lord Riddell's Intimate Diary at the Peace Conference and After*, p. 186, 4/22/20.

16. Callwell, *Henry Wilson*, 2:233–34, 4/20/20. See also, *Br. Doc.*, 2:295, Allied Conference, 1/19/20.

17. *Br. Doc.*, 8:48, S.C., 4/20/20.

18. Ibid., p. 94, 4/22/20.

19. Ibid., pp. 108, 111–12.

20. Ibid., p. 111.

21. Ibid., pp. 109-11, 113.

22. Boghos Nubar Pasha and Avetis Aharonian.

23. *Br. Doc.*, 8:117-19. S.C., 4/22/20; pp. 120-21, 4/23/20.

24. Ibid., pp. 114-15, 4/22/20.

25. Ibid., pp. 138-39, 4/23/20.

26. Ibid., p. 139. See also ibid., pp. 122-23 and p. 131, App. 3.

27. Ibid., pp. 112-13, S.C., 4/22/20; p. 140, 4/23/20, pp. 145, 156-57, 4/24/20; Callwell, *Henry Wilson*, 2:235, 4/23/20.

28. *Br. Doc.*, 8:157-58, S.C., 4/24/20.

29. The American high commissioner in Constantinople, Admiral Bristol, took this view. On September 18, 1920, he commented in a dispatch to Colby that since Armenia would receive only the Turkish territory allotted it by the president, "this would seem to impose upon him the responsibility of enforcing the Turkish evacuation of territory given to Armenia," *U.S. Doc., 1920*, 3:788.

30. *Br. Doc.*, 8:177-78, S.C., 4/25/20; pp. 217-20, 4/26/20; *U.S. Doc., 1920*, 3:779-83, Johnson to Sec. State, 4/27/20; p. 783, Colby to Wallace, 5/17/20; pp. 789-804, 11/24/20, enclosures 1 and 2; also map at back of volume; *Br. Doc.*, 13:66, Geddes to Curzon, 4/29/20; pp. 70-71, 5/11/20; pp. 71-72, 5/16/20; p. 76, 5/18/20; p. 77, Curzon to Geddes, 5/21/20; Gidney, *Mandate*, chap. 10; Kazemzadeh, *Transcaucasia*, pp. 262-63. See generally Kazemzadeh, *Transcaucasia*, chaps. 18-21; *Times* (London), 6/3/20; *International Conciliation* 151 (June 1920):13-16.

31. See above, Chapter 12; also *Br. Doc.*, 8:51, S.C., 4/20/20.

32. Kazemzadeh, *Transcaucasia*, p. 201; *Br. Doc.*, 8:129-30, S.C., 4/23/20; p. 131, App. 4; 12:594-95, Hardinge to Curzon, 4/21/20.

33. *Br. Doc.*, 8:51-52, S.C., 4/20/20; pp. 129, 136-38, 4/23/20; 12:596, Curzon to Hardinge, 4/24/20; p. 597, Wardrop to Curzon, 4/25/20; pp. 597-99, Robeck to Curzon, 4/27/20.

34. Kazemzadeh, *Transcaucasia*, pp. 202, 283-85, and generally chaps. 18-21. Carnegie Endowment for International Peace, *The Treaties of Peace, 1919-1923*, vol. 2, "Treaty of Sèvres," Articles 349-51; *Times* (London), 5/10/20; *Br. Doc.*, 12:599-633, passim. For the British Cabinet discussions regarding the evacuation, in which the War Office pressed for such action and the Foreign Office dragged its feet, see Cabinet Papers, Cab 23/21, C. 24 (20), 5/5/20; C. 30 (20), 5/21/20; C. 33 (20). 6/7/20; C. 35 (20), 7/11/20.

35. *Br. Doc.*, 7:106, 2/17/20; p. 159, 2/20/20; p. 185, 2/21/20; pp. 256-58, 2/26/20; Foreign Office, F.O. 406/43/127, Robeck to Curzon, 3/2/20, enclosure, Ryan memorandum, 2/24/20; *Le Temps*, 3/2/20; A. T. Wilson Papers, MSS 52455, Montagu to Wilson, 3/25/20; Wilson to Montagu, 3/25/20; Hirtzel to Wilson 4/15/20. The India Office and the Mesopotamian administration wanted Kurdistan included in the British Mesopotamian mandate. The French would not agree.

36. *Br. Doc.*, 7:43-44, S.C., 4/19/20; pp. 44-45, App. 5; p. 77, 4/21/20; pp. 132-34, 4/23/20; 13:65-66, Curzon to Robeck, 4/24/20.

37. See above, Chapter 9.

38. *Br. Doc.*, 8:43, 4/19/20.

39. Ibid., p. 9, S.C., 4/18/20; p. 159, 4/24/20; pp. 172-77, 4/25/20. The mandates decision was not stated in the peace treaty, but rather was incorporated in a separate agreement. Article 94 of the Treaty stated simply, "The selection of the Mandatories will be made by the Principal Allied Powers." Carnegie Endowment, *Treaties*, vol. 2, "Treaty of Sèvres."

40. *Br. Doc.* 13:251-52, Curzon to Hardinge, 4/26/20; pp. 252-53, Allenby to Curzon, 4/27/20; pp. 257-58, 5/13/20; pp. 270-73, Curzon to Cambon, 5/18/20; pp. 278-82, Cambon to Curzon, 5/31/20, enclosures; pp. 282-83, Feisal to Lloyd George, n.d.; Foreign Office,

F.O. 608/274/77/267, Hedjaz Delegation to S.C., 4/30/20; State Department, Turkey, 867.00/ 1261, Bristol to Sec. State, 5/11/20; Kedourie, *England and the Middle East,* chaps. 6 and 7; Longrigg, *Syria and Lebanon,* pp. 99–100; idem, *Iraq, 1900 to 1950,* pp. 119–21; Zeine, *Arab Independence,* chap. 7; *Times* (London), 5/11/20, 5/17/20.

41. *Br. Doc.,* 8:163–64, S.C., 4/24/20; Stein, *Balfour Declaration,* pp. 656–60.

42. *Br. Doc.,* 8:162, S.C., 4/24/20; pp. 176–77, 4/25/20.

43. Ibid., p. 164, 4/24/20.

44. Ibid., pp. 165–71; p. 176, 4/25/20.

45. For details of this dispute, see above, Chapter 12.

46. *Br. Doc.,* 8:83–89, S.C., 4/21/20; Carnegie Endowment, *Treaties,* vol. 2, "Treaty of Sèvres," Articles 101–12.

47. *Br. Doc.,* 8:9–10, Lloyd George-Millerand conversation, 4/18/20; pp. 144–45, 4/24/20; E. H. Davenport and S. R. Cooke, *The Oil Trusts and Anglo-American Relations,* pp. 54–55, 63.

48. For the texts of the Long-Berenger and Greenwood-Berenger Agreements, see *Br. Doc.,* 4:1089–92, 1114–17. For the text of the San Remo Agreement, see Foreign Office, F.O. 406/43/196, Berthelot-Cadman Oil Agreement, 4/25/20; Great Britain, *Parliamentary Papers, 1920,* Cmd. 675, "Memorandum of Agreement (San Remo, April 24, 1920) between M. Phillipe Berthelot and Prof. Sir John Cadman"; Davenport and Cooke, *Oil Trusts,* pp. 202–7; Hurewitz, *Diplomacy,* 2:75–77.

49. Great Britain, *Parliamentary Papers,* 1920, Cmd. 675, "San Remo Oil Agreement," Article 7.

50. Cabinet Papers, Cab. 24/104, C.P. 1118, Greenwood memorandum, 4/22/20.

51. Ibid.; also Cab. 24/101, C.P. 903, Long memorandum, 3/18/20.

52. A good example of the nonconcerned attitude regarding oil may be seen in the *Times* (London) editorial of June 1, 1920, which advocated that Britain not undertake a Mesopotamia mandate. The editorial stated that it would be too expensive, that only oil interests could hope to benefit from it, and that they would want a government subsidy as well. C. J. Edmonds, who was liaison officer between the Mosul Investigation Commission of the League of Nations and the British Mandate Government in 1924 has commented, "It is interesting to look back and recall how very little oil figured in our calculations. . . . I do not remember a single document in which oil was mentioned as a factor of outstanding importance" Edmonds, *Kurds,* p. 398.

53. The agreement was officially published on July 24, 1920. Neither the Italians nor the Americans were at all happy with the agreement when they learned of it. For the Italian reaction, see *Br. Doc.,* 13:342, 346–47, 363–65. For the American reaction, see ibid., pp. 66, 256–57, 273–74, 314–15, 322–23, 324–25; Lloyd George Papers, F60/4/1, Geddes to Lloyd George, 6/4/20; *U.S. Doc., 1920,* 2:651–59, 663–73; Evans, *U.S. and Partition,* pp. 297–305; De Novo, *American Interests,* pp. 176–84.

54. *U.S. Doc., 1920,* 1:1, Davis to Lansing, 2/6/20; Lansing to Davis, 2/9/20; pp. 1–2, Jay to Polk, 3/13/20; p. 2, Polk to Jay, 3/16/20; Colby to Johnson, 4/20/20; p. 3, Johnson to Colby, 4/24/20; *Br. Doc.,* 8:161, 165, S.C., 4/24/20.

55. For a discussion of Wilson's note of March 24, see above, Chapter 12.

56. For text, see *U.S. Doc., 1920,* 3:753–56, Johnson to Colby. For an earlier draft, see *Br. Doc.,* 8:31–35, S.C., 4/19/20, App. 2. See also ibid., pp. 217–19, 4/26/20.

57. Ibid., p. 21, S.C., 4/19/20.

58. Ibid.

59. This irritation was enhanced, no doubt, by continued American support of Yugoslav claims in the Adriatic at a time when the Italians were ready to accept a compromise proposal

that had been put forward by France and Britain the previous December. Ibid., vols. 7 and 8 passim.

60. Ibid., 8:63, S.C., 4/20/20.

61. Ibid., 13:57-58, Robeck to Curzon, 4/3/20; p. 59, 4/5/20; pp. 61-62, 4/11/20; p. 62, 4/15/20; *Correspondance d'Orient*, pp. 416-18, 420, 5/15/20; Davison, "Turkish Diplomacy," p. 181; Adivar, *Turkey Faces West: A Turkish View of Recent Changes and Their Origin*, p. 178; Karpat, *Turkey's Politics*, pp. 35-36; Lloyd George, *Truth*, p. 1292; Pech, *Alliés et Turquie*, p. 120, 3/19/20; pp. 120-21, 3/27/20; pp. 123-24, 4/5/20; p. 127, 4/12/20; Smith, *Turkey*, pp. 26-28, 34-36; Webster, *Turkey of Ataturk*, pp. 83, 85; *Times* (London), 3/27/20, 4/5/20, 4/14/20.

62. Adkisson, *Britain and the Kemalist Movement*, pp. 235-38; Davison, "Turkish Diplomacy," p. 181; Gaillard, *Turks and Europe*, p. 187; B. Georges-Gaulis, *La Question Turque*, p. 95; Karpat, *Turkey's Politics*, p. 36; Kemal, *Speech*, pp. 359-61. Smith, *Turkey*, pp. 32-33, and 155-57, Apps. C, D; Webster, *Turkey of Ataturk*, pp. 84-85; Kinross, *Ataturk*, p. 243.

63. Kemal, as quoted in Karpat, *Turkey's Politics*, p. 36.

64. Webster, *Turkey of Ataturk*, p. 86; also Smith, *Turkey*, pp. 38-39.

65. *Br. Doc.*, 13:67-68, Kemal to Curzon, 4/30/19; Adkisson, *Kemalist Movement*, pp. 245-47; Davison, "Turkish Diplomacy," p. 182; Adivar (Edib), *Turkey Faces West*, pp. 179-86; Kinross, *Ataturk*, pp. 248-57; Webster, *Turkey of Ataturk*, p. 86.

66. As early as April 15, the *Times* published reports that Kemal planned to form a new separate Anatolian government and state.

67. Davison, "Turkish Diplomacy," p. 181.

68. *Br. Doc.*, 8:36-37, S.C., 4/19/20; p. 48, 4/20/20; pp. 74, 90, 4/21/20; p. 94, 4/22/20.

69. The prevailing attitude at the San Remo conference was best summed up by Lloyd George when he commented that "no one believed that Mustapha Kemal would be able to drive the Greeks out of Asia Minor." Ibid., p. 92, 4/21/20.

70. Ibid., 13:68, Curzon to Webb, 5/5/20; pp. 68-70, Webb to Curzon, 5/11/20; p. 70, Derby to Curzon, 5/11/20; *Current History* 12 (April, 1920):64; (June, 1920):435; Sforza, *Diplomatic Europe*, p. 60; *Times* (London), 5/7/20.

XIV ❈ THE TREATY OF SÈVRES

WITH THE conclusion of the San Remo conference, the work pertaining to the formulation of the Turkish treaty was complete. When the treaty was presented to the Turkish delegation on May 11, a general summary of the terms was given to the press.[1] Although lacking in detail, it clearly stated the main provisions of the treaty.

Press Reaction to the Treaty

Reaction of the press [2] in Great Britain was basically favorable. It was generally agreed that the terms were harsh, yet most publications took the position that the treaty was no more than what the Turks should have expected, or than they deserved. Only a handful opposed the treaty. The *Manchester Guardian* regarded the peace terms as impossible; the *Westminster Gazette* called it an "oratorical formula, destined to mask the problems which the Allies have not been able to resolve." The *Observer* bluntly called it "artificial," "precarious" and "transitory," while *Outlook* disliked seeing the League used as a "dustbin" for all the problems the Supreme Council could not handle.[3]

Yet, even among the majority that regarded the treaty as just, there ran a strong current of uneasiness and doubt as to the ability of the powers to enforce the terms of the treaty. The *Times, Daily Telegraph, Morning Post,* and *New Statesman* all voiced concern over this issue. The press was unanimous, however, in regarding the treaty as a triumph for Venizelos and Greece.[4]

The French and Italian press saw the treaty as a tremendous victory, not so much for Greece as for Great Britain. The Italian press bitterly condemned the treaty. Newspaper editorials particularly castigated the French, whom the Italians regarded as having sold out to the British in the Near East in return for British support for some of their continental policies. So great was Italian hostility to the treaty that Nitti was obliged to state publicly that Italy would play no role in any "fatal war" that might ensue. Nevertheless, the Italians did take some comfort from the sphere of economic influence allotted to them and saw in it good opportunities for economic and commercial development.[5]

Nor was there any enthusiasm in France for the treaty, where the Italian interpretation of the French role in the negotiations met with general acceptance.[6] Tardieu used this argument in defending the government's policy in the Chamber of Deputies and *Le Temps* commented that the treaty had been negotiated at a time when Britain had France at a disadvantage, for France was completely absorbed in German affairs. The newspaper went so far as to discuss the position of the unfortunate Turkish delegates and to express the sympathy of France for them.[7]

Turkish reaction was one of shock, dismay, and indignation, but hardly resignation. Upon receiving the terms on May 11, Tewfik Pasha telegraphed home that there was no hope of getting the Greeks out of Asia Minor and that the treaty terms were "incompatible with the principles of independence."[8] When knowledge of the terms reached Constantinople the press unanimously rejected them, saying that they cast a "sentence of death" upon Turkey, and the grand vizier told de Robeck that it would be almost "impossible" to impose the treaty on the Nationalists.[9] Mustapha Kemal immediately called on all to resist, and the next few weeks witnessed a large-scale Turkish exodus from Constantinople to Asia Minor and a great increase in the number of recruits rallying to the Kemalist cause.[10]

The Nationalist–French Cease-Fire Agreement

Suddenly it became apparent that the treaty might not be signed. A Nationalist attack was launched toward Constantinople, and by the middle of June, Kemalist forces controlled Brusa and Panderma, dominating all but the immediate coastline on the Asiatic side of the Sea of Marmara. Moreover, they were in direct contact with British troops garrisoning a line across the Ismid peninsula.[11] During this same period the French, hard pressed by a series of incidents in Syria and by continued fighting in Cilicia, sent Robert de Caix, General Gouraud's right-hand man, to negotiate a truce in Cilicia with Mustapha Kemal in order that France might effect a partial withdrawal of its troops. In this he was successful and a twenty-day cease-fire went into effect on May 30. De Caix was hopeful that this was only the first step toward better relations with Kemal, and commented that a "complete and general entente of the nationalists with France appeared very possible to him."[12] In these hopes he was far too sanguine, for the truce was broken by the Kemalists even before the twenty-day period was over.[13]

Nevertheless, the signing of the cease-fire was of real significance. The very fact that a great power had made an agreement with the Nationalists was a victory for Kemal and constituted a type of unannounced de facto recognition. Certainly it was viewed in this light not only by the Nationalists but by many in the Constantinople government. Tewfik Pasha, who headed the Turkish delegation at Paris, saw in the cease-fire a sign of possible Franco-British disagreement, and he consequently sought to prolong the negotiations with the Allies as much as possible. It was this tactic that led to his replacement in Paris on June 25 by the grand vizier, Damad Ferid Pasha.[14]

Greek Intervention

By the middle of June it was obvious to all concerned that the treaty could never be put into force in the circumstances then prevailing. Two alternatives remained: either a thorough revision of the treaty or decisive military action against the Nationalists. Both the Italians and French leaned toward the former solution and made it clear that they would take no part in any military action.[15] To prevent the possibility of revision, Lloyd George decided to take the initiative. He knew that Britain could not undertake any extensive military action.[16] However, influenced by his admiration for Venizelos, and oblivious to all but his vision of a Greek empire doing Britain's work in the eastern Mediterranean, Lloyd George fully believed that Greece could undertake a limited campaign that would humble the Kemalists and force the government at Constantinople to sign the treaty. His determination in this matter was such that he rode roughshod over the protests of Churchill and Field Marshal Sir Henry Wilson, both of whom were thoroughly opposed to such action and saw little hope of its success. He dismissed all opposition from within the British government as merely political and of Tory origin, for at this time the ties that held the coalition government together were becoming quite strained, especially over the question of Irish home rule.[17]

Even the military, however, had to admit that there was no other possible solution if enforcement of the treaty were desired. At a conference of ministers held on June 18 Field Marshal Wilson conceded that assistance was desperately needed; he reluctantly concluded that Greece was the only available source from which such help could come. But he added that "his own opinion was that the operations would continue for several years and although it would be a great help to get the Greeks to come to our assistance now he did not think that such a move would really solve the problem."[18] In his personal diary Wilson was even more emphatic: "All this means war with Turkey and Russia, and will end in our being kicked out of Constantinople."[19] Wilson was convinced the Greek campaign would fail, and "then we shall be in the soup."[20]

Venizelos, however, was in London at the time and was invited to meet with the British ministers. He expressed a readiness, even eagerness, to undertake a Greek campaign, stating, as he had many times in the past, that Greek troops could easily take care of the Nationalists without any outside aid except in the form of transportation and materiel.[21] The conference of ministers, which had

already agreed that a withdrawal from Constantinople before a
"bandit like Mustapha Kemal" would constitute an intolerable blow
to British prestige and that it therefore would be in Britain's best
interest "definitely to support the Greeks," welcomed Venizelos's
assurances and authorized Field Marshal Wilson to meet with Venizelos to plan the campaign.[22]

It was now necessary to gain the concurrence of the other powers
(or, as the minutes of the conference of ministers more bluntly put
it, "to notify" them). The prime ministers were scheduled to meet
at Boulogne on June 21. Lloyd George arranged to meet privately
with Millerand at Hythe the day before. In a series of informal talks,
the French agreed to the scheme, and orders were dispatched to
the Greek commander approving the immediate start of the campaign. As usual, the Italians were informed after the fact the next
day at Boulogne, with many apologies and explanations that there
had not been time to consult with them.[23]

This decision for Greek military action taken by the political
leaders against the express advice of their top military advisors can
be understood only in terms of the status of the peace treaty in
June, 1920. That the plan had its dangers was admitted even by
Lloyd George, who stated that there was no question but that "if
this venture should fail . . . then a new situation would arise" that
would have to be "squarely faced . . . . The next three or four weeks
would determine this." [24] There was little the Italians or the French
could do but grant Lloyd George his way, for this was the only
action that could possibly bring about acceptance and enforcement
of a treaty that had been so painfully hammered out between the
Allies. To have refused to allow the Greeks to go ahead would have
been tantamount to open admission that the treaty needed total
revision. Instead, the powers decided to refuse all requests for revision
of the treaty; and the Turks, who had already been granted one
time extension in which to formulate their reply regarding the terms,
were refused another. When the reply was received, the only alteration of any import that was conceded was the addition of Turkey
to the list of nations that would be granted representation on the
Straits Commission. Otherwise, any and all protests of the Turks
were dismissed without discussion.[25]

Much to the surprise of everyone except the Greeks and Lloyd George, the Greek campaigns were successful. Thrace was occupied in five days against only token opposition, and by the middle of July, Greek forces in Asia Minor had all but cleared the Nationalists from the Straits area. Brusa and Mudania were retaken, and pressure on the British garrison at Ismid was relieved. So swift was the Greek advance that on July 13, Greek army headquarters in Asia Minor announced that the campaign was at an end, although mopping up action did continue through August.[26]

No alternative remained to the government at Constantinople but to sign the treaty. On July 22, a council of eighty prominent Turks (hastily called together since there was no parliament available) authorized, at Damad Ferid's request, the signing of the treaty. A Turkish delegation left for Paris the next day.[27]

Cancellation of the Tittoni-Venizelos Agreement

With the success of the Greek military offensive, the last obstacle to the signing of the treaty seemed to have been removed. However, at the last moment a new snag appeared. The advent of the Giolitti government in Italy in June had brought to the Ministry of Foreign Affairs Count Carlo Sforza, who had previously been Italian high commissioner in Constantinople. Sforza had long been suspected of extreme pro-Turkish sympathies, and his memoirs leave no doubt as to the extent of his opposition to the policy that the Allies had followed in relation to Turkey. It is hardly surprising that on July 18, he informed Venizelos that he intended to annul the Tittoni-Venizelos agreement, nor is it surprising that this step was taken formally a few days later.[28] Sforza later bluntly stated his reasons for doing so.

I absolutely failed to see how it could be of any use to Italy. With no undue breach of modesty, I considered that it was really not for a Great Power like Italy to have written agreements to the effect that Greece should "support" any essential point of Italian interests at the Conference. . . . But when the Foreign Minister of a great power, like Tittoni, goes so far

at the Paris Conference as to consider it an important asset to have Venizelos' support, one cannot deny that Venizelos must have had, in the eyes
of all . . . the sort of legendary power of a charmer, of a siren.[29]

  The cancellation, which was entirely within Italy's right under the
terms of the arrangement, had one very serious effect in relation
to the signing of the treaty. The Greek-Italian agreement had provided that the Dodecanese should be turned over to Greece once
the Italians had received clear title to them from Turkey. With the
renunciation of the agreement, this provision went by the boards,
and on July 26, Venizelos notified Millerand that he would be unable
to sign the treaty with Turkey until this matter had been rectified.[30]

  Italy immediately found itself under a good deal of pressure to
reach a new agreement with Greece. Although Millerand indicated
that France would sign the treaty in any case, the British at first
threatened not to sign either the treaty or the Tripartite Pact, which
Britain, unlike France and Italy, had not signed in May. Although
the British ultimately reversed their position regarding the main
treaty, they remained firm on the issue of the Tripartite Pact. This
threat was a real one for Italy, for it was this separate agreement
that gave Italy the sphere of preeminent influence in Anatolia that
constituted its total share in the Turkish plunder. Under these circumstances the Italians capitulated, and a separate agreement was
drawn up in which Italy again promised to cede to Greece all of
the Dodecanese except Rhodes. That island would be returned only
when the British returned Cyprus to Greece, and only if a plebiscite
taken at that time indicated a popular preference for Greek annexation. Should Britain not cede Cyprus, a plebiscite would be held
in Rhodes after fifteen years.[31]

Signing of the Treaty

  On August 10, 1920, in one of the exhibition rooms of the famous
china factory at Sèvres, the Turkish treaty and five other separate
treaties or agreements were signed.[32] Two, relative to minorities and
Thrace, were between the Allied powers and Greece; a third consti-

tuted a similar minorities arrangement with Armenia. In addition, signatures were affixed to the Tripartite Pact and the Italian-Greek agreement relative to the Aegean Islands.[33]

The long struggle to create a Turkish peace treaty was at an end; turning it into a Turkish peace was a task that the powers soon found they could not achieve. The Greek offensive failed in its long-term objective of eradicating Nationalist resistance, and in time Kemalist forces regained the offensive. By the spring of 1922, the Allies were voluntarily seeking to revise the treaty in favor of the Turks, and a total Nationalist military victory in the summer of 1922 resulted in the negotiation of a virtually new treaty at Lausanne in 1923. This later treaty, though retaining the portions of the Sèvres settlement that dealt with Arab mandated territories, constituted an overwhelming diplomatic victory for the Nationalist movement of Mustapha Kemal in all matters relating to the Turkish state. The Treaty of Lausanne was the only World War I peace treaty that was truly negotiated between victor and vanquished, although by that time such designations had been pretty well obliterated by the turn of events.

Evaluation

Thus the mighty labors of a year and a half brought forth a stillborn treaty. The Sèvres treaty constituted the final resolution of the Eastern Question as it had been interpreted by the European powers during the nineteenth century. It was a nineteenth-century imperialistic solution to a nineteenth-century imperial problem, a problem that had the misfortune of culminating in a new twentieth-century environment, the full ramifications of which were not fully understood by any of the statesmen involved.

Frederick Schuman, in his book *War and Diplomacy in the French Republic,* comments that all the World War I settlements were "like every dictated peace, . . . designed to consolidate the victory, to perpetuate its result, to realize the aspirations of the victors at the expense of the vanquished, to reduce the defeated States to a position of impotence, and to insure the military and political preponderance of the triumphant Powers in future world politics." [34] Certainly his judgment is correct if one is considering the Turkish treaty. At no time did the statesmen involved evidence real concern or understanding of new forces at work both at home and in the Near East. Although all gave lip service to the concept of an informed public and a government and foreign policy based upon the will of the people, none really understood what this meant or thought to take it into real account. This was as true for the apostle of the new diplomacy, President Wilson, as it was for anyone else. Wilson had had the most to do with creating the new atmosphere of diplomacy, yet he failed to recognize and work with the problem of isolationist sentiment in the United States.

Not that the people of Europe were sympathetic to Turkey; their vindictiveness and desire for national gain was both great and vocal and seemed to provide a secure basis for popular acceptance of a treaty such as that signed at Sèvres. [35] This the statesmen saw and understood. What they could not see for sometime, and what they could not really comprehend when they finally did see it, was the war weariness of the populace and its implacable opposition to any action of a military nature. This opposition was expressed both in the demands for immediate demobilization of all conscript troops and in the persistent loud demand in the press and legislative chambers for a drastic cut in military expenditures. Only the men connected with the military, Churchill, Wilson, Foch, and others, recognized the existence of the problem and tried futilely to get the statesmen to place their ambitions in line with actual national capabilities. Churchill put the matter most clearly while defending the military budget before the House of Commons in February, 1920: "I trust that, having dispersed our Armies, we shall not now take steps which will drive the Turkish people to despair, or undertake any new obligations, because our resources are not equal to their discharge." [36]

Again, the negotiators failed to recognize that the force of public opinion had finally come to the masses of the Near East and that a phrase such as "self-determination of nations" was one more likely to conflict than coincide with the interests of the European powers. Moreover, failing to recognize their own military limitations, they consistently refused to believe in the increased military capabilities of the Near Eastern peoples. Nationalism, a force of which they were well aware in European problems, seemed to them to have little real bearing on the Near East question. With the exception of President Wilson, who, at least initially, did have a personal, emotional commitment to the concept of national and political self-determination, the chief negotiators' references to national feelings constituted no more than pious mouthings of the popular slogans of the day.

Here again, the statesmen were mistaken. The Turkish Nationalist movement, which was scoffed at for close to a year, could in the end be dealt with only by the military. The French had to climax their opposition to Arab and Syrian nationalism by overthrowing the Feisal government by force in July of 1920, while the British found themselves face-to-face with a summer-long, bloody revolt in Mesopotamia.[37]

It can be said with certainty that such things as local nationalism, wishes of the people, and self-determination played no role in the Sèvres settlement. The concept of the mandate was regarded as so much window dressing by the French, and with almost as much amusement by the British. The choosing of the mandatory powers for the various areas was done through hard negotiation according to the practices of power politics, with no consideration whatsoever for the inhabitants of the area.[38] When a territory provided economic opportunities or was needed because of strategic considerations, a settlement along imperialistic lines was forthcoming. Britain and France never questioned that the men and materiel to control such areas could be found. Yet, when no national, commercial, or imperial interest could be served, solemn promises suddenly became worthless.

The classic example of this was the fate to which the powers assigned the Armenians when it was decided that the Allies could furnish no financial or military support to an Armenian state. Yet no people had received so many or so definite assurances of aid and support as had this unfortunate group. Before the commitments that had been made to the Armenian, those given to Arab, Greek or Jew paled in significance.[39]

One point, already emphasized in Chapters 9, 11, and 13, bears repeating. This is the fact that the question of oil and oil resources played a surprisingly minor role in the negotiation of the Near East settlement. Never did it provoke any lengthy or serious disagreement. The final document approved at San Remo closely paralleled the original agreement drafted a year previously by Messrs. Long and Berenger, which had been put to one side until knottier and seemingly more serious matters could be settled.

Policies and Governments

For Great Britain, the Sèvres treaty was an imperialistic settlement following the best traditions of nineteenth-century imperialism. The British sought to protect the main routes to India, and therefore made sure they received Mesopotamia and Palestine. Whatever the reasons for the initial issuance of the Balfour Declaration, there is little doubt that in 1919 and 1920 eagerness to fulfill a commitment to the Zionists was not a factor in Britain's insistence that it be given a sole mandate for Palestine.

In addition, the British sought to continue their policy of indirect control of the eastern Mediterranean. Before the war the agent of this control had been the Ottoman Empire. Now Greece was to take over that role. The choice was natural, for Greece was a maritime nation like Britain, it possessed many long-standing commercial and diplomatic ties with Great Britain, it was a Christian nation, and, most important of all, it had as its representative at the Peace Conference a man who exercised an almost hypnotic influence over all the negotiators, Eleutherios Venizelos.[40]

Lloyd George in particular was swayed by his admiration for Venizelos, and the most interesting aspect of his personal Grecophile attitude was the degree to which it influenced his attitude toward policy decisions. Certainly it is clear that he was almost alone within the British government in the extent to which he wished to carry support of Greek ambitions. His success came chiefly from the failure of others effectively to oppose him because of disagreements on other aspects of British policy. Churchill and Montagu wanted the Turks to remain in Constantinople (for different reasons); both were unfavorably inclined toward Greek claims in Asia Minor. Curzon, agreeing with them on this latter issue, vehemently opposed the retention of Constantinople by the Turks. Even on the question of Thrace, the British military at home and in Constantinople opposed the final territorial settlement, while the Foreign Office supported it.[41]

Another part of the explanation for Britain's backing of Greek claims may be found in the 1917 collapse of Tsarist Russia and that nation's subsequent withdrawal from the war. As long as Russia remained in the war. Britain had been willing to grant it a large share of postwar control in the Near East. With Russia's capitulation, a totally new situation arose. In 1919 and 1920, British policy was guided by a determination to avoid letting the vacuum created by the Russian withdrawal be filled by either France or Italy. At first it was thought that the United States might plug the gap by taking over those areas originally allotted to Russia. When this plan fell through, the British assured themselves of a preponderant influence in the Straits area through an international commission, which they would dominate as the strongest naval power. Backing this up would be an expanded Greek state, embracing both the European and Asiatic coastline of the Aegean Sea, which would serve British interests well.

In all of the negotiations of the Treaty of Sèvres, fear of Bolshevism does not appear to have been a primary issue despite the rapidly deteriorating situation in the Caucasus. At times the British cabinet did evidence some general concern regarding the extension of Bolshevik influence in Turkey. In the spring of 1920 many people believed that Kemal and the Bolsheviks had signed a military aid convention; certainly Lloyd George was convinced that Kemal was receiving Bolshevik aid.[42] Subsequent investigation has revealed no proof that this was the case, and recent scholarship has placed both the signing of a Soviet-Nationalist military convention and the beginning of·Bolshevik aid to the Nationalists well after the signing of the Treaty of Sèvres on August 10, 1920, though contact between the two governments had been established earlier.[43] In any case, in the actual inter-Allied negotiating sessions of the Turkish treaty, Bolshevism was generally not raised as an important issue in any way.

The French found themselves in the unenviable position of being dependent upon Great Britain for support on such questions as German disarmament, the Rhineland, and reparations. The situation in Europe forbade any split with the British government, and therefore the French could not afford to oppose too strenuously British ambitions in the Near East. As a result, with the exception of Syrian matters, France generally acceded to British wishes, prime examples being the Smyrna and Constantinople questions. However, long-standing French commercial and financial interests in Asia Minor made the existence of a strong Turkish state desirable, and by the summer of 1920 the French found themselves faced with a policy dilemma. The situation in Anatolia called for conciliation and support of the Nationalist regime, but such a policy would entail opposing Greek aspirations in Smyrna. To do this would mean a break with Great Britain. Moreover, it would constitute an open renunciation of previous French policy, for France had concurred in the original occupation of Smyrna and many, if not all, of the difficulties in Asia Minor could be attributed to that event.

Thus the French found themselves trapped both by previous policy decisions and by the absolute necessity of preserving British friendship. They therefore had no choice but to follow Britain's lead in officially supporting Greek military action in Anatolia in June, 1920, although they tried at the same time to assure Kemal that France really wanted to be his friend. These obviously conflicting policies were only resolved by the Nationalist victory over the Greeks in 1922.

The Italians emerged from the negotiations with the cleanest hands. This was not so much due to greater morality on the part of the Italian government as to the fact that it had no other choice. One of the central themes of the year and a half of negotiations was a constant attempt on the part of the United States, Britain, and France, and later Britain and France alone, to exclude Italy from any basic decision-making and to throw the Italians as few crumbs as possible. This was true regarding the takeover of Smyrna, the status of Constantinople, the spheres of influence, and the Greek intervention in June, 1920. In fact, if one takes into account the secret British-French discussions of December-January, the whole treaty was basically decided by two allies who purposely excluded the third. It was only natural that the Italians subsequently sought to disassociate themselves as much as possible from a treaty whose provisions did not come close to meeting their claims, and in the negotiation of which they had played a distinctly secondary role.[44]

The one concession Italy did receive was the recognition of a sphere of influence that was to be entirely within the new Turkish state. Therefore, it was imperative that Italy be on good terms with whatever Turkish authority controlled the area. On August 9, 1920, Count Sforza told the Italian Chamber of Deputies that Turkey must grow and progress rapidly, and offered "cordial and loyal collaboration of an economic and moral nature, leaving Turkish sovereignty unimpaired."[45] Although stating that this position showed Italy's high moral principles, he was honest enough to admit that such a policy would "correspond to our best interests materially in the long run."[46]

The Negotiators

From a study of the negotiations, no villain emerges. Yet there is, alas, much to criticize and unfortunately little to praise.

The United States was never at war with Turkey, refused to take part in the actual formulation of the treaty, and did not sign the final document. Its president, Woodrow Wilson, ended his official role in the Near East negotiations in June, 1919. Yet a severe judgment must be passed upon the man whose betrayal of his own ideals in supporting and abetting the Greek landing at Smyrna and in proposing a virtual French mandate for Anatolia outside of League of Nations supervision has been discussed in Chapters 4 and 5. It is precisely because the United States had no axe to grind, no material, strategic, or imperial interest in the area, that this action seems so reprehensible. At least the other nations had reasons and motives connected with what they took to be national interest; Wilson had only his blind personal dislike of the Italians, a result of the Fiume crisis.[47]

At the same time, Wilson (or better the United States) must be absolved from a charge that both then and since has often been brought forward. European leaders, particularly Lloyd George and

Curzon, were fond of blaming American indecision regarding mandates for the delay in formulating a treaty, arguing in particular that had the treaty been presented to the Turks six months earlier it could easily have been enforced.[48] Such an assertion is totally groundless for two reasons. First, the real turning point in the saga of the Turkish peace treaty was the decision on the part of all the powers to send Greek troops into Smyrna in May, 1919. It was in reaction to this that the Nationalist resistance movement appeared and grew, and it was this movement, and not the failure to present a treaty to the Turks in November, 1919, that precluded any effective enforcement of the kind of treaty the Allies sought to impose upon Turkey. Second, within a month after Wilson's return to the United States it became patent that the Versailles treaty was in for a rough time at the hands of the Senate. That this would be the case had been evident to many in Europe as early as March, 1919. Reports from the French and British ambassadors, along with those of foreign press correspondents in Washington, left little doubt that the United States would not assume any mandates, especially over territories that had belonged to a nation with which America had never been at war. The November repudiation of the treaty by the Senate was not needed to make it clear to European statesmen that America was unlikely to assume mandatory responsibilities in the Near East.[49]

Rather, blame for the delay in negotiations must be laid squarely on Anglo-French acrimony over Syria during the spring and summer of 1919.[50] The British, caught between their Arab commitments and the claims of their French ally, found themselves face-to-face with an aroused Clemenceau, who felt that the considerable French concessions relating to Palestine and Mosul made it imperative that French occupation and control of Syria should be obtained before any further discussion of Near Eastern affairs took place. Once this issue was resolved in mid-September and the French occupation of Syria was completed in November, the British and French wasted little time in making arrangements to meet in the second week of December for private and detailed discussions of the terms of the Turkish treaty. Thus, once the Syrian stalemate was broken, negotiations were quickly initiated, and it is hard to believe that any different position or attitude taken by the United States in the summer and fall of 1919 would have made an iota of difference in the speed with which the negotiations progressed.

If Wilson receives a harsh judgment, Lloyd George must run a close second. His Greek policy, at first based on what might be considered to be legitimate British interests, outran all bounds as his admiration for Venizelos increased.[51] He continually overemphasized Greek strength and minimized Turkish resistance. He appeared to be equally convinced of the barbarity of the Turk and of the totally civilized characteristics of the Asian Greek. Willing to relinquish his support for Armenian and Arab claims, he was at least consistent in supporting Greek ambitions to the end.

For both Clemenceau and Millerand, the Near East constituted a secondary front. Therefore they had the intelligence to insist upon and grasp firmly the basic component of their claims, Syria, while being willing to use other areas in the Near East as concessions to enable France to retain good relations with Britain. The cooperation of Britain in European affairs was of the utmost import to France. Thus, although their Near East interests might have called for greater opposition to British ambitions, the French leaders were willing to take Syria and for the time being remain as quiet as possible on other matters, although Millerand had the habit of making great issues out of minor details in the drafting.

Venizelos stands out as a highly persuasive and talented diplomat who knew exactly what he wanted and who was able to achieve almost all his aims at the Peace Conference. Extremely nationalistic and patriotic, he demonstrated a greed for territory and a belief in Greek capabilities that knew no bounds. Events subsequent to the signing of the Treaty of Sèvres were to show that he vastly overestimated the extent of his popular support at home and the capabilities of the Greek military machine. Yet the treaty itself must be considered in many ways as a triumph for Venizelos and a monument to his personal influence at the Peace Conference.

If one man stands out in a particularly favorable light, it is Lord Curzon. Temperamental, often peevish, given to tears and emotional outbursts, harsh and often rude to his subordinates, pompous, extremely egotistical, and quick to suspect a personal slight in any remark, Curzon, nevertheless, had a cool, dispassionate, and highly

realistic view of what could or could not be accomplished in Turkey
with the forces available.[52] An avid British nationalist and imperialist,
he at all times thought and spoke from the British point of view,
and as a negotiator proved an extremely able and aggressive defender
of British interests. At the same time, he alone was able to separate
the essential from the nonessential in the Turkish problem. Although
both the War Office and the Foreign Office were concerned about
creating an effective peace, Curzon's solution was the only one
presented during the Peace Conference that held out any hope of
being enforceable with a minimum of effort on the part of the Allies.
His scheme for the detachment of Constantinople and European
Turkey from a new Turkish state in Anatolia, coupled with the return
of Smyrna to Turkey, was a plan that would have excised the Greek
irritant that was primarily responsible for the growth of the Kemalist
movement. Equally important, it would have removed the necessity
of Allied enforcement of the treaty in Anatolia, should it subsequently appear that it was not feasible to do so. Whether or not
Kemal in the future gained control of Asia Minor, Constantinople
and the Straits would have been in Allied hands, separate from the
Turkish state, and the powers never would have found themselves
faced with the necessity of negotiating a totally new treaty on much
less favorable terms with the victorious Nationalists. Although Curzon's plan to oust the Turks from Constantinople can be severely
(and rightly) criticized from many points of view, it had the sustaining
virtue of being enforceable, and of securing for Britain what was
considered to be essential to its Near Eastern and Mediterranean
policy, without committing the British to any potentially large-scale
expenditure or military action in Asia Minor.

The Peace Treaty in Perspective

The negotiation of the Turkish treaty can shed some interesting
light also upon the whole question of the negotiation of the Treaty
of Versailles. Criticism has often been leveled at the Allied powers
for negotiating the German peace so rapidly. The argument has been
that had the powers approached the problem more slowly, allowing

the passions of war to subside, the resulting treaty would have been less vindictive, more dispassionate, and more fully attuned to the furtherance of peace in the world than was the treaty signed in June, 1919. The terms of the Sèvres treaty would seem to indicate that this would hardly have been the case.

Can it be claimed that the Turkish treaty was the better and more realistic for having been worked out during a much more lengthy period of time than the Versailles treaty, or that the negotiators showed more wisdom, vision, and tolerance in the terms they created? The answer must emphatically be in the negative. The peoples of the nations of Europe were no less vindictive in their attitudes in August, 1920, than they had been in January, 1919. Moreover, nearly two years after the war, this bitterness was beginning to be turned against the governments at home as well as against the enemy abroad. This was a result of the heightened disillusionment that usually follows a major military conflict, and it was augmented by the economic problems each nation faced in converting its industries from wartime to peacetime purposes while absorbing hundreds of thousands of returning veterans. In effect, the home governments, no longer able to ride on the swell of popularity brought on by military victory, were more susceptible to such pressures than they had been immediately following the war.[53]

At the same time there was war weariness, a desire to be rid of all things military—a condition that was far greater in 1920 than in 1919. Although this war weariness was incompatible with popular vindictiveness toward the former enemy, it was natural, it was there, and it made the negotiation of an effective and enforceable peace treaty with Turkey in 1920 an extremely difficult, indeed an almost impossible, task. There seems little reason to doubt that a similar set of conflicting attitudes and circumstances would have met the Allies in even greater form had they been attempting to formulate the German treaty in the winter and spring of 1920.

The history of the negotiations leading to the formulation of the Treaty of Sèvres can give rise to two contrasting, but not actually contradictory, final conclusions. First, the treaty was negotiated to settle the prewar Eastern question by men who saw the problem only as it had existed before the war. As such, the delay of close to two years was fatal, for it allowed a whole new set of problems and circumstances to develop in the Near East. Second, the Treaty of Sèvres was drawn up too soon for the negotiators to be able fully to assess the meaning of these new forces; the treaty failed to come to grips with the problems existing at the time it was signed. The developments of 1919–20 created such a turmoil in the Near East that it is questionable whether any treaty drawn up in the winter and spring of 1919–20 could have brought anything approaching long-range stability and peace to the Near East. Given the traditional policy attitudes of the Allies and their seeming inability or unwillingness to take these new developments realistically into account, the possibility of a stable peace virtually disappeared.

The only chance an imperialistic treaty such as that signed at Sèvres might have had for even short-term success would have been in its immediate imposition on a thoroughly defeated and prostrate Turkey. The rivalry of the European powers, complicated by Wilson's vociferous, if nonactive, participation, made this impossible. By the time the powers succeeded in formulating the treaty, its provisions no longer applied to the situation at hand. Not only had the Turkish horse escaped out the barn door, but having fed on a fodder composed of a mixture of nationalism, anti-Greek hatred and the doctrine of self-determination of nations, it was preparing to kick down the imperialistic fences so laboriously constructed by the negotiators of the Treaty of Sèvres.

1. *Correspondance d'Orient*, pp. 513–14, 6/15/20 (includes the text of Millerand's speech in giving the treaty to the Turks). *Times* (London), 5/11/20.

2. For a general summary of international press reaction, see "How Will the Turkish Treaty Work?" pp. 19–20.

3. Bardoux, *De Paris à Spa*, p. 327; *Near East*, 5/27/20, p. 752; 6/3/20, p. 789. For the negative reaction of the Indian Moslems, see C. J. C. Street, *Lord Reading*, p. 201; *Times* (London), 5/25/20.

4. Adkisson, *Britain and the Kemalist Movement*, pp. 291–92; *The Near East*, 5/20/20, pp. 717, 723; "New Empires for Old," pp. 154–55; F. H. Simonds, "Dividing Turkish Lands," pp. 607–12; *Times* (London), 5/12/20; H. C. Woods, "The Turkish Treaty," pp. 57–66.

5. France, *Bulletin périodique de la presse Italienne*, nos. 136, 137, 143; *R.F.P.: Political Review*, 5/7/20, Gaillard, *Turks and Europe*, pp. 227–37; Bardoux, *De Paris à Spa*, p. 326; *Le Temps*, 4/27/20.

6. J. Pichon has pointed out that at the time of the San Remo conference, Anglo-French relations were strained, not only over the basic question of amount and kind of reparations, but also over the recent French occupation of Frankfort and Darmstadt, which had been done without prior consultation with Britain. Pichon, *Partage*, p. 207; Cambon, *Correspondance*, 3:384–85, 6/26/20; H. Froidevaux, "Le Projet de Traité avec Turquie et la France," pp. 142–46; idem, "Les intérèts économiques français dans le Levant et la Traité de paix avec la Turquie," pp. 172–75.

7. Foreign Office. F.O. 608/278/390/390, Vansittart to Young, 6/21/20; *Le Temps*, 4/22/20, 4/25/20, 4/27/20, 5/8/20, 5/13/20, 5/14/20, 5/19/20, 5/25/20; "Britain, France, Asia and Oil," p. 255; France, *Journal Officiel, Dèbats parlementaires, Chambre des Députés, 1918–1925,* pp. 2431–45, 6/25/20; *R.F.P.: Political Review*, p. 45, 5/21/20; G. Samné, "A propos du traité turc," pp. 397–404, 5/15/20; A. Tardieu, "Réflections súr la Crise Oriental," pp. 452–53. For both French and Italian views, see Ziemke, *Neue Türkei*, pp. 119/20.

8. Pech, *Alliés et Turquie*, p. 133, 5/15/20; *Times* (London), 5/17/20; Foreign Office, F.O. 406/43/270, Robeck to Curzon, 6/8/20.

9. *Times* (London), 5/21/20; Foreign Office, F.O. 406/43/243; Robeck to Curzon, 5/27/20. See also *Br. Doc.,* 13:73, Robeck to Curzon, 5/17/20; p. 81, Curzon to Robeck, 6/5/20, and n. 1; pp. 81–83, Robeck to Curzon, 6/10/20; Kinross, *Ataturk*, p. 266.

10. Nicolson, *Curzon,* p. 249; "Turkey and Her Former Dominions: Attacks on the Peace Treaty," pp. 625–31; Pech. *Alliés et Turquie,* pp. 131–32; 5/10/20; A. Giannini, *L'Ultima fase della questione Orientale, 1913–1932,* p. 37; Gaillard, *Turks and Europe,* pp. 208–9; Kinross, *Ataturk*, p. 266; Adivar, *Ordeal,* chap. 3, and pp. 69 ff.

11. *Br. Doc.,* 13:83–84, Robeck to Curzon, 6/10/20; p. 86, 6/15/20; pp. 87–89, 6/17/20; Foreign Office, F.O. 406/43/236, Robeck to Curzon, 5/25/20; Gaillard, *Turks and Europe,* p. 223; *Times* (London), 5/31/20, 6/18/20; *Le Temps,* 6/16/20; Bardoux, *De Paris à Spa,* pp. 3, 328; Churchill, *Aftermath,* p. 398; Kinross, *Ataturk,* p. 267.

12. Pech, *Alliés et Turquie*, p. 138, 6/4/20.

13. *Br. Doc.,* 13:78, Curzon to Derby, 6/2/20; p. 79, Grahame to Curzon, 6/3/20; p. 80, 6/4/20; p. 81, Robeck to Curzon, 6/4/20; Foreign Office, F.O. 608/278/349/435, Text of Kemal-de Caix armistice, and Kemal's order to his forces, 5/28/20; 5/29/20; Cabinet Papers, Cab. 24/107, C.P. 1450, War Office memorandum, 6/8/20; State Department, Turkey, 867.00/ 1286, Knabenshue to Sec. State, 6/13/20; 1291, Bristol to Sec. State, 6/19/20, enclosure; Webster, *Turkey of Ataturk,* p. 92; Pichon, *Partage,* p. 208; Pech, *Alliés et Turquie,* p. 140, 6/17/20; Gaillard, *Turks and Europe,* p. 220; S. Duggan, "Syria and its Tangled Problems," p. 247; D. McCallum, "The French in Syria, 1919–1924," pp. 13–14; Rémusat, "Cilicie, 1918–1922," pp. 365–66.

14. Pech, *Alliés et Turquie,* pp. 134–35, 5/30/20; Webster, *Turkey of Ataturk,* p. 87.

15. *Br. Doc.,* 13:83–84, Robeck to Curzon, 6/10/20; p. 86, 6/15/20; pp. 86–87, 6/16/20; pp. 87–89, 6/17/20, p. 89, Curzon to Derby and Buchanan, 6/21/20; pp. 89–90, Robeck to Curzon, 6/23/20; pp. 90–91, Buchanan to Curzon, 6/23/20; p. 91, Derby to Curzon, 6/23/20; *Le Temps,* 6/16/20, 6/17/20, 6/21/20, 6/22/20; H. Froidevaux, "Au lendemain de la signature du traité de Sèvres," pp. 212–14; Graves, *Briton and Turk,* p. 203. The *New York Times,* in an editorial on May 5, had called on the British and the Greeks to get rid of Kemal.

16. The British made this fact clear to Venizelos. See Lloyd George Papers, F 199/9/2, Notes of conversation, Venizelos, Curzon, C.I.G.S., 3/19/20; Callwell, *Henry Wilson,* 2:230, 3/19/20; Frangulis, *Crise Mondiale,* 2:121; Pallis, *Anatolian Venture,* p. 66.

17. On June 21, Lloyd George told Lord Riddell: "Of course the military are against the Greeks. They always have been. They favour the Turks. The military are confirmed Tories. It is the Tory policy to support the Turks. They hate the Greeks. That is why Henry Wilson, who is a Tory of the most crusted kind, is so much opposed to what we have done." Riddell, *Diary,* p. 208, 6/21/20. Paul Cambon bitterly commented in a letter on June 26, 1920 that

"Lloyd George sees only through the eyes of Venizelos and we follow all the caprices of Lloyd George." *Correspondance,* 3:384–85. Count Sforza caustically commented, "Lloyd George also wanted final victory, but was decided to pay for it only with Greek blood." *Modern Europe,* p. 167. See also D. Walder, *The Chanak Affair,* pp. 83–84; Churchill, *Aftermath,* p. 407; Frangulis, *Crise Mondiale,* 2:122–24, 131; Ziemke, *Neue Türkei,* p. 118; Sachar, *Emergence,* pp. 330–35.

18. Cabinet Papers, Cab. 23/37, Conference of Ministers, no. 42, 6/18/20, App. 1.

19. Callwell, *Henry Wilson,* 2:244, 6/17/20.

20. Ibid., p. 245, 6/18/20. For additional expressions of British military opposition to an expanded Greek campaign, see *Br. Doc.,* 13:55, General Staff memorandum 4/1/20; p. 64, Webb to Curzon, 4/23/20; Cabinet Papers, Cab. 24/103, C.P. 1027, General Staff memorandum, 4/7/20; Cab. 24/106, C.P. 1380, War Office memorandum, enclosure, De Robeck to War Office.

21. Cabinet Papers, Cab. 23/27, Conference of Ministers, no. 42, 6/18/20. For earlier expressions of this view by Venizelos, see *Br. Doc.,* 1:330–32, S.C., 8/5/19; 2:236, 11/8/19; 7:67, 2/16/20; 13:20–21, Kerr to Campbell, 3/9/20; Lloyd George Papers, F 12/3/19, Curzon to Lloyd George, 3/18/20; F 199/9/2, Conversation, Venizelos, Curzon and C.I.G.S., 3/19/20; Cabinet Papers, Cab. 29/31, A.J. 140, Report of military representatives, 3/30/20.

22. Cabinet Papers, Cab. 23/37, Conference of Ministers, no. 41, 6/17/20; no. 42, 6/18/20; Lloyd George Papers F24/2/38, Hankey to Lloyd George, 6/17/20; Callwell, *Henry Wilson,* 2:244, 6/18/20.

23. *Br. Doc.,* 8:307–8, "Notes of a Conversation held at Lympne on Sunday, June 20, 1920, . . . " ; pp. 346–49, S.C., 6/21/20, at Boulogne; J. Laroche, *Au Quai D'Orsay avec Briand et Poincaré, 1913–1926,* pp. 115–16; Frangulis, *Crise Mondiale,* 2:125, 160; France, *Bulletin périodique de la presse Italian,* no. 140.

24. *Br. Doc.,* 8:348, S.C., 6/21/20.

25. Foreign Office, F.O. 608/277/284/346, Ottoman delegation to S.C., 5/28/20; 369, 6/7/20; F.O. 608/276/185/296, Turkish delegation to S.C., 6/25/20; 436, Turkish delegation to S.C., 7/8/20. A composite of these two documents was subsequently published by the Turkish government under the title, *Observations Générales présentés par la Délégation Ottomane à la Conférence de la Paix.* See also *Br. Doc.,* 8:349–51, Allied Conference at Boulogne, 6/21/20; pp. 443–49, Allied Conference at Spa, 7/7/20; pp. 544–46, 7/11/20; pp. 553–56, App. 1, Draft reply to Turkish delegation; Foreign Office, F.O. 608/276/185/432, Millerand to Turkish delegation, 7/16/20; also in F.O. 406/44/47, Vansittart to Curzon, 7/17/20; *Current History* 12 (August, 1920): 804–11; *Times* (London), 7/1/20, 7/19/20; Churchill, *Aftermath,* p. 398; Riddell, *Diary,* p. 204, 6/20/20.

26. For accounts of the Greek campaigns, see the *Times* (London), 6/24/20,ff.

27. *Br. Doc.,* 13:101–3, Robeck to Curzon, 7/17/20; pp. 105–6, 7/22/20; Foreign Office, F.O. 406/44/56, Robeck to Curzon, 7/23/20; Gaillard, *Turks and Europe,* p. 257; E. A. Powell, *The Struggle for Power in Moslem Asia,* p. 98; M. Price, *A History of Turkey, From Empire to Republic,* p. 159.

28. Frangulis, *Crise Mondiale,* 2:99–101, 103–5; Driault and Lheretier, *Grèce et la grande guerre,* p. 380.

29. Sforza, *Modern Europe,* pp. 171–72; see also *Br. Doc.,* 13:109–10, Buchanan to Curzon, 7/29/20; Foreign Office, F.O. 406/44/80, Buchanan to Curzon, 8/8/20. The Italians also had complained of Greek attacks on Italian positions during the Greek offensive in early July. F.O. 608/278/400/418 through 421, 7/10/20–7/11/20.

30. Frangulis, *Crise Mondiale,* 2:106; *Br. Doc.,* 13:108–9, Curzon to Buchanan, 7/28/20.

31. Frangulis, *Crise Mondiale,* 2:104–13; Foreign Office, F.O. 608/276/185/449, Curzon to Derby, 7/28/20; 451, Curzon to Grahame, 7/29/20; Derby to Curzon, 7/29/20; 462, Derby

to Curzon, 7/29/20; 466, Vansittart to F.O., 8/2/19; 476, Curzon to Derby (2), 8/3/20, 8/4/20; 485, Buchanan to Derby, 8/7/20; *Br. Doc.*, 13:110-12, Curzon to Buchanan, 7/30/20; pp. 114-15, Buchanan to Curzon, 8/1/20; pp. 115-16, Curzon to Buchanan, 8/3/20; pp. 112-19, Curzon to Granville, 8/5/20; pp. 120-21, Buchanan to Curzon, 8/7/20; p. 121, Grahame to Curzon, 8/9/20; *Bulletin périodique de la presse Italienne*, no. 142; *New York Times*, 8/1/20.

32. Serbia (Yugoslavia) and the Hedjaz refused to sign, the former because it would not accept a share of the Ottoman Debt, the latter because of the French mandate in Syria.

33. "La signature du traité turc," p. 255. The text of the Sèvres treaty may be found in Carnegie Endowment, *Treaties*, vol. 2; also in Great Britain, *Parliamentary Papers, 1920,* Cmd. 964; and F. L. Israel, ed., *Major Peace Treaties of Modern History, 1648-1967.* The text of the subsidiary agreements may be found in Great Britain, *Parliamentary Papers, 1920,* Cmds. 960, 963; idem, *Parliamentary Papers, 1921,* Cmd. 1390; Foreign Office, F.O. 608/276/185/510; Giannini, *Documenti per la Storia.*

34. F. L. Schuman, *War and Diplomacy in the French Republic: An inquiry into political motivations and the control of foreign policy,* p. 254.

35. See above, Chapter 1.

36. *Times* (London), 2/24/20. See also Cabinet Papers, Cab. 29/15 W.C.P. 825, Churchill memorandum, 5/21/19; Maurice *Armistices,* chap. 4 passim; Nicolson, *Curzon,* pp. 68-71; Rawlinson, *Adventures,* p. 157; Toynbee, *Western Question,* pp. 60-76; Toynbee and Kirkwood, *Turkey,* pp. 63-64; *Times* (London), 5/20/20, 6/23/20, 6/24/20; Williams, "America's Duty," pp. 215-16.

37. The French action was greeted sympathetically in much of the British press. The British government refused to consider Feisal's appeals for aid. This attitude was at least partly due to the revolt that the British were currently facing in Mesopotamia. See *Great Britain and the Near East* (August 12, 1920), p. 229; *Times* (London), 7/19/20: Great Britain, *Parliamentary Debates* (Commons), 5th ser., 132:143-88, 7/19/20.For an excellent account of the Syrian and Mesopotamian areas, 1918-1921, see Kedourie, *England and the Middle East,* chaps. 6,7. For Syria alone, see *Br. Doc.*, 13:270-323 passim; Zeine, *Arab Independence,* chap. 7. For Mesopotamia alone, see A. T. Wilson Papers, MSS 52455, Correspondence with Hirtzel and Montagu; 52456, Correspondence with Stevenson; 52459, Memorandum, "The Problems of Mesopotamia," September, 1920; Longrigg, *Iraq,* chap. 4. See also Antonius, *Arab Awakening,* pp. 314-15; A. Bruneau, *La France au Levant,* pp. 300-302; "The Case of Emir Feisal," *Current History,* pp. 249-55; *Correspondance d'Orient,* pp. 74-86, 8/15/20-8/30/20; Hourani, *Syria and Lebanon,* p. 54; Loder, *Truth,* pp. 89-98; Longrigg, *Syria and Lebanon,* pp. 102-6; McCallum "French in Syria," pp. 3-25; Sachar, *Emergence,* pp. 285-90, 366-82; G. Samné, "L' Effondrement de Fayçal," pp. 49-54; Temperley, *Peace Conference,* 6:158-61; *Le Temps,* 6/28/20, 7/21/20, 7/26/20, 7/30/20; *Times* (London), 7/17/20-7/29/20.

38. At one point in the negotiations Montagu urged Balfour, "Let us not, for Heaven's sake, tell the Moslem what he ought to think, let us recognize what they do think." To which Balfour replied, "I am quite unable to see why Heaven or any other Power should object to our telling the Moslem what he ought to think." Cabinet Papers, Cab. 29/17, W.C.P. 1057, Marginal comments on draft memorandum by Balfour, June, 1919. Curzon told the House of Lords in June, 1920, "It is quite a mistake to suppose that under the Covenant of the League or any other instrument the gift of a mandate rests with the League of Nations. It rests with the Powers who have conquered the territories, which it then falls to them to distribute." Quoted by George E. Kirk, *A Short History of the Middle East,* p. 130.

39. Ironically, in his diary, Avetis Aharonian, one of the two chief Armenian representatives at the Peace Conference, referred to the day the Treaty of Sèvres was signed as "the happiest day of my life." A. Aharonian, "From Sardarapat to Sèvres and Lausanne," *Armenian Review* 17 (Spring 1964): 8/10/20.

40. H. Kohn, *Nationalism and Imperialism in the Hither East,* pp. 247-48; Gaillard, *Turks and Europe,* p. 234.

41. Curzon remained in personal opposition to the Constantinople decision to the very end. On August 4, 1920, he told the House of Lords that regarding the cession of Constantinople to the Turks, he was not "certain in my own mind that it was a right concession" and that time would show it to be a "mistaken concession." *Parliamentary Debates* (Lords), 5th ser., 41:734 (8/4/20). See also Lloyd George Papers, F 90/1/14, Kerr to Lloyd George, Robeck memorandum, 3/9/20, and General Staff memorandum, 4/1/20; Foreign Office,F.O. 406/43/ 190, Robeck to Curzon, 4/7/20.

42. One of the prerequisites for the resumption of trade that the British demanded of the Soviet government during informal negotiations in 1920 was the cessation of aid to the Turkish nationalists. *Br.Doc.,* 12:573, Wardrop to Curzon, 3/12/20; Foreign Office,F.O. 371/5178/ E4689-345-44, Political report, Director Military Intelligence, Admiralty, 5/8/20; F.O. 371-5049/E6473-3-44, Allenby to Curzon, 6/4/20; F.O. 371/5178/E8842-345-44, Greek report of Bolshevik aid to Nationalists, 7/26/20; *Times,* (London), 2/3/20, 6/10/20; "Un Diplomate," *Cambon,* p. 310.

43. A draft treaty was initialed on August 24, 1920, but was not formally signed until seven months later. Soviet aid to the Nationalist war did not begin until the fall of 1921. See Davison, "Turkish Diplomacy," pp. 183-85; Berkes, *Secularism in Turkey,* pp. 437, 440-43; Kinross, *Ataturk,* chap. 30; X. E. Eudin and R. C. North, *Soviet Russia and the East, 1920-1927; A Documentary Survey,* pp. 106-7; Sachar, *Emergence,* pp. 417-19.

44. Nitti, *Wreck of Europe,* p. 174.

45. Mandelstam, *Probléme armenien,* p. 158.

46. Ibid. See also *Br. Doc.,* 13:98-101, Curzon to Buchanan (Sforza interview), 7/10/20.

47. See above, Chapters 1, 4 and 5.

48. See Curzon in the House of Lords, 2/10/20, as quoted in the *Times* (London), 2/11/20; Gaillard, *Turks and Europe,* p. 93; Lloyd George, *Truth,* pp. 1260, 1301; Temperley, *Peace Conference,* 6:28; Tillman, *Anglo-American Relations,* pp. 370-76; Sachar, "United States and Turkey," p. 214; Wilson, *Loyalties,* 2:214; *Br. Doc.,* 1:688-89, S.C., 9/15/19; *U.S. Doc., P.P.C.,* 11:647, Wallace to Sec. State, 9/19/19, enclosure; Lloyd George Papers, F 60/3/11, Lloyd George to Grey, 10/22/19.

49. *Br. Doc.,* 1:131-32, S.C., 7/18/19, Telegram from Wilson (n.d.); *U.S. Doc., P.P.C.,* 11:464, Steering Committee, 7/21/19; Polk Papers, Dr. 73, fol. 120, Davis to Polk, 10/14/19; Lloyd George Papers, F 89/3/4, Kerr to Lloyd George (letter to T. E. Lawrence from H. C. Lodge), 7/16/19; Sir W. Wiseman Papers, Dr. 90, fol. 7, Wiseman to Balfour, 7/18/19; Foreign Office, F.O. 608/111/385-1-11/17992, Balfour to Curzon, 8/18/19; Nevakivi, *Arab Middle East,* p. 135.

50. As late as November 14, 1919, the American Peace Commission reported to Washington that the British and the Italians had "no disposition to take up this question [Turkish treaty] at this conference." *U.S. Doc., P.P.C.,* 11:664, American Commission to Sec. State, 11/14/19. See also ibid., p. 641, House to Wilson, 9/3/19; p. 644, 9/15/19; pp. 423-24, American Commission and Technical Advisors, 9/18/19. Clemenceau told Henry White and Frank Polk on separate occasions that he welcomed the delay in the Turkish settlement and that "he would discuss no matter relating to Turkey with the British until the Syrian situation had been arranged." Buckler Papers, Dr. 51, fol. 7, Buckler to House, 7/26/19; House Papers, Dr. 16, fol. 9, Polk to Sec. State, 8/11/19; see also Evans, *U.S. and Partition,* p. 198; De Novo, *American Interests,* pp. 123-24.

51. Kinross cites Lloyd George as considering Venizelos to be "the greatest statesman Greece had thrown up since the days of Pericles." *Ataturk,* p. 165.

52. For an interesting discussion of Curzon's personal life, see Mosley, *Glorious Fault,* passim.

53. For a general discussion of the problems discussed in this and the following paragraph as they affected Great Britain, see Beloff, *Imperial Sunset*, pp. 347–49: Marwick, *The Deluge*, pp. 266–314: idem, *Britain in the Century of Total War*, pp. 142–92: C. L. Mowat, *Britain Between the Wars, 1918–1940*, chap. 1. For France, see E. Bonnefous, *Histoire Politique de la Troisième République*, vol. 3; Buell, *Contemporary French Politics:* J. Chastenet, *Cent ans de République*, vol. 5, chaps. 1–3. For Italy, see S. Hughes, *The Rise and Fall of Modern Italy*, chap. 7; Seton-Watson, *Italy*, chap. 12. For the United States, see S. Adler, *The Uncertain Giant, 1921–1941: American Foreign Policy Between the Wars*, chaps. 1–3: H. U. Faulkner, *From Versailles to the New Deal;* G. Mowry, *The Urban Nation, 1920–1960*, chap. 2; G. Soule, *Prosperity Decade; From War to Depression: 1917–1929*, chaps. 4 and 5.

APPENDIXES

APPENDIX A

ARMISTICE WITH TURKEY *

Signed 30 October 1918

I.—Opening of Dardanelles and Bosphorus and secure access to the Black Sea. Allied occupation of Dardanelles, and Bosphorus forts.

II.—Positions of all minefields, torpedo-tubes, and other obstructions in Turkish waters to be indicated, and assistance given to sweep or remove them as may be required.

III.—All available information as to mines in the Black Sea to be communicated.

IV.—All Allied prisoners of war and Armenian interned persons and prisoners to be collected in Constantinople and handed over unconditionally to the Allies.

V.—Immediate demobilization of the Turkish army, except for such troops as are required for the surveillance of the frontiers and for the maintenance of internal order. (Number of effectives and their disposition to be determined later by the Allies after consultation with the Turkish Government.)

VI.—Surrender of all war vessels in Turkish waters or in waters occupied by Turkey; these ships to be interned at such Turkish port or ports as may be directed, except such small vessels as are required for police or similar purposes in Turkish territorial waters.

VII.—The Allies to have the right to occupy any strategic points in the event of any situation arising which threatens the security of the Allies.

VIII.—Free use by the Allied ships of all ports and anchorages now in Turkish occupation and denial of their use to the enemy. Similar conditions to apply to Turkish mercantile shipping in Turkish waters for purposes of trade and the demobilization of the army.

IX.—Use of all ship-repair facilities at all Turkish ports and arsenals.

X.—Allied occupation of the Taurus tunnel system.

XI.—Immediate withdrawal of the Turkish troops from Northwest Persia to behind the pre-war frontier has already been ordered and will be carried out. Part of Trans-Caucasia has already been ordered to be evacuated by Turkish troops; the remainder is to be evacuated if required by the Allies after they have studied the situation there.

XII.—Wireless telegraphy and cable stations to be controlled by the Allies, Turkish Government messages excepted.

XIII.—Prohibition to destroy any naval, military, or commercial material.

XIV.—Facilities to be given for the purchase of coal and oil fuel, and naval material from Turkish sources after the requirements of the country have been met. None of the above material to be exported.

XV.—Allied Control Officers to be placed on all railways, including such portions of the Trans-Caucasian Railways as are now under Turkish control, which must be placed at the free and complete disposal of the Allied authorities, due consideration being given to the

* Temperley, *Peace Conference,* 1: 495-97.

needs of the population. This clause to include Allied occupation of Batoum. Turkey will raise no objection to the occupation of Baku by the Allies.

XVI.—Surrender of all garrisons in Hedjaz, Assir, Yemen, Syria, and Mesopotamia to the nearest Allied Commander; and the withdrawal of troops from Cilicia, except those necessary to maintain order, as will be determined under Clause V.

XVII.—Surrender of all Turkish officers in Tripolitania and Cyrenaica to the nearest Italian garrison. Turkey guarantees to stop supplies and communication with these officers if they do not obey the order to surrender.

XVIII.—Surrender of all ports occupied in Tripolitania and Cyrenaica, including Misurata, to the nearest Allied garrison.

XIX.—All Germans and Austrians, naval, military, and civilian, to be evacuated within one month from the Turkish dominions: those in remote districts to be evacuated as soon after as may be possible.

XX.—The compliance with such orders as may be conveyed for the disposal of the equipment, arms, and ammunition, including transport, of that portion of the Turkish Army which is demobilized under Clause V.

XXI.—An Allied representative to be attached to the Turkish Ministry of Supplies in order to safeguard Allied interests. This representative is to be furnished with all information necessary for this purpose.

XXII.—Turkish prisoners to be kept at the disposal of the Allied Powers. The release of Turkish civilian prisoners over military age to be considered.

XXIII.—Obligation on the part of Turkey to cease all relations with the Central Powers.

XXIV.—In case of disorder in the six Armenian vilayets, the Allies reserve to themselves the right to occupy any part of them.

XXV.—Hostilities between the Allies and Turkey shall cease from noon, local time, on Thursday, 31st October, 1918.

Signed in duplicate on board His Britannic Majesty's Ship *Agamemnon*, at Port Mudros, Lemnos, the 30th October, 1918.

(Signed)   ARTHUR CALTHORPE
HUSSEIN RAOUF
RECHAD HIKMET
SAADULLAH

APPENDIX B

THE SYKES-PICOT AGREEMENT *

Letter from Sir Edward Grey to M. Cambon

(Secret.)

FOREIGN OFFICE, May 16, 1916

Your Excellency,

I have the honour to acknowledge the receipt of your Excellency's note of the 9th instant, stating that the French Government accept the limits of a future Arab State, or Confederation of States, and of those parts of Syria where French interests predominate, together with certain conditions attached thereto, such as they result from recent discussions in London and Petrograd on the subject.

I have the honour to inform your Excellency in reply that the acceptance of the whole project, as it now stands, will involve the abdication of considerable British interests, but, since His Majesty's Government recognise the advantage to the general cause of the Allies entailed in producing a more favourable internal political situation in Turkey, they are ready to accept the arrangement now arrived at, provided that the co-operation of the Arabs is secured, and that the Arabs fulfill the conditions and obtain the towns of Homs, Hama, Damascus, and Aleppo.

It is accordingly understood between the French and British Governments—

1. That France and Great Britain are prepared to recognise and uphold an independent Arab State or a Confederation of Arab States in the areas (A) and (B) marked on the annexed map, under the suzerainty of an Arab chief. That in area (A) France, and in area (B) Great Britain, shall have priority of right of enterprise and local loans. That in area (A) France, and in area (B) Great Britain shall alone supply advisers or foreign functionaries at the request of the Arab State or Confederation of Arab States.

2. That in the blue area France, and in the red area Great Britain, shall be allowed to establish such direct or indirect administration or control as they desire and as they may think fit to arrange with the Arab State or Confederation of Arab States.

3. That in the brown area there shall be established an international administration, the form of which is to be decided upon after consultation with Russia, and subsequently in consultation with the other Allies, and the representatives of the Shereef of Mecca.

4. That Great Britain be accorded (1) the ports of Haifa and Acre, (2) guarantee of a given supply of water from the Tigris and Euphrates in area (A) for area (B). His Majesty's Government, on their part, undertake that they will at no time enter into negotiations for the cession of Cyprus to any third Power without the previous consent of the French Government.

* *Br. Doc.*, 4: 245-47.

5. That Alexandretta shall be a free port as regards the trade of the British Empire, and that there shall be no discrimination in port charges or facilities as regards British shipping and British goods; that there shall be freedom of transit for British goods through Alexandretta and by railway through the blue area, whether those goods are intended for or originate in the red area, or (B) area, or area (A); and there shall be no discrimination, direct or indirect, against British goods on any railway or against British goods or ships at any port serving the areas mentioned.

That Haifa shall be a free port as regards the trade of France, her dominions and protectorates, and there shall be no discrimination in port charges or facilities as regards French shipping and French goods. There shall be freedom of transit for French goods through Haifa and by the British railway through the brown area, whether those goods are intended for or originate in the blue area, area (A), or area (B), and there shall be no discrimination, direct or indirect, against French goods on any railway, or against French goods or ships at any port serving the areas mentioned.

6. That in area (A) the Bagdad Railway shall not be extended southwards beyond Mosul, and in area (B) northwards beyond Samarra, until a railway connecting Bagdad with Aleppo via the Euphrates Valley has been completed, and then only with the concurrence of the two Governments.

7. That Great Britain has the right to build, administer, and be sole owner of a railway connecting Haifa with area (B), and shall have a perpetual right to transport troops along such a line at all times.

It is to be understood by both Governments that this railway is to facilitate the connexion of Bagdad with Haifa by rail, and it is further understood that, if the engineering difficulties and expense entailed by keeping this connecting line in the brown area only make the project unfeasible, that the French Government shall be prepared to consider that the line in question may also traverse the polygon Banias-Keis Marib-Salkhad Tell Otsda-Mesmie before reaching area (B).

8. For a period of twenty years the existing Turkish customs tariff shall remain in force throughout the whole of the blue and red areas, as well as in areas (A) and (B), and no increase in the rates of duty or conversion from *ad valorem* to specific rates shall be made except by agreement between the two powers.

There shall be no interior customs barriers between any of the above-mentioned areas. The customs duties leviable on goods destined for the interior shall be collected at the port of entry and handed over to the administration of the area of designation.

9. It shall be agreed that the French Government will at no time enter into any negotiations for the cession of their rights and will not cede such rights in the blue area to any third Power, except the Arab State or Confederation of Arab States, without the previous agreement of His Majesty's Government, who, on their part, will give a similar undertaking to the French Government regarding the red area.

10. The British and French Governments, as the protectors of the Arab State, shall agree that they will not themselves acquire and will not consent to a third Power acquiring territorial possessions in the Arabian peninsula, nor consent to a third Power installing a naval base either on the east coast, or on the islands, of the Red Sea. This, however, shall not prevent such adjustment of the Aden frontier as may be necessary in consequence of recent Turkish aggression.

11. The negotiations with the Arabs as to the boundaries of the Arab State or Confederation of Arab States shall be continued through the same channel as heretofore on behalf of the two Powers.

12. It is agreed that measures to control the importation of arms into the Arab territories will be considered by the two Governments.

I have further the honour to state that, in order to make the agreement complete, His Majesty's Government are proposing to the Russian Government to exchange notes analogous to those exchanged by the latter and your Excellency's Government on the 26th April last. Copies of these notes will be communicated to our Excellency as soon as exchanged.

I would also venture to remind your Excellency that the conclusion of the present agreement raises, for practical consideration, the question of the claims of Italy to a share in any partition or rearrangement of Turkey in Asia, as formulated in article 9 of the agreement of the 26th April, 1915, between Italy and the Allies.

His Majesty's Government further consider that the Japanese Government should be informed of the arrangements now concluded.

I have, &c.
E. GREY

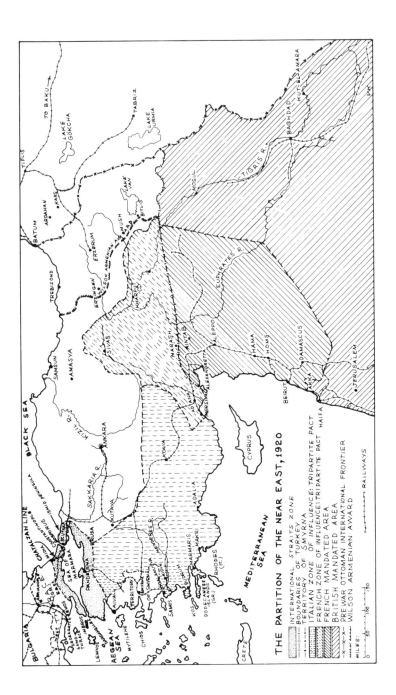

THE PARTITION OF THE NEAR EAST, 1920

INTERNATIONAL STRAITS ZONE
BOUNDARIES OF TURKEY
TERRITORY OF SMYRNA
ITALIAN ZONE OF INFLUENCE: TRIPARTITE PACT
FRENCH ZONE OF INFLUENCE: TRIPARTITE PACT
FRENCH MANDATED AREA
BRITISH MANDATED AREA
PRE-WAR OTTOMAN INTERNATIONAL FRONTIER
WILSON ARMENIAN AWARD
RAILWAYS

MILES:
0   50   100   150

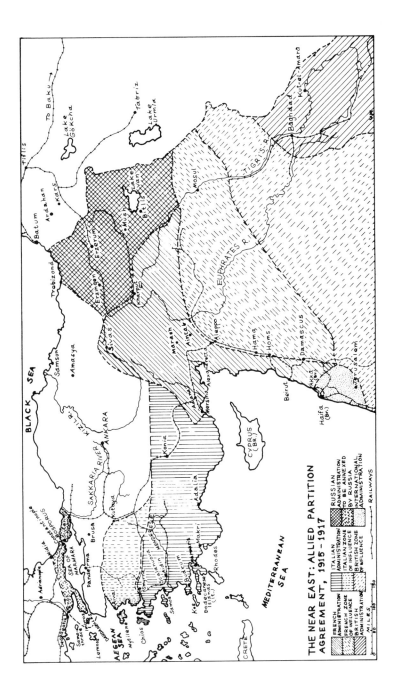

THE NEAR EAST: ALLIED PARTITION
AGREEMENT, 1915-1917

FRENCH
ADMINISTRATION

FRENCH ZONE
OF INFLUENCE

BRITISH
ADMINISTRATION

BRITISH ZONE
OF INFLUENCE

ITALIAN
ADMINISTRATION

ITALIAN ZONE
OF INFLUENCE

RUSSIAN
ADMINISTRATION

AREA TO BE ANNEXED
BY RUSSIA

INTERNATIONAL
ADMINISTRATION

RAILWAYS

MILES
0   50   100   150

BIBLIOGRAPHY

Documents and Official Sources

Armenia. *The Armenian Question Before the Peace Conference: A memorandum presented officially by the representatives of Armenia to the Peace Conference at Versailles on February 26, 1919.* New York, 1919.

L'Arménie et la question Arménienne avant, pendant et depuis la guerre. Paris, 1922. Contains documents aimed at showing how committed the Allies were to a separate Armenia, and that Armenia was for a time an existing, functioning state.

Bulgaria. Delegation to the Peace Conference. *Western Thrace; Eastern Thrace,* n.p., n.d.

Carnegie Endowment for International Peace. *The Treaties of Peace, 1919-1923.* 2 vols. New York, 1924. Volume 2 contains the text of the Treaty of Sèvres.

Dickenson, G. Lowes. *Documents and Statements Relating to Peace Proposals and War Aims, December, 1916-November, 1918.* New York, 1919.

Egypt. Delegation to the Peace Conference. *Official Correspondence, November 11, 1918-July 14, 1919.* Paris, 1919. The Egyptian White Book. Egypt was never allowed to present its claims before the Peace Conference.

———. Delegation to the Peace Conference. *Les Revendications Nationales Égyptiennes.* Paris, 1919.

Eudin, Xenia J., and Robert C. North. *Soviet Russia and the East, 1920-1927—A Documentary Survey.* Stanford, 1957.

France. *Haut Commissariat de la république française en Syrie et au Liban, La Syrie et le Liban en 1922.* Paris, 1922.

———. *Journal Officiel, Débats parlementaires, Chambre des Députés, 1918-1925.*

———. *Journal officiel, Débats parlementaires. Sénat,* April 29, 1920.

Giannini, Amedeo. *I Documenti Diplomatica della Pace Orientale.* Rome, n.d.

———. *I Documenti per la Storia della Pace Orientale, 1915-1932.* Rome, 1933. Contains text of Saint Jean de Maurienne and Tittoni-Venizelos Agreements, as well as the five minor agreements signed along with the main treaty at Sèvres in August, 1920.

Great Britain. Admiralty, Intelligence Division, Geographical Section. *Handbook of Turkey in Europe.* London, 1920.

————. Admiralty, Intelligence Division, Geographical Section. *Manual on the Turanians and Pan-Turanianism.* London, 1920.

————. Cabinet Papers, 1918-1920. Public Record Office. Cab. 21, 23, 24, 25, 27, 28, 29. A source of inestimable value, basic to this study.

————. Foreign Office. Confidential Prints, Eastern Affairs, 1919-1920. Public Record Office. F.O. 406/41-44.

————. Foreign Office. General Correspondence, 1920. Public Record Office, F.O. 371.

————. Foreign Office, Historical Section. *Handbooks prepared under the direction of the Historical Section of the Foreign Office.* London, 1920. No. 15, "The Eastern Question"; no. 16, "Turkey in Europe"; no. 17, "Albania"; no. 57, "Mohammedan History"; no. 58, "Turkey in Asia"; no. 59, "Anatolia"; no. 60, "Syria and Palestine"; no. 61, "Arabia"; no. 62, "Armenia and Kurdistan"; no. 63, "Mesopotamia"; no. 64, "Islands of the Northern and Eastern Aegean"; no. 65, "Cyprus"; no. 66, "France and the Levant"; no. 76, "Persian Gulf"; no. 162, "Zionism."

————. Foreign Office. Peace Conference of 1919-1920: British Delegation Correspondence. Public Record Office. F.O. 608. A mammoth collection, of prime importance for this study. Includes all dispatches from the Near East that were forwarded from the Foreign Office to the Peace Delegation.

————. Foreign Office. Peace Conference of 1919-1920. Public Record Office, F.O. 373, Handbooks, 1918-1919; F.O. 374, Acts of the Conferences.

————. *Parliamentary Debates,* Commons, 5th series. London, 1909-.

————. *Parliamentary Debates,* House of Lords, 5th series. London, 1909-.

————. *Parliamentary Papers, 1920,* "Agreement between France, Russia, Great Britain and Italy. Signed at London, April 26, 1915." Command 671. London, 1920.

————. *Parliamentary Papers, 1920.* "Correspondence relating to the Adriatic Question." Command 586. London, 1920.

————. *Parliamentary Papers, 1920.* "Memorandum of Agreement (San Remo, April 24, 1920) between M. Phillippe Berthelot and Prof. Sir John Cadman." Command 675. London, 1920.

————. *Parliamentary Papers, 1920.* "Treaty between the principle Allies and associated powers and Greece. Signed at Sèvres, August 10, 1920." Command 960. London, 1920.

————. *Parliamentary Papers, 1920.* "Treaty of Peace with Turkey, Signed at Sèvres, August 10, 1920." Command 964. London, 1920.

————. *Parliamentary Papers, 1920.* "Tripartite agreement between the British Empire, France and Italy respecting Anatolia. Signed at Sèvres, August 10, 1920." Command 963. London, 1920.

————. *Parliamentary Papers, 1921.* "Correspondence between H. M. Government and the United States Respecting Economic Rights in the Mandated Territories." Command 1226. London, 1921.

————. *Parliamentary Papers, 1921.* "Draft Mandates for Mesopotamia and Palestine as Submitted for the Approval of the League of Nations." Command 1176. London, 1921.

————. *Parliamentary Papers, 1921.* "Franco-British Convention, December 23, 1920, on Certain Points Connected with the Mandates for Syria and the Lebanon, Palestine and Mesopotamia." Command 1195. London, 1921.

————. *Parliamentary Papers, 1921.* "Treaty between the Allied Powers and Greece relative to Thrace. Signed at Sèvres, August 10, 1920." Command 1390. London, 1921.

————. *Parliamentary Papers, 1939.* "Correspondence between Sir Henry McMahon, His Majesty's High Commissioner at Cairo, and the Sherif Hussein of Mecca, July, 1915-March, 1916." Command 5957. London, 1939.

Parliamentary Papers, 1939. "Report of a Committee set up to consider certain correspondence which took place in the years 1915 and 1916 between Sir Henry McMahon (His Majesty's High Commissioner in Egypt) and the Sherif of Mecca in 1915 and 1916." Command 5974. London, 1939.

―――. *Parliamentary Papers, 1939.* "Statements Made on Behalf of His Majesty's Government During the Year 1918 in Regard to the Future Status of Certain Parts of the Ottoman Empire." Command, 5964. London, 1939. Contains Hogarth Declaration, Declaration to the Seven, and the Allenby Pledge.

The Greek White Book. American Hellenic Society, no. 5 and 9. New York, 1919.

Hurewitz, Jacob C. *Diplomacy in the Near and Middle East, A Documentary Record, 1535-1956.* 2 vols. New York, 1956.

India. Superintendent of Government Printing. *India in 1919.* Calcutta, 1920.

―――. Superintendent of Government Printing. *India in 1920.* Calcutta, 1921.

―――. Superintendent of Government Printing. *India in 1921-22.* Calcutta, 1922.

Israel, Fred L., ed. *Major Peace Treaties of Modern History, 1648-1967.* 4 vols. New York, 1967. Volume 3 contains the Treaty of Sèvres.

Italy. Ministere degli Affari Esteri. *I documenti diplomatici italiani, Sesta serie.* Rome, 1956. Unfortunately only one volume in this series of this highly valuable collection has as yet been published. It covers December, 1918–January, 1919.

Kemal, Mustapha Pasha. *A Speech Delivered by Ghazi Mustapha Kemal, President of the Turkish Republic, October, 1927.* Leipzig, 1929. A speech that took several days to complete and constitutes Kemal's account of the Turkish revolution.

―――. *Die Dokumente zur Rede vom 15 bis 20 Oktober, 1927.* Leipzig, n.d. Contains the text of the documents referred to by Kemal in his marathon speech. Documents are in French.

"The King-Crane Report on the Near East." *Editor and Publisher* 55 (December 2, 1922):1-27.

League of Nations. *Official Journal, 1920.* Geneva, 1921.

Lloyd George, David. *British War Aims; Statement by the Right Honorable David Lloyd George, January 5, 1918, Authorized Version as Published by the British Government.* New York, n.d.

Paris Peace Conference. American Commission to Negotiate Peace. *Principal Declarations Respecting Terms of Peace by President Wilson and the Secretary of State.* Paris, 1919.

―――. *Conference des préliminaires de paix. Composition et fonctionnement, 1er avril, 1919.* Paris, 1919.

―――. *Fonctionnement de la conférence, 1er octobre, 1919.* Paris, 1919.

―――. *La Paix de Versailles.* 12 vols. Paris, 1930. Collection of documents, including the minutes of various committees. Not useful for the topic under consideration.

"The Secret Treaty Dividing Turkey." *Nation* 3 (December, 1920):697-99. Text of the Tripartite Pact signed at Sèvres, with a good map.

Tittoni, T., and V. Scialoja. *"L'Italia alla Conferenza della Pace, Discorsi et Documenti.* Rome, 1921. Speeches of the two before the Chamber of Deputies and the Senate.

Turkey. Delegation to the Peace Conference. *Observations Générales présentées par la Délégation Ottomane à la Conference de la Paix.* n.p., n.d. A statement bitterly attacking most of the provisions of the proposed treaty.

Turquie. *Ministère des affaires étrangères, Le livre rouge. La question de Mossoul de la signature du traité d'armistice de Moudros (30 Octobre, 1918 au 1 Mars, 1925).* Constantinople, 1925. Contains British-Turk correspondence concerning the initial British occupation of Mosul and subsequent British dealings with the Kurds.

"The United States and the Armenian Mandate: Message of President Wilson to the Congress, May 24, 1920," *International Conciliation* 151 (June, 1920):271–74.

United States Congress, *Congressional Record.* 65th Cong., 2d sess., 1918. Vol. 56.

United States. Department of State. Records Relating to the Internal Affairs of Turkey, 1910–1929. National Archives, Washington, D.C. Political Affairs, 867.00.

———. Department of State. Papers of the American Commission to Negotiate Peace. National Archives, Washington, D.C. Because of the limited American participation in Near East negotiations, this collection proved far less rewarding than its British counterpart.

———. Department of State. *Papers Relating to the Foreign Relations of the United State, 1919.* 2 vols. Washington. 1934.

———. Department of State. *Papers Relating to the Foreign Relations of the United States, 1920.* 3 vols. Washington, 1935–1936.

———. Department of State. *Papers Relating to the Foreign Relations of the United States, The Lansing Papers, 1914–1920.* 2 vols. Washington, 1939–40.

———. Department of State. *Papers Relating to the Foreign Relations of the United States, The Paris Peace Conference, 1919.* 13 vols. Washington, 1942–47. A documentary record of great value, including the official minutes of the Council of Ten and the Council of Four.

Venizelos, Eleutherios. *Greece Before the Peace Congress of 1919: A Memorandum Dealing with the Rights of Greece, Submitted by Eleutherios Venizelos.* American Hellenic Society, no. 7. New York, 1919.

Woodward, E. L., and R. Butler, eds. *Documents on British Foreign Policy, 1919–1939,* Series 1. London, 1947–. An indispensable documentary collection, containing much diplomatic correspondence relative to the Near East, as well as the minutes of the December, 1919, Anglo-French discussions and the London, San Remo, and Boulogne conferences.

Personal Papers, Memoirs and Diaries

Abdullah, King. *Memoirs of King Abdullah of Trans-Jordan.* London, 1950.

Adivar, Halidé Edib. *The Turkish Ordeal.* New York, 1928.

Aharonian, Avetis. "From Sardarapat to Sèvres and Lausanne; a political diary." *Armenian Review* 15 (Fall, 1962)–17 (Spring, 1964). The installments in these issues deal with the period examined in this study.

———. "Republic of Armenia: Memorandum of Avetis Aharonian." *Nation* 108 (April 5, 1919):526–27.

Ahmed Djemal Pasha. *Memoirs of a Turkish Statesman, 1913–1919.* New York, 1922.

Armstrong, Harold C. *Turkey in Travail.* London, 1926. Memoirs.

Baker, Ray S., and William E. Dodd. *The Public Papers of Woodrow Wilson.* 3 vols. New York, 1927.

Balfour, Arthur J. Papers. On deposit in the British Museum. London, England.

———. Private Papers. On deposit in the Foreign Office archives in the Public Record Office. F.O. 800/26.

Barrère, Camille. "La Conférence de San Remo." *Revue des deux Mondes* 108 (August 1938):510–15.

Beadon, Roger H. *Some Memories of the Peace Conference.* London, 1933.

Beer, George L. Diary at the Paris Peace Conference, December, 1918–August, 1919. On deposit in Butler Library, Columbia University. New York, New York.

Bell, Gertrude L. *The Letters of Gertrude Bell.* Edited by Lady Bell. 2 vols. London, 1927.

Berenger, Henry, *Le Petrole et la France.* Paris, 1920. Unfortunately, deals almost exclusively with domestic matters. Admits that the "most instructive" chapter would be one on French diplomacy regarding petroleum since the armistice, but claims publication at that time would be premature.

Bertie, Lord Francis. *The Diary of Lord Bertie.* London, 1924.

Bliss, General Tasker. Papers. On deposit in the Library of Congress. Washington, D.C.

Bonar Law, A. Papers. On deposit in the Beaverbrook Library. London, England.

Bonsal, Stephen. *Suitors and Suppliants: The Little Nations at Versailles.* New York, 1946.

———. *Unfinished Business.* Garden City, New York, 1944.

Bowman, Humphrey E. *Middle East Window.* New York, 1942.

Bristol, Admiral Mark. Papers. On deposit in the Library of Congress. Washington, D.C.

Buckler, William L. Papers. On deposit in Sterling Memorial Library, Yale University. New Haven, Connecticut.

Burgoyne, Elizabeth, ed. *Gertrude Bell: From her Personal Papers, 1914–1926.* London, 1961.

Callwell, C. E. *Field Marshal Sir Henry Wilson, His Life and Diaries,* 2 vols. New York, 1927. A valuable contemporary source.

Cambon, Paul, *Correspondance, 1870–1924.* Edited by Henri Cambon. 3 vols. Paris, 1946. Extremely valuable collection of letters written by the French ambassador in London.

Catroux, Georges. *Deux Missions en Moyen-Orient (1919–1922).* Paris, 1958.

Cecil, Viscount Robert. *A Great Experiment.* New York, 1941. Cecil's autobiography, unfortunately of little use.

Cecil of Chelwood, Viscount E. A. Robert. Papers. On deposit in the British Museum. London, England.

Charles-Roux, François. *Souvenirs diplomatique; une grande ambassade à Rome, 1919–1925.* Paris, 1961.

Churchill, Winston S. *The World Crisis: The Aftermath, 1918–1928.* New York, 1929. Interesting comments by one of the leaders of British opposition to both Greek claims and the Turkish treaty.

Clemenceau, Georges. *Discours de paix, publiés par la Societé des amis de Clemenceau.* Paris, 1938.

———. *Grandeur and Misery of Victory,* New York, 1930.

Crespi, Silvio, *Alla Defesa d'Italia in Guerra e a Versailles, Diario, 1917–1919.* Milan, 1937.

Crowe, Sir Eyre. Private Papers. On deposit in the Foreign Archives in the Public Record Office. F.O. 800/243. Of little value for the purposes of this work.

Curzon of Kedleston, Lord George Nathaniel. Correspondence and Papers. On deposit in the Commonwealth Relations Office, India Office Library. Vols. 594–97 contain the War Cabinet Papers, 1919. Curzon's personal papers for the peace conference period were not available to the public in 1967.

———. Private Papers. On deposit in the Foreign Office Archives of the Public Record Office. F.O. 800/151. Of minimal value for the purposes of this study.

D'Abernon, Edgar V. *The Diary of an Ambassador, Viscount D'Abernon.* 3 vols. New York, 1929–30.

Day, Clive. Papers. On deposit in Sterling Memorial Library, Yale University. New Haven, Connecticut.

Edib, Halidé. See Adivar, Halidé Edib.

Edmonds, C. John. *Kurds, Turks and Arabs.* London, 1957.

Garnett, David. *The Letters of T. E. Lawrence.* New York, 1939.

Gates, Caleb F. *Not to me Only.* Princeton, N.J., 1940.

Georges-Gaulis, Berthe. *La Nouvelle Turquie.* Paris, 1924.

Giolitti, Giovanni. *Memoirs of My Life.* London, 1923.

Grew, Joseph C. Papers. On deposit in Houghton Library, Harvard University. Cambridge, Massachusetts. Of little value.

———. *Turbulent Era: A Diplomatic Record of Forty Years.* 2 vols. New York, 1952.

Hancock, W. K., and Jean Van Der Poel, eds. *Selections from the Smuts Papers.* 4 vols. Cambridge, 1966. Volume 4 covers November, 1918–August, 1919.

Hankey, Lord Maurice P. *The Supreme Control at the Paris Peace Conference 1919: A Commentary.* London, 1963. Unfortunately tends heavily toward being just a synopsis of the official minutes of the Conference.

Harbord, James G. *Leaves from a War Diary.* New York, 1925. Ends with the armistice.

Hardinge of Penhurst, Lord Charles H. *Old Diplomacy: The Reminiscences of Lord Hardinge of Penhurst Covering the Years 1880–1924.* London, 1947.

Hohler, Sir Thomas B. *Diplomatic Petrel.* London, 1942. Ends with Armistice Day, 1918, and his appointment to Constantinople.

Hoover, Herbert C. *Memoirs,* 3 vols. New York, 1951–52. Contains a brief discussion of Hoover's work in the Armenian relief program.

———. *The Ordeal of Woodrow Wilson.* New York, 1958. Primarily a memoir of Hoover's own connection with Wilson during and after the Peace Conference.

House, Edward M. Papers. On deposit in Sterling Memorial Library. Yale University. New Haven, Connecticut. A well-indexed, large collection of material, including much on the first six months of the Peace Conference. In addition to official documents the collection includes House's diary and personal correspondence.

Jones, Thomas, *Whitehall Diary.* Edited by Keith Middlemas. New York, 1969–. Vol. 1, *1916–1925.*

Lansing, Robert. Diary on deposit in Library of Congress. Washington, D.C. of little value in terms of this study.

———. *The Peace Negotiations: A Personal Narrative.* Boston, 1921.

Lawrence, Thomas E. *The Home Letters of T. E. Lawrence and His Brothers.* Oxford, 1954.

———. *Revolt in the Desert.* London, 1927.

———. *Seven Pillars of Wisdom.* London, 1935.

———. *T. E. Lawrence to his Biographer, Liddell-Hart.* New York, 1938.

———. *T. E. Lawrence to his Biographer, Robert Graves.* New York, 1938.

Lloyd George, David. Papers. On deposit in the Beaverbrook Library. London, England. A large, magnificently indexed collection including both official documents and personal correspondence.

———. *The Truth About the Peace Treaties.* 2 vols., (pages numbered consecutively). London, 1938. A distinct apologia, yet quite valuable.

———. *War Memoirs.* 6 vols. Boston, 1933–37.

Luke, Sir Harry. *Cities and Men: An Autobiography.* 2 vols. London, 1953.

Malcolm, Sir Ian. *Lord Balfour, A Memory.* London, 1930.

Mantoux, Paul. *Les Délibérations du Conseil des Quatre (24 mars – 28 juin, 1919).* 2 vols. Paris, 1955. Contains records of a number of meetings of the Council of Four at which no official minutes were kept. Based on notes taken by the chief interpreter, the actual words of the participants are recorded, and much of value that fails to appear in the official minutes, especially differences of opinion, can be found.

Marescotti, Count Luigi A. *Guerra diplomatica; ricordi e frammenti di diario (1914–1919)*. Milan, 1936. Contains records of Council of Four meetings of April 17–24 and May 7–June 2.

———. *Nouvi ricordi e frammenti di diario*. Milan, 1938. Contains minutes of Council of Four meetings in June, 1919. Also has memoranda and documents on the proceedings leading to the Saint Jean de Maurienne Agreement.

Meinertzhagen, Richard. *Middle East Diary, 1917–1956*. London, 1959.

Mezes, Sidney. Papers. On deposit in Butler Library, Columbia University, New York, New York. Deals entirely with the Inquiry period, 1917–18.

Miller, David H. *My Diary at the Conference of Paris, with Documents*. 21 vols. New York, 1928. An extensive and highly valuable collection of miscellaneous documents relating to the work of the Peace Conference.

Mordacq, Jean J., *Le Ministère Clemenceau*, 4 vols. Paris, 1930–31.

Nicolson, Harold, *Peacemaking, 1919*. Boston, 1933. An important diary written by a member of the Greek Committee and an advisor to the Big Four on the question of the division of European and Anatolian Turkey.

Nitti, Francesco. *The Wreck of Europe*. Indianapolis, 1922.

Orlando, Vittorio E. *Memorie, 1915–1919*. Edited by R. Mosca. Milan, 1960. Contains general reminiscences and comments on the Peace Conference.

Patrick, Mary M. *Under Five Sultans*. New York, 1929.

Pech, Edgar. *Les Alliés et Turquie*. Paris, 1925. Day-by-day diary of a Frenchman in Constantinople. Objective treatment.

Philby, Harry St. J. B. *Arabian Days*. London, 1948.

Pichon, Jean. *Sur la Route des Indes*. Paris, 1932. Good discussion of some of the Armenian massacres.

Poincaré, Raymond. *Au Service de la France: neuf années de souvenirs*. 10 vols. Paris, 1926. Volume 10 has a brief discussion concerning Anglo-French friction over the Turkish armistice, and early Greek ambitions to land at Smyrna.

Polk, Frank L. Papers. On deposit in Sterling Memorial Library, Yale University. New Haven, Connecticut. Particularly valuable for material relevant to the negotiations concerning Thrace in the summer of 1919.

Rawlinson, Sir Alfred. *Adventures in the Near East, 1918–1922*. New York, 1924. Sheds light on British attempts to sound out Kemal in the fall of 1919.

Riddell, Baron George A. *Lord Riddell's Intimate Diary of the Peace Conference and After, 1918–1923*. New York, 1934.

Rodd, Sir James Rennell. *Social and Diplomatic Memories, 1884–1919*. London, 1922–25.

Ryan, Sir Andrew. *The Last of the Dragomans*. London, 1951. Memoirs of a member of the British High Commission in Constantinople.

Samuel, Viscount Herbert L. *Grooves of change, a book of Memoirs by the Rt. Hon. Viscount Samuel*. New York, 1946.

Seymour, Charles. *The Intimate Papers of Colonel House*. 4 vols. Boston, 1926. A valuable collection based upon Seymour's work in the House Papers currently on deposit at Yale University.

———. *Letters from the Paris Peace Conference*. Edited by H. B. Whiteman, Jr. New Haven, Conn., 1965.

———. Papers. On deposit in Sterling Memorial Library, Yale University. New Haven, Connecticut.

Sforza, Count Carlo. *Diplomatic Europe Since the Treaty of Versailles*. New Haven, Conn., 1928.

———. *Makers of Modern Europe.* Indianapolis, 1930. Was high commissioner in Constantinople. Admits contacts with and sympathy for Kemalist forces from the time the resistance was organized. A study of leading personalities, full of first person reminiscences.

Shotwell, James T. *At the Paris Peace Conference.* New York, 1937.

———. *Autobiography.* Indianapolis, 1961. Of little value for the purposes of this study.

———. Papers. On deposit in Butler Library, Columbia University. New York, New York.

Sonnino, Baron Sidney. Papers relating to World War I in the Archive of Baron Sidney Sonnino. Ann Arbor, Mich.: University Microfilms, 1969. Reels 17-24, 41-54. A vast and important collection, primarily of official Italian State telegrams, but including in the last eight reels a miscellaneous collection of papers, correspondence, and memoranda.

Steed, H. Wickham. *Through Thirty Years, 1892-1922, A Personal Narrative,* 2 vols. London, 1924. Interesting sidelights provided by a man who at the time of the Peace Conference was editor of the *Times* (London).

Storrs, Sir Ronald. *Orientations.* London, 1937.

Thompson, Charles T. *The Peace Conference Day by Day: A Presidential Pilgrimage leading to the Discovery of Europe.* New York, 1920.

Townshend, Sir Charles V. F. *My Campaign.* New York, 1920.

Vansittart, Lord Robert. *The Mist Procession: The Autobiography of Lord Vansittart.* London, 1958.

Weizmann, Chaim. *Trial and Error.* 2 vols. Philadelphia, 1949.

Westermann, William L. Personal Diary at the Peace Conference in Paris, December, 1918–July, 1919. On deposit in Butler Library, Columbia University. New York, New York. A member of the Greek Committee, Westermann bitterly opposed President Wilson's support of Greek claims in Asia Minor.

Wilson, A. T. *Loyalties, Mesopotamia.* 2 vols. London, 1930–31. Memoirs of the acting civil commissioner for Mesopotamia in 1919-20.

———. Papers. On deposit in the British Museum. London, England.

Wilson, Woodrow. Papers. Series V-A, Peace Conference, 1919. On deposit in the Library of Congress. Washington, D.C. Of great general use.

Wiseman, Sir William. Papers. On deposit in Sterling Memorial Library, Yale University. New Haven, Connecticut.

Yale, William. Papers. On deposit in Sterling Memorial Library, Yale University. New Haven, Connecticut. Of particular interest is a report written by Yale concerning his attempt to negotiate a Near East settlement in the early fall of 1919.

Yalmin, Ahmed Emin. *Turkey in My Time.* Norman, Oklahoma, 1956. Memoirs of a Turkish journalist.

Young, Sir Hubert. *The Independent Arab.* London, 1933.

Biographies

Adam, George. *The Tiger, Georges Clemenceau, 1841-1929.* New York, 1930.

Aldington, Richard. *Lawrence of Arabia, A Biographical Enquiry.* London, 1955. An attempt to prove that Lawrence was little more than a humbug and a fake.

Armstrong, Harold C. *Grey Wolf, Mustafa Kemal: An Intimate Study of a Dictator.* London, 1932.

Azan, Paul J. *Franchet d'Esperey.* Paris, 1949.

Baker, Ray S. *Woodrow Wilson and World Settlement.* 3 vols. Garden City, New York, 1923. Volume 3 contains a collection of documents.

Beaverbrook, William M. Aitken, Baron. *The Decline and Fall of Lloyd George.* London, 1963.

Benoist-Méchin, Jacques. *Le Loup et le léopard, Mustapha Kemal; ou, La Mort d'un empire.* Paris, 1954.

Bruun, Geoffrey. *Clemenceau.* Cambridge, Mass., 1943. Some information regarding the presidential election, nothing regarding the Eastern Question.

Butler, James R. M. *Lord Lothian, Philip Kerr, 1882–1940.* London, 1960.

Collier, Basil. *Brasshat: A Biography of Field-Marshal Sir Henry Wilson.* London, 1961.

"Un Diplomate." *Paul Cambon, Ambassadeur de France, 1843–1924.* Paris, 1937.

Dugdale, Blanche. *Arthur James Balfour.* 2 vols. New York, 1937. Contains many documents, but few pertaining to the Near East settlement. Of particular interest is Balfour's avowal that Wilson was told early of the existence and content of the secret treaties.

Edwards, H. Hugh. *David Lloyd George, The Man and the Statesman.* 2 vols. New York, 1929.

Erlanger, Philippe. *Clemenceau.* Paris, 1968.

Eubank, Keith. *Paul Cambon: Master Diplomatist.* Norman, Oklahoma, 1960.

Garrety, John A. *Henry Cabot Lodge: A Biography.* New York, 1953.

Gibbons, Herbert A. *Venizelos.* Boston, 1920.

Graves, Robert. *Lawrence and the Arabian Adventure.* New York, 1928.

Huddleston, Sisley. *Poincaré: A Biographical Portrait.* London, 1924.

Jackson, John H. *Clemenceau and the Third Republic.* New York, 1948.

Jones, Thomas. *Lloyd George.* Cambridge, Mass., 1951.

Kinross, Lord. *Ataturk: A Biography of Mustafa Kemal, Father of Modern Turkey.* New York, 1965.

Lansing, Robert. Diary on deposit in Library of Congress. Washington, D.C. of little value character studies of selected individuals with whom the author was in close contact. Venizelos is included among the "others."

Leslie, Shane. *Mark Sykes, His Life and Letters.* London, 1923.

Liddell-Hart, Basil H. *T. E. Lawrence, In Arabia and After.* London, 1943.

Lord, John. *Duty, Honor, Empire: The Life and Times of Colonel Richard Meinertzhagen.* New York, 1970.

Martet, Jean. *Georges Clemenceau.* New York, 1930.

Mikusch, Dagobert von. *Mustapha Kemal: Between Europe and Asia.* New York, 1931.

Monnerville, Gaston. *Clemenceau.* Paris, 1968.

Mosley, Leonard. *The Glorious Fault: The Life of Lord Curzon.* New York, 1960.

Mousa, Suleiman. *T. E. Lawrence; an Arab View.* London, 1966.

Nevins, Allan. *Henry White: Thirty Years of American Diplomacy.* New York, 1930. Contains many excerpts from White's correspondence.

Nicolson, Harold. *Curzon: The Last Phase, 1919–1925.* London, 1934. Sympathetic to the Foreign Office and to policies it tried to follow.

Orga, Irfan. *Phoenix Ascendant: The Rise of Modern Turkey.* London, 1958. A generally favorable biography of Kemal.

Orga, Irfan, and Margarite Orga. *Ataturk.* London, 1962.

Owen, Frank. *Tempestuous Journey: Lloyd George, His Life and Times,* New York, 1955.

Palmer, Frederick. *The Life and Letters of Tasker Bliss.* New York, 1934.

Ronaldshay, Earl of. *See* Zetland, Lawrence J.

Spender, Harold. *The Prime Minister, David Lloyd George.* New York, 1920.

Street, Cecil J. C. *Lord Reading.* London, 1928. Brief comment on Indian Moslem agitation concerning Constantinople.

Suarez, Georges. *Briand.* 4 vols. Paris, 1940. Vol. 4, *1916-1918.*

Thomson, Malcolm. *David Lloyd George, The Official Biography.* London, n.d.

Waley, Sir David. *Edwin Montagu, A Memoir and An Account of His Visits to India.* New York, 1964.

―――――. "Life of the Hon. Edwin Samuel Montagu." 2 vols. Typescript. British Commonwealth Relations Office, India Office Library. Contains much material not in the published volume.

Wavell, Sir Archibald P. *Allenby, A Study in Greatness.* 2 vols. London, 1940-44.

Weisgal, Meyer W., and Joel Carmichael, eds. *Chaim Weizmann, A Biography by Several Hands.* New York, 1963.

Young, Kenneth. *Arthur James Balfour; The Happy Life of the Politician, Prime Minister, Statesman and Philosopher, 1848-1930.* London, 1963.

Zetland, Lawrence J., Earl of Ronaldshay. *The Life of Lord Curzon, being the authorized biography of George Nathaniel, Marquess Curzon of Kedleston, K.G.* 3 vols. New York, 1928. The standard work on Lord Curzon. Volume 3 has extensive material on the Near East settlement.

Monographs and General Historical Works

Abbott, George F. *Greece and the Allies, 1914-1922.* London, 1922. Generally anti-Venizelos.

Abelous, Frédéric. *L' Evolution de la Turquie dans ses rapports avec les éstrangères.* Toulousse, 1928.

Adivar, Halidé Edib. *Turkey Faces West: A Turkish View of Recent Changes and Their Origin.* New Haven, Conn., 1930.

Adkisson, Laura M. *Great Britain and the Kemalist Movement for Turkish Independence, 1919-1923.* Ann Arbor, Mich.: University Microfilms, 1958. Should be used with caution.

Adler, Selig. *The Uncertain Giant, 1921-1941: American Foreign Policy Between the Wars.* New York, 1965.

Albin, Pierre. *La Conférence de la Paix, Paris-Versailles, janvier-juin 1919; documents contemporains.* Paris, 1921. Consists of bound index to articles in *Le Monde Nouveau Diplomatique et Economique.*

Albrecht-Carrié, René. *Italy at the Paris Peace Conference.* New York, 1938.

Ancel, J. *Manuel Historique de la Question d'Orient, 1792-1923.* Paris, 1923.

Anderson, Matthew S. *The Eastern Question, 1774-1923.* New York, 1966. The best general survey.

Antonius, George. *The Arab Awakening: The Story of the Arab National Movement.* New York, 1939. Subsequent scholarship indicates it should be used with caution. Still a useful source.

Atamian, Sarkis. *The Armenian Community.* New York, 1955.

Bailey, Thomas A. *Woodrow Wilson and the Lost Peace.* New York, 1944.

Baker, Ray S. *What Wilson Did at Paris.* New York, 1919.

Bardoux, Jacques. *De Paris à Spa*. Paris, 1921. Has an excellent chapter dealing with French and British press and public reaction to the publication of the Turkish peace treaty in May, 1920.

———— *Lloyd George et la France*. Paris, 1923. Anti-Lloyd George, but also critical of French lackadaisical attitudes.

Barton, James L. *Near East Relief, 1915-1930*. New York, 1943.

Bass, John F. *The Peace Tangle*. New York, 1920.

Bassett, John S. *The League of Nations, A Chapter in World Politics*. New York, 1928.

Beer, George L. *African Questions at the Paris Peace Conference*. New York, 1923.

Beloff, Max. *Imperial Sunset*. New York, 1970. Vol. 1, *Britain's Liberal Empire, 1897-1921*.

Berkes, Niyazi. *The Development of Secularism in Turkey*. Montreal, 1964.

Birdsall, Paul. *Versailles, Twenty Years After*. New York, 1941.

Bishop, Donald G. *The Administration of British Foreign Relations*. Syracuse, N.Y., 1961.

Bississo, Saadi. *La Politique Anglo-Sioniste en Palestine*. Paris, 1937.

Black, Cyril E., and Ernst C. Helmreich. *Twentieth Century Europe*. 2d ed. rev. New York, 1959.

Blaisdell, Donald C. *European Financial Control in the Ottoman Empire*. New York, 1929. Good survey of the history of the Ottoman Debt.

Bonnefous, Édouard, *Historie Politique de la Troisième République*. 2d ed. 7 vols. Paris, 1968. Vol. 3, *L'Apres-Guerre, 1919-1924*.

Bourgeois, Émile. *Manuel historique de politique étrangère*. 4 vols. Paris, 1893-1926. Volume 4 pertains to the period under consideration.

Brémond, Édouard. *La Cilicie en 1919-1920*. Paris, 1921.

———— *Le Hedjaz dans la Guerre Mondiale*. Paris, 1931.

Brown, Carrol, and Theodore Ion. *Persecution of the Greeks in Turkey Since the Beginning of the European War*. American Hellenic Society, no. 3, New York, 1918.

Bruneau, André. *La France au Levant*. Paris, 1932. Has text of Gouraud ultimatum to Feisal in July, 1920.

Buell, Raymond L. *Contemporary French Politics*. New York, 1920.

Bujac, Colonel Emile. *Les Campagnes de l'Armée Hellénique, 1918-1922*. Paris, 1930.

Bullard, Sir Reader. *Britain and the Middle East from Earliest Times to 1950*. London, 1951.

Cassavetes, Nicholas J. *The Question of Northern Epirus at the Peace Conference*. New York, 1919. Pro-Greek propaganda.

Chastenet, Jacques. *Cent ans de République*. 9 vols. Paris, 1970. Vol. 5, *Les années d'illusions, 1918-1931*.

Chirol, Sir Valentine. *The Occident and the Orient*. Chicago, 1924.

Cohn, Josef. *Englund und Palästina*. Berlin, 1931.

Coke, Richard. *The Arab's Place in the Sun*. London, 1929.

Costopoulo, Stavro. *L'Empire de l'Orient*. Paris, 1925.

Cumming, Henry H. *Franco-British Rivalry in the Post War Near East*. New York, 1938.

Davenport, E. H., and S. R. Cooke. *The Oil Trusts and Anglo-American Relations*. London, 1923. Good discussion of the organization of the British petroleum executive.

Davison, Roderic, "Turkish Diplomacy from Mudros to Lausanne," In *The Diplomats, 1919-1939*, edited by Gordon A. Craig and Felix Gilbert. Princeton, N.J., 1953.

Delaisi, Francis. *Oil, Its Influence on Politics*. London, 1922.

De la Tramerye, Pierre E. *The World Struggle for Oil*. New York, 1924.

DeNovo, John A. *American Interests and Policies in the Middle East, 1900-1939.* Minneapolis, Minn., 1963. Based on extensive research in documentary and manuscript collections as well as existing secondary sources. An excellent general survey.

Dillon, Emile J. *The Inside Story of the Peace Conference.* New York, 1920.

Driault, Édouard. *La Grand Idée, la Renaissance de l'Hellénisme.* Paris, 1920.

———. *La Question d'Orient depuis ses origins jusqu'à la paix de Sèvres.* Paris, 1926.

Driault, Édouard, and Michel Lheretier. *Histoire diplomatique de la Grèce de 1821 a nos jours.* 5 vols. Paris, 1926. Vol 5, *La Grèce et la grande guerre de la revolution Turque au traite de Lausanne, 1908-1923.* Superceded by documentary collections. Has a good deal on the deliberations of the Committee on Greek Affairs.

Dukagjin, Basrî Bey, of. *Le Monde Oriental et l'Avenir de la Paix.* Paris, 1920.

Earle, Edward M. *Turkey, the Great Powers and the Bagdad Railway.* New York, 1923.

Edib, Halidé. *See* Adivar, Halidé Edib.

ESCO Foundation, *Palestine, A Study of Jewish, Arab and British Policies.* 2 vols. New Haven, Conn., 1947.

Evans, Laurence. *United States Policy and the Partition of Turkey, 1914-1924.* Baltimore, Md., 1965.

Fabre-Luce, Alfred. *La Crise des Alliances.* Paris, 1922. A diatribe against Britain and the weakness of French Policy.

Faulkner, Harold U. *From Versailles to the New Deal.* New Haven, Conn., 1950.

Ferriman, Z. Duckett. *Greece and Tomorrow.* American Hellenic Society, no. 2. New York, 1918.

Fisher, Sidney N. *The Military in the Middle East.* Columbus, Ohio, 1963.

Fitzsimons, M. A. *Empire by Treaty: Britain and the Middle East in the Twentieth Century.* Notre Dame, Ind., 1964.

Frangulis, Antoine F. *La Grèce et la Crise Mondiale.* 2 vols. Paris, 1926. Excellent, though pro-Greek coverage of the question of Greek claims. Anti-Venizelos. Many documents.

Frischwasser-Ra'anan, Heinz F. *The Frontiers of a Nation,* London, 1955. Good study of the forces and diplomacy leading to the formation of the Palestine mandate.

Fuad, Ali. *La Question des détroits.* Paris, 1928.

Gaillard, Gaston. *The Turks and Europe.* London, 1921. Concerned with the negotiation of the Treaty of Sèvres. Pro-Turkish, anti-British, now outdated by publication of documents. Chief present value is in discussion of public opinion.

Gelfand, Lawrence E. *The Inquiry: American Preparation for Peace 1917-1919.* New Haven, Conn., 1963. By far the most thorough and systematic coverage of the Inquiry yet undertaken.

Georges-Gaulis, Berthe. *Angora, Constantinople, Londres: Mustapha Kémal et la politique anglaise en Orient.* Paris, 1922.

———. *La Question Turque.* Paris, 1921.

Giannini, Amedeo. *L'Ultima fase della questione Orientale, 1913-1932.* Rome, 1933. Conventional. Has map showing division of spheres as formulated in the Tripartite Pact.

Gidney, James B. *A Mandate for Armenia.* Kent, Ohio, 1967.

Gontaut-Biron, Roger de. *Comment la France s'est installée en Syrie (1918-1919).* Paris, 1922. Anti-British, but criticizes French government for lack of concrete plans for the Near East. Gives a good deal of press reaction. Detailed discussion of December, 1919, discussions between Kemal and Picot.

———. *D'Angora à Lausanne, les étapes d'une déchéance.* Paris, 1924.

———. *La France et la question de Moussoul.* Paris, 1923.

Gordon, Leland J. *American Relations with Turkey, 1830-1930; an economic interpretation.* Philadelphia, 1932.

Gottlieb, Wolfram W. *Studies in Secret Diplomacy during the First World War.* London, 1957. Good account of the negotiations of the early secret agreements between France, Britain, and Russia concerning the planned partition of Turkey.

Graves, Philip. *Briton and Turk.* London, 1941.

Grosbois, Jacques. *La Turquie et les détroits.* Paris, 1945.

Guinn, Paul. *British Strategy and Politics, 1914-1918.* Oxford, 1965.

Hacobian, A. P. *Armenia and the War.* New York, n.d.

Haddad, George. *Fifty Years of Modern Syria and Lebanon.* New York, 1950.

Hanna, Paul L. *British Policy in Palestine.* Washington, D.C., 1942.

Haskins, Charles H., and Robert H. Lord. *Some Problems of the Peace Conference.* Cambridge, Mass., 1920. Of little value.

Hellas and Unredeemed Hellenism. American Hellenic Society, no. 11. New York, 1920. Contains articles concerning Greek claims in Asia Minor. See especially George Bourdon, "The Italians in the Ottoman Empire."

Helmreich, Ernst C. *The Diplomacy of the Balkan Wars, 1912-1913.* Cambridge, Mass., 1938.

Hocking, William E. *The Spirit of World Politics, with Special Studies of the Near East.* New York, 1932.

Hourani, A. H. *Syria and Lebanon: A Political Essay.* New York, 1946. Maintains that British and French interests were essentially the same, rather than different, in the area.

House, Edward M., and Charles Seymour, eds., *What Really Happened at Paris: The Story of the Peace Conference, 1918-1919.* New York, 1921.

Hovannisian, Richard G. *Armenia on the Road to Independence, 1918.* Berkeley, Calif., 1969.

Howard, Harry N. *The King-Crane Commission.* Beirut, 1963.

_____. *The Partition of Turkey, 1913-1923.* Norman, Okla., 1931. An admirable and detailed study; the section dealing with the Treaty of Sèvres is based primarily on an examination of the Miller diary.

Huddleston, Sisley. *Peace-making at Paris.* London, 1919.

Hudson, Geoffrey F. *Turkey, Greece and the Eastern Mediterranean.* Oxford, 1939.

Hughes, Serge. *The Rise and Fall of Modern Italy.* New York, 1967.

Hurewitz, Jacob C. *Middle East Dilemmas; the background of United States policy.* New York, 1953.

Ivanov, Iordan. *Les Bulgares devant le Congres de la paix.* Berne, 1919. Has population statistics purporting to show that Thrace was Bulgarian at the close of the war.

Jäckh, Ernst. *The Rising Crescent: Turkey Yesterday, Today and Tomorrow.* New York, 1944.

Jäschke, Gotthard, and Eric Pritsch. *Die Türkei seit dem Weltkriege: Geschichtskalender, 1918-1928.* Berlin, 1929. A useful calendar of events.

Karpat, Kemal. *Turkey's Politics: The Transition to a Multi-Party System.* Princeton, N.J., 1959.

Kazemzadeh, Firuz. *The Struggle for Transcaucasia, 1917-1921.* New York, 1951. An important work, dealing chiefly with events in the area with relatively little emphasis on the workings of the Peace Conference.

Kedourie, Elie. *England and the Middle East: The Destruction of the Ottoman Empire, 1914-1921.* London, 1956. A very valuable study, using a wide variety of sources, including many Arabic. Concerned generally with events in the Near East and less with the peace negotiations. Chapter 6 on Syria was particularly valuable for the purpose of this study.

Kirk, George E. *A Short History of the Middle East.* Washington, D.C., 1949.

Kohn, Hans. *A History of Nationalism in the East.* New York, 1929. Contains a good analysis of British interests and connections in the Near East.

———. *Nationalism and Imperialism in the Hither East.* New York, 1932.

La Chesnais, Pierre G. *Les peuples de la Transcaucasie pendant la guerre et devant la paix.* Paris, 1921.

Larcher, Commandant M., *La Guerre Turque dans la Guerre Mondiale.* Paris, 1926. Concerned primarily with Turkey's participation in the war.

Laroche, Jules. *Au Quai D'Orsay avec Briand et Poincaré, 1913–1926.* Paris, 1957.

Lenszowski, George. *The Middle East in World Affairs.* 2d ed. rev. Ithaca, N.Y., 1956.

Leslie, Shane. *Salutation to Five.* London, 1951.

Lewis, Bernard. *The Emergence of Modern Turkey.* New York, 1961.

Lewis, Geoffrey L. *Turkey.* London, 1955.

The Liberation of the Greek People in Turkey. London, 1919.

Loder, John de Vere. *The Truth about Mesopotamia, Palestine and Syria.* London, 1923. Contains a good account of the Mesopotamia uprising of 1920.

Longrigg, Stephen. *Iraq, 1900 to 1950.* New York, 1956.

———. *Oil in the Middle East: Its Discovery and Development.* New York, 1954.

———. *Syria and Lebanon Under the French Mandates.* New York, 1958. Thorough.

Loris-Melikov, *La Révolution russe et la nouvelles républiques transcaucasiennes.* Paris, 1920.

Loti, Pierre, *La Mort de Notre Chère France en Orient.* Paris, 1920. Good example of French pro-Turk attitude. Hates Greeks and British. Contains a document which is claimed to be the secret Anglo-Turk agreement of September 12, 1919.

———. *Les Alliés qu'il nous faudrait.* Paris, 1919. A collection of pro-Turk essays.

Lugan, Alphonse. *Les Problémes internationaux et le Congrès de la Paix.* Paris, 1919. French propaganda.

Luke, Harry C. *Mosul and its Minorities.* London, 1925.

Luquet, J. *La Politique des mandates dans le Levant.* Paris, 1923.

Lyautey, Pierre. *Le Drame oriental et le Rôle de la France.* Paris, 1924.

Lybyer, Albert H. *The Question of the Near East.* New York, 1921.

Macartney, Maxwell, and Paul Cremona. *Italy's Foreign and Colonial Policy, 1914–1937.* New York, 1938.

McCallum, Robert B. *Public Opinion and the Last Peace.* New York, 1944.

Mandelstam, André. *La société des nations et les puissances devant le probléme arménien.* Paris, 1926. Good treatment of the Armenian question.

Manuel, Frank. *The Realities of American Palestine Relations.* Washington, D.C., 1949. A thorough study, utilizing all available materials in Washington.

Marlowe, John. *A History of Modern Egypt and Anglo-Egyptian Relations, 1800–1956.* 2d ed. Hamden, Conn., 1965.

Marston, Frank S. *The Peace Conference of 1919: Organization and Procedure.* New York, 1944.

Marwick, Arthur, *Britain in the Century of Total War.* Boston, 1968.

———. *The Deluge: British Society and the First World War.* Boston, 1965.

Massey, William T. *Allenby's Final Triumph.* London, 1920.

Maurice, Sir Frederick B. *The Armistices of 1918.* New York. A critical discussion of events leading to the signing of the armistices. Feels Britain justified, but not judicious, in signing alone an armistice the terms of which were too hastily formulated.

Mayer, Arno J. *Politics and Diplomacy of Peacemaking: Containment and Counterrevolution at Versailles, 1918-1919.* New York, 1967. An excellent study, interrelating national domestic situations with the work of the Peace Conference.

Mears, Eliot G., ed. *Modern Turkey,* New York, 1924.

Mileff, Milu. *La Bulgarie et les Détroits.* Paris, 1927.

Mills, John S., and M. B. Chrussachi. *The Question of Thrace—Greeks, Bulgars and Turks.* London, 1919. A series of maps aimed at showing that historically Thrace has always been Greek rather than Turkish or Bulgarian.

Miller, David H. *The Drafting of the Covenant.* 2 vols. New York, 1928.

Minorskii, Vladimir F. *The Mosul Question.* Paris, 1926.

Monroe, Elizabeth. *Britain's Moment in the Middle East, 1914-1956.* Baltimore, 1963.

Mowat, Charles. *Britain Between the Wars, 1918-1940.* Chicago, 1955.

Mowat, Robert B. *A History of European Diplomacy, 1914-1925.* 3 vols. London, 1927.

Mowry, George E. *The Urban Nation, 1920-1960.* New York, 1965.

Nevakivi, Jukka. *Britain, France and the Arab Middle East, 1914-1920.* London, 1969.

Noble, George B. *Policies and Opinions at Paris, 1919.* New York, 1935.

Northedge, Frederick S. *The Troubled Giant: Britain Among the Great Powers, 1916-1939.* New York, 1967.

Ostrorog, Léon. *The Turkish Problem.* London, 1919.

Paillarès, Michel. *Le Kémalisme devant les Alliés.* Constantinople, 1922.

Pallis, Alexander A. *Greece's Anatolian Venture and After.* London, 1937.

Papadopoulos, Alexander. *Persecutions of the Greeks in Turkey before the European War.* New York, 1919.

Pernot, Maurice. *La Question Turque.* Paris, 1923. An objective study, tending to indict both Britain and France, and stating that no Near East policy would be successful until the two powers learned to cooperate.

Peters, Richard. *The Story of the Turks: From Empire to Democracy.* New York, 1959.

Philby, Harry St. J. B. *Arabia.* New York, 1930.

Phillipson, Coleman, and Noel Buxton. *The Question of the Bosphorus and Dardanelles.* London, 1917.

Pichon, Jean. *Le Partage du Proche-Orient.* Paris, 1938. Valuable.

Powell, Edward A. *The Struggle for Power in Moslem Asia.* New York, 1924.

Price, Clair. *The Rebirth of Turkey.* New York, 1923.

Price, M. Philips. *A History of Turkey: From Empire to Republic.* London, 1956.

Puaux, René. *Constantinople et la Question d'Orient.* Paris, 1920. Well-argued pro-Greek pamphlet. Supports League of Nations, is opposed to British and French imperialism in the Near East.

———. *La Déportation et le Rapatriement des Grecs en Turquie.* Paris, 1919. Pro-Greek.

Redan, Pierre. *La Cilicie et le problème Ottoman.* Paris, 1921.

Richard, Henry. *La Syrie et la Guerre.* Paris, 1916. A vehement advocate of vigorous French action in a large Syria.

Robinson, Richard D. *The First Turkish Republic: A Case Study in National Development.* Cambridge, Mass., 1963.

Royal Institute of International Affairs. *British Interests in the Mediterranean and Middle East.* Oxford, 1958.

———. *The Middle East, a Political and Economic Survey.* 3d ed. London, 1958.

Sachar, Howard M. *The Emergence of the Middle East.* New York, 1969.

———— "The United States and Turkey, 1914–1927—The Origins of Near Eastern Policy." Ph.D. dissertation, Harvard University, 1953.

Safrastian, Arshak. *Kurds and Kurdistan*. London, 1948.

Samné, Georges. *La Syrie*. Paris. 1921. Vehemently pro-French and anti-British.

Schemsi, Kara. *Les Turcs et le Panhellénisme*. Geneva, 1918. A violent attack on Greece and Greek claims.

Schlicklin, Jean. *Angora; l'aube de la Turquie nouvelle (1919–1922)*. Paris, 1922.

Schuman, Frederick L. *War and Diplomacy in the French Republic: An Inquiry into Political Motivations and the Control of Foreign Policy*. New York, 1931.

Seton-Watson, Christopher. *Italy from Liberalism to Fascism, 1870–1925*. London, 1967.

Seymour, Charles. *Geography, Justice and Politics at the Paris Peace Conference*. New York, 1951.

Shotwell, James, and Francis Deak. *Turkey at the Straits*. New York, 1940.

Shwadran, Benjamin. *The Middle East, Oil and the Great Powers*. 2d ed. New York, 1959.

Smith, Daniel M. *The Great Departure: The United States and World War I, 1914–1920*. New York, 1965.

Smith, Elaine D. *Turkey: Origins of the Kemalist Movement and the Government of the Grand National Assembly, (1919–1923)*. Washington, D.C., 1959. Rambling and poorly organized. Uses Turkish sources extensively.

Soteriadis, George. *An Ethnological Map Illustrating Hellenism in the Balkan Peninsula and Asia Minor*. London, 1918.

Soule, George. *Prosperity Decade: From War to Depression, 1917–1929*. New York, 1947.

Sousa, Nasim. *The Capitulatory Regime of Turkey, its History, Origin and Nature*. Baltimore, Md., 1933. The most thorough study of the capitulations.

Spector, Ivar. *The Soviet Union and the Muslim World, 1917–1958*. Seattle, Wash., 1959.

Speiser, Ephraim A. *The United States and the Near East*. Cambridge, Mass., 1947.

Stein, Leonard. *The Balfour Declaration*. London, 1961. An excellent, scholarly study. The epilogue deals briefly with the Peace Conference.

Stoddard, Lathrop. *The New World of Islam*. New York, 1922.

Sykes, Christopher. *Two Studies in Virtue*. New York, 1953. Includes a study of Balfour, in relation to the Balfour Declaration.

Temperley, Harold W. V. *A History of the Peace Conference*. 6 vols. London, 1920–24. An early and still standard study of the work of the Peace Conference. Volume 6 deals with Near Eastern affairs.

Thomas, Lewis, and Richard Frye. *The United States and Turkey and Iran*. Cambridge, Mass., 1951.

Thompson, John M. *Russia, Bolshevism and the Versailles Peace*. Princeton, N.J., 1966. Significant in its lack of any real mention of Bolshevism in relation to the Turkish peace settlement.

Tillman, Seth P. *Anglo-American Relations at the Paris Peace Conference of 1919*. Princeton, N.J., 1961.

Topf, Erich. *Die Staatenbildungen in den Arabischen Teilen der Türkei seit dem Weltkriege nach Entstehung, Bedeutung und Lebensfähigkeit*. Hamburg, 1929.

Toynbee, Arnold J., *The Western Question in Greece and Turkey*. London, 1923. Good discussion of the Greek campaign in Asia Minor.

Toynbee, Arnold J., and Kenneth P. Kirkwood. *Turkey*. New York, 1927. A good summary of the treaty terms and of the reaction in Constantinople to the treaty.

Ullman, Richard. *Anglo-Soviet Relations, 1917–1921*. 3 vols. Princeton, N.J., 1961–. Vol. 2, *Britain and the Russian Civil War. November, 1918–February, 1920*.

Walder, David. *The Chanak Affair*. London, 1969.

Webster, Donald E. *The Turkey of Ataturk: Social Process in the Turkish Reformation.* Philadelphia, 1939. Good study of the Kemalist movement.

Wilson, Trevor. *The Downfall of the Liberal Party, 1914–1935.* Ithaca, N.Y., 1966.

Wormser, George M. *La République de Clemenceau.* Paris, 1961.

Yale, William. *The Near East, A Modern History.* Ann Arbor, Mich., 1958.

Yalmin, Ahmed Emin. *Turkey in the World War.* New Haven, Conn., 1930. Has a chapter on treatment of minorities during the war.

Young, George. *Constantinople.* New York, 1926.

Zeine, Zeine N. *The Struggle for Arab Independence: Western Diplomacy and the Rise and Fall of Faisal's Kingdom in Syria.* Beirut, 1960. Chronological account. Chapters on the Peace Conference are often little more than a series of quotations from documents. Seems to be unaware of the Anglo-French discussions in December, 1919, and mentions only in passing the Conference of London in February–March, 1920. Makes use of Arab sources.

Ziemke, Kurt. *Die Neue Türkei, 1914–1929.* Stuttgart, 1930.

Newspapers and Periodicals

"America for expelling the Turk." *Literary Digest* 64 (March 20, 1920):30–31.

"American Military Mission to Armenia." *International Conciliation* 151 (June, 1920):275–312. Report on Armenia by the Harbord Commission.

Andreades, A. "La Grèce devant le Congrès de la Paix." *Revue Politique et Parlementaire* (February, 1919).

Armenian Review. Spring, 1949–Spring, 1952. A series of twelve articles dealing with the American (Harbord) Military Mission to Armenia. The Spring, 1950 issue contains a record of an interview between Kemal and Harbord.

"Baffling feature of the latest crisis over Turkey." *Current Opinion* 68 (April, 1920): 458–63.

"The Balkans and Turkey." *Current History* 11 (March, 1920): 431–35.

Bennett, E. N. "Our Anatolian policy and the Suppressed Report." *English Review* 30 (April, 1920): 357–62.

Bliss, W. D. P. "Armenia's Struggle for Independence." *Current History* 11 (January, 1920):138–44.

Bourdon, G. "The Italians in the Ottoman Empire." In *Hellas and Unredeemed Hellenism.* American Hellenic Society, no. 11. New York, 1920.

"Britain, France, Asia and Oil." *Contemporary Review* 118 (August, 1920):253–63.

Bryce, Lord James. "The Future of Armenia." *Contemporary Review* 114 (December, 1918):604–11.

_____. "The Settlement of the Eastern Question." *Contemporary Review* 117 (January, 1920): 1–9.

Burrows, Ronald M. "The Unity of the Greek Race." *Contemporary Review* 115 (February, 1919):153–64.

Buxton, H. "Armenia, some recent impressions." *Contemporary Review* 117 (April, 1920):497–500.

Buzanski, Peter. "The Interallied Investigation of the Greek Invasion of Smyrna, 1919." *The Historian* 25 (May, 1963):325–43.

Caix, Robert de. "The Question of Syria." *New Europe* 12 (August 28, 1919):145–49; (September 4, 1919):169–74.

"The Case of Emir Feisal."*Current History* 13 (February, 1921):249–55.

Correspondance d'Orient, May, 1919–August, 1920.

"The Crime in Turkey." *Nation* 111 (July 3, 1920):5.

Current History. March, 1919–June, 1920.

Curry, G. "Woodrow Wilson, Jan Smuts and the Versailles Settlement." *American Historical Review* 66 (July, 1961):968–86.

"Dangerous Complications in Syria—The Massacres at Marash." *Current History* 12 (April, 1920):108–12.

DeNovo, John A. "The Movement for an Aggressive American Oil Policy Abroad, 1918–1920." *American Historical Review* 61 (July, 1956):854–76.

Driault, Édouard. *Before Constantinople.* Pamphlet, translated from *Revue Bleu* (December 21–28, 1918–January 4–11, 1919). Vehemently glorifies France and Greece.

Duggan, Stephen. "Syria and Its Tangled Problems" *Current History* 13 (February, 1921):238–48.

Dumont-Wilden. "La Question de Constantinople." *Revue Politique et Littéraire* 58 (March 13, 1920):151–54.

"Effects of America's Exit from the Near East." *Current Opinion* 68 (February, 1920):162–65.

"Europe's Perplexity over the Upheaval in Turkey." *Current Opinion* 67 (December, 1919):284–85.

"Explosive Conditions in the Near East." *World's Work* 40 (May, 1920):20–22.

"The Fate of Constantinople." *New Statesman* 14 (January 10, 1920):396–97.

France. Ministères de la Guerre et des Affaires Étrangères, *Bulletin périodique de la presse Italienne.* Paris, December, 1919–August, 1920. A good summary of Italian press attitude.

France, Anatole. "Greece and the Peace." *L'Humanité,* February 3, 1919.

Frangulis, A. F. "Les Revendications de la Grèce." *Le Monde Nouveau Diplomatique et Économique,* March 6, 1919, pp. 7–10.

Freer, Mary R. "Did President Wilson Contradict Himself on the Secret Treaties?" *Current History* 30 (June, 1929):435–43.

Fregier, C. "Lettres d'Athenes." *Journal des Débats,* February 7, 1919, pp. 228–29.

Froidevaux, H. "Au lendemain de la signature du traité de Sèvres." *L'Asie Française,* July–August, 1920, pp. 212–14.

———. "L'Announce de la Paix avec Turquie." *L'Asie Française,* January, 1920, pp. 6–10.

———. "Les Intérêts économiques francais dans le Levant et le Traité de paix avec la Turquie." *L'Asie Française,* June, 1920, pp. 172–75.

———. "Le Projet de Traité avec la Turquie et la France." *L'Asie Française,* May, 1920, pp. 142–46.

"The Future of Turkey," *Spectator* 123 (July 12, 1919):40–41. Claims Lloyd George's offer of Constantinople to the Turks in January, 1918, was made only as an inducement for immediate Turkish withdrawal from the war.

Gates, C. F. "Making of the Turkish Republic." *Current History* 34 (April, 1931): 89–93.

Gautherot, Gustave. "Syria and the Hedjaz: A French View." *Current History* 12 (April, 1920):113–16. Reprinted from *La France Nouvelle.*

Gauvain, A. "Les Alliés en Orient." *Journal des Débats,* June 25, 1920, pp. 1034–35.

Gerard, J. W. "Civilization's Surrender to Barbarism: Proposed Retention of the Turks in Europe." *Independent* 101 (March 6, 1920):345.

Great Britain and the Near East. See *The Near East.*

Great Britain. General Staff, War Office. *Daily Review of the Foreign Press: Allied Press Supplement.* 6 vols. London, November 6, 1918–July 30, 1919. Vols. 5 and 6.

Haim, Sylvia G. "The Arab Awakening: A Source for Historians." *Die Welt des Islams,* n.s. 2 (1953).

Hanotaux, G. "The Question of the Dardanelles." *Living Age* 304 (January 31, 1920):263–65.

Harbord, J. G. "Investigating Turkey and Trans Caucasia." *World's Work* 40 (May, 1920):35–47.

———. "Mustapha Kemal Pasha and his Party." *World's Work* 40 (June, 1920):176–93.

Hibben, Paxton. "Arbitrating for Armenia." *New Republic* 23 (June 16, 1920):86–90.

———. "Asia Minor Muddle." *New Republic* 23 (August 11, 1920):304–6.

Hovannisian, Richard G. "The Allies and Armenia, 1915–1918." *Journal of Contemporary History* 3 (January, 1968):145–68.

"How Will the Turkish Treaty Work?" *Literary Digest* 66 (August 28, 1920):19–20.

Howard, Harry N. "An American Experiment in Peace Making: The King-Crane Commission." *The Moslem World* 32 (April, 1942):122–46.

———. "The United States and Turkey: American policy in the Straits Question (1914–1963)," *Balkan Studies* 4 (1963):225–50.

"L'Importance des Intérêts Français dans L'Empire Ottoman," *L'Aise Française,* October, 1919, pp. 179–83.

International Conciliation 751 (June, 1920).

Journal des Débats, September 19, 1919.

Kidwal of Gadia, M. H. "Sultan of Turkey and Constantinople." *Saturday Review* 127 (June 28, 1919):632.

Le Temps (Paris). December, 1918–August, 1920.

Loti, Pierre. "The Turks: A Plea for Justice." *Living Age* 300 (January 11, 1919):65–67.

Louis, W. Roger. "Great Britain and the African Peace Settlement of 1919." *American Historical Review* 71 (April, 1966):875–92.

Lybyer, Albert H. "Turkey under the Armistice." *Journal of International Relations* 12 (April, 1922):447–73.

McCallum, D. "The French in Syria, 1919–1924." *Journal of the Central Asian Society* (1925):3–25.

Machray, R. "The Arab Question." *Fortnightly Review* 113 (February, 1920):249–60.

Mandelstam, A. "The Turkish Spirit." *New Europe* 15 (April 22, 1920):39–45.

Miguel, Pierre. "Le Journal des Débats et la paix de Versailles." *Revue Historique* 232 (October–December, 1964):379–414.

Montgomery, A.E. "The Making of the Treaty of Sèvres of 10 August 1920." *The Historical Journal* 15 (December, 1972): 775–87.

"Near East Chaos." *Nation* 111 (September 4, 1920):261–62.

"New Empires for Old." *New Statesman* 15 (May 15, 1920):154–55.

"The New National Movement in Turkey." *Living Age* 304 (January 3, 1920):266–67.

New York Times. January, 1919–August, 1920.

Pech, E. "Les alliés et le mandat sur la Turquie." *L'Acropole* 1:320–28.

Pinon, R. "La Liquidation de l'Empire ottoman." *Revue des Deux Mondes,* 6th ser. 53 (September 1, 1919):128–60.

"The Problem of Turkey." *Current History* 11 (February, 1920):270–75.

"La Question de Syrie et la Paix." *L'Asie Française,* October, 1918–January, 1919, pp. 119–31.

"The Question of Thrace, an Official Greek View." *The New Europe* 112 (August 21, 1919):134–37.

Rémusat. "Cilicie, 1918–1922." *Revue des Science Politiques* 54 (July, 1931):348–91.

A Review of the Foreign Press: Political Review. London. A very useful survey, covering the period from November 14, 1919 to June 11, 1920.

Robinson, L. R. "Turkey looks eastward." *Nation* 110 (March 13, 1920):327–30.

Saint-Brice. "L'Accord Syrien." *Correspondance d'Orient,* September 30, 1919, pp. 145–52.

Samné, Georges. "A propos du traité turc." *Correspondance d'Orient,* May 15, 1920, pp. 397–404.

———. "L'Effondrement de Faycal." *Correspondance d'Orient,* August 15-30, 1920, pp. 49-54.

———. "French Interests in Syria." *Living Age* 299 (December 7, 1918):608–13.

———. "Les variations de l'Émir Faycal et le nationalisme turc." *Correspondance d'Orient,* February 22, 1920, pp. 149–52.

"La Signature du traité turc." *Journal des Débats* 255 (August 13, 1920).

Simonds, Frank H. "Dividing Turkish Lands." *Review of Reviews* 61 (June, 1920):607–12.

———. "Greek vs. Turk, a new phase of the Eastern Question." *Review of Reviews* 62 (August, 1920):159-68.

Smith, W. G. "Armenian Tragedy." *Catholic World* 111 (July, 1920):485–92.

"Struggle for Asia." *Living Age* 304 (March 27, 1920):768–71.

"The Sultan of Turkey and the Caliphate." *Contemporary Review* 110 (August, 1916):199-205.

Taillandier, Saint-René. "La France et la Syrie, notre oeuvre dans le Levant et son avenir." *Revue des Deux Mondes,* 6th ser. 49(February 15, 1919):771-804.

"The Tangled Turkish Question." *Current History* 12 (May, 1920):323-30.

Tardieu, André. "Mossoul et le pétrole." *L'Illustration,* June 20, 1920. An important statement defending Clemenceau's policy in relation to Mosul.

———. "Reflections sur la Crise Oriental," *L'Illustration,* December 11, 1920, pp. 452-53.

The Near East (later *Great Britain and the Near East*), January 9, 1920, p. 39; January 22, 1920, p. 109; February 5, 1920, p. 177; May 27, 1920, p. 752; July 3, 1920, p. 789; August 12, 1920, p. 229.

Times (London). October, 1918–August, 1920.

Toynbee, Arnold J. "Meaning of the Constantinople Decision." *New Europe* 14 (February 19, 1920):129–31.

———. "The Question of the Caliphate." *Contemporary Review* 117 (February, 1920):192-96.

———. "Review of the Turkish Problem." *New Europe* 14 (January 15, 1920):1-5.

———. "San Remo and Turkey." *New Europe* 15 (May 6, 1920):73-75.

———. "Turkey in Suspence." *New Europe* 15 (April 15, 1920):16-18.

"Trying to Carve Turkey." *Literary Digest* 67 (December 4, 1920):17-18.

"Turkey and her former Dominions, Attacks on the Peace Treaty." *Current History* 12 (July, 1920):625-31.

"Turkey at the Coming Peace Conference." *Literary Digest* 63 (December 13, 1919):21-22.

"The Turkish Danger." *Saturday Review* 129 (June 19, 1920):556.

"The Turks to Stay in Europe." *Current History* 12 (April, 1920):103-8.

Tyrrell, F. H. "Great Britain, Turkey and Germany." *Asiatic Review,* n.s. 7 (November 15, 1915): 365-78.

Williams, A. "Armenia, British Pledges and the Near East." *Contemporary Review* 121 (April, 1922):418-425.

Williams, T. "America's Duty to Turkey." *Independent* 99 (August 16, 1919):215-16.

Wilson, Trevor. "The Coupon and the British General Election of 1918." *Journal of Modern History* 36 (March, 1964):28-42.

Woods, H. C. "Anatolian War." *Fortnightly Review* 116 (September, 1921):492-550.

———. "The Future of Turkey." *Asiatic Review,* n.s. 15 (October, 1919):637-40.

———. "The Future of Turkey." *Contemporary Review* 115 (June, 1919):628-36.

———. "Sèvres, Before and After." *Fortnightly Review* 118 (October, 1922):545-60.

———. "The Turkish Treaty." *Fortnightly Review* 114 (July, 1920): 57-66.

INDEX